A Guide and Reference

S0-CAE-727

HOW TO WRITE ANYTHING

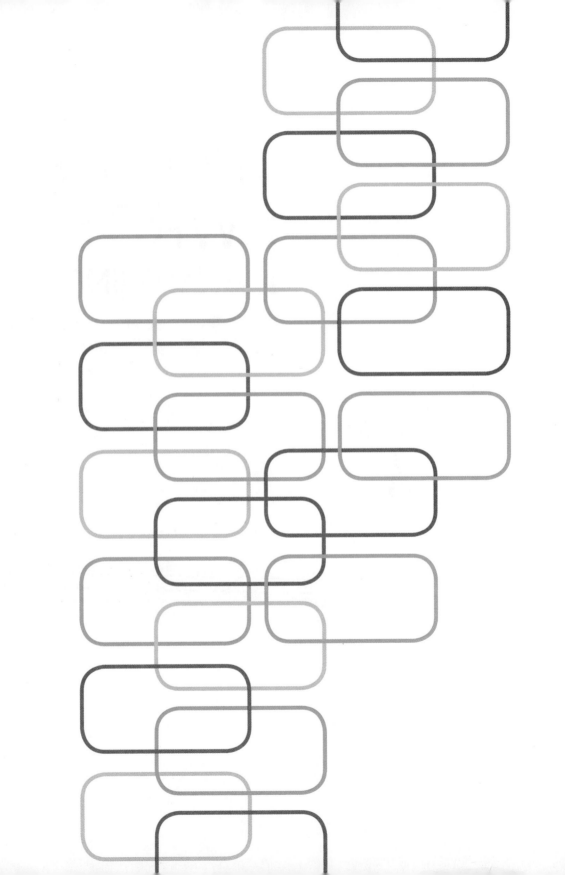

HOW TO WRITE ANYTHING

A Guide and Reference

John J. Ruszkiewicz

UNIVERSITY OF TEXAS, AUSTIN

BEDFORD/ST. MARTIN'S

Boston ◆ New York

For Bedford/St. Martin's

Executive Editor: Leasa Burton
Senior Developmental Editor: Ellen Darion
Senior Production Editor: Deborah Baker
Senior Production Supervisor: Dennis J. Conroy
Marketing Manager: Molly Parke
Editorial Assistants: Melissa Cook, Sarah Guariglia
Copyeditor: Mary Lou Wilshaw–Watts
Art Director and Text Design: Anna Palchik
Cover Design: Nancy Goulet
Composition: Aptara
Printing and Binding: RR Donnelley and Sons

President: Joan E. Feinberg
Editorial Director: Denise B. Wydra
Editor in Chief: Karen S. Henry
Director of Marketing: Karen Melton Soeltz
Director of Editing, Design, and Production: Marcia Cohen
Assistant Director of Editing, Design, and Production: Elise Kaiser
Managing Editor: Elizabeth M. Schaaf

Library of Congress Control Number: 2008925888

3   2   1   0   9   8
f   e   d   c   b   a

For information, write: Bedford/St. Martin's, 75 Arlington Street, Boston, MA 02116 (617–399–4000)

ISBN–10: 0–312–45226–8
ISBN–13: 978–0–312–45226–1

Acknowledgments:

"2007 Porsche 911 Turbo." Brief quote from *Road & Track,* June 2006 issue. Copyright © 2006. Reprinted with permission.

Jane E. Brody. "Gene-Altered Food: A Case Against Panic." From *The New York Times,* Health & Fitness Section, December 5, 2000 issue, page 8. Copyright © 2000 The New York Times. Used by permission and protected by the Copyright Laws of the United States. The printing, copying, redistribution, or retransmission of the Material without express written permission is prohibited.

Acknowledgments and copyrights are continued at the back of the book on pages 554–58, which constitute an extension of the copyright page. It is a violation of the law to reproduce these selections by any means whatsoever without the written permission of the copyright holder.

Preface

How to Write Anything is not a humble title. You might wonder whether any book, especially one designed expressly as a compact guide for college writers, should promise so much. The simple answer is *no*; the more intriguing one is *maybe*.

What, after all, do writers do when they face an assignment? They try to grasp what the project entails; they look for examples of the genre; they wrestle with basic language and research skills. *How to Write Anything* guides college writers through these stages for their most common academic and professional assignments. In doing so, it lays out strategies to follow in any situation that requires purposeful writing.

But rarely do different writers work in the same order, and the same writer is likely to follow different paths for different projects. *How to Write Anything* doesn't define a single process of writing or imagine that all students using it will have the same skills and interests. Instead, a modular chapter organization and an innovative system of cross references encourage students to navigate the book's materials to find exactly the information they want at the level of specificity they need—which pretty much sums up the rationale for the book. If many college guides to composition test the patience of teachers and students alike by their sheer size and kitchen-sink approach to instruction, *How to Write Anything* is both more focused and more flexible, marrying the rich perspectives of a full rhetoric to the efficiency of a brief handbook.

A Guide and Reference

The Guide, in Parts 1 and 2, covers a wide range of genres that instructors frequently assign in composition classes or that students encounter in other undergraduate courses. Each chapter lays out the basics of a genre, such as narrative or argument, then redefines the writing process as a flexible series of rhetorical choices—Exploring Purpose and Topic; Understanding Audience; Finding and Developing Materials; Creating a Structure; and Choosing a Style and Design. These choices provide students with a framework for writing in any situation and in any genre, and encourage writers to explore the range of possibilities within genres. The explanations here are direct, practical, and economical. If writers do need more help with a particular topic, targeted cross references make it easy to find in the Reference section.

The Reference section (Parts 3 through 9) covers key aspects of the writing process—with separate parts devoted to Ideas; Shaping and Drafting; Style; Revising and Editing; Research and Sources; Media and Design; and Common Errors. While the topics will seem familiar to most writing instructors, the fresh and lively material here is designed to expand points introduced in the Guide. For instance, a writer might turn to these sections to find specific techniques for generating ideas or arguments or guidance for making a formal style feel more friendly. The organization of *How to Write Anything* lets students quickly find what they need without getting bogged down in other material.

A Flexible Writing Process

Writers get started, develop ideas, and revise in different ways. *How to Write Anything* acknowledges this by asking students to think about their *own* process and what they need help with. Rather than merely walking them through a lockstep, linear writing sequence, the text encourages students to actively choose the order of topics that best fits their situation.

At the beginning of each Guide chapter, "How to Start" questions anticipate where students get stuck when writing and direct them to specific materials within the chapter for help. For example, one writer might need advice about finding a topic, while another will already have a topic but need help with audience, or developing or organizing ideas.

In this hyperlinked era, we know how important it is for supporting information to be intuitive, easy to find, and above all, relevant and useful. With this in mind, the cross references between the Guide and Reference sections target only the topics that students are most likely to need help with for the assignment at hand. The cross references' simple language and unobtrusive design result in clean, uncluttered pages that make it easy for students to find the exact help they need and to stay focused on their own writing. For a visual explanation of how these elements work, see the "How to Use This Book" tutorial on pages xlvi–xlvii.

Professional and Student Writing

How to Write Anything contains over 30 readings, carefully chosen to illustrate key principles and show how genres change in response to different contexts and audiences. Writers intuitively look to such models to understand patterns of composition or points of rhetoric, style, and mechanics. So every chapter in the Guide includes many complete examples of the genres under discussion, most of these texts annotated to show how they meet criteria set down in *How to Write Anything*. Each of the assignments offered at the end of these chapters is tied to a particular reading in the chapter, so students can use the sample texts both as models and as springboards for discussion and exploration.

Just as important, the models in *How to Write Anything* are approachable. Some represent the work of published professionals; other show how college students themselves have approached similar assignments. The student samples are especially inventive—chosen to motivate undergraduates to take comparable risks with their own writing.

"How To" Visual Tutorials

Throughout the book, students will recognize a world they already live in, one which assumes that composing occurs in more than just words. But learning occurs in more than just words too. Savvy readers of telegraphic text messages and quick-cut visuals will no doubt appreciate the direct yet context-rich advice in the book's "How To" Visual Tutorials. Through drawings, photographs, and screen shots, these tutorials show step-by-step instructions for challenging topics, ranging from how to browse the Internet for ideas to how to cite a variety of materials in both MLA and APA formats.

The Visual Tutorials are just one example of *How to Write Anything*'s appealing visual style, a style well-suited to readers accustomed to blogging, texting, and using the Internet. The variety of illustrations and humorous visual commentary here can't help but draw readers in and keep them interested.

Invitation to Write

How to Write Anything was designed and edited to be compact and readable. But it retains a personal voice, frank and occasionally humorous, on the grounds that a textbook without character won't convince students that their own prose should have a style adapted to real audiences. And if some chapters operate like reference materials, they still aren't written coldly or dispassionately—not even the final section on Common Errors.

So if *How to Write Anything* seems like an ambitious title, maybe it's because learning to write should be a heady enterprise, undertaken with confidence and optimism. My hope is that this book will encourage students to grasp the opportunities that the writing affords and gain the satisfaction that comes from setting ideas (and words) into motion.

Acknowledgments

The following reviewers were very helpful through several drafts of this book:

Angela K. Albright, NorthWest Arkansas Community College; Glenn Blalock, Baylor University; Miriam Chirico, Eastern Connecticut State University; Ron Christiansen, Salt Lake Community College; Michelle Cox, Bridgewater State College; Mark Crane, Utah Valley State College; Anthony Edgington, University of Toledo; Caroline L. Eisner, University of Michigan; Jessica Fordham Kidd, University of Alabama; Maureen Fitzpatrick, Johnson County Community College; Hank Galmish, Green River Community College; John Gides, California State University–Northridge; Steffen Guenzel, The University of Alabama; Virginia Scott Hendrickson, Missouri State University; Lynn Lewis, University of Oklahoma; Leigh A. Martin, Community College of Rhode

Island; Sandie McGill Barnhouse, Rowan-Cabarrus Community College; Miles McCrimmon, J. Sargeant Reynolds Community College; Erica Messenger, Bowling Green State University; Mary Ellen Muesing, University of North Carolina–Charlotte; Mark Reynolds, Jefferson Davis Community College; Bridget F. Ruetenik, Penn State Altoona; Wendy Sharer, East Carolina University; Marti Singer, Georgia State University; William H. Thelin, University of Akron; James G. Van Belle, Edmonds Community College; Carol Westcamp, University of Arkansas–Fort Smith; and Mary K. Zacharias, San Jacinto College Central.

All books are collaborations, but I have never before worked on a project that more creatively drew upon the resources of an editorial team and publisher. *How to Write Anything* began with the confidence of Joan Feinberg, president of Bedford/St. Martin's, that we could develop a groundbreaking brief rhetoric. She had the patience to allow the idea to develop at its own pace and then assembled an incredible team to support it. I am grateful for the contributions of Denise Wydra, Editorial Director; Karen Henry, Editor in Chief; and Leasa Burton, Executive Editor. I am also indebted to the designers who labored over *How to Write Anything* at greater length and with more care than I have ever seen in thirty years of publishing: Anna Palchik, Art Director and designer of the text; Deborah Baker, Senior Production Editor; and designer Nancy Goulet. Special thanks to Sarah Guariglia, who conceived the Visual Tutorials and took the photographs, and to Peter Arkle for his drawings. They all deserve credit for the distinctive and accessible visual style of *How to Write Anything*.

For their marketing efforts, I am grateful to the guidance offered by Karen Melton Soeltz, Karita dos Santos, and Molly Parke. And for all manner of tasks including art research, coordinating reviews, and permissions, I thank Melissa Cook.

But my greatest debt is to Ellen Darion, who was my splendid editor on this lengthy project: always confident about what we could accomplish, patient when chapters went off-track, and perpetually good-humored. If *How to Write Anything* works, it is because Ellen never wavered from our original high aspirations for the book. Her hand is in every chapter, every choice of reading, and every assignment. She and Leasa Burton also oversaw the complex design as well and created its splendid Visual Tutorials.

Finally, I am extraordinarily grateful to my former students whose papers or paragraphs appear in *How to Write Anything*. Their writing speaks for itself, but I have been inspired, too, by their personal dedication and character. These are the sort of students who motivate teachers, and so I am very proud to see their work published in *How to Write Anything*: Marissa Dahlstrom, Manasi Deshpande, Micah T. Eades, Ryan Hailey, Wade Lamb, Cheryl Lovelady, Shane McNamee, Melissa Miller, Matthew Nance, Ricky Patel, Miles Pequeno, Heidi Rogers, Tobias Salinger, Kanaka Sathasivan, Scott Standley, and Annie Winsett.

Correlation to the Council of Writing Program Administrators' (WPA) Outcomes Statement

How to Write Anything helps students build proficiency in the four categories of learning that writing programs across the country use to assess their work: rhetorical knowledge; critical thinking, reading, and writing; writing processes; and knowledge of conventions. For a complete, detailed correlation to specific WPA outcomes, see the instructor's manual, *Teaching with How to Write Anything*, at bedfordstmartins.com/howtowrite.

Note on MLA Documentation

As you may know, the Modern Language Association publishes two versions of its guidelines for documenting sources. The *MLA Style Manual and Guide to Scholarly Publishing* is for scholars and graduate students. The *MLA Handbook for Writers of Research Papers* is for undergraduate and high school students. In May 2008, the guide for scholars was updated with new guidelines for documenting sources. The Modern Language Association strongly discouraged publishers from updating texts intended for undergraduates to reflect the changes in the scholars' guide. Accordingly, the coverage of MLA documentation in *How to Write Anything* reflects the guidelines for undergraduates as put forth in the current edition of the *MLA Handbook for Writers of Research Papers*. When the Modern Language Association publishes the new edition of this book (anticipated in the spring of 2009), student copies of *How to Write Anything* will be reprinted to reflect these new guidelines.

Classroom and Professional Support

CompClass for How to Write Anything <bedfordstmartins.com/compclass> is the first online course space shaped by the needs of composition students and instructors. In *CompClass,* students can read assignments, do their work, and see their grades all in one place; and instructors can easily monitor student progress and give feedback right away. Along with the *How to Write Anything e-Book, CompClass* comes preloaded with the innovative digital content that Bedford/St. Martin's is known for. To order *CompClass* packaged with *How to Write Anything,* use ISBN 0–312–56151–2.

Re:Writing Plus <bedfordstmartins.com/rewritingplus> neatly gathers our collections of premium digital content into one online library for composition. Check out hundreds of model documents; *i•cite visualizing sources,* which brings research to life through animation, tutorials, and hands-on practice; and *Peer Factor,* the first ever peer-review game. New for January 2009: *VideoCentral,* where real writers talk about what it means to write at work, at school, and to change the world. Available stand-alone or packaged at a discount with the print book. To order *Re:Writing Plus* packaged with *How to Write Anything,* use ISBN 0–312–56153–9.

How to Write Anything e-Book <bedfordstmartins.com/howtowrite> is available online, all the time. Easy to search and use, the e-book is integrated with all the free resources available on the book companion site. Available stand-alone or packaged for free with the print book. To order the *How to Write Anything e-Book* packaged with the print book, use ISBN 0–312–56235–7.

Book Companion Site <bedfordstmartins.com/howtowrite> for *How to Write Anything* includes a wealth of free resources, additional examples of the genres covered in the book, checklists for analyzing each genre, the complete instructor's manual, and more.

Teaching with *How to Write Anything*. Available on the book companion site, the instructor's manual features sample syllabi, thorough coverage of each genre treated in the book, correlations to the Council of Writing Program Administrators' (WPA) Outcomes Statement, and more. Each chapter also includes teaching tips, suggestions for prompting class discussion, and additional writing activities and assignments.

Brief Contents

guide

reference

Contents

guide

Part 1 Genres 2

1 Narrative 4

8   Rhetorical Analysis   222

reference

guide

Genres

Need a form that you don't see here? Try "Special Assignments," p. 252.

How to start
- Need a **topic**? See page 9.
- Need to choose the right **details**? See page 12.
- Need to **organize the events** in your story? See page 14.

1

Narrative

describes
events in
people's lives

You may never have been asked to write a narrative, but chances are you've shared bits and pieces of your life story in writing. In doing so, you've written personal narratives. *Personal* does not necessarily mean you're baring your soul. Instead, it implies that you're telling a story from a unique perspective, providing details only you could know and insights only you could have.

- You want more people to think about bicycling to work, so you share your own experiences as an urban cyclist.

- Your application for a scholarship must include a personal statement of no more than five hundred words explaining how your life has prepared you for a career as a pharmacist.

- To work at the campus writing center, you prepare a literacy biography explaining your own experiences with writing and language.

- Your insurance company demands a detailed explanation of your most recent traffic accident—the one involving your mother's Caravan and a Starbucks that formerly served your neighborhood.

- A community group is collecting stories about the lives of local citizens, past and present, and you decide to tell your grandparents' story.

UNDERSTANDING NARRATIVES.   Narratives may describe almost any human activity that writers choose to share with readers: school, family, work experiences, personal tragedies, travel, sports, growing up, relationships, and so on. Stories can be told in words or through other media, including photographs, film, songs, cartoons, and more. Expect a narrative you write to do the following.

Tell a story.   In a narrative, something usually happens. Maybe all you do in the paper is reflect on a single moment when something peculiar caught your attention. Or your story could follow a simple sequence of events—the classic road-trip script. Or you might spin a tale complicated enough to seem like an actual plot, with a connected beginning, middle, and end. In every case, though, you need to select specific events that serve your purpose in writing, whatever it may be. Otherwise you're just rambling.

StoryCorps Story-Booth   StoryCorps is a national project of Sound Portraits Productions meant to inspire people to record one another's stories in sound. Photo of the Story-Corps StoryBooth, courtesy of StoryCorps. Learn more at www.storycorps.net.

Make a point—usually.   Your point may depend on your specific reason for writing a narrative. If your insurance agent asks about your recent auto wreck, she probably just wants to know who hit whom and how you are involved in the incident. But most narratives will be less cut-and-dry and more reflective, enabling you to connect with audiences more subtly—to amuse, enlighten, and, perhaps, even to change them. ○ Some narratives are therapeutic too, enabling you to confront personal issues or to get a weight off your chest.

Observe details closely.   What makes a narrative memorable and brings it to life are its details—the colors, shapes, textures, sounds, and smells that you convey to readers through language or other media. Those physical impressions go a long way toward convincing readers that a story is credible and honest. They assure readers that you were close enough to an experience to have an insider's perspective. So share your reactions with readers, conveying specific information as events unfurl. But don't fall back on clichés to make your points. Give readers evidence that the story really belongs to you.

Sara Smith, a college student, keeps a journal both to explore ideas that are important to her and so skill have a reservoir of events and memories for writing assignments. Does this journal entry suggest any paper topics to you?

My Dad friended me last night. How lame is that? Last month he didn't know how to send an e-mail and all of a sudden he has his own page on Facebook. It's really sad, it's worse than sad, it's pathetic. He's lonely. Has no friends. So he puts up a picture of us — a father and his very happy daughter, both with the Albert Einstein crazy hair except his is grey and mine is brown, both beaming — to show people what a good family guy he is. There should be an age limit or something, for Facebook.

develop a thesis
p. 336

Wall Street Journal columnist Peggy Noonan uses narrative to introduce her argument that Americans need a common language to ensure they can work out problems together. More than just an opening anecdote, the personal narrative is key to her argument—it both engages readers and raises the issue of a single national language above mere politics. In particular, note how Noonan's descriptive details shift as her story of a meeting on a city street develops.

From "We Need to Talk"

Peggy Noonan

July 6, 2007

It is late afternoon in Manhattan on the Fourth of July, and I'm walking along on Lexington and 59th, in front of Bloomingdale's. Suddenly in my sight there's a young woman standing on a street grate. She is short, about 5 feet tall, and stocky, with a broad brown face. She is, I think, Latin American, maybe of Indian blood. She has a big pile of advertisements in her hand, and puts one toward me. "MENS SUITS NEW YORK—40% to 60% Off Sale!—Armani, Canali, Hugo Boss, DKNY, Zegna. TAILOR ON PREMISES. EXCELLENT SERVICE. LARGE SELECTION." Then the address and phone number.

You might have seen this person before. She's one of a small army of advertisement giver-outers in New York. Which means her life right now consists of standing in whatever weather and trying to give passersby a thing most of them don't want. If this is her regular job, she spends most of her time being rebuffed or ignored by busy people blurring by. You should always take an advertisement, or ten, from the advertisement giver-outers, just to give them a break, because once they give out all the ads, they can go back and get paid. So I took the ad and thanked her and walked on.

And then, half a block later, I turned around. I thought of a woman I'd met recently who had gone through various reverses in life and now had a new job, as a clerk in the back room of a store. She was happy to

Uses factual details to describe subject, a woman distributing advertising fliers.

Second paragraph provides contextual information and describes a simple action.

Turning around marks a shift in thought and action.

have it, a new beginning. But there was this thing: They didn't want to pay for air conditioning, so she sweltered all day. This made her want to weep, just talking about it. Ever since that conversation, I have been so grateful for my air conditioning. I had forgotten long ago to be grateful for it.

Anyway, I look back at the woman on the street grate. It's summer and she's in heavy jeans and a black sweatshirt with a hood. On top of that, literally, she's wearing a sandwich board—MENS SUITS NEW YORK. Her hair is long and heavy, her ponytail limp on her shoulders. She's out here on a day when everybody else, as she well knows—the streets are not crowded—is at a ball game or the beach. Everyone else is off.

So I turned around and went back. I wanted to say something—I don't know what, find out where she was from, encourage her. I said hello, and she looked at me and I patted her arm and said, "Happy Fourth of July, my friend." She was startled and then shy, and she smiled and made a sound, and I realized: She doesn't speak English. "God bless you," I said, because a little while in America and you know the word *God* just as ten minutes in Mexico and you learn the word *Dios*. And we both smiled and nodded and I left.

I went into Bloomingdale's and wrote these words: "We must speak the same language so we can hearten each other."

The question of whether America should have an "official language," of whether English should be formally declared our "national language," is bubbling, and will be back, in Congress, the next few sessions.

Noonan now describes her subject in greater and more sympathetic detail.

Story climaxes with a few phrases of dialogue.

Concludes narrative with her thesis— leading into her more formal argument in remainder of column.

Exploring purpose and topic

Writing a narrative on your own, you usually don't have to search for a topic. You know what events you want to record in a journal or diary or what part of your life you want to share in e-mails with friends. You'll know your audience well enough, too, to tune your story to the people likely to read it.

Assigned to write a narrative in school, you face different choices. Typically, such an assignment directs you to narrate an event that has changed or shaped you. Or perhaps an instructor requests a story that explores an aspect of your personality or reveals something about the communities to which you belong. Consider the following strategies when no topic ideas present themselves.

topic ◀

Brainstorm, freewrite, build lists, and use memory prompts to find a topic for a narrative. Talk with others, too, about their choices of subjects or share ideas on a class Web site. Trading ideas might jog your own memory about an incident or moment worth retelling.

Choose a manageable subject. You may be drawn to those life-changing events so obvious they seem cliché: deaths, graduations, car wrecks, winning hits, or first love. But understand that to make such topics work, you have to make them fresh for readers who've likely undergone similar experiences—or seen the movie. If you find an angle on such familiar events that belong specifically to you and can express it originally, you might take the risk. O

Alternatively, you can opt to narrate a slice of life rather than the whole side of beef—your toast at a wedding rather than the three-hour reception, a single encounter on a road trip rather than the entire cross-country adventure, or the scariest part of the night you were home alone when the power went out, rather than a minute-by-minute description. Beginning with your general topic, mine it for the dozens of more manageable stories within.

get an idea
p. 308

Understanding your audience

People like to read other people's stories, so the audiences for narratives are large, diverse, and receptive. (Even many diarists secretly hope that someone someday will find and read the confidential story of their lives.) Most of these eager readers probably expect a narrative to make some point or reveal an insight. Typically, they hope to be moved by the piece, to learn something from it, or perhaps to be amused by it.

You can capitalize on those expectations, using stories to introduce ideas that readers might be less open to if presented more formally (see Peggy Noonan's "We Need to Talk," p. 7).

Sometimes, however, your audience is quite specific. For instance, people within well-defined social, political, ethnic, or religious groups often write to share the experiences of their lives. Women and members of minority groups have used such narratives to document the adversities they face or to affirm their solidarity. Similarly, members of religious groups recall what it was like to grow up Jewish or Catholic or Baptist—and their readers appreciate when a story hits a familiar note. Of course, the best of these personal narratives often attract readers from outside the target audience too. ○

Of course, you might decide finally that the target audience of a narrative is yourself. Even then, be demanding. Think about how your story might sound ten or twenty years from now. Whatever the audience, you have choices to make.

A Classic Narrative Arc
You'll need to decide where to start your story and where to stop. The plan shown in this illustration is effective because the action unfolds in a way that meets audience expectations.

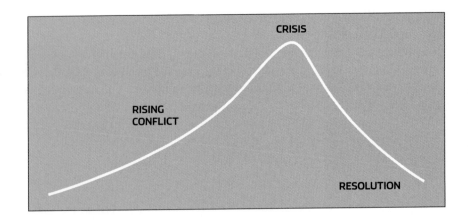

CRISIS

RISING CONFLICT

RESOLUTION

respect your readers
p. 374

Select events that will keep readers engaged.   Consider what parts of your topic will matter to readers. Which events represent high points in the action or moments that could not logically be omitted? Select those and consider cutting the others. Build toward a few major moments in the story that support one or two key themes.

Pace the story effectively.   Readers do want the story to move ahead, but not always at the same speed. Early on, they may want to learn about the characters involved in the action or to be introduced to the setting. You can slow the narrative to fill in these details and also to set up expectations for what will follow. For instance, if a person plays a role later in the story, introduce him or her briefly in the early paragraphs. If a cat matters, show the cat. But don't dwell on incidentals: Keep the story moving.

Tailor your writing to your intended readers.   An informal story written for peers may need brisk action as well as slang and dialogue to sound convincing—though you shouldn't use rough language for cheap effects. In a narrative written for an academic audience, you should slow the pace and use neutral language. But don't be too cautious. You still want the story to have enough texture to make your experiences seem authentic.

For instance, when writing a personal statement for an application to an academic program, keep a tight rein on the way you present yourself. ○ Here, for example, is a serious anecdote offered in an application to graduate school. You could easily imagine it told much more comically to friends.

> During my third year of Russian, I auditioned for the role of the evil stepsister Anna in a stage production of *Zolushka*. Although I welcomed the chance to act, I was terrified because I could not pronounce a Russian *r*. I had tried but was only able to produce an embarrassing sputter. Leading up to the play, I practiced daily with my professor, repeating "ryba" with a pencil in my mouth. When the play opened, I was able to say *"Kakoe urodstvo!"* with confidence. This experience gave me tremendous pride, because through it I discovered the power to isolate a problem, seek the necessary help, and ultimately solve it. I want to pass this power along to others by becoming a Russian language instructor.
>
> –Melissa Miller

refine your tone
p. 374

Finding and developing materials

▶ develop
   details

When you write about an event soon after it occurs—for instance, an accident report for an insurance claim—you might have the facts fresh in mind. Yet even in such cases, evidence helps back up your recollections. That's why insurance companies encourage drivers to carry a disposable camera in their cars in case they have a collision. The photo freezes details that human memory, especially under pressure, could ignore or forget. Needless to say, when writing about events in the more distant past, other memory prompts will help.

Consult documents.   A journal, if you keep one, provides a handy record for personal narratives such as a job history or family chronicle. Even a daily planner or PDA (personal digital assistant) might hold the necessary facts to reconstruct a series of events: Just knowing when certain meetings occurred jogs your thinking.

Consult images.   Photographs and videos provide material for personal narratives of all sorts. Not only do they document people and places, but they may also generate ideas, calling to mind far more than just what appears in the images. In writing a personal narrative, such prompts may stimulate your memory about past events and, just as important, the feelings those events generated. Visual images also remind you of the physical details—the shapes, colors, and textures—that add authenticity to a narrative and assure readers you're a sharp observer.

Trust your experiences.   In gathering materials for a narrative (or searching for a subject), you may initially be skeptical about your credentials for the assignment: you might think, "What have I done worth writing about"? ○ Most people underestimate their own expertise. First-year college students, for example, are usually experts about high school or certain kinds of music or hanging out at the mall or dealing with difficult parents. You don't have to be a celebrity to observe life or have something to say about it.

find a topic
p. 308

Here's humorist David Sedaris—who's made a career writing about his very middle-class life from his unique personal perspective—describing the problem:

> When I was teaching—I taught for a while—my students would write as if they were raised by wolves. Or raised on the streets. They were middle-class kids and they were ashamed of their background. They felt like unless they grew up in poverty, they had nothing to write about. Which was interesting because I had always thought that poor people were the ones who were ashamed. But it's not. It's middle-class people who are ashamed of their lives. And it doesn't really matter what your life was like, you can write about anything. It's just the writing of it that is the challenge. I felt sorry for these kids, that they thought that their whole past was absolutely worthless because it was less than remarkable.
>
> —David Sedaris, interviewed in *January Magazine*, June 2000

Photographs such as this one taken at a celebration after the Boston Red Sox won the 2007 World Series may recall not only the scene but also the moment the photo was taken, who was there, and so on.

Creating a structure

organize
events

Don't be intimidated by the idea of organizing a narrative. ○ You know a great deal about narrative structure from watching films or TV. All the complex plot devices you see in dramas or comedies—from foreshadowing to flashback, even to telling a story backward (as in the film *Memento*)—can be adapted to narratives you create in prose. But you need to plan ahead, know how many words or pages you have to tell your story, and then be sure you connect your incidents with effective transitional words and phrases.

Consider a simple sequence.   In a simple sequence, one event follows another chronologically. This structure has its complications, but it's a natural choice for narrative. Journals and diaries probably have the simplest sequential structures, with writers just recording one event after another without connecting them by anything much more than a date.

> First event
>
> Next event
>
> Next event
>
> Final event

Build toward a climax.   Narratives become much more complex if you want to present a set of incidents that lead to a *climax* or an *epiphany*. A climax is the moment when the action of a story peaks, takes an important turn, or is resolved. An epiphany is a moment of revelation when a writer or character suddenly sees events in a new light.

> First event
>
> Next event
>
> Next event
>
> Climax and/or epiphany
>
> Final event

connect ideas
p. 350

Narratives can have both structural features and often do—it's only logical that a major event in life would trigger heightened awareness or new understanding. In creating a structure for this kind of narrative, you can begin by deciding what that important event will be and then choosing other elements and incidents that lead up to or explain it. Everything not connected to that moment should probably be cut from the story. ◯

Similarly, when you want a narrative to make a specific point, include only events and incidents that reinforce your theme, directly or indirectly. Cut any actions that don't contribute to that point, however much you love them. Or refocus your narrative on the moment you do love.

Use images to tell a story.   In some cases, you may use images to accompany your narrative or to illustrate a sequence of events. ◯ An illustrated timeline is a simple form of this kind of narrative, as are baby books or yearbooks. More complex stories about your life or community can be told by combining your words and pictures in photo-essays or other media productions.

Fisherman with His Catch, a 32-inch, 18-pound Striped Bass   Note how the photograph conveys far more than the numerical statistics alone would.

revise for details
p. 386

think visually
p. 500

Choosing a style and design

Narratives are usually written in middle or low styles. That's because both styles nicely mimic the human voice through devices such as contractions and colloquialisms. Both styles are also comfortable with *I*, the point of view of many stories. A middle style may work in reaching academic or professional audiences. But a low style, dipping into slang and unconventional speech, can more accurately capture many moments in life and so feel more authentic. It's your choice.

Style is important because narratives get their energy and textures from sentence structures and vocabulary choices. In general, narratives require tight but evocative language—*tight* to keep the action moving, *evocative* to capture the gist of events. In a first draft, run with your ideas and don't do much editing. Flesh out the skeleton as you have designed it and then go back to see that the story works technically: Characters should be introduced and developed, locations identified and colored, events clearly explained and sequenced, key points made memorably and emphatically. You'll likely need several drafts to get these major items into shape.

Then look at your language and allow plenty of time for it. Begin with Chapter 32, "Vigorous, Clear, Economical Style." When you get the language right, your readers get the impression that you have observed events closely. Here are some options for your narrative.

Need help seeing the big picture? See "How to Revise Your Work" on pp. 390–91.

Don't hesitate to use first person—*I.* Most personal narratives are about the writer and so use first-person pronouns without apology. ○ (Third-person perspective tends to be used by essayists and humorists.)

A narrative often must take readers where the *I* has been, and using the first-person pronoun helps make writing authentic. Consider online journalist Michael Yon's explanation of why he reports on the Iraq War using *I* rather than a more objective third-person perspective:

> I write in first person because I am actually there at the events I write about. When I write about the bombs exploding, or the smell of blood, or the bullets snapping by, and I say *I*, it's because I was there. Yesterday a sniper shot at us, and seven of my neighbors were injured by a large bomb. These

define your style
p. 366

are my neighbors. These are soldiers. . . . I feel the fire from the explosions, and am lucky, very lucky, still to be alive. Everything here is first person.

–Glenn Reynolds, *An Army of Davids*

Use figures of speech such as similes, metaphors, and analogies to make memorable comparisons.

Similes make comparisons by using *like* or *as: He used his camera* like *a rifle.* Metaphors drop the *like* or *as* to gain even more power: *His camera was a rifle aimed at enemies.* An *analogy* extends the comparison: *His camera became a rifle aimed at his imaginary enemies, their private lives in his crosshairs.*

People use comparisons eagerly, some so common they've been reduced to invisible clichés: *hit me like a ton of bricks; dumb as an ox; clear as a bell.* Use similes and metaphors in a narrative fresher than these and yet not contrived or strained. Here's science writer Michael Chorost effortlessly using both a metaphor (*spins up*) and a simile (*like riding a roller coaster*) to describe what he experiences as he awaits surgery.

I can feel the bustle and clatter around me as the surgical team spins up to take-off speed. It is like riding a roller coaster upward to the first great plunge, strapped in and committed.

–*Rebuilt: How Becoming Part Computer Made Me More Human*

In choosing verbs, favor active rather than passive voice.

Active verbs propel the action (*Agnes signed the petition*) while passive verbs slow it down by an unneeded word or two (*The petition was signed by Agnes*). ○

Since narratives are all about movement, build sentences around strong and unpretentious verbs. Edit until you get down to the bone of the action and produce sentences as effortless as these from Joseph Epstein, describing the pleasures of catching plagiarists. ○ Verbs are highlighted in this passage; you'll find only one passive verb *is followed* in the mix.

In thirty years of teaching university students I never encountered a case of plagiarism, or even one that I suspected. Teachers I've known who have caught students in this sad act report that the capture gives one an odd sense of power. The power derives from the authority that resides behind the word *gotcha*. This is followed by that awful moment–a veritable sadist's

improve your sentences
p. 378

avoid plagiarism
p. 431

Mardi Gras—when one calls the student into one's office and points out the odd coincidence that he seems to have written about existentialism in precisely the same words Jean-Paul Sartre used fifty-two years earlier.

—"Plagiary, It's Crawling All Over Me," *Weekly Standard,* March 6, 2006

Use powerful and precise modifiers.   In most cases, one strong word is better than several weaker ones (*freezing* rather than *very cold; doltish* rather than *not very bright*). ○ Done right, proper modifiers can even make you hungry.

My friend Barbara got the final stretch of the trip, a southwestern route of burritos and more burritos: with and without rice, with and without sour cream, planned burritos and serendipitous burritos.

We pulled off the highway near Odessa, Texas, to hunt down a Taco Villa and, across the street, espied something called JumBurrito, an even smaller Texas chain. Taco Villa's grilled chicken burrito had a profusion of chicken that indeed tasted grilled, while JumBurrito's combination burrito redeemed dull beef with vibrant avocado.

Neither approximated the majesty of the burrito I loved most, which I ate in Dallas, at a Taco Cabana. A great burrito is a balancing act, and the proportions of ground beef, beans, sour cream, and diced tomatoes in Taco Cabana's plump, heavy Burrito Ultimo (three Wet Naps) were spot on.

—Frank Bruni, "Life in the Fast-Food Lane," *New York Times*, May 24, 2006

Use dialogue to propel the narrative and to give life to your characters.   What people say and how they say it can reveal a great deal about them without much commentary from you. But be sure the words your characters speak sound natural: *No* dialogue is better than awkward dialogue. Dialogue ordinarily requires quotation marks and new paragraphs for each change of speaker. But keep the tags simple: You don't have to vary much from *he said* or *she said*.

"My dear Mr. Bennet," said his lady to him one day, "have you heard that Netherfield Park is let at last?"

Mr. Bennet replied that he had not.

"But it is," returned she; "for Mrs. Long has just been here, and she told me all about it."

Mr. Bennet made no answer.

> The difference between the almost right word and the right word is really a large matter—it's the difference between the lightning bug and the lightning.

—Mark Twain

improve your sentences
p. 378

"Do not you want to know who has taken it?" cried his wife, impatiently.

"*You* want to tell me, and I have no objection to hearing it." This was invitation enough.

–Jane Austen, *Pride and Prejudice*

If you are using dialogue — say it aloud as you write it. Only then will it have the sound of speech.

—John Steinbeck

Develop major characters through language *and* action.   Search for the precise adjectives and adverbs to describe their looks (*cheery, greedily*) and their manners (*tight, conceitedly, smarmy*) or, even better, have them reveal their natures by their actions (*glancing in every mirror; ignoring the staff to fawn over the bigwigs*). In fact, you'll probably need to do both. Here's how one writer describes a classmate (ouch!) with whom she is partnered on a group project:

> Jane dragged me to her dorm one weekend to help her crunch the numbers. Her phone started ringing, but she told me to ignore it. The answering machine clicked on as a whiny, southern voice pleaded, "Jane, honey, where *are* yew? Daddy and I have been trying to reach you for three days, but you haven't answered your dorm or cell phones. Please, call us so we'll know that you're okay. We love you very much, Sweetie."
>
> Jane's annoyance rivaled the desperation in her mother's voice. She had always claimed to love her family, but she barely batted an eye at her mom's concern for her well-being. "I don't have time for her right now," Jane stated coldly as she continued typing.
>
> –Bettina Ramon, "Ambition Incarnate"

Develop the setting to set the context and mood.   Show readers where and when events are occurring if the setting makes a difference—and that will be most of the time. Location (Times Square; dusty street in Gallup, New Mexico; your bedroom), as well as climate and time of day (cool dawn, exotic dusk, broiling afternoon), will help readers get a fix on the story. But don't churn out paragraphs of description just for their own sake; readers will skate right over them. Consider, too, whether photographs attached to the narrative might help readers grasp the setting and situation. Don't use images as an excuse to avoid writing; rather, consider how they complement text, and so may have a legitimate place in your story. **O**

think visually
p. 500

Examining models

LITERACY NARRATIVE   Such a piece typically narrates the processes by which a person learns to read or write or acquires an intellectual skill or ability. In "Strange Tools," author Richard Rodriguez explains how he developed his habits of reading. The selection is from *Hunger of Memory* (1981), in which Rodriguez explains how his life has followed the pattern of "the scholarship boy," described by Richard Hoggart as a youth from a lower-class background whose pursuit of education separates him from his community.

Strange Tools

RICHARD RODRIGUEZ

Sets the scene.

From an early age I knew that my mother and father could read and write both Spanish and English. I had observed my father making his way through what, I now suppose, must have been income tax forms. On other occasions I waited apprehensively while my mother read onion-paper letters airmailed from Mexico with news of a relative's illness or death. For both my parents, however, reading was something done out of necessity and as quickly as possible. Never did I see either of them read an entire book. Nor did I see them read for pleasure. Their reading consisted of work manuals, prayer books, newspapers, recipes.

Richard Hoggart imagines how, at home,

> . . . [The scholarship boy] sees strewn around, and reads regularly himself, magazines which are never mentioned at school, which seem not to belong to the world to which the school introduces him; at school he hears about and reads books never mentioned at home. When he brings those books into the house they do not take their place with other books which the family are reading, for often there are none or almost none; his books look, rather, like strange tools.

Hoggart's "scholarship boy" is a key theme in Rodriguez's work.

In our house each school year would begin with my mother's careful instruction: "Don't write in your books so we can sell them at the end of the year." The remark was echoed in public by my teachers, but only in part: "Boys and girls, don't write in your books. You must learn to treat them with great care and respect."

Narrates early experiences as a reader.

OPEN THE DOORS OF YOUR MIND WITH BOOKS, read the red and white poster over the nun's desk in early September. It soon was apparent to me that reading was the classroom's central activity. Each course had its own book. And the information gathered from a book was unquestioned. READ TO LEARN, the sign on the wall advised in December. I privately wondered: What was the connection between reading and learning? Did one learn something only by reading it? Was an idea only an idea if it could be written down? In June, CONSIDER BOOKS YOUR BEST FRIENDS. Friends? Reading was, at best, only a chore. I needed to look up whole paragraphs of words in a dictionary. Lines of type were dizzying, the eye having to move slowly across the page, then down, and across. . . .The sentences of the first books I read were coolly impersonal. Toned hard. What most bothered me, however, was the isolation reading required. To console myself for the loneliness I'd feel when I read, I tried reading in a very soft voice. Until: "Who is doing all that talking to his neighbor?" Shortly after, remedial reading classes were arranged for me with a very old nun.

At the end of each school day, for nearly six months, I would meet with her in the tiny room that served as the school's library but was actually only a storeroom for used textbooks and a vast collection of *National Geographics*. Everything about our sessions pleased me: the smallness of the room; the noise of the janitor's broom hitting the edge of the long hallway outside the door; the green of the sun, lighting the wall; and the old woman's face blurred white with a beard. Most of the time we took turns. I began with my elementary text. Sentences of astonishing simplicity seemed to me lifeless and drab: "The boys ran from the rain. . . . She wanted to sing. . . . The kite rose in the blue." Then the old nun would read from her favorite books, usually biographies of early American presidents. Playfully she ran through complex sentences, calling the words alive with her voice, making it seem that the author somehow was speaking directly to me. I smiled just to listen to her. I sat there

Details give experiences impact.

and sensed for the very first time some possibility of fellowship between a reader and a writer, a communication, never *intimate* like that I heard spoken words at home convey, but one nonetheless *personal*.

One day the nun concluded a session by asking me why I was so reluctant to read by myself. I tried to explain; said something about the way written words made me feel all alone—almost, I wanted to add but didn't, as when I spoke to myself in a room just emptied of furniture. She studied my face as I spoke; she seemed to be watching more than listening. In an uneventful voice she replied that I had nothing to fear. Didn't I realize that reading would open up whole new worlds? A book could open doors for me. It could introduce me to people and show me places I never imagined existed. She gestured toward the bookshelves. (Bare-breasted African women danced, and the shiny hubcaps of automobiles on the back covers of the *Geographic* gleamed in my mind.) I listened with respect. But her words were not very influential. I was thinking then of another consequence of literacy, one I was too shy to admit but nonetheless trusted. Books were going to make me "educated." *That* confidence enabled me, several months later, to overcome my fear of the silence.

> Most action occurs in Rodriguez's thoughts.

In fourth grade I embarked upon a grandiose reading program. "Give me the names of important books," I would say to startled teachers. They soon found out that I had in mind "adult books." I ignored their suggestion of anything I suspected was written for children. (Not until I was in college, as a result, did I read *Huckleberry Finn* or *Alice's Adventures in Wonderland*.) Instead, I read *The Scarlet Letter* and Franklin's *Autobiography*. And whatever I read I read for extra credit. Each time I finished a book, I reported the achievement to a teacher and basked in the praise my effort earned. Despite my best efforts, however, there seemed to be more and more books I needed to read. At the library I would literally tremble as I came upon whole shelves of books I hadn't read. So I read and I read and I read: *Great Expectations*; all the short stories of Kipling; *The Babe Ruth Story*; the entire first volume of the *Encyclopaedia Britannica* (A–ANSTEY); the *Iliad*; *Moby-Dick*; *Gone with the Wind*; *The Good*

Earth; Remond; Forever Amber; The Lives of the Saints; Crime and Punishment; The Pearl. . . . Librarians who initially frowned when I checked out the maximum ten books at a time started saving books they thought I might like. Teachers would say to the rest of the class, "I only wish the rest of you took reading as seriously as Richard obviously does."

Growing skill as a reader causes conflict for Rodriguez.

But at home I would hear my mother wondering, "What do you see in your books?" (Was reading a hobby like her knitting? Was so much reading even healthy for a boy? Was it the sign of "brains"? Or was it just a convenient excuse for not helping around the house on Saturday mornings?) Always, "What do you see . . . ?"

Getting older, Rodriguez examines why he reads.

What *did* I see in my books? I had the idea that they were crucial for my academic success, though I couldn't have said exactly how or why. In the sixth grade I simply concluded that what gave a book its value was some major idea or theme it contained. If that core essence could be mined and memorized, I would become learned like my teachers. I decided to record in a notebook the themes of the books that I read. After reading *Robinson Crusoe*, I wrote that its theme was "the value of learning to live by oneself." When I completed *Wuthering Heights*, I noted the danger of "letting emotions get out of control." Rereading these brief moralistic appraisals usually left me disheartened. I couldn't believe that they were really the source of reading's value. But for many more years, they constituted the only means I had of describing to myself the educational value of books.

Rodriguez concludes by raising doubts about the skills he has acquired.

In spite of my earnestness, I found reading a pleasurable activity. I came to enjoy the lonely good company of books. Early on weekday mornings, I'd read in my bed. I'd feel a mysterious comfort then, reading in the dawn quiet—the bluegray silence interrupted by the occasional churning of the refrigerator motor a few rooms away or the more distant sound of a city bus beginning its run. On weekends I'd go to the public library to read, surrounded by old men and women. Or, if the weather was fine, I would take my books to the park and read in the shade of a tree. A warm summer evening was my favorite reading time. Neighbors would leave for vacation and I would water their lawns. I would sit through the twilight on the front porches or in backyards, reading to the cool, whirling sounds of the sprinklers.

I also had favorite writers. But often those writers I enjoyed most I was least able to value. When I read William Saroyan's *The Human Comedy,* I was immediately pleased by the narrator's warmth and the charm of his story. But as quickly I became suspicious. A book so enjoyable to read couldn't be very "important." Another summer I determined to read all the novels of Dickens. Reading his fat novels, I loved the feeling I got—after the first hundred pages—of being at home in a fictional world where I knew the names of the characters and cared about what was going to happen to them. And it bothered me that I was forced away at the conclusion, when the fiction closed tight, like a fortune-teller's fist—the futures of all the major characters neatly resolved. I never knew how to take such feelings of a novel's meaning. Still, there were pleasures to sustain me after I'd finish my books. Carrying a volume back to the library, I would be pleased by its weight. I'd run my fingers along the edge of the pages and marvel at the breadth of my achievement. Around my room, growing stacks of paperback books reinforced my assurance.

I entered high school having read hundreds of books. My habit of reading made me a confident speaker and writer of English. Reading also enabled me to sense something of the shape, the major concerns, of Western thought. (I was able to say something about Dante and Descartes and Engels and James Baldwin in my high school term papers.) In these various ways, books brought me academic success as I hoped that they would. But I was not a good reader. Merely bookish, I lacked a point of view when I read. Rather, I read in order to acquire a point of view. I vacuumed books for epigrams, scraps of information, ideas, themes—anything to fill the hollow within me and make me feel educated. When one of my teachers suggested to his drowsy tenth-grade English class that a person could not have a "complicated idea" until he had read at least two thousand books, I heard the remark without detecting either its irony or its very complicated truth. I merely determined to compile a list of all the books I had ever read. Harsh with myself, I included only once a title I might have read several times. (How, after all, could one read a book more than once?) And I included only those books over a hundred pages in length. (Could anything shorter be a book?)

There was yet another high school list I compiled. One day I came across a newspaper article about the retirement of an English professor at a nearby state college. The article was accompanied by a list of the "hundred most important books of Western Civilization." "More than anything else in my life," the professor told the reporter with finality, "these books have made me all that I am." That was the kind of remark I couldn't ignore. I clipped out the list and kept it for the several months it took me to read all of the titles. Most books, of course, I barely understood. While reading Plato's *Republic,* for instance, I needed to keep looking at the book jacket comments to remind myself what the text was about. Nevertheless, with the special patience and superstition of a scholarship boy, I looked at every word of the text. And by the time I reached the last word, relieved, I convinced myself that I had read *The Republic.* In a ceremony of great pride, I solemnly crossed Plato off my list.

MEMOIR   In the following essay, Miles Pequeno uses a narrative about a chess match to describe a changing relationship with his father. The paper was written in response to an assignment in an upper-division college writing class.

Pequeno 1

Miles Pequeno

Instructor's Name

Course Title

Date

Check. Mate?

"Checkmate! Right? You can't move him anywhere, right? I got you again!" I couldn't control my glee. For good measure, I even grabbed my rook, which stood next to his king, and gave him a posthumous beating. The deposed king tumbled from the round table and onto the hardwood floor with a thud. The sound of sure victory. Being eight, it was easy to get excited about chess. It gave me not only at least a few minutes of Dad's attention and approval, but the comfort of knowing I'd taste victory every time. Either Dad was letting me always win, or I was the prodigy he wanted me to be. I always liked to believe it was the latter.

The relationship I had with my father was always complicated. I loved him and he loved me; that much was understood. But his idea of fatherhood was a little unorthodox (or maybe too orthodox, I'm not sure which). We didn't play catch in the yard, but he did make flash cards to teach me my multiplication tables when I was still in kindergarten. He didn't take me to Astros games, but he made sure I knew lots of big words from the newspaper. We were close, but only on his terms.

> Narrative opens with dialogue and action.

> Uses particular details to explain relationship with father.

Pequeno 2

Save for the ever-graying hair near his temples, he looks much the same now as he did when I was little: round belly, round face, and big brown eyes that pierced while they silently observed and inwardly critiqued. His black hair, coarse and thick, and day-or-two-old beard usually gave away his heritage. He came to our suburb of Houston from Mexico when he was a toddler, learned English watching Spider-Man cartoons, and has since spent his life catching up, constantly working at moving up in the world. Even more was expected of me, the extension of his hard work and dreams for the future. I had no idea at the time, but back when I was beating him at chess as a kid, I myself was a pawn. He was planning something.

Then a funny thing happened. After winning every game since age eight, the five-year win streak ended. I lost. This time, Dad had decided to take off the training wheels. Just as he was thrust into the real world unceremoniously with my birth when he was but eighteen years old, I was forced to grow up a little early, too. The message was clear: Nothing is being handed to you anymore, Son.

This abrupt lesson changed my outlook. I no longer wanted to make Dad proud; I wanted to equal or better him. I'd been conditioned to seek his attention and approval, and then the rug was pulled from beneath my feet. I awoke to the realization that it was now my job to prove that the student could become the teacher.

I spent time after school every day playing chess against the artificial intelligence of my little Windows 95 computer. I knew what problems I had to correct because Dad was sure to point them out in the days after forcing that first loss. I had trouble using my queen. Dad always either knocked her out early or made me too afraid to put her in play. The result was my king slaughtered time and time

Using first person, Pequeno draws on personal experience to describe and characterize father.

Notice how a metaphor here (*training wheels*) blossoms into an analogy about growing up.

Provides background information here important later in story.

Pequeno 3

again as his bride, the queen, sat idle on the far side of the board.

Our chess set was made of marble, with green and white hand-carved pieces sitting atop the thick, round board. Dad kept the set next to the TV and, most nights, we'd take it down from the entertainment center and put it on the coffee table in front of the sofa, where we sat side by side and played chess while halfway paying attention to the television. One night after Mom's spaghetti dinner, I casually walked into the living room to find Dad sitting sipping a Corona and watching the Rockets game. Hakeem Olajuwon was having a great night. Usually, if Dad was really into something on TV, we'd go our separate ways and maybe play later. This night, I picked up the remote control from the coffee table. Off.

"Let's play," I said resolutely. I grabbed the marble chess set, with all the pieces exactly where I had put them in anticipation of this game. The board seemed heavier than usual, carrying it to the coffee table. I sat down next to him on the sofa and stared at the pieces, suddenly going blank. The bishops might as well have been knights. I froze as Dad asked me what color I wanted. Traditionally, this had been merely a formality. I'd always picked white before because I wanted to have the first move. That was the rule: White moves first, green next.

"Green."

Then it all came back to me. The certainty of my declaration surprised him. He furrowed his brows slightly and leaned back just enough to show good-natured condescension.

"You sure? That means I go first."

"I'm sure. Take white."

So he began his attack. He started off controlling one side of the board, slowly advancing. The knights led the charge, with the

> Paragraph sets the physical scene for climactic chess match.

> First dialogue since opening signals rising action.

> "Combat" metaphor in next few paragraphs moves story forward.

Pequeno 4

pawns waiting in the wings to form an impenetrable wall around the royal family, who remained in their little castle of two adjacent spaces.

Every move was made with painful precision. Now and then after my moves, he'd sigh and sink a little into the sofa. He'd furrow those big black brows, his eyes darting quickly from one side of the board to the other, thinking two or three moves ahead. Some of his mannerisms this time were completely new, like the hesitation of his hand as he'd reach for a piece and then jerk it back quickly, realizing that my strategy had shut more than a few doors for him.

Eventually I worked up the courage to thrust the queen into action. She moved with great trepidation at first, never attacking, merely sneaking down the board. In the meantime, Dad's advancing rooks and knights were taking out my line of pawns, which I'd foolishly put too far into play. Every risk either of us took was clearly calculated. Sometimes he'd mutter to himself, slowly realizing this game wasn't as usual.

Things were looking good. Even if I didn't win, I'd already won a victory by challenging him. But that wasn't what I had practiced for. It wasn't why I'd turned off the television, and it certainly wasn't why I was concentrating so hard on these white-and-green figurines.

I was locked in. This was more than father and son. This was an epic battle between generals who knew each other well enough to keep the other at bay. But I was advancing. Sure, there were losses, but that was the cost of war. I had a mission.

My queen finally reached his king unharmed.

"Check."

I uttered the word silently. As the game had progressed, gaining intensity and meaning, there was no conversation. In its place were sporadic comments, muttered with deference. So when I said

Another extended analogy.

Pequeno 5

"check," I made sure not to make a big deal of it. I said it quietly, softly. I didn't want to jinx myself with bragging, and I certainly didn't want to get too excited and break my own concentration. As his king scrambled for a safe hiding place my knights continued their advance. I had planned for this stage of the game several moves before, which was apparently at least one move more than Dad was thinking ahead. Check again. More scrambling, and another check. It seemed I had him cornered. Then. . . .

"Check." It wasn't the first time I had him in check, and I didn't expect it to be the last in this game.

"Mate," he whispered, faint hints of a smile beginning to show on the corners of his mouth, pushing his cheeks up slightly. I hadn't realized that I had won until he conceded defeat with that word. Raising his eyebrows, he leaned back into the cushion of the sofa. He looked a little tired.

"Mate?" I wasn't sure he was right. I didn't let myself believe it until I stared at these little marble men. Sure enough, his desperate king was cornered.

"Good game, Son."

And that was it. There was his approval right there, manifesting itself in that smile that said "I love you" and "you sneaky son of a bitch" at the same time. But I didn't feel like any more of a man than I had an hour before. In fact, I felt a little hollow. So I just kept my seat next to him, picked up the remote control again, and watched the Rockets finish off the Mavericks. Business as usual after that. I went back to my room and did some homework, but kept the chess game at the forefront of my mind.

Note that story climax occurs mostly through dialogue.

Father's smile signals change in father-son relationship.

Pequeno 6

"Wait a second. Had he let me win? Damn it, I'd worked so hard just for him to toy with me again, even worse than when he'd let me beat him before. No, there's no way he let me win. Or maybe he did. I don't know."

I walked back into the living room.

"Rematch?"

So we played again, and I lost. It didn't hurt, though. It didn't feel nearly as bad when he first took off the training wheels. This was a different kind of defeat, and it didn't bother me one bit. I had nothing left to prove. If I'd lost, so what? I'd already shown what I could do.

But what if he'd let me win?

Again, so what? I had made myself a better player than I was before. I didn't need him to pass me a torch. I'd taken the flame myself, like a thirteen-year-old Prometheus. After that night, I was my own man, ready for everything: high school, my first girlfriend, my parents' divorce, my first job, moving away to college, starting a career. I never lost the feeling that I could make everything work if I just chose the right moves. I still live by that principle.

> Initial doubts about followup match lead to *epiphany* in final paragraph—sudden moment of insight.

GRAPHIC NOVEL (EXCERPT)   In *Persepolis* (2003), Marjane Satrapi uses the medium of graphic novel to narrate the story of her girlhood in Iran. As she grew up, she witnessed the overthrow of the shah and the Islamic Revolution, and the subsequent war with Iraq. The selection on the following pages describes life under the shah.

▶

HE TOOK PHOTOS EVERY DAY. IT WAS STRICTLY FORBIDDEN. HE HAD EVEN BEEN ARRESTED ONCE BUT ESCAPED AT THE LAST MINUTE.

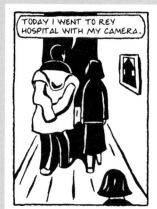

TODAY I WENT TO REY HOSPITAL WITH MY CAMERA.

PEOPLE CAME OUT CARRYING THE BODY OF A YOUNG MAN KILLED BY THE ARMY. HE WAS HONORED LIKE A MARTYR. A CROWD GATHERED TO TAKE HIM TO THE BAHESHTE ZAHRA CEMETERY.

THEN THERE WAS ANOTHER CADAVER, AN OLD MAN CARRIED OUT ON A STRETCHER. THOSE WHO DIDN'T FOLLOW THE FIRST ONE WENT OVER TO THE OLD MAN, SHOUTING REVOLUTIONARY SLOGANS AND CALLING HIM A HERO.

HERE IS ANOTHER MARTYR.

WELL, I WAS TAKING MY PHOTOS WHEN I NOTICED AN OLD WOMAN NEXT TO ME. I UNDERSTOOD THAT SHE WAS THE WIDOW OF THE VICTIM. I HAD SEEN HER LEAVE THE HOSPITAL WITH THE BODY.

PLEASE! STOP IT! STOP IT!

WHAT? WHAT IS IT?

STOP IT!

WHO ARE YOU?

HIS WIDOW!

ARE YOU A ROYALIST?

NO, BUT MY HUSBAND DIED OF CANCER...

1. **Literacy Narrative:** After reading Richard Rodriguez's "Strange Tools" (p. 20), write a literacy narrative of your own, recalling teachers or assignments that helped (or hindered) you in learning to read or write. Describe books that changed you or ambitions you might have to pursue a writing or media career. However, you don't have to be an aspiring writer to make sense of this assignment. Remember that there are many kinds of literacy. The narrative you write may be about your encounters with paintings, films, music, fashion, architecture, or maybe even video games.

2. **Memoir:** Using Miles Pequeno's "Check. Mate?" as a model (p. 26), compose a short narrative describing how an individual (like Pequeno's father) changed your life or made you see the world in a different way. Make sure readers gain a strong sense both of this person and your relationship to him or her.

3. **Reflection:** Make a point about your school or community the way Peggy Noonan does in her piece about Manhattan on the Fourth of July ("We Need to Talk," p. 7). If appropriate, supplement the narrative with a photo.

4. **Visual Narrative:** *Persepolis* (p. 32) demonstrates that a story can be told in various media: This graphic novel even became an animated film in 2007. Using a medium other than words alone, tell a story from your own life or from your community. Draw it, use photographs, craft a collage, create a video, record interviews, or combine other media suited to your nonfiction tale.

5. **Reflection:** Narrate your experiences about a *place*—from the past or present—that show why this environment is an important part of your life. You can introduce readers to characters you met there, thoughts or emotions the place evokes, or incidents that occurred in this setting, whether it is a coffeehouse, stage, newspaper office, club, or even a library. You can tell this story in words, in a photoessay, or in a video.

How to start
- Need a **topic**? See page 45.
- Need to **find information**? See page 48.
- Need to **organize that information**? See page 50.

2 Report

provides readers with reliable information

You've been preparing reports since the second grade when you probably used an encyclopedia to explain why volcanoes erupt or who Franklin Roosevelt was. Today, the reports you write may be more ambitious.

- You research a term paper on global warming, trying to separate scientific evidence from political claims.

- You write up the results of your chemistry, biology, or physics labs hoping your words do less damage than the experiments did.

- You write a sports column for your campus newspaper, describing the complexities of NCAA regulations on major collegiate sports. You focus on recruiting.

- You prepare a PowerPoint presentation for your history class to show that weather—more than English naval tactics—doomed the Spanish Armada of 1588.

- You study the annual reports issued by a major company for the past decade to compare growth projections with actual performance.

UNDERSTANDING REPORTS.   As you might guess, reports make up one of the broadest genres of writing. If you use Google to search the term online, you will turn up an unwieldy two billion items, beginning with the *Drudge Report* and moving on to sites that cover everything from financial news to morbidity studies. Such sites may not resemble the term papers, presentations, and lab reports you'll typically prepare for school. But they'll share at least some of the goals you'll have when drafting academic reports.

Stephen Colbert parodies the concept of *report* in his nightly putdown of pompous cable-TV pundits, *The Colbert Report*. *Time*, on the other hand, promises to provide readers with accurate information about the aftermath of Katrina in a "special report." But does the magazine undermine its objectivity by rendering a verdict on the cover: "It's pathetic"?

Present information.   Obviously, people read reports to discover what they don't already know or confirm what they do. They expect what they read to be timely and accurate. And sometimes, the information or data you present *will* be new (as in *news*), built from recent events or the latest research. But just as often, your reports will repackage data from existing sources. *Are cats and dogs really color-blind?* The answer to such a question is already out there for you to find—if you know where to look.

Find reliable sources.   The heart and soul of any report will be reliable sources that provide or confirm information—whether they are "high government officials" quoted anonymously in news stories or articles listed in the bibliographies of college term papers. If asked to write a report about a topic new to you, immediately plan to do library and online research. ○

But the information in reports is just as often generated by careful experiments and observations. Even personal experience may sometimes provide material for reports, though anecdotes need corroboration to be convincing.

Aim for objectivity.   Writers and institutions (such as newspapers or government agencies) know that they'll lose credibility if their factual presentations seem incomplete or biased. Of course, smart readers understand that reports on contentious subjects—global warming, intelligent design, or stem-cell research, for example—may lean one way or another. In fact, you may develop strong opinions based on the research you've done. But readers of reports usually prefer to draw their own conclusions.

Present information clearly.   Readers expect material in reports and reference material to be arranged (and perhaps illustrated) for their benefit. ○ So when you present information, state your claims quickly and support them with data. You'll gain no points for surprises, twists, or suspense in a report. In fact, you'll usually give away the game on the first page of most reports by announcing not only your thesis but also perhaps your conclusions.

find a topic
p. 308

think visually
p. 500

This very brief report—actually a news item—from *Astronomy* magazine explains a recent astronomical discovery. Brief as it is, it shows how reports work.

Uranus's Second Ring-Moon System

LAURA LAYTON

Saturn isn't the only planet to harbor a complex ring structure. In 1986, NASA's *Voyager 2* spacecraft sent back images of a family of ten moons and a system of rings orbiting Uranus. New images from the Hubble Space Telescope (HST) increase those numbers.

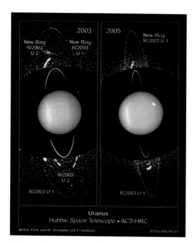

The Hubble telescope imaged Uranus's two newly discovered rings in 2003 and 2005. *NASA, ESA, and M. Showalter of the SETI Institute.*

On December 22, planetary astronomer Mark Showalter of the SETI Institute and Jack Lissauer of the NASA Ames Research Center announced the discovery of two additional moons and two large outer rings. HST's Advanced Camera for Surveys (ACS) imaged new moons Cupid and Mab as well as two faint, dusty rings from July 2003 through August 2005.

Newly discovered moon Cupid orbits in the midst of a swarm of inner moons known as the Portia group, so named after the group's largest moon. The Portia group lies just outside Uranus's inner ring system and

Title is simple, factual.

Opening paragraphs present new information and sources.

Facts are presented clearly and objectively.

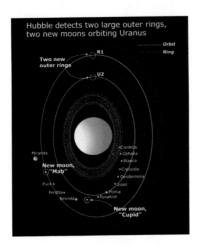

Hubble detects two large outer rings, two new moons orbiting Uranus

The features and locations of Uranus's known moons and rings.   *NASA, ESA, and A. Field of STScI.*

inside the planet's larger, classical moon group of Belinda, Perdita, Puck, and Miranda. Mab, the smaller of the two newly detected moons, orbits outside the inner moon group and Cupid, but interior to Uranus's four outer moons.

A second ring system was also detected around Uranus and imaged by Hubble. Rings R/2003 U 1 and R/2003 U 2 (R1 and R2, respectively) both lie outside the orbit of the inner ring system. Researchers believe micron-size dust is a main constituent of these rings.

What is not clear is how these rings formed. Meteoroid impacts on Uranus's moons that eject fine dust may feed the rings or collisions among existing rings may produce new ones. Either way, the moons' small sizes and surface areas keep any ejected material from falling back to their surfaces and reaccreting. According to Showalter, "Dust material is coming off of Mab and spreading out to make this [R1] ring." It's not apparent what body provides the material for the inner (R2) ring. Lissauer theorizes that a disrupted moon may have been a source.

Showalter believes Uranus's ring-moon system is unstable and exhibits chaotic evolution. Since the last observations were made, Uranus's moons changed orbit. This has long-term implications for Uranus's ring-moon system. "Long-term changes to the system include collisions and crossing ring systems," adds Lissauer.

One thing is for sure, says Lissauer — "Our solar system is a dynamic place."

—*Astronomy,* December 28, 2005

Images and captions illustrate discovery.

Authorities are quoted.

Exploring purpose and topic

When assigned a report, think about the kinds of information you need to present. Will your report merely answer a factual question about a topic and deliver basic information? Or are you expected to do a more in-depth study? Or might the report deliver new information based on your own recent research or experiments? Consider your various options as you select a topic.

topic ◀

Answer questions.   For this kind of report, include basic facts and, perhaps, an overview of key features, issues, or problems. Think of an encyclopedia as a model: When you look up an article there, you usually aren't interested in an exhaustive treatment of a subject.

Assigned a report intended to answer basic questions, you can choose topics that would otherwise seem overly ambitious. So long as all that readers expect is an overview, not expertise, you could easily write two or three fact-filled pages on "Memphis and the Blues" or "The Battle of Marathon" by focusing on just a few key figures, events, and concepts. Given this opportunity, select a topic that introduces you to new ideas or perspectives— this could, in fact, be the rationale for the specific assignment.

Review what is already known about a subject.   Instructors who ask you to write five- or ten-page reports on specific subjects in a field— for example, to explain banking practices in Japan or to describe current trends in museum architecture—doubtless know plenty about those subjects

Field research is one way to deliver new information.

already. They want you to look at the topic in some depth to increase what you know. But the subject may also be evolving rapidly because of ongoing research or current events.

So consider updating an idea introduced in a lecture or textbook: You might be surprised by how much you can add to what an instructor has presented. If workers are striking in Paris again, make that a focal point of your general report on European Union economic policies; if your course covers globalism, consider how a world community made smaller by jet travel complicates the response to epidemic diseases. In considering topics for in-depth reports, you'll find "research guides"especially helpful. ○ You may also want to consult librarians or experts in the field you're writing about. ○

Report new knowledge.   Many schools encourage undergraduates to conduct original research in college. In most cases, this work is done under the supervision of an instructor in your major field, and you'll likely choose a topic only after developing expertise in some area. For a look at research topics students from different schools have explored, use Google to search "undergraduate research journal."

If you have trouble finding a subject for a report, try the brainstorming techniques suggested in Chapter 17, both to identify topic ideas and to narrow them to manageable size.

Establish credibility.   Because they draw on sources, speak in reasonable tones, and document their claims, reports often seem more respectable than even responsible editorials or op-ed pieces. Not surprisingly then, people and organizations use reports to boost their credibility. On the Web site of any major group embroiled in controversy you will usually find—if you look hard enough—reports, white papers, fact sheets, and other data to back up the organization's major claims. Most credible groups feel an obligation to provide such information. Academic reports you write may serve this function, providing the solid facts and evidence for ideas you will explore later in more advanced work.

refine your search
p. 406

ask for help
p. 325

Understanding your audience

You probably know that you should tailor any report to its potential readers. Well-informed audiences expect detailed reports that use technical language, but if your potential audience includes a range of readers, from experts to amateurs, design your work to suit them all. Perhaps you can use headings to ease novices through your report while simultaneously signaling to more knowledgeable readers what sections they might skip. ○ Make audience-sensitive moves like this routinely, whenever you are composing.

But sometimes it's not the content that you must tailor for potential readers: It's how readers perceive *you*. They'll look at you differently, according to the expertise you bring to the project. What are the options?

Suppose you are the expert.   This may be the typical pose of most professional writers of reports, smoothly presenting material they know well enough to teach. But knowledgeable people still often make two common mistakes in presenting information. Either they assume an audience is as informed as they are, and so omit the very details and helpful transitions that many readers need, or they underestimate the intelligence of their readers and consequently weary them with trivial and unnecessary explanations. ○ Readers want a confident guide but also one who knows when—*and when not*—to define a term, provide a graph, or supply some context.

Suppose you are the novice.   In a typical academic report, you're likely dealing with material relatively new to you. Your expertise on language acquisition in childhood may be only a book chapter and two journal articles thick, but you may still have to write ten pages on the topic to pass a psychology course. Moreover, you not only have to provide information in a report but you also have to convince an expert reader—your instructor—that you have earned the credentials to write about this subject.

Suppose you are the peer.   For some reports, your peers may be your primary audience. That's often the case with oral presentations in class. You know that an instructor is watching and likely grading the content—including your topic, organization, and sources. But that instructor may also be watching how well you adapt that material to the interests and capabilities of your colleagues. ○

Tips for Writing Credible Reports

- Choose a serious subject you know you can research.
- Model the project on professional reports in that area.
- Select sources recognized in the field.
- Document those sources correctly.
- Use the discipline's technical vocabulary and conventions.

design your work
p. 517

respect your readers
p. 374

understand oral
reports p. 298

Finding and developing materials

▶ find information

Once you have settled on a research topic and thesis, plan to spend time online, in a library, or in the field gathering the data you need for your report. Look beyond reference works such as dictionaries and encyclopedias toward resources used or created by experts in the field, including scholarly books published by university presses, articles in professional journals, government reports (also known as white papers), oral histories, and so on. Find materials that push you well beyond what you knew at the outset of the project. The level of the works you read may intimidate you initially, but that's a signal that you are learning something new—an outcome your instructor probably intended.

Sometimes, you will write reports based on information you discover yourself, either under the controlled conditions of a scientific experiment or through interviews, fieldwork, polling, or news-gathering. ○ It's not easy to summarize all the rules that govern such work. They vary from major to major, and some you learn in courses devoted to research methods. But even informal field research requires systematic procedures and detailed record keeping so that you can provide readers with data they can verify. To get reports right, follow these basic principles.

Base reports on the best available sources.   You can't just do an online search on a topic and hope for the best. The quality of material on Web sites (and in libraries, for that matter) varies widely. You will embarrass yourself quickly if you don't develop procedures and instincts for evaluating sources. Look for materials—including data such as statistics and photographic reproductions—supported by major institutions in government, business, and the media and offered by reliable authors and experts. For academic papers, take your information whenever possible from journals and books published by university presses and professional organizations. ○

With Web materials, track them back to their original sources. Use the Google search engine for "Korean War," for instance, and you find an item that seems generic—except that its URL indicates a military location (.mil). Opening the URL, however, you discover that a government institution— the Naval Historical Center—supports the site. So its information is likely to be credible but will reflect the perspectives of the Department of the Navy. That's information you need to know as you read material from the site.

> Need help finding relevant sources? See "How to Browse for Ideas" on pp. 312–13.

understand lab reports
p. 290

find reliable sources
p. 415

Some Online Sites for Locating Facts and Information

- **Alcove 9: An Annotated List of Reference Sites** (http://www.loc.gov/rr/main/alcove9/) A collection of online reference sites maintained by the Library of Congress.
- **Bartleby.com: Great Books Online** (http://www.bartleby.com/) Includes online versions of key reference and literary works, from *Gray's Anatomy* to the *Oxford Shakespeare*.
- **Biography on A&E** (http://www.biography.com/search/) A collection of 25,000 brief biographies, from Julius Caesar to Orlando Bloom.
- **Fedstats** (http://www.fedstats.gov/) *The* site for finding information gathered by the federal government. Also check out FirstGov.gov (http://www.firstgov.gov/).
- **The Internet Public Library** (http://www.ipl.org) Provides links to material on most major academic fields and subjects. Includes reference collections as well.
- **The World Factbook** (http://www.cia.gov/cia/publications/factbook/index.html) Check here for data about any country—compiled by the CIA.

Base reports on multiple sources.   Don't rely on a limited or narrow selection of material. Not all ideas or points of view deserve equal coverage, but neither should you take any particular set of claims for granted. Above all, avoid the temptation to base a report on a single source, even one that *is* genuinely excellent. You may find yourself merely paraphrasing the material, not writing a report of your own.

Fact-check your report.   It's a shame to get the big picture in focus in a report and then lose credibility because you slip up on a few easily verifiable facts. In a lengthy project, these errors might seem inevitable or just a nuisance. But misstatements can take on a life of their own and become lore—like the initial and exaggerated reports of crime and mayhem during Hurricane Katrina. So take the extra few minutes it requires to get details right.

Creating a structure

▶ organize
information

How does a report work? Not like a shopping mall—where the escalators and aisles are designed to keep you wandering and buying, deliberately confused. Not like a mystery novel that leads up to an unexpected climax, or even like an argument, which steadily builds in power to a memorable conclusion. Instead, reports lay all their cards on the table right at the start and hold no secrets. They announce what they intend to do and then do it, providing clear markers all along the way.

Clarity doesn't come easily; it only seems that way when a writer has been successful. You have to know a topic intimately to explain it to others. Then you need to choose a pattern that supports what you want to say. Among structures you might choose for drafting a report are the following, some of which overlap.

Organize by date, time, or sequence. Drafting a history report, you may not think twice about arranging your material chronologically: In 1958, the USSR launched *Sputnik,* the first Earth satellite; in 1961, the USSR launched a cosmonaut into Earth orbit; in 1969, the United States put two men on the moon. This structure puts information into a relationship readers understand immediately as a competition. You'd still have blanks to fill in with facts and details to tell the story of the race to the moon, but a chronological structure helps readers keep complicated events in perspective.

By presenting a simple sequence of events, you can use time to organize many kinds of reports, from the scoring in football games to the movement of stock markets to the flow of blood through the human heart. ○

Organize by magnitude or order of importance. Many reports present their subjects in sequence, ranked from biggest to smallest (or vice versa); most important to least important; most common/frequent to least; and so on. Such structures assume, naturally, that you have already done the research to position the items you expect to present. At first glance, reports of this kind might seem tailored to the popular media: "10 Best Restaurants in Seattle," "100 Fattest American Cities." But you might also use such a structure to report on the disputed causes of a war, the multiple effects of a stock-market crash, or even the factors responsible for a disease.

shape your work
p. 340

Organize by division.   It's natural to organize some reports by division—that is, by breaking a subject into its major parts. A report on the federal government, for example, might be organized by treating each of its three branches in turn: executive, legislative, and judicial. A report on the Elizabethan stage might examine the separate parts of a typical theater: the heavens, the balcony, the stage wall, the stage, the pit, and so on. Of course, you'd then have to decide in what order to present the items, perhaps spatially or in order of importance. You might even use an illustration to clarify your report.

The Swan Theatre
The architectural layout of this Elizabethan theater, shown in this 1596 sketch by Johannes de Witt, might suggest the structure of a report describing the theater.

Organize by classification. Classification is the division of a group of concepts or items according to specified and consistent principles. Reports organized by classification are easy to set up when you borrow a structure that is already well established—such as those below. A project becomes more difficult when you try to create a new system—perhaps to classify the various political groups on your campus or to describe the behavior of participants in a psychology experiment.

- **Psychology** (by type of study): abnormal, clinical, comparative, developmental, educational, industrial, social

- **Plays** (by type): tragedy, comedy, tragicomedy, epic, pastoral, musical

- **Nations** (by form of government): monarchy, oligarchy, democracy, dictatorship

- **Passenger cars** (by engine placement): front engine, mid engine, rear engine

- **Dogs** (by breed group): sporting, hound, working, terrier, toy, nonsporting, herding

Organize by position, location, or space. Organizing a report spatially is a powerful device for arranging ideas—even more so today, given the ease with which material can be illustrated. ○ A map, for example, is a report organized by position and location. But it is only one type of spatial structure.

You use spatial organization in describing a painting from left to right, a building from top to bottom, a cell from nucleus to membrane. A report on medical conditions might be presented most effectively via cutaways that expose different layers of tissues and organs. Or a report on an art exhibition might follow a viewer through a virtual 3-D gallery.

Organize by definition. Typically, definitions begin by identifying an object by its "genus" and "species" and then listing its distinguishing features, functions, or variations. This useful structure is the pattern behind most entries in dictionaries, encyclopedias, and other reference works.

○

think visually
p. 500

It can be readily expanded too, once the genus and species have been established: *Ontario* is a *province of Canada* between Hudson Bay and the Great Lakes. That's a good start, but what are its geographical features, history, products, and major cities—all the things that distinguish it from other provinces? You could write a book, let alone a report, based on this simple structure.

Organize by comparison/contrast.   You've been comparing and contrasting probably since the fourth grade, but that doesn't make this principle of organization any less potent for college-level reports. ◯ You compare and contrast to highlight distinctions that might otherwise not be readily apparent. Big differences are usually uninteresting: That's why *Consumer Reports* doesn't test Nikon SLRs against disposable cameras. But the differences between Nikons and Canons? That might be worth exploring.

Organize by thesis statement.   Obviously, you have many options for organizing a report; moreover, a single report might use several structural patterns. So it helps if you explain early in a project what its method of organization will be. That idea may be announced in a single thesis sentence, a full paragraph (or section), or even a PowerPoint slide. ◯

SENTENCE ANNOUNCES STRUCTURE

In the late thirteenth century, Native Puebloans may have abandoned their cliff dwellings for several related reasons, including an exhaustion of natural resources, political disintegration, and, most likely, a prolonged drought.

–Kendrick Frazier, *People of Chaco: A Canyon and Its Culture*

PARAGRAPH EXPLAINS STRUCTURE

In order to detect a problem in the beginning of life, medical professionals and caregivers must be knowledgeable about normal development and potential warning signs. Research provides this knowledge. In most cases, research also allows for accurate diagnosis and effective intervention. Such is the case with Cri Du Chat Syndrome (CDCS), also commonly known as Cat Cry Syndrome.

–Marissa Dahlstrom, "Developmental Disorders: Cri Du Chat Syndrome"

understand evaluation
p. 102

develop a thesis
p. 336

Choosing a style and design

Reports are typically written in a formal or *high* style—free of emotional language that might make them sound like arguments. ○ To separate fact from opinion, scientific and professional reports usually avoid *I* and other personal references as well as devices such as contractions and dialogue. Reports in newspapers, magazines, and even encyclopedias may be less formal: You might detect a person behind the prose. But the style will still strive for impartiality, signaling that the writer's opinions are (or, at least, *should* be) less important than the facts reported.

Why tone down the emotional, personal, or argumentative temper of the language in reports? It's a matter of audience. The moment readers suspect that you are twisting language to advocate an agenda or moving away from a sober recital of facts, they will question the accuracy of your report. So review your drafts to see if a word or phrase might be sending wrong signals to readers. Give your language the appearance of neutrality, balance, and perspective.

Present the facts cleanly.   Get right to the point and answer key questions directly: *Who? What? Where? When? How? Why?* Organize paragraphs around topic sentences so readers know what will follow. Don't go off on tangents. Keep the exposition controlled and focus on data. When you do, the prose will seem coolly efficient and trustworthy.

Keep out of it.   Write from a neutral, third-person perspective, avoiding the pronouns *I* and *you*. Like all guidelines, this one has exceptions, and it certainly doesn't apply across the board to other genres of writing. But when perusing a report, readers don't usually care about the writer's personal opinion unless that writer's individual experiences are part of the story.

Avoid connotative language.   Maintaining objectivity is not easy because language is rife with *connotations*—the powerful cultural associations that may surround words, enlarging their meanings and sometimes imposing value judgments. Connotations make *shadowy* and *gloomy* differ from *dark*; *porcine* and *tubby,* from *overweight.* What's more, words' connotations are not the same for every reader. One person may have no problem with a

define your
style p. 366

term like *slums,* but another person living in *low-income housing* may beg to differ. Given the minefield of potential offenses that writing can be, don't use loaded words when more neutral terms are available and just as accurate. Choose *confident,* not *overweening* or *pompous;* try *corporate official* rather than *robber baron*—unless, of course, the more colorful term fits the context.

Cover differing views fairly, *especially* those you don't like. The neutrality of reports is often a fiction. You need only look at the white papers or fact sheets on the Web sites of various groups to appreciate how data presentation can sometimes be biased. But a report you prepare for a course or a professional situation should represent a good-faith effort to run the bases on a subject, touching all its major points. An upbeat report on growth in minority enrollment on your campus might also have to acknowledge areas where achievements have been lagging. A report on the economic boom that occurred during Bill Clinton's presidency (1993–2001) might also have to cover the dot-com bust and slide into recession at the end of his term.

Pay attention to elements of design. Clear and effective design is particularly important in reports. **O** If your paper runs more than a few pages and readily divides into parts, consider using headings or section markers to help readers follow its structure and locate information. Documents such as term papers and lab reports may follow specific formulas, patterns, and templates that you will need to learn.

Much factual information is best presented graphically. This is especially the case with numbers and statistics. So learn to create or incorporate charts, graphs, photos, and illustrations, and also captions into your work. Software such as Microsoft Word can create modest tables and simple graphics; generate more complex tables and graphs with software such as Excel. And remember that any visual items should be purposeful, not ornamental.

design your work
p. 517

Examining models

INFORMATIVE REPORT   In "Gene-Altered Foods: A Case Against Panic," health and nutrition expert Jane E. Brody summarizes what is known about genetically modified foods to correct false impressions about them. The article originally appeared in the *New York Times*.

Gene-Altered Foods: A Case Against Panic

Jane E. Brody

December 5, 2000

Ask American consumers whether they support the use of biotechnology in food and agriculture and nearly 70 percent say they do. But ask the question another way, "Do you approve of genetically engineered (or genetically modified) foods?" and two-thirds say they do not.

Yet there is no difference between them. The techniques involved and the products that result are identical. Rather, the words "genetic" and "engineer" seem to provoke alarm among millions of consumers.

The situation recalls the introduction of the MRI (for magnetic resonance imaging), which was originally called an NMR, for nuclear magnetic resonance. The word *nuclear* caused such public concern, it threatened to stymie the growth of this valuable medical tool.

The idea of genetically modified foods, known as GM foods, is particularly frightening to those who know little about how foods are now produced and how modern genetic technology, if properly regulated, could result in significant improvements by reducing environmental hazards, improving the nutritional value of foods, enhancing agricultural productivity, and fostering the survival worldwide of small farms and the rural landscape.

Without GM foods, Dr. Alan McHughen, a biotechnologist at the University of Saskatchewan, told a recent conference on agricultural biotechnology at Cornell, the earth will not be able to feed the ever-growing billions of people who inhabit it.

> Thesis: People don't understand GM foods and fear what they don't understand.

Still, there are good reasons for concern about a powerful technology that is currently imperfectly regulated and could, if inadequately tested or misapplied, bring on both nutritional and environmental havoc. To render a rational opinion on the subject and make reasoned choices in the marketplace, it is essential to understand what genetic engineering of foods and crops involves and its potential benefits and risks.

GENETICS IN AGRICULTURE

Headings mark off key topics in report.

People have been genetically modifying foods and crops for tens of thousands of years. The most commonly used method has involved crossing two parents with different desirable characteristics in an effort to produce offspring that express the best of both of them. That and another approach, inducing mutations, are time-consuming and hit-or-miss and can result in good and bad characteristics.

Genetic engineering, on the other hand, involves the introduction into a plant or animal or micro-organism of a single gene or group of genes that are known quantities, genes that dictate the production of one or more desired elements, for example, the ability to resist the attack of insects, withstand herbicide treatments, or produce foods with higher levels of essential nutrients.

Explains how genetic engineering works.

Since all organisms use the same genetic material (DNA), the power of the technique includes the ability to transfer genes between organisms that normally would never interbreed.

Thus, an antifreeze gene from Arctic flounder has been introduced into strawberries to extend their growing season in northern climates. But contrary to what many people think, this does not make the strawberries "fishy" any more than the use of porcine insulin turned people into pigs.

Dr. Steven Kresovich, a plant breeder at Cornell, said, "Genes should be characterized by function, not origin. It's not a flounder gene but a cold tolerance gene that was introduced into strawberries."

As Dr. McHughen points out in his new book, *Pandora's Picnic Basket: The Potential and Hazards of Genetically Modified Foods,* people share about 7,000 genes with a worm called *C. elegans.* The main

Sources add authority.

difference between organisms lies in the total number of genes their cells contain, how the genes are arranged, and which ones are turned on or off in different cells at different times.

CURRENT AND POTENTIAL BENEFITS

An insecticidal toxin from a bacterium called *Bacillus thuringiensis* (Bt) has been genetically introduced into two major field crops, corn and cotton, resulting in increased productivity and decreased use of pesticides, which means less environmental contamination and greater profits for farmers. For example, by growing Bt cotton, farmers could reduce spraying for bollworm and budworm from seven times a season to none. Bt corn also contains much lower levels of fungal toxins, which are potentially carcinogenic.

Offers five paragraphs of evidence in support of GM foods.

"The genetic introduction of herbicide tolerance into soybeans is saving farmers about $200 million a year by reducing the number of applications of herbicide needed to control weed growth," said Leonard Gianessi, a pesticide analyst at the National Center for Food and Agricultural Policy, a research organization in Washington.

Genetically engineered pharmaceuticals are already widely used, with more than 150 products on the market. Since 1978, genetically modified bacteria have been producing human insulin, which is used by 3.3 million people with diabetes.

Future food benefits are likely to accrue directly to the consumer. For example, genetic engineers have developed golden rice, a yellow rice rich in beta carotene (which the body converts to vitamin A) and iron. If farmers in developing countries accept this crop and if the millions of people who suffer from nutrient deficiencies will eat it, golden rice could prevent widespread anemia and blindness in half a million children a year and the deaths of one million to two million children who succumb each year to the consequences of vitamin A deficiency.

Future possibilities include peanuts or shrimp lacking proteins that can cause life-threatening food allergies, fruits and vegetables with longer shelf lives, foods with fewer toxicants and antinutrients, meat and dairy products and oils with heart-healthier fats, and foods that deliver vaccines.

REAL AND POTENTIAL RISKS

GM foods and crops arrived without adequate mechanisms in place to regulate them. Three agencies are responsible for monitoring their safety for consumers, farmers, and the environment: the Food and Drug Administration, the Department of Agriculture, and the Environmental Protection Agency. But the drug agency says its law does not allow it to require premarket testing of GM foods unless they contain a new substance that is not "generally recognized as safe."

For most products, safety tests are done voluntarily by producers. The recent recall of taco shells containing GM corn that has not been approved for human consumption was done voluntarily by the producer. The agency is now formulating new guidelines to test GM products and to label foods as "GM-free," but says it lacks a legal basis to require labeling of GM foods.

"In the current environment, such a label would be almost a kiss of death on a product," said Dr. Michael Jacobson, director of the Center for Science in the Public Interest, a nonprofit consumer group. "But it may be that the public is simply not going to have confidence in transgenic ingredients if their presence is kept secret."

The introduction of possible food allergens through genetic engineering is a major concern. If the most common sources of food allergens—peanuts, shellfish, celery, nuts, milk, or eggs—had to pass through an approval process today, they would never make it to market.

But consumers could be taken unaware if an otherwise safe food was genetically endowed with an allergen, as almost happened with an allergenic protein from Brazil nuts. Even if known allergenic proteins are avoided in GM foods, it is hard to predict allergenicity of new proteins.

> Remains objective, reporting both sides: GM foods still need regulation.

△

Explains that technology poses real risks.

A potentially serious environmental risk involves the "escape" of GM genes from crops into the environment, where they may harm innocent organisms or contaminate crops that are meant to be GM-free.

Dr. Jacobson concluded, "Now is the time, while agricultural biotechnology is still young, for Congress and regulatory agencies to create the framework that will maximize the safe use of these products, bolster public confidence in them, and allow all of humankind to benefit from their enormous potential." Two congressional bills now under discussion can do much to assure safer use of agricultural biotechnology, he said.

Reports that Congress can act to address these risks.

ACADEMIC REPORT   Academic reports often support clear and straightforward thesis statements. The following short report does that in explaining the dual mission of Frank Gehry's celebrated Guggenheim Museum Bilbao. The paper below is not only based on sources but also on information gathered at the museum, in Spain's Basque Country.

Winsett 1

Annie Winsett

Instructor's Name

Course Title

Date

Inner and Outer Beauty

The Guggenheim Bilbao, designed by North American architect Frank Gehry (b. 1929), is a recent addition to the Solomon R. Guggenheim Foundation, a conglomeration of museums dedicated to modern American and European art. Home to several

Thesis suggests a paper with two parts.

Winsett 2

permanent works and host to visiting expositions, the Guggenheim Bilbao is itself an artistic wonder, perhaps more acclaimed than any of the art it houses. In design, the building meets the requirements of a proper museum, but it also signifies the rejuvenation of Spain's Basque country.

Like any museum, the Guggenheim Bilbao is dedicated to preserving and presenting works of art. Paintings and sculptures are here to be protected. So the thick glass panes of the Bilbao serve not only to let in natural light, but also provide escape for the heat generated by the titanium outsides of the structure. The unconventional metal plating of the Guggenheim, guaranteed to last up to one hundred years, actually ensures its survival as well. Similarly, the floor material will be able to withstand the many visitors to come.

Fig. 1. The Guggenheim Museum Bilbao

Winsett offers a photograph to convey Bilbao's extraordinary design.

Winsett 3

First section of paper explains how the avant-garde building functions as a museum.

Even though the outside of the Guggenheim Bilbao appears to be composed of irregular forms only, the interior houses nineteen functional galleries. The alternating rooms and curving walkways around a central atrium provide an extensive journey through the world of art. So the unusual exterior structure actually allots a vast amount of wall and floor display space and serves the wide variety of art it houses more than adequately.

"But" at beginning of paragraph signals that report is moving into its second section.

But the Guggenheim Bilbao was created to do more. In 1991, having noted the economic depression facing one of its main industrial cities, the Basque Country government proposed that the Solomon R. Guggenheim Foundation locate its next museum in Bilbao (Guggenheim). As part of a massive revitalization involving the city's port, railways, and airport, the new museum would enhance the cultural identity of the city. Perhaps a conventional structure would have met the need for societal enrichment.

Yet the Basque government achieved much more by selecting a design by Frank Gehry. Designed with computers, the museum presents an original and striking three-dimensional form not possible using conventional design methods. From above, it appears that its metal-coated solids extend from a central skylight in the shape of a flower (Bilbao.net). The building also suggests a ship on the river's shore with edges that swoop upward in a hull-like fashion. The "scales" of metal that surround the structure's steel frame are like those of a fish. Undoubtedly, the design references the museum's coastal and riverside environment.

Paper uses several online sources.

Report explains how museum represents city of Bilbao.

Whatever its intended form, Gehry's building captures the spirit of a renewed Bilbao in the twenty-first century. For instance, Gehry managed to incorporate the city's mining industries in the

Winsett 4

structural materials. The titanium plates reflect both the beautiful Basque sky and the core of the Basque economy. Also crucial is the tourism such an incomparable structure might generate. Though most of Gehry's works incorporate the unique materials and forms seen in Bilbao, the Guggenheim is individual and original. And travelers have flocked here to experience the futuristic titanium masterpiece. As hoped, Bilbao and the Basque Country have earned a revived place in the international community. At the 2004 Venice Biennial, the Basque Country was recognized for the most successful urban regeneration project in the world, at the heart of which was the Guggenheim museum (Euskadi.net).

Winsett 5

Works Cited

Bilbao Metropoli-30: Association for the Revitalization of
    Metropolitan Bilbao. Bilbao Metropoli-30. 30 Oct. 2006
    <http://www.bm30.es/Welcome_uk.html>.

Bilbao.net. 30 Oct. 2006. The Bilbao City Council. 30 Oct. 2006
    <http://www.bilbao.net/nuevobilbao/jsp/bilbao/homeModulos.
    jsp?idioma=I&color=rojo>.

Euskadi.net. 2004. Eusko Jaurlaritza-Gobierno Vasco. 7 Nov. 2006.
    <http://www.lehendakaritza.ejgv.euskadi.net:80/r48-7413/en/>.

Guggenheim Bilbao. 26 Oct. 2006. The Solomon R. Guggenheim
    Foundation. 29 Oct. 2006 <http://www.guggenheim-bilbao.es/
    ingles/home.htm>.

Blood Cells for Sale

There's More to Blood Banking Than Just Bagging Blood

EMILY HARRISON · PHOTOGRAPH BY CARY WOLINSKY

This is not a bag of blood. Granted, it did begin as a blood donation, drawn from the arm of a volunteer donor in Massachusetts. Within hours of collection, though, that precursory pint of warm whole blood had been centrifuged, fractionated, and decanted into a red blood cell concentrate laced with a cocktail of chemical buffers and nutrients. The ruddy yield, shown here, is one chilled unit of processed blood product, suitable for a patient desperately in need of red cells. Such units—screened, packaged, and tracked through their life cycles in keeping with the dictates of the U.S. Food and Drug Administration—are manufactured with assembly-line efficiency to optimize the safety and utility of a precious, limited resource.

A half-liter unit of whole blood, when spun, separates into layers. The 275-milliliter top layer of lemon-yellow plasma is rich in platelet cells, which are principal to blood clotting. The 225-ml bottom layer of red cells (erythrocytes), which shuttle oxygen and carbon dioxide around the body, is skimmed with a slick of the immune system's white cells (leukocytes). Because different patients need varying boosts for different blood functions, packaging these layers separately lets each whole blood donation help several people. And reducing unnecessary biological material, such as the leukocytes in the red cell concentrate, lowers the risk that a patient's immune system will reject a transfusion.

Synthetic blood replacements, which would carry no disease risk and could be manufactured in surplus, have an enormous potential market. Although several are in development, nothing can yet take the place of genuine blood cells grown by the human body.

COST OF LIVING

The product of 24 hours of processing, this unit of leukocyte-reduced
AS-3 red cells costs $220. A typical kidney transplant surgery requires
1–2 units; a heart transplant requires 4–6. Car accident victims consume
as many as 20 units.

Keeping Tabs
A unique bar code on each
package lets blood banks
monitor their inventory and
anonymously link each unit
to donor information in a
central database. The same
bar code labels four small
tubes of blood collected at
the time of donation and
sent to testing laboratories
for disease screening and
blood typing.

**Sustainable
Envelopment**
Living red cells have needs,
even in refrigerated stor-
age. The preservative AS-3
provides them with sodium
citrate, sodium phosphate,
adenine, sodium chloride,
and dextrose, which act
as anticoagulants, maintain
the cells' structural integrity,
and sustain their metabolism.
AS-3 also dilutes the red cell
concentrate so that it flows
freely through tubes and
needles into blood vessels.

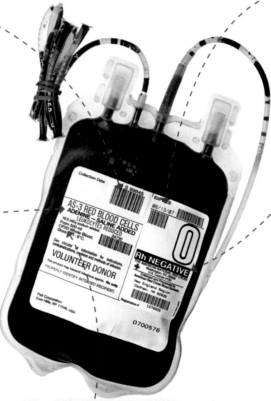

Sanguine Expiration
Red cells endure 42 days
at 1 to 6 degrees Celsius,
over a month longer than
platelets last at their optimal
temperature of 20 to 24
degrees C. If a temporary
glycerol preservative is added
to the red cells, they can be
frozen for up to one year, but
the stress of being frozen and
having the glycerol washed
out reduces their post-thaw
shelf life to one day.

Type Treatment
Blood type is determined by
sugar-and-protein chains,
called antigens, that tag the
red cells' surfaces. The body
rejects cells bearing antigens
that do not match its own, so
the most universally useful
blood type of transfusions
is O negative—which carries
neither the common A and B
antigens nor the Rh antigen.
If researchers could pin down
a procedure for stripping
blood cells of their antigens,
it could expand the useful-
ness and safety of the blood
supply.

Clot Stopper
Once outside the body, blood has a natural
tendency to clot and dry. To counter that,
an anticlotting solution called CP2D is added
to the whole blood at the time of donation.

VISUAL REPORT This report by Michael Kupperman originally appeared in *The Believer* magazine.

1. **Informative Report:** Jane E. Brody draws on her expertise in health and nutrition to write "Gene-Altered Foods: A Case Against Panic" (p. 56). Write a similar report on a subject you already know a great deal about, using your experience to correct false impressions general readers less knowledgeable than you might have about the topic. Be certain to look for new information to keep the report fresh and to base all claims you make on reputable sources and authorities.

2. **Visual Report:** Design a report that, like "Blood Cells for Sale" (p. 64) and "What's in Your Glass of Water?" (facing page), combines words and images to convey information. Use charts, photographs, drawings, diagrams, annotations, and so on. Your word processor or more specialized graphic software (like PowerPoint or InDesign) will help you produce a handsome but sensible project.

3. **Academic Report:** Write a factual academic report based on subjects or ideas in courses outside your major—in other words, on topics generally new to you. Like Annie Winsett in "Inner *and* Outer Beauty" (p. 60), narrow your subject to a specific claim that you can explain in several pages. Use respectable sources and document them in proper Modern Language Association (MLA) or American Psychological Association (APA) style. (For MLA style, see p. 437; for APA style, see p. 474.)

4. **Informative Report:** Imagine that you've been asked to prepare a report on some natural phenomena (like the rings of Uranus, see p. 43) to a group of ninth graders—one of the toughest audiences in the world. In a brief report, engage them with a topic of your choosing, perhaps reflecting your own interest in an offbeat subject. Design the report as a paper, oral presentation, or Web site and base it on reliable sources, which you should cite in some form within the report.

How to start

- Need a **topic**? See page 74.
- Need **support for your argument**? See page 80.
- Need to **organize your ideas**? See page 84.

3 Argument

asks readers to consider debatable ideas

It doesn't take much to spark an argument these days—a casual remark, a political observation, a dumb joke that hurts someone's feelings. Loud voices and angry gestures may follow, leaving observers upset and frustrated, wishing that we could all just get along. But arguments aren't polarizing or hostile by nature, not when people more interested in generating light than heat offer them. Arguments should make us smarter and better able to deal with problems in the world. In fact, you probably make such constructive arguments all the time without raising blood pressures, at least not too much.

- In a letter to the editor, you challenge an op-ed that compares the impact of gasoline prices on a family budget today compared with twenty years ago because figures used in the article haven't been adjusted for inflation.

- You point out that an attendance policy announced on the Web site for a course you plan on taking may be invalid because it contradicts several key university policies.

- You argue that high school officials across the country have adopted "zero tolerance" disciplinary policies as a convenient way of avoiding the tough decisions that competent administrators are paid to make.

68

UNDERSTANDING ARGUMENTS. Arguments come in many shapes to serve different purposes. Subsequent chapters in this section cover some forms often assigned in the classroom, including *causal analyses, proposals,* and *literary analyses.* But even less specialized arguments have distinctive features. In your projects, you'll aim to do the following.

Offer levelheaded and disputable claims. You won't influence audiences by making points no one cares about or calls into question. In any argument, something clear and specific ought to be at stake. Maybe you want to change readers' minds about an issue or reaffirm what they already believe. In either case, you'll need a well-defined and appropriately qualified point, either stated or implied, if you expect to influence levelheaded audiences. ○

Poster by Ben Shahn, 1968 This poster illustrates the words of British pacifist and parliamentarian John Morley (1838–1923). Note how the style of Shahn's typography and crayon figure complement each other to make a memorable argument out of Morley's sober observation.

Ben Shahn, "You have not converted a man because you have silenced him." 1968. Offset lithograph, 45 inches x 30 inches (114.2 x 76.2 cm). Smithsonian American Art Museum, Washington, D.C. , USA © Estate of Ben Shahn / Licensed by VAGA, New York, NY. Photo credit: Smithsonian American Art Museum, Washington, D.C. / Art Resource, NY. / Art Resource, NY.

develop a thesis
p. 336

Offer good reasons to support a claim.   Without evidence and supporting reasons, a claim is just an assertion—and little better than a shout or a slogan. Slogans do have their appeal in advertising and politics. But they don't become arguments until they are developed through full-bodied thinking and supported by a paper trail of evidence.

Respond to opposing claims and points of view.   You won't be able to make a strong case until you can honestly paraphrase the logic of those who see matters differently. ○ And, in your own arguments, you will seem smarter and more fair when you acknowledge these other *reasonable* opinions even as you refute them. Also be prepared to address less rational claims temperately, but firmly.

Use language strategically—and not words only.   Opinions clothed in good sense still need to dress for the occasion. You have to find the right words and images to carry a case forward. Fortunately, you have many options to make words memorable. Design is increasingly important, too: Your choice of medium may ultimately determine who sees your message. ○

Do you think this Nike advertisement is more than just a slogan? If so, what argument do you think it makes?

It goes without saying that many appeals you encounter daily do not measure up to the criteria of serious argument. We've all been seduced by claims just because they are stylish, hip, or repeated so often that they begin to seem true. But if much persuasion doesn't seem fair or sensible, that's all the more reason to reach for a higher standard.

restate ideas
p. 428

work with visuals
p. 504

Journal Article

Here's an argument by writer and editor Robert Kuttner that raises serious questions about the uses college admissions officers make of school rankings and the consequent effects of their actions on students. Kuttner's word choices leave little doubt how strongly he feels about the subject. But the piece also gains power from the way it is written: The author invites readers to share his outrage. Kuttner also offers colleges a simple avenue for change: *Just say* no.

American Prospect

Posted: February 27, 2006
From: Robert Kuttner

College Rankings or Junk Science?

Connotative words (*feverish, infecting*) suggest Kuttner's view.

It's approaching that season when students and their parents anxiously await college admissions decisions. But increasingly, an equally feverish process is infecting the other side of the transaction and distorting the process of who gets financial aid.

Colleges these days engage in an ever-more-frantic competition for "rankings," driven almost entirely by the annual *U.S. News & World Report* issue on "America's Best Colleges." *U.S. News* is so dominant that when a dean boasts that his school is ranked in the top ten or a president's bonus is based on whether his college makes it into the top fifty he invariably refers to *U.S. News*.

Massive efforts by admissions departments, deans, and college presidents are devoted to gaming the *U.S. News* ranking system, published every August. This includes everything from manipulating who is considered a part-time student (which raises the reported performance of full-time students) to giving students temporary research jobs in order to raise the placement score reported to *U.S. News*. But the easiest single way to raise rankings is by enrolling students with ever-higher SAT scores.

Explains the problem he sees with *U.S. News*'s college rankings.

If the average score of your entering freshman class increases, the *U.S. News* ranking will probably improve, too. And if your ranking goes up, the presumed prestige of the college will follow. More

Doesn't name specific sources in article.

kids will apply, more applicants will choose your college rather than brand X, and, best of all, more families will pay sticker price.

Explains how rankings influence admissions policies.

This competition spawns many evils that should shame a higher-education system devoted to intellectual honesty. But perhaps the worst thing about it is what the ranking obsession is doing to the allocation of financial aid. More and more scholarship money is being shifted from aid based on financial need to aid based on "merit."

Anticipates potential objection to his argument.

That sounds nice — who could be opposed to merit? But today's "merit scholarships" are primarily bait to attract students with very high SAT scores who don't need the aid. The flip side is less aid available to students from less affluent families, who can't attend college without aid, or who must sacrifice academic work to paid jobs, or who graduate with staggering debt loads.

There is, of course, a limited pot of financial aid. One reason tuitions keep relentlessly rising is that some of the tuition money goes to underwrite financial-aid budgets. That would be defensible, even laudable if colleges were "taxing" affluent families in order to redistribute aid money to less affluent ones. But when higher tuitions spin off scholarships for other affluent kids intended mainly to raise rankings, the result is to doubly raise barriers to poor and middle-class kids, with both higher tuition barriers and diminished aid.

One result: poorer performance by poorer kids. Forty percent of all college students from the most affluent quarter of the population get a bachelor's degree within five years. For kids in the bottom income quarter, the figure is just six percent, according to a new book, *Strapped*, by Tamara Draut.

Finally names a source.

Offers more evidence for claim.

Another consequence: Affluent families pass their affluence along to their children. According to studies by Anthony P. Carnevale and Steven J. Rose, nearly three-quarters of students at elite universities are from the wealthiest quarter of the population. Just 3 percent are from the bottom quarter.

The *U.S. News* process for ranking colleges and universities has been almost universally condemned by specialists as junk science. Publishing a data-rich guide to colleges is a service. What's bogus is the supposed ranking. As any statistician will tell you, you can't reasonably combine entirely unrelated variables (test scores, reputation, placements, spending per student, student aid, etc.) into a single linear index. Worse, the criteria and their weightings are arbitrary. It's hard enough for colleges to come up with financial aid based on need, without a spurious ranking contest creating inducements to subsidize the already privileged.

The data sent by colleges to *U.S. News* are self-reported and unaudited. Also, many of the factors are entirely subjective to begin with. One dean told me that when she rates reputations of other comparable graduate schools, she hasn't a clue how to rate more than a few. There is also the all-too-human temptation to downgrade the near competition.

Oregon's Reed College, for more than a decade, has stopped cooperating with *U.S. News*. The college's president, Colin Diver, writing in the *Atlantic*, reported that liberation from this annual hazing has freed Reed to "pursue our own educational philosophy, not that of some magazine." Reed has thrived.

Others should follow Reed's lead and just boycott this travesty.

Appeals to authority (*any statistician*) to undercut rankings.

Kuttner's thesis: He endorses action against college rankings.

Exploring purpose and topic

▶ topic

In a college assignment, you could be asked to write an argument or be given a topic area to explore, but you probably won't be told what your claim should be. That decision has to come from you, drawing on your knowledge, experiences, and inclinations. So choose topics about which you genuinely care—not issues routinely defined in the media as controversial. You'll likely do a more credible job defending your choice *not* to wear a helmet when cycling than explaining, one more time, why the environment should concern us all. And if environmental matters do roil you, stake your claim on a specific ecological problem—perhaps from within your community—that you might actually change by the power of your rhetoric. ◯

If you really are stumped, the Yahoo Directory's list of "Issues and Causes"—with topics from *abortion* to *zoos*—offers problems enough to keep both liberal Susan Sarandon *and* conservative Jon Voight busy to the end of the century. To find it, click on "Society and Culture" on the site's main Web directory (http://dir.yahoo.com). ("Society and Culture" itself offers a menu of intriguing topic areas.) Once you have an issue or even a specific claim, you'll need to work it like bread dough.

Arguments take many different forms, but finger-pointing is rarely a good persuasive tool.

get an idea
p. 308

Learn *much* more about your subject.   Do basic library and online research to get a better handle on it—*especially* when you think you already have all the answers. Chances are, you don't.

State a preliminary claim, if only for yourself.   Some arguments fail because writers never examine their own thinking. Instead, they wander around their subjects, throwing out ideas or making contradictory assertions, hoping perhaps that readers will assemble the random parts. To avoid this misdirection, begin with a *claim*—a complete sentence that states a position you will then have to defend. Though you will likely change this initial claim, such a statement will keep you on track as you explore a topic. Even a simple sentence helps:

> College ranks published annually by *U.S. News & World Report* do more harm than good.
>
> Westerners should be less defensive about their cultures.
>
> People who oppose gay marriage don't know what they are talking about.

Qualify your claim to make it reasonable.   As you learn more about a subject, revise your topic idea to reflect the complications you encounter. Your tentative thesis will likely grow longer, but the topic will actually narrow because of the issues and conditions you've specified. You'll also have less work to do, thanks to qualifying expressions such as *some, most, a few, often, under certain conditions, occasionally, when necessary,* and so on. Other qualifying expressions are highlighted below.

> The statistically unreliable college ratings published by *U.S. News* usually do more harm than good to students because they lead admissions officers to award scholarships on the basis of merit rather than need.
>
> Westerners should be more willing to defend their cultural values and intellectual achievements if they hope to defend freedom against its enemies.
>
> Many conservative critics who oppose gay marriage unwittingly undermine their own core principles, especially monogamy and honesty.

Examine your core assumptions.   Claims may be supported by reasons and evidence, but they are based on assumptions. *Assumptions* are the principles and values on which we ground our beliefs and actions. Sometimes those assumptions are controversial and stand right out. At other times, they're so close to us, they seem invisible—they are part of the air we breathe. Expect to spend a paragraph defending any assumptions your readers might find controversial. ○

CLAIM

The statistically unreliable college ratings published by *U.S. News & World Report* usually do more harm than good to students because they lead admissions officers to award scholarships on the basis of merit rather than need.

ASSUMPTION

Alleviating need in our society is more important than rewarding merit.
[Probably controversial]

CLAIM

Westerners should be more willing to defend their cultural values and intellectual achievements if they hope to defend freedom against its enemies.

ASSUMPTION

Freedom needs to be defended at all costs.
[Possibly noncontroversial for some audiences in many democracies]

CLAIM

Many conservative critics who oppose gay marriage unwittingly undermine their own core principles, especially monogamy and honesty.

ASSUMPTION

People should be consistent about their principles.
[Probably noncontroversial]

develop ideas
p. 346

Understanding your audience

Retailers know audiences. In fact, they go to great lengths to pinpoint the groups most likely to buy their fried chicken or video games. They then tailor their images and advertising pitches to those specific customers. You'll play to audiences the same way when you write arguments—if maybe a little less cynically.

Understand that you won't ever please everyone in a general audience, even if you write bland, colorless mush—because then some readers will regard you as craven and spineless. In fact, how readers imagine you *as the person presenting an argument* may determine their willingness to consider your claims at all.

Specific topics simply touch groups of readers differently, so you will need to consider a variety of approaches when imagining the audiences for your arguments.

Consider and control your ethos.   People who study persuasion describe the character that writers create for themselves within an argument as their *ethos*—the voice and disposition they choose to give their case. It is a powerful concept, worth remembering. Surely you recognize when writers are coming across as, let's say, appealingly confident or stupidly nasty. And don't you respond in kind, giving ear to the likable voice and dismissing the malicious one? A few audiences—like those for political blogs—may actually prefer a writer with a snarky ethos. But most readers respond better when writers seem reasonable, knowledgeable, and fair—neither insulting those who disagree with them nor making those who share their views embarrassed to have them on their side.

Control your ethos in an argument by adjusting the style, tone, and vocabulary: For instance, contractions can make you seem friendly (or too casual); an impressive vocabulary suggests that you are smart (or maybe just pompous); lots of name-dropping makes you seem hip (or perhaps pretentious). You may have to write several drafts to find a suitable ethos for a particular argument. O And, yes, your ethos may change from paper to paper, audience to audience.

Need help supporting your argument? See "How to Use the Writing Center" on pp. 328–29.

revise and edit
p. 386

Consider your own limits.   If you read newspapers and magazines that mostly confirm your own political views, you might be in for a wake-up call when you venture an opinion beyond your small circle of friends. Tread softly. There are good reasons people don't talk politics at parties. When you do argue about social, political, or religious issues, be respectful of those who work from premises different from your own.

Consider race and ethnicity.   The different lives people live as a result of their heritage plays a role in many claims you might make about education, politics, art, religion, or even athletics. Be sensitive without being gutless. ○

Consider gender and sexual orientation.   These issues almost always matter, often in unexpected ways. Men and women, whether straight or gay, don't inhabit quite the same worlds. But, even so, you shouldn't argue, either, as if all men and all women think the same way—or should. False assumptions about gender can lead you into a minefield.

Gender attitudes develop early, along with some argument strategies.

respect your readers
p. 374

Consider income and class.   People's lives are often defined by the re-alities of their economic situations—and the assumptions that follow from privilege, poverty, or something in between. Think it would be just dandy to have an outdoor pool on campus or a convenient new parking garage? You may find that not everyone is as eager or as able as you to absorb the costs of such proposals to improve campus life. And if you intend to complain about fat cats, ridicule soccer moms, or poke fun at rednecks, is it because you can't imagine them among your readers?

Consider religion and spirituality.   Members of different organized religions manage to insult each other almost without trying, more so now perhaps as religion routinely takes center stage in the political and diplo-matic arena. People within the same denomination often hold incompatible views. And the word *atheist* can engender negative reactions in certain audi-ences. It takes skill and good sense to keep the differences in mind when your topic demands it.

Consider age.   Obviously, you'd write differently for children than for their parents on almost any subject, changing your style, vocabulary, and allusions. But consider that people at different ages really have lived dif-ferent lives. The so-called greatest generation never forgot the Depression; youngsters today will remember the destruction of the World Trade Center Towers on September 11, 2001, and the school shootings in Littleton, Colorado. They'll grow up with different attitudes, values, heroes, and villains. A writer has to be savvy enough to account for such differences when constructing an argument.

Finding and developing materials

You could write a book by the time you've completed the research for some arguments. Material is out there on every imaginable subject, and the research techniques you use to prepare a report or term paper should work for arguments too. Since arguments often deal with current events and topics, start with a resource such as the Yahoo "Issues and Causes" directory mentioned earlier. Explore your subject, too, in *LexisNexis,* if your library gives you access to this huge database of newspaper articles. ○

▶ develop
support

As you gather materials, though, consider how much space you have to make your argument. Sometimes a claim has to fit within the confines of a letter to the editor, an op-ed column in a local paper, or a fifteen-minute PowerPoint lecture. Aristotle, still one of the best theorists on persuasion, thought arguments *should* be brief, with speakers limiting examples to the *minimum* necessary to make a case—no extra points for piling on. So gather big, and then select only the best stuff for your argument.

List your reasons.   You'll come up with reasons to support your claim almost as soon as you choose a subject. Write those down. Then start reading and continue to list new reasons as they arise, not being too fussy at this point. Be careful to paraphrase these ideas so that you don't inadvertently plagiarize them later.

Then, when your reading and research are complete, review your notes and try to group the arguments that support your position. It's likely you'll detect patterns and relationships among these reasons, and an unwieldy initial list of potential arguments may be streamlined into just three or four—which could become the key reasons behind your claim. Study these points and look for logical connections or sequences. Readers will expect your ideas to converge on a claim or lead logically toward it. ○

ORIGINAL

Why ethanol won't solve our energy problems

- Using ethanol in cars actually increases NOx emissions.
- Ethanol requires more energy to make it than it produces.
- Ethanol reduces range: You can't drive as far on a gallon.
- Ethanol can plug up fuel systems of older cars.
- Ethanol produces much less energy per gallon than gas.
- Creating ethanol contributes to global warming.

refine your search
p. 406

shape your work
p. 340

- Ethanol is cheaper than gas only because of massive farm subsidies.
- Ethanol harms performance in cars.
- Ethanol damages engines.
- Everyone's just on another eco bandwagon.
- Ethanol drives up crop prices, and thus food prices.

STREAMLINED

Why ethanol won't solve our energy problems

- Ethanol hurts performance of vehicles significantly.
- Ethanol is expensive to produce.
- Ethanol harms the environment.

Assemble your hard evidence.   Gather examples, illustrations, testimony, and numbers to support each main point. Record these items as you read, photocopying the data or downloading it carefully into labeled files. Take this evidence from the most reputable sources and keep track of all bibliographical information (author, title, publication info, URL) just as you would when preparing a term paper—even if you aren't expected to document your argument. You want that data on hand in case your credibility is later challenged.

If you borrow facts from a Web site, do your best to track the information down to its actual source. For example, if a blogger quotes statistics from the U. S. Department of Agriculture, take a few minutes to find the table or graph on the USDA Web site itself and make sure the numbers are reported accurately. ○

Think of hard evidence as a broad category that might also include photographs, video clips, or physical objects. Audiences do have a fondness for smoking guns—those pieces of indisputable evidence that clinch an argument. If you find one, use it.

Cull the best quotations.   You've done your homework for an assignment, reading the best available sources. So prove it in your argument by quoting from them intelligently. Choose quotations that do one or more of the following:

analyze claims and
evidence p. 420

Creating a structure

▶ organize
ideas

It's easy to sketch a standard structure for arguments: One that leads from claim to supporting reasons to evidence and even accommodates a counter-argument or two.

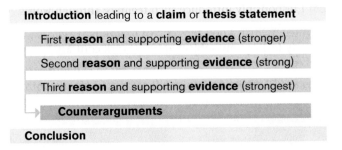

Introduction leading to a **claim** or **thesis statement**

First **reason** and supporting **evidence** (stronger)

Second **reason** and supporting **evidence** (strong)

Third **reason** and supporting **evidence** (strongest)

Counterarguments

Conclusion

The problem is you won't read many effective arguments, either in or out of school, that follow this template. The structure isn't defective, just too simple to describe the way arguments really move when ideas matter. Some controversies need lots of background to get rolling; some require detours to resolve other issues first; and a great many arguments work best when writers simply lay out the facts and allow readers to draw their own conclusions—or be nudged toward them.

You won't write a horrible paper if you use the traditional model because all the parts will be in place. Thesis? Check. Three supporting reasons? Check. Counterarguments? Check. But your argument will sound exactly like what it is: A writer going through the motions instead of engaging with ideas. Here's how to get your ideas to breathe in an argument—while still hitting all the marks.

Spell out what's at stake. When you write an argument, you start a disagreement, so you'd better explain why. ○ Do you hope to fix a looming problem? Then describe what your concern is and make readers share it. Do you intend to correct a false notion or bad reporting? Then be sure to tell readers what setting the record straight accomplishes. Appalled by the apathy of voters, the dangers of global warming, the infringements of free speech on campus? Then explain what makes such issues matter today and why readers should pay attention.

develop a thesis
p. 336

Don't just jump into a claim: Take a few sentences or paragraphs to set up the situation. Quote a nasty politician or tell an eye-popping story or two. Get readers invested in what's to come.

Make a point or build toward one.   Arguments can unfurl just as reports do, with unmistakable claims followed by reams of supporting evidence. But they can also work like crime dramas, in which the evidence in a case builds toward a compelling conclusion—your thesis perhaps. Consider the ethanol issue. You could argue straight up that this fuel causes more problems than it solves. Or you could open by wondering if ethanol really is the miracle fuel some claim it to be and then offer evidence that contradicts the media hype. In both cases, readers get the same claim and reasons. But the first approach might work better for readers already interested in environmental issues while the second might grab those who aren't by arousing their curiosity. This is your call. O

Address counterpoints when necessary, not in a separate section.   *Necessary* is when your readers start thinking to themselves, "Yeah, but what about . . . ?" Such doubts likely surface approximately where your own do—and, admit it, you have *some* misgivings about your argument. So take them on. Strategically, it rarely makes sense to consign major objections to a lengthy section near the end of a paper. That's asking for trouble. Do you really want to offer a case for the opposition just when your readers are finishing up?

On the plus side, dealing with opposing arguments can be like caffeine for your writing, sharpening your attention and reflexes. Here's Ann Hulbert, for example, eager to take on those who now argue that it's boys who are being shortchanged in schools by curriculums and modes of teaching that favor girls:

> Other complaints about boy-averse pedagogy also don't quite add up – in part because they contradict one another. Sommers blamed a touchy-feely, progressive ethos for alienating boys in the classroom; males, she argued, thrive on no-nonsense authority, accountability, clarity, and peer rivalry. But now *Newsweek* blames roughly the opposite atmosphere for boy trouble:

order ideas
p. 342

the competitive, cut-and-dried, standardized-test-obsessed (and recess-
less) pedagogical emphasis of the last decade. So much speculative
certainty doesn't really shed much light on the puzzle of what's deterring
young men from college.

— "Will Boys Be Boys?" Slate.com, February 1, 2006

Hold your best arguments for the end.   Of course, you want strong
points throughout the paper. But you need a high note early on to get
readers invested and then another choral moment as you finish to send
them out the door humming. If you must summarize an argument, don't
let a flat recap of your main points squander an important opportunity to
influence readers. End with a rhetorical flourish that reminds readers how
compelling your arguments are. ○

A pithy phrase, an ironic twist, and a question to contemplate can also
lock down your case. Here's Maureen Dowd, bleakly—and memorably—
concluding an argument defending the job journalists have done covering
the Iraq War:

Journalists die and we know who they are. We know they liked to cook and
play Scrabble. But we don't know who killed them, and their killers will
never be brought to justice. The enemy has no face, just a finger on a
detonator.

— "Live from Baghdad: More Dying," *New York Times*, May 31, 2006

Journalists undergo training to
prepare for the dangers they
are likely to face in conflict
zones.

shape an ending
p. 359

Choosing a style and design

Arguments vary widely in style. An unsigned editorial you write to represent the opinion of a newspaper might sound formal and serious. Composing an op-ed under your own name, you'd likely ease up on the echoing parallel clauses and allow yourself more personal pronouns. Arguing a point in an alternative newsletter, you might even slip into the lingo of its vegan or survivalist subscribers. Routine adjustments like these really matter when you need to attract and hold readers.

You should also write with sensitivity since some people reading arguments may well be wavering, defensive, or spoiling for a fight. There's no reason to distract them with fighting words if you want to offer a serious argument. Here's how political commentator Ann Coulter described a politically active group of 9/11 widows who she believed were using their status to shield their opinions of the Iraq War from criticism:

> These broads are millionaires, lionized on TV and in articles about them, reveling in their status as celebrities and stalked by grief-arazzis. I have never seen people enjoying their husbands' death so much.
>
> – *Godless: The Church of Liberalism* (2006)

Any point Coulter might make simply gets lost in her breathtaking idiom of attack.

There are many powerful and aggressive ways to frame an argument without resorting to provocative language or fallacies of argument. Following are some of those strategies. O

Invite readers with a strong opening.   Arguments—like advertisements—are usually discretionary reading. People can turn away the moment they grow irritated or bored. So you have to work hard to keep them invested in your ideas. You may need to open with a little surprise or drama. Try a blunt statement, an anecdote, or a striking illustration if it helps—maybe an image, too. Or consider personalizing the lead-in, giving readers a stake in the claim you are about to make. Following is a remarkable opening paragraph from an argument by Malcolm Gladwell on the wisdom of banning dogs by breed. When you finish, ask yourself whether Gladwell has earned your attention. Would you read the remainder of the piece?

read critically
p. 317

One afternoon last February, Guy Clairoux picked up his two-and-a half-year-old son, Jayden, from day care and walked him back to their house in the west end of Ottawa, Ontario. They were almost home. Jayden was straggling behind, and, as his father's back was turned, a pit bull jumped over a back-yard fence and lunged at Jayden. "The dog had his head in its mouth and started to do this shake," Clairoux's wife, JoAnn Hartley, said later. As she watched in horror, two more pit bulls jumped over the fence, joining in the assault. She and Clairoux came running, and he punched the first of the dogs in the head, until it dropped Jayden, and then he threw the boy toward his mother. Hartley fell on her son, protecting him with her body. "JoAnn!" Clairoux cried out, as all three dogs descended on his wife. "Cover your neck, cover your neck." A neighbor, sitting by her window, screamed for help. Her partner and a friend, Mario Gauthier, ran outside. A neighborhood boy grabbed his hockey stick and threw it to Gauthier. He began hitting one of the dogs over the head, until the stick broke. "They wouldn't stop," Gauthier said. "As soon as you'd stop, they'd attack again. I've never seen a dog go so crazy. They were like Tasmanian devils." The police came. The dogs were pulled away, and the Clairouxes and one of the rescuers were taken to the hospital. Five days later, the Ontario legislature banned the ownership of pit bulls. "Just as we wouldn't let a great white shark in a swimming pool," the province's attorney general, Michael Bryant, had said, "maybe we shouldn't have these animals on the civilized streets."

– "Troublemakers," *New Yorker*, February 6, 2006

Write vibrant sentences.   You can write arguments full throttle, using a complete range of rhetorical devices, from deliberate repetition and parallelism to dialogue and quotation. Metaphors, similes, and analogies fit right in too. The trick is to create sentences with a texture rich enough to keep readers hooked, yet lean enough to advance an argument. In the following three paragraphs, follow the highlighting to see how Thomas L. Friedman uses parallelism and one intriguing metaphor after another to argue in favor of immigration legislation after witnessing the diversity in a high school graduation class in Maryland. ○

improve your sentences
p. 378

There is a lot to be worried about in America today: a war in Iraq that is getting worse not better, an administration whose fiscal irresponsibility we will be paying for for a long time, an education system that is not producing enough young Americans skilled in math and science, and inner cities where way too many black males are failing. We must work harder and get smarter if we want to maintain our standard of living.

But if there is one reason to still be optimistic about America it is represented by the stunning diversity of the Montgomery Blair class of 2006. America is still the world's greatest human magnet. We are not the only country that embraces diversity, but there is something about our free society and free market that still attracts people like no other. Our greatest asset is our ability to still cream off not only the first-round intellectual draft choices from around the world but the low-skilled–high-aspiring ones as well, and that is the main reason that I am not yet ready to cede the twenty-first century to China. Our Chinese will still beat their Chinese.

This influx of brainy and brawny immigrants is our oil well – one that never runs dry. It is an endless source of renewable human energy and creativity. Congress ought to stop debating gay marriage and finally give us a framework to maintain a free flow of legal immigration.

– "A Well of Smiths and Xias," *New York Times*, June 7, 2006

Ask rhetorical questions.   The danger of rhetorical questions is that they can seem stagy and readers might not answer them the way you want. But the device can be very powerful in hammering a point home. Good questions also invite readers to think about an issue in exactly the terms that a writer prefers. Here's George Will using rhetorical questions to conclude a piece on global warming.

In fact, the earth is always experiencing either warming or cooling. But suppose the scientists and their journalistic conduits, who today say they were so spectacularly wrong so recently, are now correct. Suppose the earth is warming and suppose the warming is caused by human activity. Are we sure there will be proportionate benefits from whatever climate change can be purchased at the cost of slowing economic growth and spending trillions? Are we sure the consequences of climate change – remember, a thick sheet of ice once covered the Midwest – must be bad?

Or has the science-journalism complex decided that debate about these questions, too, is "over"?

– "Let Cooler Heads Prevail," *Washington Post*, April 2, 2006

Use images and design to make a point.　If we didn't know it already (and we did), the video and photographic images from 9/11, Abu Ghraib, and Hurricane Katrina clearly prove that persuasion doesn't occur by words only. We react powerfully to what we see with our own eyes.

And yet words still play a part because most images become *focused* arguments only when accompanied by commentary—as commentators routinely prove when they put a spin on news photographs or video. And because digital technology now makes it so easy to incorporate nonverbal media into texts, whether on a page, screen, or PowerPoint slide, you should always consider how just the right image might enhance the case you want to make. And now you don't always have to start with words. A series of photographs might be shaped into a photo-essay every bit as powerful as a conventional op-ed piece.

In fact, you already have the tools on your computer to create posters, advertisements, slides, and brochures, all of which may be instruments of persuasion. **O**

Photographs of people trapped on rooftops by flooding from Hurricane Katrina became an important element of that story, and the argument that followed.

work with visuals
p. 504

Examining models

ARGUMENT FROM PERSONAL EXPERIENCE   In "Protecting What Really Matters," Shane McNamee offers a rationale for gay marriage and a good deal more. McNamee makes strong personal and emotional connections with readers by sharing portions of his life, while he assembles a logical chain of reasons for supporting his claim about gay marriage. He wrote this essay in response to an assignment in a college writing class.

McNamee 1

Shane McNamee

Instructor's Name

Course Title

Date

Protecting What Really Matters

Some consider me an anomaly. As a gay man with certain conservative values, I've seen ideologues of all types distort homosexuality to advance their political agendas. Regardless of how sexual orientation is determined or defined, we should treat the subject with candor. I'll volunteer to go first.

Stereotypical gay culture doesn't suit me. I hate shopping, and you'll never see me inside a gay dance club. Hearing about such places from my gay friends creeps me out. If one craves mindless conversation or a one-night stand, he might find it there. And you're right if you think that some in the gay community regard youthful beauty more highly than traditional Christian values like chastity and committed relationships. But if your identity were criticized by defenders of traditional values from the time you hit puberty, wouldn't you yearn for alternative ideals?

Gay Americans can't have their cake, much less eat it. Conservatives tell homosexuals to suppress their emotions and

> Establishes a trustworthy ethos.

> Rhetorical question leads readers to identify with McNamee's dilemma.

91

McNamee 2

desires for a lifetime. When these bottled-up feelings explode in a burst of liberation, conservatives scold a lack of restraint. I'm all for encouraging monogamy, but many who advocate it also don't want gay marriage. With such limited options, no wonder so many gay men and women say, "The hell with you guys. You don't want me to do anything, so I'll do whatever I please."

Is homosexuality wrong? The U.S. military and the Catholic Church share similar party lines here: No--if homosexuality means nothing beyond same-sex physical attraction. But if you act on such thoughts, the plot thickens.

Military officers usually won't ask if you don't tell. They're concerned that openly gay servicemembers will hurt morale--never mind that Australia, Britain, Canada, and Israel allow openly gay servicemembers and have seen positive morale effects (Human Rights Campaign). If their subordinates seem less-than-straight and can be implicated with photos, eyewitness testimony, or a written statement from the accused, they'll likely face dishonorable discharge. I didn't like those prospects while in air force ROTC my freshman year of college. Pretending to be heterosexual at times and asexual at others proved tiresome. So I quit.

Whereas the military strictly enforces its policies, the typical Catholic Church is more relaxed. A Catholic priest, despite any ambivalence he may feel about the issue, will give you the Vatican's stance: Once you cross the line from temptation to indulgence--by acting on your homosexual desires--you commit a sin and risk going to hell. This condemnation stems from three mistakes made by those who cite the Bible passages most commonly used against

Paragraphs about the military and Church both explore how homosexuality is tolerated so long as homosexuals deny their nature.

McNamee 3

homosexuals: mistranslation, taking a verse out of context, and reading too much into vague wording of scripture.

Uses sources to challenge religious strictures.

Though many see the Bible as the inerrant word of God, its sixty-six different books have been written by an unknown number of people throughout 1,200 years. God may have dictated to the original authors, but I doubt that God edits every translation of original scripture. Since few people know Aramaic and other relevant ancient languages, what prevents scholars from tacking their bias onto an ambiguous translation? Furthermore, we trust that the original authors were pure of heart. Saint Paul gives us room for pause.

Conservative Christians sometimes quote Paul in their attacks on homosexuality, forgetting that Jesus was mute on the subject. Modern believers should also know that Paul's values sometimes differed from Jesus'. If you admire this former persecutor of Christians, maybe you'll agree with his opinion that a woman shouldn't "teach or have authority over a man; she is to keep silent. . . ." Paul is not the only reason why we need to think more critically about the Bible.

Offers logical reasons to question scriptural interpretations.

Look at the passage that inspired the word sodomy: "Then the LORD rained upon Sodom and upon Gomorrah brimstone and fire from the LORD out of heaven. . . ." (Gen. 19:24). Many preachers interpret these lines as God punishing the Sodomites for trying to rape the angels who visit Lot. Others argue that this passage begs us to be hospitable hosts. Even if we accept the first interpretation as truth, angel-rape is a far cry from consensual homosexual relation-ships. Rape involves coercion and violence; loving relationships require free will and respect. Other infamously antigay Bible pas-sages refer to child molestation and cavorting pagans. In fact,

McNamee 4

nowhere does the Bible refer to "homosexuality." The word didn't exist back then. Scripture that supposedly condemns same-sex intercourse typically involves other factors: rape, prostitution, sex with minors, etc. Homosexual relationships between consenting adults go unmentioned.

Biblical interpretations aside, some think that homosexuals mistake lust for love--a reasonable opinion at first glance. Most scientists and ministers would agree that human sexuality is tricky. Alfred Kinsey's research from the 1940s indicates that heterosexuals act on occasional same-sex attractions (Kinsey Institute). Are these people merely confused, deviating from their prescribed sexual destinies? Perhaps, if you accept the premise that sexual orientation is permanently fixed.

Considering a growing scientific consensus, Christians should at least acknowledge evidence that homosexuality has a genetic basis. A recent study conducted by Dr. Brian Mustanski from the University of Illinois at Chicago supports earlier scientific forays into sexual orientation by building "on previous studies that have consistently found evidence of genetic influence on sexual orientation" (WebMD). Mustanski scoured the human genome for genetic material shared among hundreds of sets of brothers, both gay and straight. He found that regions of DNA from three chromosomes were shared by 60% of gay brothers, more than the 50% expected from chance alone. These findings suggest that homosexuality, while not determined solely by genetics, results from more than just social factors.

Environmental variables certainly help establish sexuality, but if we're going to play that game, here's some personal history: (1) I

Uses both research and personal experience to question Western attitudes toward homosexuality.

Uses scientific evidence to argue key point.

McNamee 5

was never molested; (2) my relationship with my father has always
been peachy; and (3) I rarely saw homosexuals on TV or otherwise
as a youngster--not until after I already suspected that I was
different from other boys. These facts disprove those who believe
that homosexuality is caused by traumatic childhood experience, a
distant father, or indoctrination. And just so we're clear, most
geneticists now believe that human traits depend on the interaction
between both our genes and our environment--trait-expressing
DNA segments are triggered by environmental stimuli, including
both chemical and social agents.

Yet science is only one source of authority. Practically speaking,
human experience is more relevant than academic debate. If God is as
great as we all hope, I think He'd want us to be happy with whomever
we love. Last summer I found someone who makes me happy.

I love Jonathan Miguel Jiménez, and I'm not afraid to say it.
We're from different backgrounds and are of two minds when it
comes to politics. He's much more liberal than I am. Though we have
our disagreements, these debates add to the joy we derive from our
relationship. JJ has already taught me more about myself and about
crafting a solid argument than a lifetime of personal reflection and
formal education.

> Risks his relationship with readers with frank declaration.

If openly embracing homosexuality still bothers you, forget for the
moment the rainbow flags and pink triangles. Gay pride is not about
being homosexual; it's about the integrity and courage it takes to be
honest with yourself and your loved ones. It's about spending life with
whomever you want and not worrying what the government or the
neighbors think. Let's protect that truth, not some rigid view of sexual

> Throughout, argument is both personal and political.

McNamee 6

Responsibility
for action on
gay marriage
is laid on
readers.

orientation or marriage. Keep gay marriage out of your church if you like,

but if you value monogamy as I do, give me an alternative that doesn't

involve dishonesty or a life of loneliness. Many upstanding gay citizens

yearn for recognition of their loving, committed relationships. Unless you

enjoy being lied to and are ready to send your gay friends and family on

a Trail of Queers to Massachusetts or Canada--where gay marriage is

legal--then consider letting them live as they wish.

McNamee 7

Works Cited

Human Rights Campaign. Impact of Lifting the Ban: Other Agencies

     and Countries That Allow Open Service. 5 Jan. 2008 <http://

     www.hrc.org/issues/4882.htm>.

Kinsey Institute. "Kinsey's Heterosexual-Homosexual Rating Scale."

     June 1999. 10 Jan. 2008 <http://www.kinseyinstitute.org/

     resources/ak-hhscale.html>.

WebMD. "Is There a Gay Gene?" 28 Jan. 2005. 23 Jan. 2008 <http://

     www.webmd.com/sex-relationships/news/20050128/

     is-there-gay-gene>.

ARGUMENT ABOUT A PUBLIC ISSUE   Writing during the run-up to the American invasion of Afghanistan, Anna Quindlen argues in "Uncle Sam and Aunt Samantha" that, should a military draft be necessary, women must be included. The piece appeared in *Newsweek* in November 2001.

Uncle Sam and Aunt Samantha

ANNA QUINDLEN

One out of every five new recruits in the United States military is female.

The Marines gave the Combat Action Ribbon for service in the Persian Gulf to twenty-three women.

Two female soldiers were killed in the bombing of the USS *Cole*.

The Selective Service registers for the draft all male citizens between the ages of eighteen and twenty-five.

What's wrong with this picture?

As Americans read and realize that the lives of most women in this country are as different from those of Afghan women as a Cunard cruise is from maximum-security lockdown, there has nonetheless been little attention paid to one persistent gender inequity in U.S. public policy. An astonishing anachronism, really: While women are represented today in virtually all fields, including the armed forces, only men are required to register for the military draft that would be used in the event of a national security crisis.

Since the nation is as close to such a crisis as it has been in more than sixty years, it's a good moment to consider how the draft wound up in this particular time warp. It's not the time warp of the Taliban, certainly, stuck in the worst part of the thirteenth century, forbidding women to attend school or hold jobs or even reveal their arms, forcing them into sex and marriage. Our own time warp is several decades old. The last time the draft was considered seriously was twenty years ago, when registration with the Selective Service was restored by Jimmy Carter after the Soviet invasion of,

Defines a clear problem.

yep, Afghanistan. The president, as well as army chief of staff, asked at the time for the registration of women as well as men.

Amid a welter of arguments—women interfere with esprit decorps, women don't have the physical strength, women prisoners could be sexually assaulted, women soldiers would distract male soldiers from their mission—Congress shot down the notion of gender-blind registration. So did the Supreme Court, ruling that since women were forbidden to serve in combat positions and the purpose of the draft was to create a combat-ready force, it made sense not to register them.

But that was then, and this is now. Women have indeed served in combat positions, in the Balkans and the Middle East. More than forty thousand managed to serve in the Persian Gulf without destroying unit cohesion or failing because of upper-body strength. Some are even now taking out targets in Afghanistan from fighter jets, and apparently without any male soldier's falling prey to some predicted excess of chivalry or lust.

> Two paragraphs provide background information.

Talk about cognitive dissonance. All these military personnel, male and female alike, have come of age at a time when a significant level of parity was taken for granted. Yet they are supposed to accept that only males will be required to defend their country in a time of national emergency. This is insulting to men. And it is insulting to women. Caroline Forell, an expert on women's legal rights and a professor at the University of Oregon School of Law, puts it bluntly: "Failing to require this of women makes us lesser citizens."

> Forell states what is, in effect, Quindlen's thesis.

Neither the left nor the right has been particularly inclined to consider this issue judiciously. Many feminists came from the antiwar movement and have let their distaste for the military in general and the draft in particular mute their response. In 1980 NOW released a resolution that buried support for the registration of women beneath opposition to the draft, despite the fact that the draft had been re-designed to eliminate the vexing inequities of Vietnam, when the sons of the working class served and the sons of the Ivy League did not. Conservatives, meanwhile, used an equal-opportunity draft as the linchpin of opposition to the Equal Rights Amendment, along with the terrifying specter of unisex bathrooms. (I

> Concedes fault on all sides.

have seen the urinal, and it is benign.) The legislative director of the right-wing group Concerned Women for America once defended the existing regulations by saying that most women "don't want to be included in the draft." All those young men who went to Canada during Vietnam and those who today register with fear and trembling in the face of the Trade Center devastation might be amazed to discover that lack of desire is an affirmative defense.

Parents face a series of unique new challenges in this more egalitarian world, not the least of which would be sending a daughter off to war. But parents all over this country are doing that right now, with daughters who enlisted; some have even expressed surprise that young women, in this day and age, are not required to register alongside their brothers and friends. While all involved in this debate over the years have invoked the assumed opposition of the people, even ten years ago more than half of all Americans polled believed women should be made eligible for the draft. Besides, this is not about comfort but about fairness. My son has to register with the Selective Service this year, and if his sister does not when she turns eighteen, it makes a mockery not only of the standards of this household but of the standards of this nation.

It is possible in Afghanistan for women to be treated like little more than fecund pack animals precisely because gender fear and ignorance and hatred have been codified and permitted to hold sway. In this country, largely because of the concerted efforts of those allied with the women's movement over a century of struggle, much of that bigotry has been beaten back, even buried. Yet in improbable places the creaky old ways surface, the ways suggesting that we women were made of finer stuff. The finer stuff was usually porcelain, decorative and on the shelf, suitable for meals and show. Happily, the finer stuff has been transmuted into the right stuff. But with rights come responsibilities, as teachers like to tell their students. This is a responsibility that should fall equally upon all, male and female alike. If the empirical evidence is considered rationally, if the decision is divested of outmoded stereotypes, that's the only possible conclusion to be reached.

"Fairness" is premise for key argument.

Only stereotypes prevent reasonable change in U.S. draft policy. Conclusion shows how elements of Quindlen's argument connect.

VISUAL ARGUMENT

"Vampire Energy" appeared in the January/February 2008 issue of *GOOD* magazine, an online periodical. While the image conveys a great deal of information, it also makes an explicit argument for energy conservation.

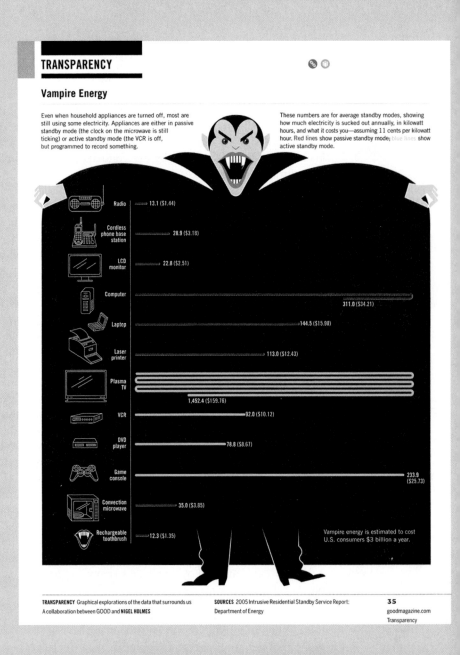

TRANSPARENCY

Vampire Energy

Even when household appliances are turned off, most are still using some electricity. Appliances are either in passive standby mode (the clock on the microwave is still ticking) or active standby mode (the VCR is off, but programmed to record something.

These numbers are for average standby modes, showing how much electricity is sucked out annually, in kilowatt hours, and what it costs you—assuming 11 cents per kilowatt hour. Red lines show passive standby mode; blue lines show active standby mode.

Radio — 13.1 ($1.44)

Cordless phone base station — 28.9 ($3.18)

LCD monitor — 22.8 ($2.51)

Computer — 311.0 ($34.21)

Laptop — 144.5 ($15.90)

Laser printer — 113.0 ($12.43)

Plasma TV — 1,452.4 ($159.76)

VCR — 92.0 ($10.12)

DVD player — 78.8 ($8.67)

Game console — 233.9 ($25.73)

Convection microwave — 35.0 ($3.85)

Rechargeable toothbrush — 12.3 ($1.35)

Vampire energy is estimated to cost U.S. consumers $3 billion a year.

TRANSPARENCY Graphical explorations of the data that surrounds us. A collaboration between GOOD and **NIGEL HOLMES**

SOURCES 2005 Intrusive Residential Standby Service Report: Department of Energy

35

goodmagazine.com
Transparency

1. **Argument from Personal Experience:** Write an argument that draws heavily on your personal experiences but potentially affects a large segment of the public, in the manner of Shane McNamee's "Protecting What Really Matters" (p. 91). Be sure, though, that your argument also draws on a range of outside sources.

2. **Argument about a Public Issue:** As Anna Quindlen does in "Uncle Sam and Aunt Samantha" (p. 97), assemble the facts about a controversy on your campus or in your community — academic, social, political, or religious — and take a stand on the issue. Gather the necessary background information and keep abreast of day-to-day developments, following coverage of the issue in multiple sources when possible. Finally, offer a perspective of your own and defend your claim authoritatively in an essay short enough to serve as an op-ed piece in your campus or local newspaper.

3. **Visual Argument:** In "Vampire Energy," *GOOD* magazine supports an argument about energy usage by making factual information powerfully visual (p. 100). Design a visual argument of your own that not only offers a specific claim (e.g., *Drill here, drill now*) but also presents visual evidence to support or extend it.

4. **Online Argument:** If you have the technical skills, design a Web site or blog that focuses on an issue — local or national — that you believe deserves more attention. Using current sites or blogs as models, be sure your project introduces the topic, explains your purpose, provides a forum for feedback, and includes both images and links relevant to the topic and online community.

How to start
- Need a **topic**? See page 107.
- Need **criteria for your evaluation**? See page 110.
- Need to **organize your criteria and evidence**? See page 113.

4 Evaluation

makes a claim about the value of something

Evaluations—in the forms of commentary and criticism—are so much a part of our lives that you might only notice them when they are specifically assigned. The others just happen.

- On a course evaluation, you explain in detail how your physics instructor made a mystifying subject you detested relevant and clear.

- After reviewing the draft of a friend's short story, you send her an e-mail explaining why it needs a thorough reorganization and rewrite.

- You run an increasingly popular blog featuring reviews of recent Hollywood movies from your particular red-state point of view.

- You sort through two dozen brochures and Web sites trying to find a 10-megapixel digital SLR camera that would meet your semiprofessional needs and very amateur budget.

- It's late August, time once again to go ballistic when *Sports Illustrated* fails even to rank your team among the top-ten prospects for the NCAA national title in football. How can the editors be so stupid? You're more than willing to explain.

UNDERSTANDING EVALUATIONS.   It's one thing to offer an opinion, an entirely different matter to back up a claim with reasons and evidence. Only when you do will readers (or listeners) take you seriously. But you'll also have to convince them that you know *how* to evaluate a book, a social policy, even a cup of coffee by reasonable standards. It helps when you use objective standards to make judgments, counting and measuring the road to excellence. But evaluations frequently involve people debating matters of taste. Here's how to frame this kind of argument. ○

Make value judgments.   You'll either judge something as good, bad, or indifferent when you write an evaluation or challenge an opinion someone else has offered. Of course, fair judgments can be quite complex: Even movie critics who do thumbs-up-or-down routines don't offer those verdicts until after they first talk about their subjects in detail.

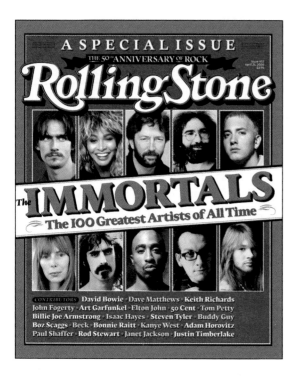

Popular magazines frequently evaluate or rank artists and celebrities, and their work. Cover photo from *Rolling Stone*, April 21, 2005. ©Rolling Stone LLC 2005. All rights reserved. Reprinted by permission.

understand argument
p. 68

Establish and defend criteria.   *Criteria* are the standards by which objects are measured: *A good furnace should heat a home quickly and efficiently. Successful presidents leave office with the country in better shape than when they entered.* When readers will generally agree with your criteria, you need to explain little about them. When they won't, you have to defend them. ○ And sometimes you'll break new ground—as happened when critics first asked, *What is good Web design?* and *Which are the best blogs?* In such cases, new criteria of evaluation had to be invented and rationalized.

Offer convincing evidence.   Evidence in the form of facts, statistics, testimony, examples, and good reasons provides the link between an evaluative claim and the criteria used to make it. If good furnaces heat homes quickly and efficiently, then you'd have to supply data to show that a product you judged faulty didn't meet those minimal standards. (It might be noisy and unreliable to boot.) Evidence will obviously vary from subject to subject, anything from hard numbers to harrowing tales of personal woe. ○

Offer useful advice.   Some evaluations are just for fun: Consider all the hoopla that arguments about sports rankings generate. But most evaluations, when done right, also provide practical information—some of it offered in clever forms that make it easy for readers to find and consult. So evaluations do important work, whether they rank humidifiers, books, or candidates in a city-council race.

Here's a review of the type millions of people consult annually when they consider spending $25,000 or more to buy a new car. You'll note that the following review of a Toyota Camry Hybrid not only describes the product in detail but also attempts to match the vehicle to its likely buyers. Many different criteria of evaluation are embedded in the review, some of them relating specifically to a hybrid vehicle designed to enhance fuel economy, not driving pleasure.

develop ideas
p. 346

interview and observe
p. 412

Erik B. Johnson's review in *Automobile* magazine acknowledges the merit of the new Camry for readers considering a hybrid vehicle, offering good reasons to examine it in the showroom. But Johnson leaves readers to make the final judgment with their checkbooks.

2007 Toyota Camry Hybrid

ERIK B. JOHNSON

Opening paragraph establishes criteria for hybrid.

With fuel prices in flux and environmental concerns deepening, the seductive song of the hybrid sirens is louder than ever, despite increasing skepticism about hybrid vehicles' positive effects on wallets and the environment. Perhaps the problem is that there hasn't yet been a fuel-sipping hybrid sedan for the common family man. The current hybrid sedans are either too conspicuous (Toyota Prius), too small (Honda Civic Hybrid), or too focused on performance rather than economy (Lexus GS450h and Honda Accord Hybrid). But Toyota's latest gasoline/electric model, the Camry Hybrid, is a fastball grooved right down the Everyman's strike zone. With it, Toyota aims to bring hybrid ownership to the masses; after all, the 2007 Camry on which it is based is the successor to the best-selling car in America.

Toyota Camry Hybrid

The Camry Hybrid is a comfortable and unassuming machine as long as you drive it calmly over smooth pavement, where you'll enjoy generally placid ride characteristics. But stay away from pockmarked roads, where the Hybrid's body control goes limp (likely due to the extra weight of the hybrid system), poor damping allows unwanted vibrations into the cabin, and severe bumps cause kickback through the steering wheel.

One of the Hybrid's oddest attributes is the relationship between its throttle, engine speed, and engine sound. The accelerator has long travel and is desensitized to all but the most urgent stomps; when you mash the pedal, the continuously variable transmission revs the engine endlessly, making it sound not unlike a broken food processor. All of this makes the car seem unbearably sluggish, but in an extremely scientific test—OK, a drag race—the Hybrid outpulled its conventional four-cylinder twin by a hefty margin.

Over a day of driving in urban and suburban settings, the Camry Hybrid returned 37 mpg, which is close to the EPA's combined estimate of 39 mpg. (Unlike the Accord Hybrid, the Camry Hybrid will run solely on battery power for several minutes if you go easy on the gas.) But before you fill out that Sierra Club application, consider that a regular four-cylinder Camry LE with a five-speed automatic achieved 31 mpg on the same route.

It would seem almost foolish to opt for the Hybrid, if not for its compelling price. Most hybrids command a lofty premium over nonhybrid versions of the same vehicle, but at $26,480, the equipment-heavy Camry Hybrid is only about $1,500 more than a similarly outfitted four-cylinder Camry XLE. Is 6 mpg worth the additional cash? It almost doesn't matter, because the Hybrid's negatives—including its smaller trunk, due to the hybrid system's components—won't be enough to dissuade people from plunking down the extra money if they really want one. Simply put, hybrids make a lot of people feel good, and, in the end, that's just as valid a reason to buy a car as avant-garde styling or world-class handling.

> Author makes important observation: The car sounds and feels slower than it is.

> Compares mileage figures to provide evidence for consumers.

Exploring purpose and topic

Most evaluations you're required to prepare for school or work come with assigned topics. But to choose an object to evaluate, follow different strategies, depending on what you hope to accomplish. ○

Evaluate a subject you know well. This is the safest option, built on the assumption that everyone is an expert on something. Years of reading *Gourmet* magazine or playing tennis might make it natural for you to review restaurants or tennis rackets. You've accumulated not only basic facts but also lots of tactile knowledge—the sort that gives you confidence when you make a claim. So go ahead and demonstrate your expertise.

topic ◀

Evaluate a subject you need to investigate. Perhaps you are considering graduate schools to apply to, looking for family-friendly companies to work for, or thinking about purchasing an HDTV. To make such choices, you'll need more information. So kill two birds with a single assignment: Use the school project to explore the issues you face, find the necessary facts and data, and make a case for (or against) Michigan State, Whole Foods, or Sharp.

Evaluate a subject you'd like to know more about. How do wine connoisseurs tell one cabernet from another and rank them so confidently? How would a college football championship team from the fifties match up against more recent winning teams? Use an assignment to settle questions like these that you an d your friends may have debated late into an evening.

Keep an open mind. Whatever your topic, you probably shouldn't begin an evaluation already knowing the outcome—hating a book before you read it or dead set against any chilies not grown in Hatch, New Mexico. Follow your criteria and data to the reasonable choice—even if it's one you don't prefer. Don't review what you can't treat fairly.

A fair evaluation requires an open mind.

find a topic
p. 308

Understanding your audience

Your job as a reviewer is made easier when you can assume readers might be interested in your opinions. Fortunately, most people consult evaluations and reviews willingly, hoping to find specific information: *Is the latest Tony Hillerman novel up to snuff? Who's the most important American architect working today? Mets or Marlins in the NL East this year?* But you'll still have to gauge the level of potential readers and make appropriate adjustments.

Write for experts.   Knowledgeable readers can be a tough audience because they bring to a subject strong, maybe inflexible, opinions. But if you know your stuff, you can take on the experts because they know their stuff too: You don't have to provide tedious background information or discuss criteria of evaluation in detail. You can use the technical vocabulary experts share and make allusions to people and concepts they'd recognize. Here's a paragraph from *Road & Track* that isn't making concessions to the general public:

> The new Variable Turbine Geometry technology is not new, having been used on diesels for years. It works by adding vanes outside the turbine that can change pitch with an electric motor. The vanes focus exhaust flow onto the turbine blades at low throttle opening, but at larger flow rates, i.e., high rpm, they open up to decrease the restriction. Porsche's breakthrough in applying this to a gasoline engine centers on the materials that are used to control thermal expansion due to the hotter exhaust gases from gasoline engines.
>
> – Shaun Bailey, "2007 Porsche 911 Turbo," June 2006

Need help thinking about your audience? See "How to Revise Your Work" on pp. 390–91.

Write for a general audience.   You have to explain more to general audiences than to specialists, clarifying your criteria of evaluation, providing background information, and defining key terms. But general readers usually are willing to learn more about a topic. Here's noted film critic Roger Ebert doing exactly that:

> *The Lake House* tells the story of a romance that spans years but involves only a few kisses. It succeeds despite being based on two paradoxes: time travel and the ability of two people to have conversations that are, under the terms established by the film, impossible. Neither one of these

problems bothered me in the slightest. Take time travel: I used to get distracted by its logical flaws and contradictory time lines. Now in my wisdom I have decided to simply accept it as a premise, no questions asked. A time-travel story works on emotional, not temporal, logic.

–rogerebert.com, June 16, 2006

Write for novices.   You have a lot of explaining to do when readers are absolutely fresh to a subject and need lots of background information. For instance, because *Consumer Reports* reviews a range of products well beyond the expertise of any individual, the editors always take care to explain how they make their judgments, whether the subject be washing machines, waffles, or Web sites. Do the same yourself. Take special care to define technical terms for your readers.

Are buffalo dangerous? For some audiences, you have to explain *everything*.

The following, for example, is a warning attached to camera reviews at Digital Photography Review, a Web site that examines photographic equipment in detail; "If you're new to digital photography you may wish to read the Digital Photography *Glossary* before diving into this article (it may help you understand some of the terms used)." Clicking the link leads to a fully illustrated dictionary of terms meant to help amateurs understand the qualities of a good digital camera.

Finding and developing materials

Assigned to write a review, it makes sense to research your subject thoroughly, even one you think you know pretty well. Online research is easy: Do a quick Web search to see if your notions are still current in a world where opinions change rapidly. ○

For many subjects (and products especially), it's easy to discover what others have already written, particularly when a topic has a distinctive name. Just type that name followed by the word *review* into Google's search window and see what pops up. But don't merely parrot opinions you find in sources: Challenge conventional views whenever you can offer better ones. (At one time, most critics thought good poetry should rhyme—until some poets and critics argued otherwise.) Make a fresh and distinctive case of your own. To do that, focus on criteria and evidence.

develop criteria

Decide on your criteria.   Get them firmly in mind, even if you're just evaluating pizza. Should the crust be hard or soft? The sauce red and spicy, or white and creamy? How thick should pizza be? How salty? And, to all these opinions—*why*?

Didn't expect the *why*? You really don't have a criterion until you attach a plausible reason to it. ○ The rationale should be clear in your own mind even if you don't expect to expound on it in the review or evaluation itself: *Great pizza comes with a soft crust that wraps each bite and topping in a floury texture that merges the contrasting flavors.* More important, any criteria you use will have to make sense to readers either on its own (*Public art should be beautiful*) or after you've explained and defended it (*Public art should be scandalous because people need to be jolted out of conformist thinking*).

Look for hard criteria.   It helps when criteria are countable or observable. You'll seem objective when your criteria at least *seem* grounded in numbers. Think, for example, of how instructors set numerical standards for your performance in their courses, translating all sorts of activities, from papers to class participation, into numbers. Teachers aren't alone in deferring to numbers. Following, for example, are the criteria CNET Reviews follows for evaluating televisions, as explained on its Web site:

refine your search
p. 406

develop a thesis
p. 336

Design (30 percent of the total rating): We look at not only the overall aesthetics of the product but also its interface and included remote. An uninspiring but functional design will rate a 5. Higher scores will be given for a well-designed remote with backlit buttons, a clear onscreen navigation system, and particularly sleek cosmetics.

Features (30 percent of the total rating): The range of features is considered in determining this portion of the rating. From picture-in-picture (PIP) and 2:3 pull-down to the appropriate number of A/V inputs, we consider everything this product delivers to the consumer. A set that comes armed with a suitable number of inputs and basic features will earn a 5. Products with more inputs, individual input memories, or other extras will earn a better rating.

Performance (40 percent of the total rating): We consider picture quality to be the most important criteria for displays, so we give it the most weight. A score of 5 represents a television that can produce a serviceable picture with only a reasonable amount of adjustment. Sets with a particularly sharp picture; rich, accurate color; deep black levels; and good video processing will earn a higher score.

Argue for criteria that can't be measured.   How do you measure the success or failure of something that can't be objectively calculated—a student dance recital, Scorsese's latest film, or the new abstract sculpture just hauled onto the campus? Do some research to find out how such topics are customarily discussed. Get familiar with what sensible critics have to say about whatever you're evaluating—contemporary art, fine saddles, good teaching, TV crime dramas. If you read carefully, you'll find values and criteria deeply embedded in all your sources. ○

In the following, for example, James Morris explains why he believes American television is often better than Hollywood films. Morris's criteria are highlighted.

> What I admire most about these shows, and most deplore about contemporary movies, is the quality of the scripts. The TV series are devised and written by smart people who seem to be allowed to let their intelligence show. Yes, the individual and ensemble performances on several of the series are superb, but would the actors be as good as they are if they were miming the action? TV shows are designed for the small screen and cannot rely, as movies do,

read closely
p. 317

on visual and aural effects to distract audiences. If what's being said on TV isn't interesting, why bother to watch? Television is rigorous, right down to the confinement of hour or half-hour time slots, further reduced by commercials. There's no room for the narrative bloat that inflates so many Hollywood movies from their natural party-balloon size to Thanksgiving-parade dimensions.

—"My Favorite Wasteland," *Wilson Quarterly*, Autumn 2005

Stand by your values.   Make sure you define criteria that apply to more than just the individual case you are examining at the moment. Think about what makes socially conscious rap music, world-class sculpture, a great president. For instance, you may have a special fondness for Jimmy Carter, but should criteria for great presidents be measured by what they do *after* they leave office? Similarly, you might admire artists or actors who overcome great personal tragedies on their paths to stardom. But to make such heroics a *necessary* criterion for artistic achievement might look like special pleading.

Gather your evidence.   In writing an evaluation, some of your evidence will come from secondary sources, especially when assessing something like a government program or historical event. Before offering an opinion on the merit of Social Security or the wisdom of Truman's decision to drop atomic bombs to end World War II, expect to do critical reading. Weigh the evidence and arguments you find in these sources before you offer your own judgment—and then cite some of these sources for evidence and support. ○

Other evidence will come from careful observation. When judging a book, a movie, a restaurant, or an art exhibit, for instance, take careful notes not only of your initial impressions but also of the details that support or explain them. When appropriate, take time to measure, weigh, photograph, and interview your subjects. If it makes sense to survey what others think about an issue (about a campus political issue, for example), keep a record of such opinions. Finally, be willing to alter your opinion when the evidence you gather in support of a hypothesis heads in a direction you hadn't expected. (See Scott Standley's "Rock the Vote: Useful Harm?" on p. 121.)

analyze claims and evidence p. 420

Creating a structure

As with other arguments, evaluations have distinct parts that can be built into a pattern or structure.

organize ◀ criteria

Choose a simple structure when your criteria and categories are predictable. A basic review might announce a subject and make a claim, list criteria of evaluation, present evidence to show whether the subject meets those standards, and draw conclusions. Here's one version of that pattern with the criteria discussed all at once, at the opening of the piece.

Introduction leading to an **evaluative claim**

    Criteria of evaluation stated and, if necessary, defended

        Subject measured by first **criterion + evidence**

        Subject measured by second **criterion + evidence**

        Subject measured by additional **criteria + evidence**

Conclusion

And here's a template with the criteria of evaluation introduced one at a time.

Introduction leading to an **evaluative claim**

    First criterion of evaluation stated and, if necessary, defended

        Subject measured by first **criterion + evidence**

    Second criterion stated/defended

        Subject measured by second **criterion + evidence**

    Additional criteria stated/defended

        Subject measured by additional **criteria + evidence**

Conclusion

You might find structures this tight and predictable, for instance, in job-performance reviews at work or in consumer magazines. Once a pattern is established for measuring TVs, computers, paint sprayers, even teachers (consider those forms you fill in at the end of the term), it can be repeated for each new subject and results can be compared.

Yet what works for hardware and tech products is not quite so convincing when applied to music, books, or other subjects that are more than the sum of their parts. Imagine a film critic whose *every* review marched through the same predictable set of criteria: acting, directing, writing, set design, cinematography, and costumes. When a subject can't be reviewed via simple categories, you will need to decide which of its many possible aspects deserve attention. ○

Choose a focal point.   Look for features that you and your readers will surely notice, that is, what makes you react strongly and intellectually to the subject. You could, in fact, organize an entire review around one or more shrewd insights, and many reviewers do. The trick is to make connections between key or controlling ideas and various aspects of your subject. Look carefully at Rob Sheffield's review of Green Day's *American Idiot* (p. 119) and you'll discover that what holds it together are the writer's expressions of surprise that an aging punk band can still do relevant work. Sheffield makes that point at both the beginning and the end of the evaluation:

> Tell the truth: Did anybody think Green Day would still be around in 2004? Ten years ago, when they blew up into the hot summer band of 1994, they were snotty little Berkeley, California, punk kids who sounded ready to pogo off the face of the earth in three-chord tantrums such as "Basket Case."
>   . . . Against all odds, Green Day have found a way to hit their thirties without either betraying their original spirit or falling on their faces.

Compare and contrast.   Another obvious way to organize an evaluation is to examine differences. Strengths and weaknesses stand out especially well when similar subjects are examined critically, as in the following opening paragraph of a review in the *Wall Street Journal*:

shape your work
p. 340

We've been testing this new iMac, and our verdict is that it's the gold
standard of desktop PCs. To put it simply: No desktop offered by Dell
or Hewlett-Packard or Sony or Gateway can match the new iMac G5's
combination of power, elegance, simplicity, ease of use, built-in software,
stability, and security. From setup to performing the most intense tasks, it's
a pleasure to use. And, contrary to common misconceptions, this Mac is
competitively priced, when compared with comparably equipped midrange
Windows PCs; and it handles all common Windows files, as well as the
Internet and e-mail, with aplomb.

−Walter S. Mossberg and Catherine Boehret, "A Gold Standard for PCs,"
November 30, 2005

To keep extended comparisons on track, the simplest structure is to
evaluate one subject at a time, running through its features completely
before moving on to the next. Let's say you decided to contrast economic
conditions in France and Germany. Here's how such a paper might look in a
scratch outline if you focused on the countries one at a time. ○

France and Germany: An Economic Report Card

  I. France
    A. Rate of growth
    B. Unemployment rate
    C. Productivity
    D. Gross national product
    E. Debt

 II. Germany
    A. Rate of growth
    B. Unemployment rate
    C. Productivity
    D. Gross national product
    E. Debt

order ideas
p. 342

The disadvantage of evaluating subjects one at a time is that actual comparisons, let's say, of rates of employment in the outline above, might appear pages apart. So in some cases, you might prefer a comparison-contrast structure that looks at features point by point.

France and Germany: An Economic Report Card

  I. Rate of growth
    A. France
    B. Germany
  II. Unemployment rate
    A. France
    B. Germany
  III. Productivity
    A. France
    B. Germany
  IV. Gross national product
    A. France
    B. Germany
  V. Debt
    A. France
    B. Germany

Choosing a style and design

Depending on the aim of the review you are composing and your stance within it, evaluations can be written in any style, from high to low. ○ You should also look for opportunities to present evaluations visually.

Use a high or formal style.   Technical reviews tend to be the most formal and impersonal: They may be almost indistinguishable from reports, spelling out findings in plain, unemotional language. Such a style gives the impression of scientific objectivity, even though the work may reflect someone's agenda. For instance, here's a paragraph in formal style from the National Assessment of Educational Progress summarizing the performance of American students in science.

> At grade 8, there was no overall improvement. In 2005, 59 percent of students scored at or above the *Basic* level. An example of the knowledge and skills at the *Basic* level is being able to compare changes in heart rate during and after exercise. Twenty-nine percent performed at or above the *Proficient* level. Identifying the energy conversions that occur in an electric fan is an example of the knowledge and skills at the *Proficient* level.
>
> —*Nation's Report Card*, 2005 Science Assessment (http://nationsreportcard .gov/science_2005)

Use a middle style.   When the writer has a more direct stake in the work—as is typical in restaurant or movie reviews, for example—the style moves more decisively toward the middle. Even though a reviewer may never use *I*, you still sense a person behind the writing, making judgments and offering opinions. That's certainly the case in these two paragraphs by Clive Crook, written shortly after the death of noted economist John Kenneth Galbraith: Words, phrases, even sentence fragments that humanize the assessment are highlighted.

> Galbraith, despite the Harvard professorship, was never really an economist in the ordinary sense in the first place. In one of countless well-turned pronouncements, he said, "Economics is extremely useful as a form of employment for economists." He disdained the scientific pretensions and formal apparatus of modern economics—all that math and number

crunching—believing that it missed the point. This view did not spring from mastery of the techniques: Galbraith disdained them from the outset, which saved time.

Friedman, in contrast, devoted his career to grinding out top-quality scholarly work, while publishing the occasional best seller as a sideline. He too was no math whiz, but he was painstakingly scientific in his methods (when engaged in scholarly research) and devoted to data. All that was rather beneath Galbraith. Brilliant, yes; productive, certainly. But he was a bureaucrat, a diplomat, a political pundit, and a popular economics writer of commanding presence more than a serious economic thinker, let alone a great one.

—"John Kenneth Galbraith, Revisited," *National Journal*, May 15, 2006

Use a low style.   Many reviews get chummy with readers and so personal they verge on arrogance. You probably want evaluations you write for academic or work assignments to be relatively low-key in style, focused more on the subject than on you as the reviewer. But you have an enormous range of options—all the more reason to look at models of the kind of evaluation you will be preparing. For examples of highly personal reviews using an informal style, check those of products on Amazon.com.

Present evaluations visually.   Comparisons work especially well when presented via tables, charts, or graphs. ○ Readers see relationships that could not be explained quite as efficiently in words alone.

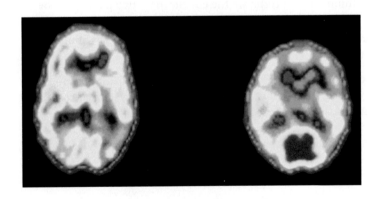

PET scan of two human brains.   To evaluate patients, doctors use comparison and contrast as a diagnostic tool. The brain on the left reflects normal brain activity; that on the right shows the brain activity of a schizophrenic.

display data
p. 514

Examining models

MUSIC REVIEW   Rob Sheffield couldn't know how successful Green Day's CD *American Idiot* would be when he reviewed it in September 2004 for *Rolling Stone,* well before it won multiple Grammys and a huge following. But his review holds up because he examines the music in its context, recognizing weaknesses, yet admitting its unanticipated strengths. The review also demonstrates how demanding a colloquial style, with its idiosyncratic vocabulary and in-the-know allusions, can be.

Green Day: *American Idiot*

ROB SHEFFIELD

Tell the truth: Did anybody think Green Day would still be around in 2004? Ten years ago, when they blew up into the hot summer band of 1994, they were snotty little Berkeley, California, punk kids who sounded ready to pogo off the face of the earth in three-chord tantrums such as "Basket Case." Between Billie Joe Armstrong's adenoidal snarl and Tre Cool's maniac drums, Green Day seemed like a Saturday-morning-cartoon version of *The Young Ones,* three cheeky monkeys who came to raid the bar and disappear. But here they are with *American Idiot*: a fifty-seven-minute politically charged epic depicting a character named Jesus of Suburbia as he suffers through the decline and fall of the American dream. And all this from the boys who brought you *Dookie.*

American Idiot is the kind of old-school rock opera that went out of style when Keith Moon still had a valid driver's license, in the tradition of the Who's *Tommy,* Yes's *Relayer,* or Styx's *Kilroy Was Here.* Since Green Day are punk rockers, they obviously have a specific model in mind: Hüsker Dü's 1984 *Zen Arcade,* which showed how a street-level hardcore band could play around with storytelling without diluting the primal anger of the music. On *American Idiot,* the thirteen tracks segue together,

This sentence serves as thesis. Surprise—this music is serious.

Provides information to locate American Idiot musically.

119

expanding into piano balladry and acoustic country shuffles. The big statement "Jesus of Suburbia" is a nine-minute five-part suite, with Roman-numeral chapters including "City of the Damned," "Dearly Beloved," and "Tales of Another Broken Home."

American Idiot could have been a mess; in fact, it is a mess. The plot has characters with names such as St. Jimmy and Whatsername, young rebels who end up on the "Boulevard of Broken Dreams." But the individual tunes are tough and punchy enough to work on their own. You can guess who the "American Idiot" is in the bang-up title tune, as Armstrong rages against the "subliminal mind-fuck America" of the George W. Bush era: "Welcome to a new kind of tension / All across the alien nation." Green Day have always swiped licks from the Clash, even back when they were still singing about high school shrinks and whores, so it makes sense for them to come on like Joe Strummer. The other Clash flashback is "Are We the Waiting," a grandiose ballad evoking Side Three of *London Calling.* "Wake Me Up When September Ends" is an acoustic power ballad, a sadder, more adult sequel to "Good Riddance (Time of Your Life)." Even better, there are punk ravers such as "Give Me Novocaine," "Extraordinary Girl," and "Letterbomb," which bites off a big juicy chunk of the Cheap Trick oldie "She's Tight."

Since rock operas are self-conscious and pompous beasts by definition, Green Day obligingly cram all their bad ideas into one monstrously awful track, the nine-minute "Homecoming," which sounds like the Who's "A Quick One While He's Away" without any of the funny parts. But aside from that, *Idiot* does a fine job of revving up the basic Green Day conceit, adding emotional flavor to top-shelf Armstrong songs. They don't skimp on basic tunefulness—not even in the other big nine-minute track, "Jesus of Suburbia," which packs in punk thrash, naked piano, glockenspiel, Beach Boys harmonies, and a Springsteen-style production number about a 7-Eleven parking lot where there are some mystical goings-down indeed. Against all odds, Green Day have found a way to hit their thirties without either betraying their original spirit or falling on their faces. Good Charlotte, you better be taking notes.

> Claim seems paradoxical: CD is a mess, but it works.

> Major weakness in the CD acknowledged.

> Sheffield summarizes the accomplishments of *American Idiot.*

EVALUATION OF A PUBLIC SERVICE CAMPAIGN   Scott Standley was initially turned off by the idea that Rock the Vote—an organization dedicated to bringing more young Americans to the polls—relies on celebrities and star power to raise civic awareness. A look at actual evidence changed his mind about the group's campaign during a recent election. Standley wrote this paper in response to an assignment in a college writing class.

Standley 1

Scott Standley

Instructor's Name

Course Title

Date

Rock the Vote: Useful Harm?

I was planning on writing a paper that revealed the absurdities of using celebrity influence for political purposes. I was going to base my accusations in my generation's deep immersion in harmful levels of celebrity exposure. I would suggest that this toxic influence has lulled us into a sedentary, apathetic lifestyle and that campaigns like Rock the Vote only contribute to this behavior by perpetuating the importance of celebrity. My conclusion was going to be killer. Instead of encouraging political action, I was going to claim that Rock the Vote detracts from it by promulgating the very thing that creates widespread apathy: a celebrity-laden culture of unbalanced priorities and revoltingly trivial lifestyles. After formulating my perfect ending, I decided that some actual evidence would be a good idea, so I sat down and watched some of Rock the Vote's TV spots on YouTube.

What I heard on one of their commercials went something like this:

Opening paragraph outlines plan for an essay of evaluation Standley did *not* write.

Standley 2

Script from a
Rock the Vote
ad is key piece
of evidence
for paper.

If you care about the environment, if you care about the
cost of education, if you care whether there's a military
draft. Politicians are passing laws that affect the air we
breathe, the water we drink, who fights the war in Iraq,
how much you pay for your college education, and who
makes the sacrifices, the many issues that will be decided
this election. Don't keep your opinions to yourself. Show
you care. Vote. The most important thing I can do is the
same thing you can do. Vote on November 2nd. ("Vote!")

If I had read this script prior to seeing the actual commercial, I
can tell you I would have been very pleased to know that it had
been broadcast on national television. Looking purely at the textual
aspect of this commercial, I see a very important and legitimate
attempt at getting a higher voter turnout. Of course, this is only one
script from a bigger ad campaign and cannot vouch for all of Rock
the Vote, but in itself, I see a message that I wish more people
received. Politicians profoundly influence our lives! I would hope
everyone knew that and applied that realization to their actions.

Analysis of
the script
causes an
opinion shift.

One explanation offered for lower voting numbers among 18-25
year olds is that they don't yet fully understand how deeply
government policy can influence their lives. I find this point
legitimate when I recall my days of political ambivalence in high
school and notice similar attitudes in younger people now. The
dialogue in Rock the Vote's script directly attacks this problem of
political cluelessness among youth. By simply listing some of the
many political issues that heavily influence young voters, the

Standley 3

commercial, if nothing else, is at least showing why we should care who staffs our government's ranks. The only part in the script that panders to celebrity status is the line, "The most important thing I can do is the same thing you can do." Even this is mild in terms of celebrity focus, so I don't find it particularly appalling or shameful. So I consider the text of the "Rock the Vote" ad to be beneficial to anyone watching. It is a direct reminder of the connection between our vote and the behavior of our government.

Moving past the script of Rock the Vote's commercial, we come to its more controversial feature: the conveyors of the message. The cast for this commercial includes Justin Timberlake, Leonardo DiCaprio, and Samuel Jackson, three of the best-known figures in the world of pop culture. Does this casting demean the message being delivered? Do these actors somehow strip the argument of its validity? I would like to think that a good argument maintains itself regardless of its source. One could argue that these celebrities have absolutely no background or credentials in politics, and so they are illegitimate spokesmen for a political movement--but is that really even the point? If some brilliant scientist discovered a cure for a disease but used his suave and attractive assistant to explain the method to the public, would his cure be any less valuable? Clearly the scientist would be the higher authority in the matter, but letting a more appealing figure relay the message shouldn't matter if the cure works. Would Rock the Vote's political message be more legitimate if spoken by a political scientist from Harvard as opposed to Justin Timberlake? I say that it doesn't really matter: An argument's legitimacy stands regardless who delivers it. While a credible ethos is always desirable, public service announcements are designed to spread awareness. The truth is,

---

Raises second major issue of evaluation.

Key premise is: Those delivering message don't really affect its content.

Offers reasons to defend Rock the Vote's strategies.

Middle style is both personal and serious.

Standley 4

when it comes to gaining the public's attention, a famous face can be vastly more effective than an impressive résumé.

But I haven't abandoned the opinion that our celebrity-laden culture has created unbalanced priorities and trivial lifestyles. What I realized is that pinning this problem on groups like Rock the Vote doesn't make much sense. Rock the Vote is using long-established social systems and hierarchies to reach potential voters who would otherwise be unreachable. While the power celebrities wield may be a regrettable feature of our culture, I can't blame Rock the Vote for exploiting this fact. I have long been politically informed, and every day I see reasons for political action that are far stronger than endorsements from Top-40 musicians. This is why I initially reacted so vehemently to Rock the Vote. Given that, I know that plenty of young, nonvoters do need motivation and that many of them won't find it until they flip the channel to find a favorite celebrity offering compelling reasons to take the government's behavior seriously.

Standley 5

Works Cited

"Vote!" Video. 10 April 2008. RocktheVote. <http://
www.youtube.com/watch?v=MFbOhdlmZCU>.

MOVIE POSTERS

These posters (here and on the next page) from two film versions of the Zorro legend, *The Mark of Zorro* (1940) and *The Legend of Zorro* (2005), are not, in themselves, evaluations. But their stark differences in theme, design, and style seem to embody significant changes in cultural values over sixty-five years and are, therefore, well worth comparing and evaluating.

The Mark of Zorro (1940)

The Legend of Zorro (2005)

Assignments

1. **Cultural Evaluation:** Drawing on your expertise as a consumer of popular culture (the way Rob Sheffield does in his *Rolling Stone* review of *American Idiot*—see p. 119), explain why you admire a book, movie, television series, musical piece, artist, or performer that most people do not. For instance, you might argue that *Gilligan's Island* is as sophisticated a situation comedy as *Seinfeld*. Or, taking the opposite tack, explain why you don't share the public's enthusiasm for some widely admired artist or entertainment. Write a review strong enough to change someone's mind.

2. **Cultural Evaluation:** Assess a public figure or social movement you believe deserves serious and detailed appreciation. In other words, don't write a paper simply describing the person or group as good or bad, talented or pathetic, successful or unsuccessful. Instead, offer readers a careful evaluation of what they do and accomplish, perhaps using Scott Standley's "Rock the Vote: Useful Harm?" (see p. 121) as a model.

3. **Evaluation of Visual Texts:** Compare and evaluate two or more visual texts that you believe embody different values the way the Zorro movie posters on pages 125–26 do. You might, for example, compare political campaign videos (readily available on YouTube), book covers, product packages, or even fashions.

4. **Cultural Evaluation:** Evaluate a program or facility on your campus that you believe works especially well or is atrociously run. Imagine your audience is an administrator with the power to reward or shut down the operation.

5. **Product Review:** Choose a product that you own or use regularly, anything from a Coleman lantern to Dunkin' Donuts coffee. Limit the evaluation to one well-designed page (preferably with graphics), perhaps creating a structure that might be used to review other similar items.

How to start ➤

- Need a **topic**? See page 134.
- Need to identify **possible causes**? See page 138.
- Need to **organize your analysis**? See page 141.

5 Causal Analysis

examines *why* or *what if* something happens

We all do causal analyses daily. Someone asks, "Why?" We reply, "Because . . ." and then offer reasons and explanations. Such a response comes naturally.

- An instructor asks for a ten-page paper examining the root causes of a major armed conflict during the twentieth century. You choose to write about the Korean War because you know almost nothing about it.

- An uncle has been diagnosed with macular degeneration. You go online to learn the causes of this eye disease and its likely consequences.

- The provost of your university has proposed to tie fee increases to the rate of inflation. You prepare a response that shows this move would damage student services and discourage the development of new programs.

- You notice that most students now walk across campus chatting on cell phones or listening to music. You wonder if this phenomenon has any relationship to a recent drop in the numbers of students joining campus clubs and activities.

UNDERSTANDING CAUSAL ANALYSIS.   From global warming to childhood obesity to high school students performing poorly on standardized tests, the daily news is full of issues framed by *why* and *what if* questions. Take childhood obesity. The public wants to know why we have a generation of overweight kids. Too many burgers? Not enough dodge ball? People worry, too, about the consequences of the trend. Will these portly children grow into obese adults? Will they develop medical problems? We're interested in such questions because they really do matter, and we're often eager to find solutions. But solid analyses of cause and effect require persistence, precision, and research. ○ Even then, you'll often have to deal with a world that seems complicated or contradictory. Not every problem or issue can—or should—be explained simply.

Don't jump to conclusions.   It's just plain hard to say precisely which factors, past or present, are responsible for a particular event, activity, or

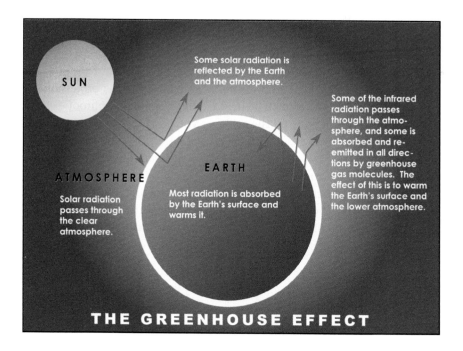

The Greenhouse Effect
Many scientists agree that the greenhouse effect, an increase in the concentration of certain atmospheric gases, is leading to climate change that will have dangerous consequences for us and our environment.

analyze claims and
evidence p. 415

behavior. And it is even tougher to project how events or actions happening now might alter the future. So you shouldn't make a causal claim lightly, and you should qualify it carefully or perhaps offer your thesis tentatively. ○

Dealing with causes and effects will quickly teach you humility—even if you *don't* jump to hasty conclusions. In fact, many causal analyses begin by undercutting or correcting someone else's prior claims, dutifully researched and sensibly presented.

Appreciate the limits of causal analysis.   There are no easy answers when investigating causes and effects. The space shuttle *Columbia* burned up on reentry because a 1.67-pound piece of foam hit the wing of the 240,000-pound craft on liftoff. Who could have imagined such an unlikely sequence of events? Yet investigators had to follow the evidence relentlessly to its conclusion.

But if the aim of causal analyses is to find correct explanations, the fact remains that you'll usually have to offer answers that are merely plausible or probable. That's because causal analyses—especially outside the hard sciences—typically deal with imprecise or unpredictable forces and phenomena and sometimes require a leap of imagination.

Offer sufficient evidence for claims.   Your academic and professional analyses of cause and effect will be held to a high standard of proof— particularly in the sciences. ○ The evidence you provide may be a little looser in the popular media, where readers will entertain some anecdotal and casual examples. But even there, back up your claims with a preponderance of plausible evidence, not hearsay.

For instance, you may have an interesting theory that a successful third political party will develop in the United States to end the deadlock between Democrats and Republicans. But without supporting facts and analysis, all you have is speculation — not causal analysis.

develop a thesis
p. 336

understand lab reports
p. 290

Tobias Salinger's "Unplugging Ads, Not Conversations" offers one explanation for the popularity of iPods among students and young people. Like many examinations of popular culture, this causal analysis is both speculative and argumentative and very much attuned to its audience. The piece originally appeared in the *Daily Texan*, a student newspaper at the University of Texas at Austin. As you'll see, Salinger doesn't pretend to examine the iPod phenomenon exhaustively. Instead, he wants to correct the mistaken analyses of various social commentators he mocks as "geezers."

Unplugging Ads, Not Conversations

Tobias Salinger

June 28, 2006

Young people are always picking up habits that infuriate old geezers. If they're not wearing their pants so low that their damn underwear is showing, they have baseball caps on backward. If they're not growing their hair down to their waists, they're constantly fornicating. Whippersnappers are a constant source of aggravation for sensible adults.

> Comic opening raises a serious causal issue: Why don't older people understand youth?

These days, the elders have found another youth fad that gets on their nerves: iPods. Just look at college campuses, they say. Those spoiled brats strut around with their iPods in their ears like they own the whole world or something.

The geezer world is raging at this newfangled music player. George F. Will, the spokesman for perturbed yet prudent old fogeys, considers devices like the iPod a threat to our moral fabric. In a November 20 column, Will found no coincidence in the seemingly unrelated facts that two teens were caught having sex in a school auditorium and that *Desperate Housewives* can now be watched on a video iPod.

> Focuses on claim made by George Will.

"The connection is this: Many people have no notion of propriety when in the presence of other people, because they are not actually in the presence of other people, even when they are in public," Will wrote.

Christine Rosen is a fellow at the Ethics and Public Policy Center, a think tank that analyzes current events using Judeo-Christian morals. In a piece on the iPod in the May 15 edition of *The NewsHour with Jim Lehrer*, she said people use devices like the iPod to shut out ideas that they don't want to hear.

"We don't have to hear or see things we haven't already programmed into our iPods or into our TiVos," Rosen said. "And so, in that sense, I think it can have a narrowing effect on what we encounter on a day-to-day basis."

Summarizes causal claim he will dispute.

In other words, we use iPods because we no longer value human interaction or manners. The music in our ears purportedly takes us into our own world, a place where nobody else matters.

I can understand these reservations. They should know, however, that iPod users are more than happy to take out their earphones when they see someone they know. We would just rather listen to our favorite music than car engines, construction vehicles, and other noise pollution.

Refutes that claim with commonsense observation.

Some people see a young man enjoying his music, a ball game or a favorite show. Others see an isolationist who doesn't want to engage with society or his surroundings. Is the truth somewhere in between?

Offers more
serious claim.

Furthermore, if critics like Rosen and Will weren't so busy being annoyed with whippersnappers, they would see that gadgets like iPods and DVRs are revolutions in consumer choice. MP3 players are liberating us from the curse that is commercial radio music.

Instead of choosing between Top 40 "mix" stations that play every song you've heard way too much, "classic rock" stations that have continuous loops of Aerosmith, the Steve Miller Band, and the Eagles, and "oldies" stations that make you feel like you're wearing Depends, we get to actually choose our music, free of commercials.

Offers evidence
for his claim.

The TiVo turns the same great trick on the corporate broadcast channels. The only thing we tech-savvy kids are tuning out is crappy programming and advertisements.

MP3 players are also on the cutting edge of the fastest-growing grassroots democracy anywhere: Internet piracy.

You can now easily get almost any piece of music off the Web, download it to your computer, and listen to it on your iPod. When you do this, you have effectively sidestepped the dominant means of communication and all the paradigms that go with it. No matter how hard authorities like the federal government and record companies try, it's getting easier to obtain free music and movies off the Internet. That fact should render any attempt by telecommunications companies to stop Net neutrality as unenforceable as a ban on illegal immigrants.

Anticipates
objection and
states thesis,
suggesting
outcome of
his causal
analysis.

None of this means that the popularity of the iPod is some sort of victory against the evil empire. Products like MP3 players are just more consumer goods for our materialistic society to obsess over. But that doesn't mean that they're not helpful in changing the world we're going to inherit from the old geezers.

Exploring purpose and topic

▶ topic

To find a topic for a causal analysis, begin a sentence with *why* or *what if* and then finish it, drawing on what you may already know about a trend or problem. ○

> Why are American high schools producing fewer students interested in science?
>
> Why is the occurrence of juvenile asthma spiking?
>
> Why do so few men study nursing or so few women study petroleum engineering?

There are, of course, many other ways to phrase questions about cause and effect in order to attach important conditions and qualifications.

> What if scientists figure out how to stop the human aging process—as now seems plausible within twenty years? What are the consequences for society?
>
> How likely is it that a successful third political party might develop in the United States to end the deadlock between Republicans and Democrats?

As you can see, none of these topics would just drop from a tree—like the apocryphal apple that supposedly inspired Isaac Newton to ponder gravity. They require knowledge and thinking. So look for potential cause-and-effect issues in your academic courses or professional life. Or search for them in the culture and media—though you should probably shy away from worn-out

This graph from *The Onion* (September 12, 2005) parodies causal analysis.

Reprinted with permission of THE ONION. Copyright © 2008, by ONION, INC. www.theonion.com.

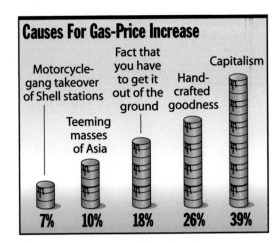

Causes For Gas-Price Increase

| Motorcycle-gang takeover of Shell stations | Teeming masses of Asia | Fact that you have to get it out of the ground | Hand-crafted goodness | Capitalism |

7% 10% 18% 26% 39%

find a topic
p. 308

subjects—global warming, obesity, plagiarism—unless you can offer a fresh insight (as Salinger does with iPods, see p. 131).

Following are some approaches to finding a subject.

Look again at a subject you know well.   It may be one that has affected you personally or might in the future. Or a topic you think is ripe for rethinking because of insights you can offer. For instance, you may have experienced firsthand the effects of high-stakes testing in high school or have theories about why people your age still smoke. Offer a hypothesis.

Look for an issue new to you.   Given a choice of topics for an academic paper, choose a subject you've always wanted to know more about (for example, the Korean War). You probably won't be able to offer a thesis or hypothesis until after you've done some research, but that's the appeal of this strategy. The material is fresh and you are energized. ◯

Examine a local issue.   Is there an issue you can explore or test with personal research or observation? ◯ Look for recent changes and examine why these changes happened or what the consequences may be. With a community issue, talk to the people responsible or affected. Tuition raised? Admissions standards lowered? Speech code modified? Why, or what if?

Choose a subject with many dimensions.   An issue that is complicated and challenging will simply push you harder and sharpen your thinking. Don't rush to judgment; remain open-minded about contrary evidence, conflicting motives, and different points of view.

Tackle an issue that seems settled.   If you really have guts, look for a phenomenon that most people assume has been adequately explained. Tired of the way Republicans, feminists, Wall Street economists, vegans, funda-mentalists, or the women on *The View* smugly explain the way things are? Pick one sore point and offer a different—and better—causal analysis.

find a topic
p. 308

interview and observe
p. 412

Understanding your audience

Audiences for cause-and-effect analysis are diverse, but it may help to distinguish between a readership you create by drawing attention to a subject and readers who come to your work because it deals with a topic they already care about.

Create an audience.   In some situations, you must set the stage for your causal analysis by telling readers why they should be concerned by the phenomenon you intend to explore. ○ Assume they are smart enough to become engaged by a topic once they appreciate its significance—and how it might affect them. But you first have to make that case. That's exactly what the editors of the *Wall Street Journal* do in an editorial noting the sustained decrease in traffic deaths that followed a congressional decision ten years earlier to do away with a national 55-mph speed limit. (The complete editorial appears on pp. 146–48.)

Anticipate readers who might ask, Why does this issue matter?

This may seem noncontroversial now, but at the time the debate was shrill and filled with predictions of doom. Ralph Nader claimed that "history will never forgive Congress for this assault on the sanctity of human life." Judith Stone, president of the Advocates for Highway and Auto Safety, predicted to Katie Couric on NBC's *Today Show* that there would be "6,400 added highway fatalities a year and millions of more injuries." Federico Peña, the Clinton administration's secretary of transportation, declared: "Allowing speed limits to rise above 55 simply means that more Americans will die and be injured on our highways."

– "Safe at Any Speed," July 7, 2006

Write to an existing audience.   In many cases, you'll enter a cause-and-effect debate on topics already on the public agenda. You may intend to reaffirm what people now believe or, more controversially, ask them to rethink their positions. But in either case, you'll likely be dealing with readers as knowledgeable (and opinionated) on the subject as you are. Still, they'll lend you an ear, at least briefly, because the subject already matters to them. They may routinely pay attention to topics such as traffic safety, sustainability, the tax code, and so on. In the following opening paragraphs from a lengthy article about urban sprawl, notice how author Robert Bruegmann addresses an audience that he assumes is quite well-informed.

develop a thesis
p. 336

There is overwhelming evidence that urban sprawl has been beneficial for many people. Year after year, the vast majority of Americans respond to batteries of polls by saying that they are quite happy with where they live, whether it is a city, suburb, or elsewhere. Most objective indicators about American urban life are positive. We are more affluent than ever; home ownership is up; life spans are up; pollution is down; crime in most cities has declined. Even where sprawl has created negative consequences, it has not precipitated any crisis.

> Assumes readers understand what *urban sprawl* means.

So what explains the power of today's antisprawl crusade? How is it possible that a prominent lawyer could open a recent book with the unqualified assertion that "sprawl is America's most lethal disease"? Worse than drug use, crime, unemployment, and poverty? Why has a campaign against sprawl expanded into a major political force across America and much of the economically advanced world?

> Presumes readers know that sprawl has critics.

> Poses a question readers might entertain.

I would argue that worries about sprawl have become so vivid not because conditions are really as bad as the critics suggest but precisely because conditions are so good. During boom years, expectations can easily run far ahead of any possibility of fulfilling them. A fast-rising economy often produces a revolution of expectations. I believe these soaring expectations are responsible for many contemporary panics.

> Offers causal claim likely to engage readers.

—"How Sprawl Got a Bad Name," *American Enterprise*, June 2006

This aerial view of a housing development depicts what some people call "urban sprawl."

Finding and developing materials

Expect to do as much research for a causal analysis as for any fact-based report or argument. Even when you speculate about popular culture, as Tobias Salinger did earlier, you need to show that you have considered what others have written on the subject. ○

Be careful not to ascribe the wrong cause to an event just because two actions might have occurred close in time or have some other fragile connection. Does the economy really improve after tax cuts? Do children in fact do better in school if they have participated in Head Start programs? Exposing faulty causality in situations like these can make for powerful arguments. ○ You can avoid faulty analyses by appreciating the various kinds of genuine causal relationships outlined below.

▶ consider causes

Understand necessary causes.   A *necessary cause* is any factor that must be in place for something to occur. For example, sunlight, chlorophyll, and water are all necessary for photosynthesis to happen. Remove one of those elements from the equation and the natural process simply doesn't take place. But since none of them could cause photosynthesis on its own, they are necessary causes, but not sufficient (see *sufficient cause* below).

On a less scientific level, necessary causes are those that seem so important that we can't imagine something happening without them. You might argue, for example, that a team could not win a World Series without a specific pitcher on the roster: Remove him and the team doesn't get to the play-offs. Or you might claim that, while fanaticism doesn't itself cause terrorism, terrorism doesn't exist without fanaticism. In any such analysis, it helps to separate necessary causes from those that may be merely *contributing* (see *contributing factors* on p. 140).

Understand sufficient causes.   A *sufficient cause,* in itself, is enough to bring on a particular effect. Not being eighteen would be a sufficient cause for being arrested for drinking alcohol in the United States. But there are many other potential sufficient causes for getting arrested. In a causal argument, you might need to establish which of several possible sufficient causes is the one actually responsible for a specific event or phenomenon— assuming that a single explanation exists. A plane might have crashed

refine your search
p. 406

read critically
p. 317

because it was overloaded, ran out of fuel, had a structural failure, encountered severe wind shear, and so on.

Understand precipitating causes.   Think of a *precipitating cause* as the proverbial straw that finally breaks the camel's back. In itself, the factor may seem trivial. But it becomes the spark that sets a field gone dry for months ablaze. By refusing to give up her bus seat to a white passenger in Montgomery, Alabama, Rosa Parks triggered a civil rights movement in 1955, but she didn't actually cause it: The necessary conditions had been accumulating for generations.

Understand proximate causes.   A *proximate cause* is nearby and often easy to spot. A corporation declares bankruptcy when it can no longer meet its massive debt obligations; a minivan crashes because a front tire explodes; a student fails a course because she plagiarizes a paper. But in an analysis, getting the facts right about such proximate causes may just be your starting point as you work toward a deeper understanding of a situation. As you might guess, proximate causes may sometimes also be sufficient causes.

Understand remote causes.   A *remote cause*, as the term suggests, may act at some distance from an event but is intimately related to it. That bankrupt corporation may have defaulted on its loans because of a decade of bad management decisions; the tire exploded because it was underinflated and its tread worn; the student resorted to plagiarism *because* she ran out of time *because* she was working two jobs to pay for a Hawaiian vacation *because* she wanted a memorable spring break to impress her friends—a string of remote causes. Remote causes—which are usually contributing factors as well (see p. 140)—are what make many causal analyses challenging and interesting: Figuring them out is like detective work.

Understand reciprocal causes.   You have a *reciprocal* situation when a cause leads to an effect which, in turn, strengthens the cause. Consider how creating science internships for college women might encourage more women to become scientists who then sponsor more internships, creating

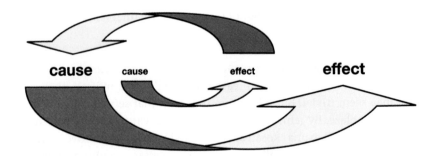

cause   cause   effect   **effect**

yet more female scientists. Many analyses of global warming describe reciprocal relationships, with CO_2 emissions supposedly leading to warming, which increases plant growth or alters ocean currents, which in turn releases more CO_2 or heat and so on.

Understand contributing factors.   When analyzing social or cultural issues, you'll often spend time assessing factors too general or ambiguous to be called necessary, sufficient, or even remote causes but which, nonetheless, might play a role in explaining an event. To account for an outbreak of high school violence in the late 1990s, social critics quickly identified a host of potential factors: divorce, guns, video games, goth culture, bullying, cliques, movies, psychosis, and so on. Though none of these explanations was entirely convincing, they couldn't simply be dismissed either. Many factors that might contribute to violence were (and remain) in play within the culture of American high schools.

Need help assessing your own work? See "How to Use the Writing Center," on pp. 328–29.

Come to conclusions thoughtfully.   Causal analyses do often require some imagination: You are playing detective with the complexities of life and so you may need to think outside the box. But you also have to give your notions the same tough scrutiny that you would give any smart idea. Just because a causal explanation is clever or novel doesn't mean it's right.

Don't oversimplify situations or manipulate facts.   By acknowledging any weaknesses in your own analyses, you may actually enhance your credibility or lead a reader toward a better conclusion than what you've come up with. Sometimes, you may have to be content with solving only part of a problem.

Creating a structure

Take introductions seriously. They are unusually important and often quite lengthy in causal analyses; you'll often need more than one paragraph to provide enough detail for readers to appreciate the significance of your subject. The following brief paragraph might seem like the opener of a causal essay on the failures of dog training. ○

> For thousands of years, humans have been training dogs to be hunters, herders, searchers, guards, and companions. Why are we doing so badly? The problem may lie more with our methods than with us.
>
> – Jon Katz, "Train in Vain," Slate.com, January 14, 2005

In fact, *seven* paragraphs precede this one to set up the causal claim. Those paragraphs help readers (especially dog owners) recognize a problem many will find familiar. The actual first paragraph has Katz narrating a dog-owner's dilemma.

> Sam was distressed. His West Highland terrier, aptly named Lightning, was constantly darting out of doors and dashing into busy suburban Connecticut streets. Sam owned three acres behind his house, and he was afraid to let the dog roam any of it.

By paragraph seven, Katz has offered enough similar details and situations to provoke a crisis in dogdom, a problem that leaves readers hoping for an explanation.

organize ◀ ideas

> The results of this failure are everywhere: Neurotic and compulsive dog behaviors like barking, biting, chasing cars, and chewing furniture — sometimes severe enough to warrant antidepressants — are growing. Lesser training problems — an inability to sit, stop begging, come, or stay — are epidemic.

Following your introduction, you have several options for developing analyses of cause and effect.

Explain why something happened.   If you are simply offering plausible causes to explain a phenomenon, your structure will be quite simple. You'll move from an introduction that explains that phenomenon to a thesis or

shape a beginning
p. 354

hypothesis. Then you will work through your list of factors toward a conclusion. In a persuasive paper, you'd build toward the most convincing explanation supported by the best evidence.

Introduction leading to a **causal claim**

First cause explored + **reasons/evidence**

Next cause explored + **reasons/evidence** . . .

Best cause explored + **reasons/evidence**

Conclusion

Explain the consequences of a phenomenon.   A structure similar to that immediately above lends itself to exploring the effects that follow from some action, event, policy, or change in the status quo. Once again, begin with an introduction that fully describes a situation you believe will have consequences; then work through those consequences, connecting them as you need to. The conclusion could then draw out the implications of your paper.

Introduction focusing on a **change** or **cause**

First effect proposed + **reasons**

Other effect(s) proposed + **reasons** . . .

Assessment and conclusion

Suggest an alternative view of cause and effect.   A natural strategy is to open a causal analysis by refuting someone else's faulty claim and then offering your own. After all, we often think about causality when someone makes a claim we disagree with. It's a structure used in this chapter by both Tobias Salinger (p. 131) and Liza Mundy (p. 149).

Introduction questioning a **causal claim**

Reasons to doubt claim offered + **evidence**

Alternative cause(s) explored . . .

Best cause examined + **reasons/evidence**

Conclusion

Explain a chain of causes.   Quite often, causes occur simultaneously and so in presenting them you have to make judgments about their relative importance. But maybe just as often, you'll be describing causes that operate in sequence: A causes B, B leads to C, C trips D, and so on. In such a case, you might use a sequential pattern of organization, giving special attention to the links (or transitions) in the chain. ○

Introduction suggesting a **chain** of **causes/consequences**

First link presented + **reasons/evidence**

Next link(s) presented + **reasons/evidence** . . .

Final link presented + **reasons/evidence**

Conclusion

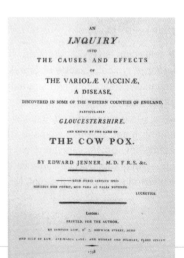

People have been writing causal analysis for centuries. Here is the title page of Edward Jenner's 1798 publication, *An Inquiry into the Causes and Effects of the Variolae Vaccinae.* Jenner's research led to an inoculation that protected human beings from smallpox.

shape your
work p. 340

Choosing a style and design

When you analyze cause and effect, you'll often be offering an argument or exploring an idea for an audience you need to interest. You can do that through both style and design.

Consider a middle style.   Even causal analyses written for fairly academic audiences incline toward the middle style because of its flexibility: It can be both familiar and serious. ○ Here Robert Bruegmann, discussing the causes of urban sprawl, uses language that is simple, clear, and colloquial—and almost entirely free of technical jargon.

> When asked, most Americans declare themselves to be against sprawl, just as they say they are against pollution or the destruction of historic buildings. But the very development that one individual targets as sprawl is often another family's much-loved community. Very few people believe that they themselves live in sprawl or contribute to sprawl. Sprawl is where other people live, particularly people with less good taste. Much antisprawl activism is based on a desire to reform these other people's lives.

Adapt the style to the subject matter.   Friendly as it is, a middle style can still make demands of readers, as the following passage from an essay by Malcolm Gladwell demonstrates. To explain author Steve Johnson's theory that pop culture is making people smarter, Gladwell uses extremely intricate sentences filled with pop-culture allusions and cultural details. Yet he maintains a sense of voice too: Notice how he uses italics to signal how a word should be read. This is middle style at its complex best, making claims and proving them in a way that keeps readers interested.

> As Johnson points out, television is very different now from what it was thirty years ago. It's *harder*. A typical episode of *Starsky and Hutch*, in the 1970s, followed an essentially linear path: two characters, engaged in a single story line, moving toward a decisive conclusion. To watch an episode of *Dallas* today is to be stunned by its glacial pace—by the arduous attempts to establish social relationships, by the excruciating simplicity of the plotline, by how *obvious* it was. A single episode of *The Sopranos*, by contrast, might follow five narrative threads, involving a dozen characters who weave in and out of the plot. Modern television also

define your style
p. 366

requires the viewer to do a lot of what Johnson calls "filling in," as in a *Seinfeld* episode that subtly parodies the Kennedy assassination conspiracists, or a typical *Simpsons* episode, which may contain numerous allusions to politics or cinema or pop culture. The extraordinary amount of money now being made in the television aftermarket – DVD sales and syndication – means that the creators of television shows now have an incentive to make programming that can sustain two or three or four viewings.

– "Brain Candy," *The New Yorker*, May 16, 2005

Use appropriate supporting media.   Causal analyses have no special design features. But, like reports and arguments, they can employ charts that summarize information and graphics that illustrate ideas. *USA Today*, for instance, uses its daily "snapshots" to present causal data culled from surveys. Because causal analyses usually have distinct sections or parts (see "Creating a structure," p. 141), they do fit nicely into PowerPoint presentations. **O**

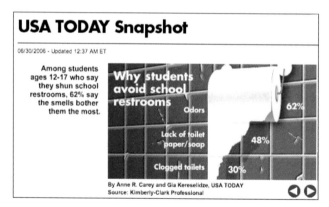

By Anne R. Carey and Gia Kereselidze, USA TODAY
Source: Kimberly-Clark Professional

A graphic like this one reflects a statistical approach to causality, polling people to find out why they do what they do.

work with visuals
p. 504

Examining models

EDITORIAL The editors of the *Wall Street Journal* are pleased that federal legislation no longer dictates how fast people in the states may drive. To make their point, the editors remind readers how much the predicted consequences of abolishing the national 55-mph speed limit in 1995 differed from the actual effects.

Safe at Any Speed

WITH HIGHER SPEED LIMITS, OUR HIGHWAYS HAVE BEEN GETTING SAFER

Editors of the *Wall Street Journal*

Friday, July 7, 2006 12:01 A.M.

It's another summer weekend, when millions of families pack up the minivan or SUV and hit the road. So this is also an apt moment to trumpet some good, and underreported, news: Driving on the highways is safer today than ever before.

In 2005, according to new data from the National Highway Safety Administration, the rate of injuries per mile traveled was lower than at any time since the Interstate Highway System was built fifty years ago. The fatality rate was the second lowest ever, just a tick higher than in 2004.

As a public-policy matter, this steady decline is a vindication of the repeal of the 55-miles-per-hour federal speed-limit law in 1995. That 1974 federal speed limit was arguably the most disobeyed and despised law since Prohibition. "Double nickel," as it was often called, was first adopted to save gasoline during the Arab oil embargo, though later the justification became saving lives. But to Westerners with open spaces and low traffic density, the law became a symbol of the heavy hand of the federal nanny state. To top it off, Congress would deny states their own federal highway construction dollars if they failed to comply.

In repealing the law, the newly minted Republican majority in Congress declared that states were free to impose their own limits.

> Key claim is that abolishing national speed limit made sense.

> Background information explains the 55-mph speed limit.

Many states immediately took up this nod to federalism by raising their limits to 70 or 75 mph. Texas just raised its speed limit again on rural highways to 80.

> **Analysis of effects begins here.**

This may seem noncontroversial now, but at the time the debate was shrill and filled with predictions of doom. Ralph Nader claimed that "history will never forgive Congress for this assault on the sanctity of human life." Judith Stone, president of the Advocates for Highway and Auto Safety, predicted to Katie Couric on NBC's *Today Show* that there would be "6,400 added highway fatalities a year and millions of more injuries." Federico Peña, the Clinton administration's secretary of transportation, declared: "Allowing speed limits to rise above 55 simply means that more Americans will die and be injured on our highways."

Higher Speed Limits, More Safety

	1995	2005	% Decline
Highway fatality rate*	1.73	1.46	16%
Injuries*	143	90	37
Crashes*	560	375	33
Pedestrian deaths	5,584	4,674	16

*Per 100 million vehicle miles traveled

Source: National Highway Traffic Safety Administration, 2006.

We now have ten years of evidence proving that the only "assault" was on the sanctity of the truth. The nearby table shows that the death, injury, and crash rates have fallen sharply since 1995. Per mile traveled, there were about 5,000 fewer deaths and almost one million fewer injuries in 2005 than in the mid-1990s. This is all the more remarkable given that a dozen years ago Americans lacked today's distraction of driving while also talking on their cell phones.

> **Dire predictions are undermined by statistics.**

More facts
offered to
prove dire
predictions
were wrong.

Of the thirty-one states that have raised their speed limits to more than 70 mph, twenty-nine saw a decline in the death and injury rate and only two—the Dakotas—have seen fatalities increase. Two studies, by the National Motorists Association and by the Cato Institute, have compared crash data in states that raised their speed limits with those that didn't and found no increase in deaths in the higher speed states.

Article
presents
positive
effects of
higher speed
limits.

Jim Baxter, president of the National Motorists Association, says that by the early 1990s "compliance with the 55-mph law was only about 5 percent—in other words, about 95 percent of drivers were exceeding the speed limit." Now motorists can coast at these faster speeds without being on the constant lookout for radar guns, speed traps, and state troopers. Americans have also arrived at their destinations sooner, worth an estimated $30 billion a year in time saved, according to the Cato study.

Editors make
an important
qualification.

The tragedy is that 43,000 Americans still die on the roads every year, or about 15 times the number of U.S. combat deaths in Iraq. Car accidents remain a leading cause of death among teenagers in particular. The Interstate Highway System is nonetheless one of the greatest public works programs in American history, and the two-thirds decline in road deaths per mile traveled since the mid-1950s has been a spectacular achievement. Tough drunk-driving laws, better road technology, and such improving auto safety features as power steering and brakes are all proven life savers.

We are often told, by nanny-state advocates, that such public goods as safety require a loss of liberty. In the case of speed limits and traffic deaths, that just isn't so.

Editors
conclude
by offering
a political
implication.

EXPLORATORY ESSAY   Liza Mundy, a writer for the *Washington Post,* offers a classic kind of causal analysis—one in which readers are asked to consider a subject from an entirely different point of view. That shift in perspective illuminates her subject and raises unexpected and scary consequences.

Slate.com

Posted: Wednesday, May 3, 2006, at 10:20 AM ET
From: Liza Mundy

What's Really behind the Plunge in Teen Pregnancy?

Identifies a trend that needs a causal explanation.

May 3 — in case you didn't know it — was "National Day to Prevent Teen Pregnancy." In the past decade, possibly no social program has been as dramatically effective as the effort to reduce teen pregnancy, and no results so uniformly celebrated. Between 1990 and 2000, the U.S. teen pregnancy rate plummeted by 28 percent, dropping from 117 to 84 pregnancies per 1,000 women aged 15–19. Births to teenagers are also down, as are teen abortion rates. It's an achievement so profound and so heartening that left and right are eager to take credit for it, and both can probably do so. Child-health advocates generally acknowledge that liberal sex education and conservative abstinence initiatives are both to thank for the fact that fewer teenagers are ending up in school bathroom stalls sobbing over the results of a home pregnancy test.

Poses question about causality.

What, though, if the drop in teen pregnancy isn't a good thing, or not entirely? What if there's a third explanation, one that has nothing to do with just-say-no campaigns or safe-sex educational posters? What if teenagers are less fertile than they used to be?

Offers a startling hypothesis.

Not the girls — the boys?

Reminds readers how contentious studies of causality can be.

It's a conversation that's taking place among a different and somewhat less vocal interest group: scientists who study human and animal reproduction. Like many scientific inquiries, this one is hotly contested and not likely to be resolved anytime soon. Still, the fact that it's going on provides a useful reminder that not every social trend is the sole result of partisan policy initiatives and think-tank-generated outreach efforts. It reminds us that a drop in something as profound as fertility, in human creatures of any age, might also have something to do with health, perhaps even the future of the species.

The great sperm-count debate began in 1992, when a group of Danish scientists published a study suggesting that sperm counts declined globally by about 1 percent a year between 1938 and 1990. This study postulated that "environmental influences," particularly widely used chemical compounds with an impact like that of the female hormone estrogen, might be contributing to a drop in fertility among males. If true, this was obviously an alarming development, particularly given that human sperm counts are already strikingly low compared to almost any other species. "Humans have the worst sperm except for gorillas and ganders of any animal on the planet," points out Sherman Silber, a high-profile urologist who attributes this in part to short-term female monogamy. Since one man's sperm rarely has to race that of another man to the finish, things like speed and volume are less important in human sperm than in other animals, permitting a certain amount of atrophy among humans.

The Danish study set an argument in motion. Other studies were published showing that sperm counts were staying the same; still others showed them going up. In the late 1990s, however, an American reproductive epidemiologist named Shanna Swan published work confirming the Danish findings. In a well-respected study published in *Environmental Health Perspectives,* Swan, now at the University of Rochester Medical Center, found that sperm counts are dropping by about 1.5 percent a year in the United States and 3 percent in Europe and Australia, though they do not appear to be falling in the less-developed world. This may not

New causal factor is presented and explored.

Detailed paragraphs present evidence that sperm counts are dropping.

sound like a lot, but cumulatively — like compound interest — a drop of 1 percent has a big effect. Swan showed, further, that in the United States there appears to be a regional variation in sperm counts: They tend to be lower in rural sectors and higher in cities, suggesting the possible impact of chemicals (such as pesticides) particular to one locality.

Swan is part of a group of scientists whose work suggests that environmental changes are indeed having a reproductive impact. Under the auspices of a women's health group at Stanford University and an alliance called the Collaborative on Health and the Environment, some of these scientists met in February 2005 at a retreat in Menlo Park, California, to discuss their findings. Among the evidence presented are several trends that seem to point to a subtle feminization of male babies: a worldwide rise in hypospadias, a birth defect in which the urethral opening is located on the shaft of the penis rather than at the tip; a rise in cryptorchidism, or undescended testicles; and experiments Swan has done showing that in male babies with high exposure to compounds called phthalates, something called the anogenital distance is decreasing. If you measure the distance from a baby's anus to the genitals, the distance in these males is shorter, more like that of . . . girls.

Wildlife biologists also talked about the fact that alligators living in one contaminated Florida lake were found to have small phalli and low testosterone levels, while females in the same lake had problems associated with abnormally high levels of estrogen. In 1980, the alligators' mothers had been exposed to a major pesticide dump, which, some believe, was working like an estrogen on their young, disrupting their natural hormones. A report later published by this group pointed out that similar disruptions have been found in a "wide range of species from seagulls to polar bears, seals to salmon, mollusks to frogs." As evidence that a parent's

Analysis assumes a knowledgeable, not expert, audience.

exposure to toxicants can powerfully affect the development of offspring, the example of DES, or diethylstilbestrol, was also, of course, offered. Widely given to pregnant women beginning in the late 1930s under the mistaken assumption that it would prevent miscarriage, DES left the women unaffected but profoundly affected their female fetuses, some of whom would die of cancer, others of whom would find their reproductive capacity compromised. The consensus was that the so-called chemical revolution may well be disrupting the development of reproductive organs in young males, among others. This research is controversial, certainly, but accepted enough, as a hypothesis, that it appears in developmental-biology textbooks.

Tellingly, the U.S. government is also taking this conversation seriously. Together, the National Institutes of Health and the U.S. Centers for Disease Control are sponsoring a longitudinal effort to study the effect of environment on fertility. This study will track couples living in Texas and Michigan, following their efforts to become pregnant. The aim is to determine whether toxicants are affecting the reproductive potential of female and male alike.

It will be welcome information. In the United States, good statistics about infertility are strikingly hard to come by. There is no government-sponsored effort to track male fertility rates, even though male-factor problems account for half of all infertility. Even among women, who are regularly interrogated about reproductive details, it's difficult to get a good handle on developments. For years, government researchers included only married women in the category of "infertility," creating a real problem for demographers and epidemiologists looking for trends. The National Center for Health Statistics created a second category called "impaired fecundity," which includes any woman, of any marital category, who is trying to get pregnant and not having luck.

Explains what other causal studies are needed.

Puts qualifications and limits on available statistics.

And the "impaired fecundity" category contains findings that may have a bearing on the are-young-men-more-infertile-than-their-fathers question. In the United States, "impaired fecundity" among women has seen, over several decades, a steady rise. And while much attention has focused on older women, the most striking rise between 1982 and 1995 took place among women under twenty-five. In that period, impaired fecundity in women under twenty-five rose by 42 percent, from 4.3 percent of women to 6.1 percent. Recently published data from 2002 show a continued rise in impaired fecundity among the youngest age cohort.

In a 1999 letter to *Family Planning Perspectives,* Swan sensibly proposed "that the role of the male be considered in this equation." If sperm counts drop each year, then the youngest men will be most acutely affected, and these will be the men who are having trouble impregnating their partners. In 2002, Danish researchers published an opinion piece in *Human Reproduction* noting that teen pregnancy rates (already much lower than in the United States) fell steadily in Denmark between 1985 and 1999. Unlike in the United States, in Denmark there have been no changes in outreach efforts to encourage responsible behavior in teens: no abstinence campaigns, no big new push for condom distribution. Wider social trends notwithstanding, they note that "it seems reasonable also to consider widespread poor semen quality among men as a potential contributing factor to low fertility rates among teenagers."

Among other things, the sperm-count debate reminds us that we should not be smug about the success of teen-pregnancy prevention efforts. We may not want today's teenagers to become pregnant now, but we certainly want them to become pregnant in the future, providing they want to be. If nothing else, the sperm-count hypothesis shows that when it comes to teenagers and sexual behavior, there's always something new to worry about.

Last paragraph warns against jumping to conclusions too quickly.

CULTURAL ANALYSIS   Charles Paul Freund's "The Politics of Pants," a summary of James Sullivan's book *Jeans: A Cultural History of an American Icon,* argues that consumers, not manufacturers or marketers, determine the cultural significance of products — such as jeans. In fact, Levi Strauss, the original manufacturer of blue jeans, had a hard time understanding why young people in the middle of the twentieth century adopted jeans as a symbol of freedom and protest. Maybe the pictures say it all?

The Politics of Pants

CHARLES PAUL FREUND

In the 1950s, Levi Strauss & Co. decided to update the image of its denim clothes. Until then, the company had been depending for sales on the romantic appeal of the gold rush and the rugged image of the cowboy. Hell, it was still calling its signature pants, the ones with the copper rivets, "waist overalls." It didn't want to abandon the evocative gold-rush connection, but the postwar world was filling with consumption-minded creatures called "teenagers," and it seemed time to rethink the company's pitch.

So in 1956 Levi Strauss tried an experiment, releasing a line of black denim pants it called Elvis Presley Jeans. It was the perfect endorsement. On the branding level, it was a successful marriage of an old product and its developing new character. People had long worn denim for work, or to "westernize" themselves; now a new set of customers was wearing it to identify themselves with the postwar scene of rebellious urban (and suburban) outliers. Upon the release of Elvis's 1956 hit movie *Jailhouse Rock,* writes James Sullivan in *Jeans: A Cultural History of an American Icon* (Gotham Books), "black

Elvis Presley made jeans hip, but he didn't like them.

Jeans were once for cowboys or actors who played them.

jeans became the rage of the season." That transition would eventually make undreamed-of profits for Levi Strauss and its many competitors.

The endorsement was wonderfully revealing from within too. Elvis actually disliked denim. To him, as to most people from real working-class backgrounds, it was just a reminder of working hard and being poor. The less denim Elvis wore, the happier he was. As for the company suits at Levi Strauss, they had no idea where their new customers would take them. The company was a lot more comfortable dealing with a safe, midcult crooner like Bing Crosby. In 1951 Levi Strauss had presented Crosby with a custom-made denim tuxedo jacket, just the kind of empty PR stunt the company bosses understood. The eroticizing Presley was unknown territory to them, and they nearly fumbled the whole bad boy connection—one that had already emerged via Presley, Brando, James Dean, and even the Beats[1]—that would help put their product on nearly every pair of hips in the Western world (and on plenty of hips everywhere else too).

---

[1]**Brando, James Dean, and even the Beats:** In the early 1950s, actors Marlon Brando and James Dean were known for their roles in disaffected-youth films such as *The Wild One* and *Rebel Without a Cause*. The "Beat Generation" of young poets came to prominence in the late 1950s and early 1960s, subsequently affecting the wider youth culture.

In fact, as Sullivan, a former critic for the *San Francisco Chronicle,* tells the story, the denim industry worked hard to undermine its own success. When jeans started making a transition from working clothes to something darker—the preferred style of the dreaded "juvenile delin-quent"—the industry got worried. When school districts started pro-mulgating antidungaree "dress codes," it panicked. Suddenly a Denim Council sprang up to persuade adults that jeans were "Right for School." Young people who wore denim, the industry group argued, were exem-plary citizens who studied hard and who honored their fathers and mothers. Happily for Levi's, Wrangler, and Lee (and for Jordache, Guess, Lucky, and the wave of designers to come) nobody paid much attention to the Denim Council.

It was civil libertarians who took care of the dress codes, with a legal strategy the industry never would have dreamed of. Groups challenged the codes as, in Sullivan's words, "an imposition on freedom of expres-sion." In fact, the industry old-timers still don't get it. Looking back on

Cool personi-fied: James Dean, as Jett Rink in *Giant.*

the emergence of jeans wearing as an issue of "expression," one such old-timer can still tell Sullivan, "Amazing . . . Just for a pair of pants."

This series of events takes up just a few pages in one chapter of Sullivan's 303-page book. But I've focused on it because it is a stellar example of a primary market issue that many people — not only markets' critics but some of their defenders too — have failed to acknowledge. It's neither makers nor marketers who successfully attach meaning to the products they want to sell. It's the consumers who impute meaning to those products they choose to buy.

The anthropologist Grant Mc-Cracken has done a lot of scholarly work to elucidate this distinction, and the *New Yorker*'s Malcolm Gladwell has been a pioneer in reporting it. His famous 1997 piece "The Coolhunt" focused on consultants who attempt to monitor "coolness" as it is attached to — and detached from — consumer goods by a hierarchy of influential buyers. Gladwell offered case studies of brands, such as Hush Puppies shoes, that had become cool (for a while, anyway) without the manufacturer or its ad people ever having a clue. Jeans conquered the world — Levi's 501s are the single most successful garment ever designed — not because of the denim industry's efforts to give them meaning but in spite of them.

How to scare parents, in the 1950s: Brando in leather and denim.

The rest of Sullivan's book is addressed to the culture, the fashion, and of course the business of jeans. The last of these threads is the most valuable, since it is probably the least known and the most revealing. Who knew, for example, that leisure suits were introduced by Lee? (And what does *that* episode say about the marketers' conception, let alone control, of a product's meaning?) Sullivan's book is as comprehensive on its subject as you are likely to want, if not more so. Jeans and Jack Kerouac.[2] Jeans and the dude ranch. Jeans and the advent of the zipper. Jeans and punk. Jeans and disco. Jeans and the indigo trade. Thousand-dollar Jeans. Collectible jeans. Even pants (not jeans) and Brigham Young,[3] who in 1830 charged that trousers with buttons in front were "fornication pants."

There's even jeans and the color blue. Sullivan has penned an ode to blueness that goes on for four pages. ("The deeper blue becomes," he quotes the artist Wassily Kandinsky as saying, "the more urgently it summons man toward the infinite.") Best of all, though, is jeans and Vladimir Nabokov,[4] despite the fact that Nabokov has nothing much to say about jeans.

Sullivan uses Nabokov inventively, quoting from his 1955 novel, *Lolita*, to demonstrate how the narrator's "refined" sensibility is transformed by a whole world of low-end culture that has become — for him — eroticized. The novel's motels and shopping strips, writes Sullivan, "are the consummate low-culture backdrops for Lolita's jeans, sneakers, and lollipops." It's not just Lolita that Nabokov's intellectual narrator has fallen for. And if you don't see what eroticized low-end culture has to do with the triumph of American jeans, then Elvis really has left the building, and you've gone with him.

---

[2]**Jack Kerouac:** "Beat" writer; his novel *On the Road* was one of the best-known works to come out of the Beat Generation.

[3]**Brigham Young:** Influential nineteenth-century leader of the Church of Jesus Christ of Latter-day Saints (better known as the Mormon Church).

[4]**Vladimir Nabokov:** Russian writer of fiction; best known for his novel *Lolita*.

Assignments

1. **Opinion:** Like Tobias Salinger in "Unplugging Ads, Not Conversations" (p. 131), you've probably objected to a superficial explanation for a phenomenon you know well. It might be college faculty explaining lamely why grades are inflated or why students browse the Web during classes. Or maybe you belong to a group that has been the subject of causal analyses verging on prejudicial. If so, refute the faulty analysis of cause and effect by offering a more plausible explanation.

2. **Opinion:** Using the *Wall Street Journal*'s editorial "Safe at Any Speed" as a model (p. 146), develop a cause-and-effect analysis to suggest that some other causal prediction may have gone awry—particularly something in the public sector. Like the *WSJ* editors, be sure to explain what factors made the prediction go wrong. What changed or what consequences couldn't be easily foreseen or anticipated?

3. **Exploratory Essay:** Liza Mundy's analysis of cause and effect in "What's Really behind the Plunge in Teen Pregnancy?" (p. 149) has significant cultural and political implications. Locate a similarly challenging analysis in a national newspaper or news magazine. Then write a detailed response to the causal issues it raises, suggesting, for instance, why you find it convincing or speculating about how society might respond to its conclusions. You'll find many analyses covering topics such as the environment, terrorism, education, religion, culture, and so on.

4. **Cultural Analysis:** Like Charles Paul Freund dealing with jeans (p. 154), identify a trend you have noticed or some significant change in society or culture. It might relate to music, films, choice of majors, political preferences, and so on. Write an analysis of the phenomenon, considering either causes or potential consequences of this fashion. Then illustrate the trend with images that suggest its cultural reach or significance. Spend some time in the opening of your paper describing the trend and proving that it is real.

How to start

- Need a **topic**? See page 166.
- Need to come up with a **solution**? See page 170.
- Need to **organize your ideas**? See page 172.

6 Proposal

defines a problem & suggests a solution

Proposals are written to try to solve problems. You'll usually write a proposal to initiate an action or change. At a minimum, you hope to alter someone's thinking—even if only to recommend leaving things as they are.

- You write to your academic advisor suggesting that a service-learning experience would be a better senior project for you than writing a traditional thesis—given your talents and interests.

- Noticing the difficulty students with disabilities have navigating campus, you make a plan to enhance accessibility the keystone of your campaign for a seat on student government.

- Your major has so many requirements that most students take five or six years to graduate—adding tens of thousands of dollars to the cost of their degrees. You think it's high time for faculty to rethink the program.

- You show your banker why loaning you money to open a barbecue restaurant would make sound fiscal sense, especially since no one else in town serves decent brisket and ribs.

UNDERSTANDING PROPOSALS.   *Got an issue or a problem? Good—let's deal with it.* That's the logic driving most proposals, both the professional types that pursue grant money and less formal propositions that are part of everyday life, academic or otherwise. Like causal analysis, proposal is another form of argument. ○

Although grant writing shares some of the elements of informal proposals, it is driven by rigid formulas set by foundations and government agencies, usually covering things like budgets, personnel, evaluation, outcomes, and so on. Informal proposals are much easier. Though they may not bring large sums of cash your way, they're still important tools for addressing problems. A sensible proposal can make a difference in any situation—be it academic, personal, or political.

Following are some moves you'll need to make in framing a proposal. Not every proposal needs to do each of these things. In a first-round pitch,

Buy Nothing Day   Imagine that you want people to consider an economic system *not* based on growth and exploitation of the natural environment. How might you get their attention? By proposing a day without shopping to highlight the evils of capitalism and rampant consumerism. In the United States, Buy Nothing Day occurs on the Friday after Thanksgiving—traditionally one of the biggest shopping days of the year.

understand argument
p. 68

you might just test whether an idea will work at all; a more serious plan headed for public scrutiny would have to punch the ticket on more of the items.

Define a problem.   Set the stage for a proposal by describing the specific situation, problem, or opportunity in enough detail that readers *get it*: They see a compelling need for action. In many cases, a proposal needs to explain what's wrong with the status quo.

Target the proposal.   To make a difference, you have to reach people with the power to change a situation. That means first identifying such individuals (or groups) and then tailoring your proposal to their expectations. Use the Web or library, for example, to get the names and contact information of government or corporate officials. ○ When the people in power *are* the problem, go over their heads to more general audiences with clout of their own: voters, consumers, women, fellow citizens, the elderly, and so on.

Consider reasonable options.   Your proposal won't be taken seriously unless you have weighed all the workable possibilities, explaining their advantages and downsides. Only then will you be prepared to make a case for your specific ideas.

Make specific recommendations.   Explain what you propose to do about the situation or problem; don't just complain that someone else has gotten it wrong. The more detailed your solution is, the better.

Make realistic recommendations.   You need to address two related issues: *feasibility* and *implementation*. A proposal is feasible if it can be achieved with available resources and is acceptable to the parties involved. And, of course, a feasible plan still needs a plausible pathway to implementation: *First we do this; then we do this.*

plan a project
p. 400

The following proposal originally appeared in *Time* (August 21, 2005). Its author Barrett Seaman doesn't have the space to do much more than alert the general public (or, more likely, parents of college students) to the need for action to end alcohol abuse on campuses. Still, he does have a surprising suggestion to offer about dealing with bingeing — one most readers might not initially favor. More important, the brief essay does what a proposal must: It makes a plausible case and gets people talking.

How Bingeing Became the New College Sport

BARRETT SEAMAN

In the coming weeks, millions of students will begin their fall semester of college, with all the attendant rituals of campus life: freshman orientation, registering for classes, rushing by fraternities and sororities, and, in a more recent nocturnal college tradition, "pregaming" in their rooms.

Pregaming is probably unfamiliar to people who went to college before the 1990s. But it is now a common practice among eighteen-, nineteen- and twenty-year-old students who cannot legally buy or consume alcohol. It usually involves sitting in a dorm room or an off-campus apartment and drinking as much hard liquor as possible before heading out for the evening's parties. While reporting for my book *Binge,* I witnessed the hospitalization of several students for acute alcohol poisoning. Among them was a Hamilton College freshman who had consumed twenty-two shots of vodka while sitting in a dorm room with her friends. Such hospitalizations are routine on campuses across the nation. By the Thanksgiving break of the year I visited Harvard, the university's health center had admitted nearly seventy students for alcohol poisoning.

When students are hospitalized — or worse yet, die from alcohol poisoning, which happens about 300 times each year — college presidents tend to react by declaring their campuses dry or shutting down fraternity houses. But tighter enforcement of the minimum drinking age of twenty-one is not the solution. It's part of the problem.

Defines problem he intends to address: bingeing known as pregaming.

Proposal draws on research the author has done.

Points out that current solutions to college drinking don't work.

Over the past forty years, the United States has taken a confusing approach to the age-appropriateness of various rights, privileges, and behaviors. It used to be that twenty-one was the age that legally defined adulthood. On the heels of the student revolution of the late '60s, however, came sweeping changes: The voting age was reduced to eighteen; privacy laws were enacted that protected college students' academic, health, and disciplinary records from outsiders, including parents; and the drinking age, which had varied from state to state, was lowered to eighteen.

Explains factors responsible for the spike in alcohol abuse.

Then, thanks in large measure to intense lobbying by Mothers Against Drunk Driving, Congress in 1984 effectively blackmailed states into hiking the minimum drinking age to twenty-one by passing a law that tied compliance to the distribution of federal-aid highway funds—an amount that will average $690 million per state this year. There is no doubt that the law, which achieved full fifty-state compliance in 1988, saved lives, but it had the unintended consequence of creating a covert culture around alcohol as the young adult's forbidden fruit.

Drinking has been an aspect of college life since the first western universities in the fourteenth century. My friends and I drank in college in the 1960s—sometimes a lot but not so much that we had to be hospitalized. Veteran college administrators cite a sea change in campus culture that began, not without coincidence, in the 1990s. It was marked by a shift from beer to hard liquor, consumed not in large social settings, since that is now illegal, but furtively and dangerously in students' residences.

In my reporting at colleges around the country, I did not meet any presidents or deans who felt that the twenty-one-year age minimum helps their efforts to curb the abuse of alcohol on their campuses. Quite the opposite. They thought the law impeded their efforts since it takes away the ability to monitor and supervise drinking activity.

Points out that current law makes it harder to deal with bingeing.

Offers specific proposal tentatively, posed as question.

What would happen if the drinking age was rolled back to eighteen or nineteen? Initially, there would be a surge in binge drinking as young adults savored their newfound freedom. But over time, I predict, U.S. college students would settle into the saner approach to alcohol I saw on the one campus I visited where the legal drinking age is eighteen: Montreal's

Proposal stands up to tests of feasibility, acceptability, and practicality.

McGill University, which enrolls about two thousand American under-graduates a year. Many, when they first arrive, go overboard, exploiting their ability to drink legally. But by midterms, when McGill's demanding academic standards must be met, the vast majority have put drinking into its practical place among their priorities.

A culture like that is achievable at U.S. colleges if Congress can muster the fortitude to reverse a bad policy. If lawmakers want to reduce drunk driving, they should do what the Norwegians do: Throw the book at offenders no matter what their age. Meanwhile, we should let the pregamers come out of their dorm rooms so that they can learn to handle alcohol like the adults we hope and expect them to be.

States his thesis, and then offers precedents for students behaving more responsibly with lower drinking age.

Do current strict drinking laws in the United States actually encourage students to abuse alcohol?

Exploring purpose and topic

Most people will agree to reasonable proposals—as long as it doesn't cost them anything. So moving audiences from *I agree* to *I'll do something about it* takes
a powerful act of persuasion. And for that reason, proposals are usually framed as arguments, requiring all the strategies used in that genre. ○

▶ topic

Occasionally, you'll be asked to solve a particular problem in school or on the job. Having a topic assigned makes your task a little easier, but you can bet that any problem assigned will be complex and open to multiple solutions. Otherwise, there would be no challenge to it.

When choosing your own proposal topic, keep the following standards in mind. ○

Look for a genuine issue.   Spend the first part of your project defining a problem readers will care about. You may think it's a shame no one retails Prada close to campus, but your classmates could plausibly be more concerned with outrageous student fees or the high price of gasoline. Go beyond your own concerns in settling on a problem.

Look for a challenging problem.   It helps if others have tried to fix it in the past, but failed—and for reasons you can identify. Times change, attitudes shift, technology improves: All of these can be factors that make what seemed like an insoluble problem in the past more manageable now. Choose a serious topic to which you can bring fresh perspectives.

> Need help deciding what to write about? See "How to Browse for Ideas" on pp. 312–13.

Look for a soluble problem.   Challenges *are* good, but impossible dreams are for Broadway musicals. Parking on campus is the classic impasse—always present, always frustrating. Steer clear of problems no one has ever solved, unless you have a *really* good idea.

Look for a local issue.   It's best to leave "world peace" to celebrity activists like Bono. You can investigate a problem in your community more credibly, talking with people involved or searching local archives for material. ○
Doing so makes it easier to find an audience you can influence, including people potentially able to change the situation. It's more likely you'll get the attention of your dean of students than the secretary of state.

understand argument
p. 68

find a topic
p. 308

interview and
observe p. 412

Understanding your audience

While preparing a proposal, keep two audiences in mind—one fairly narrow and the other more broad. The first group includes people who could possibly do something about a problem; the second are general readers who could influence those in the first group by bringing the weight of public opinion down on them. And public opinion makes a difference.

Writers adjust for audience all the time in offering proposals. Grant writers especially make it a point to learn what agencies and institutions expect in applications. Quite often, it takes two or three tries to figure out how to present a winning grant submission. You won't have that luxury with most academic or political pieces, but you can certainly study models of successful proposals, noting how the writers raise an issue with readers, provide them with information and options, and then argue for a particular solution.

Write to people who can make a difference.   A personal letter you might prepare for the dean of students to protest her policies on downloading MP3 files onto university-controlled servers would likely have a respectful and perhaps legalistic tone, pointing to case law on the subject and university policies on freedom of speech. You'd also want to assure the dean of your good sense and provide her with sound reasons to consider your case.

You'd be in good company adopting such a strategy. Listen to how matter-of-factly environmentalist David R. Brower argues—in a famous proposal—that the gates of the massive Glen Canyon Dam should be opened and the waters of Lake Powell drained. Radical stuff, but his strategy was sensible. For one thing, he argued, the artificial reservoir leaked.

> One of the strongest selling points [for removing the dam] comes from the Bureau of Reclamation itself. In 1996, the bureau found that almost a million acre-feet, or 8 percent of the river's flow, disappeared between the stations recording the reservoir's inflow and outflow. Almost 600,000 acre-feet were presumed lost to evaporation. Nobody knows for sure about the rest. The bureau said some of the loss was a gain—being stored in the banks of the reservoir—but it has no idea how much of that gain it will ever get back. Some bank storage is recoverable, but all too likely the region's downward-slanting geological strata are leading some of Powell's waters

into the dark unknown. It takes only one drain to empty a bathtub, and we don't know where, when, or how the Powell tub leaks. A million acre-feet could meet the annual domestic needs of 4 million people and at today's prices are worth $435 million in the Salt Lake City area—more than a billion on my hill in Berkeley, California.

— "Let the River Run Through It," *Sierra,* March/April 1997

Rally people who represent public opinion.   Imagine you've had no response from the dean of students on the file-sharing proposal you made. Time to take the issue to the public, perhaps via an op-ed or letter sent to the student paper. Though still keeping the dean firmly in mind, you'd now also write to stir up student and community opinion. Your new piece could be more emotional than your letter and less burdened by legal points—though still citing facts and presenting solid reasons for allowing students to download music files to university computers. ○

The fact is that people often need a spur to move them—that is, some strategy that frames an issue to help them find their part in it. Again, you'd be in good company in leading an audience to your position. In 1962 when President John F. Kennedy proposed a mission to the moon, he did it in language that stirred a public reasonably skeptical about the cost and challenges of such an implausible undertaking.

OCEAN HILLS Community Meeting

Learn About the New Mall

Scheduled To Speak:

Mayor Tom Smith
Planning Comissioner Laura Tarkle
Principal Jack Snow

Followed by an open discussion and question period

Thursday Night
7:00 PM

Andrews Middle School Auditorium
23434 Sycamore Blvd.
Ocean Hills

Proposals to very small or targeted groups can be as simple as this unadorned but clear and direct leaflet.

refine your tone
p. 374

JFK Aims High
In 1962, the president challenged Americans to go to the moon; in 2008, we were asked to pump up our tires.

There is no strife, no prejudice, no national conflict in outer space as yet. Its hazards are hostile to us all. Its conquest deserves the best of all mankind, and its opportunity for peaceful cooperation may never come again. But why, some say, the moon? Why choose this as our goal? And they may well ask why climb the highest mountain? Why, thirty-five years ago, fly the Atlantic? Why does Rice play Texas?

We choose to go to the moon. We choose to go to the moon in this decade and do the other things, not because they are easy, but because they are hard, because that goal will serve to organize and measure the best of our energies and skills, because that challenge is one that we are willing to accept, one we are unwilling to postpone, and one which we intend to win, and the others, too.

—Rice Stadium "Moon Speech," September 12, 1962

Finding and developing materials

Proposals might begin with whining and complaining (*I want my MP3s!*), but they can't stay in that mode long. Like any serious work, proposals must be grounded in solid thinking and research.

What makes them distinctive, however, is the sheer variety of strategies you might use in a single document. To write a convincing proposal, you may have to narrate, report, argue, evaluate, and explore cause and effect. A proposal can be a little like old-time TV variety shows, with one act following another, displaying a surprising range of talent. Here's how you might develop those various parts.

The Journalist's Questions

Who?   What?
Where?   When?
Why?   How?

Define the problem. First, research the existing problem fully enough to explain it to your readers. Run through the traditional journalist's questions—*Who? What? Where? When? Why? How?*—to be sure you've got the basics of your topic down cold. When appropriate, interview experts or people involved with an issue; for instance, in college communities, the best repositories of institutional memory will usually be staff. ○

Even when you think you know the topic well, spend time locating any documents that might provide hard facts to cite for skeptical readers. For instance, if you propose to change a long-standing policy, find out when it was imposed, by whom, and for what reasons.

▶ consider
solutions

Examine prior solutions. If a problem is persistent, other people have certainly tried to solve it—or perhaps they caused it. In either case, do the research necessary to figure out, as best you can, what happened in these earlier efforts. But expect controversy. Your sources may provide different and contradictory accounts that you will have to sort out in a plausible narrative.

Once you know the history of an issue, shift into an evaluative mode to explain why earlier solutions or strategies did not work. ○ Provide reliable information so that readers can later make comparisons with your own proposal and appreciate its ingenuity.

Make a proposal.   Coming up with a proposal may take all the creativity you can muster, to the point where a strong case can be made for working collaboratively when that's an option. ○ You'll benefit from the additional feedback. Be sure to write down your ideas as they emerge so you can see what exactly you are recommending. Be specific about numbers and costs.

For instance, if you propose that high school students in your district take a course in practical economics (balancing a checkbook, credit card use, etc.) to better prepare them for adult responsibilities, do the research necessary to figure out who might teach such classes and how many new instructors the school district would have to hire. Your results could preempt an implausibly expensive proposal or suggest more feasible alternatives for handling the problem that you see.

Defend the proposal.   Any ideas that threaten the status quo will surely provoke arguments. That's half the fun of offering proposals. So prove your position, using all the tools of argument available to you, from the logical and factual to the emotional. It is particularly important to anticipate objections, because readers invested in the status quo will have them in spades. Take time to define a successful solution to a problem, and point out every way your solution meets that definition. Above all, you've got to show that your idea will work.

Be prepared, too, to show that your plan is feasible—that is to say, that it can be achieved with existing or new resources. For example, you might actually solve your school's traffic problems by proposing a monorail linking the central campus to huge new parking garages. But who would pay for the multimillion-dollar system? Still, don't be put off too easily by the objection that *we can't possibly do that.* A little ingenuity goes a long way—it's part of the problem-solving process.

Figure out how to implement the proposal.   Readers will want assurances that your ideas can be implemented: Show them how. Figure out what has to happen to meet your goals: where new resources will come from, how personnel can be recruited and hired, where brochures or manuals will be printed, and so on. Provide a timetable.

collaborate
p. 314

Creating a structure

organize
ideas

Proposals follow the mental processes many people go through in dealing with issues and problems, and some of these problems have more history and complications than others. ○ Generally, the less formal the proposal, the fewer structural elements it will have. So you should adapt the proposal paradigm below to your purposes, using it as a checklist of *possible* issues to consider in your own project.

Introduction defining a **problem** or an **issue**

Nature of the **problem**

Prior **solution(s)** + **reason(s)** for inadequacy

New **proposal**

Explanation

Rationale

Comparisons and/or **counterarguments**

Feasibility

Implementation

Conclusion

You might use a similar structure when you intend to explore the effects that follow from some action, event, policy, or change in the status quo. Once again, you'd begin with an introduction that fully describes the situation you believe will have consequences; then you would work through those consequences, connecting them as necessary. Your conclusion could then draw out the implications of your paper.

shape your work
p. 340

Examining models

PROPOSAL FOR CHANGE Michael Gurian's "Disappearing Act," which appeared in the *Washington Post,* is an example of a proposal that focuses more on defining a problem than on offering a solution. As Gurian himself notes late in his piece, not much happens until the public takes notice of an issue. "Disappearing Act" bases its arguments on both personal experience and various studies and statistics. But the tight confines of a newspaper feature preclude the documentation readers might want to follow up on for Gurian's claims.

Disappearing Act

WHERE HAVE THE MEN GONE?
NO PLACE GOOD

Michael Gurian

Sunday, December 4, 2005

In the 1990s, I taught for six years at a small liberal-arts college in Spokane, Washington. In my third year, I started noticing something that was happening right in front of me. There were more young women in my classes than young men, and on average, they were getting better grades than the guys. Many of the young men stared blankly at me as I lectured. They didn't take notes as well as the young women. They didn't seem to care as much about what I taught—literature, writing, and psychology. They were bright kids, but many of their faces said, "Sitting here, listening, staring at these words—this is not really who I am."

That was a decade ago, but just last month, I spoke with an administrator at Howard University in the District. He told me that what I observed a decade ago has become one of the "biggest agenda items" at Howard. "We are having trouble recruiting and retaining male students," he said. "We are at about a 2-to-1 ratio, women to men."

Howard is not alone. Colleges and universities across the country are grappling with the case of the mysteriously vanishing male. Where men once dominated, they now make up no more than 43 percent of students at American institutions of higher learning, according to 2003

> Identifies genuine and challenging issue.

> Suggests problem has long-term consequences.

175

statistics, and this downward trend shows every sign of continuing unabated. If we don't reverse it soon, we will gradually diminish the male identity, and thus the productivity and the mission, of the next generation of young men, and all the ones that follow.

The trend of females overtaking males in college was initially measured in 1978. Yet despite the well-documented disappearance of ever more young men from college campuses, we have yet to fully react to what has become a significant crisis. Largely, that is because of cultural perceptions about males and their societal role. Many times a week, a reporter or other media person will ask me: "Why should we care so much about boys when men still run everything?"

Tries to rally audience.

It's a fair and logical question, but what it really reflects is that our culture is still caught up in old industrial images. We still see thousands of men who succeed quite well in the professional world and in industry—men who get elected president, who own software companies, who make six figures selling cars. We see the Bill Gateses and John Robertses and George Bushes—and so we're not as concerned as we ought to be about the millions of young men who are floundering or lost.

Defines problem as one of class—rich vs. poor.

But they're there: The young men who are working in the lowest-level (and most dangerous) jobs instead of going to college. Who are sitting in prison instead of going to college. Who are staying out of the long-term marriage pool because they have little to offer to young women. Who are remaining adolescents, wasting years of their lives playing video games for hours a day, until they're in their thirties, by which time the world has passed many of them by.

The old industrial promise—"That guy will get a decent job no matter what"—is just that, an old promise. So is the old promise that a man will be able to feed his family and find personal meaning by "following in his father's footsteps," which has vanished for millions of males who are not raised with fathers or substantial role models. The old promise that an old boys' network will always come through for "the guys" is likewise gone for many young men who have never seen and will never see such a network (though they may see a dangerous gang). Most frightening, the old promise that schools will take care of boys and educate them to succeed is also breaking down, as boys dominate the

Explains why prior solutions do not work now.

failure statistics in our schools, starting at the elementary level and continuing through high school.

Of course, not every male has to go to college to succeed, to be a good husband, to be a good and productive man. But a dismal future lies ahead for large numbers of boys in this generation who will not go to college. Statistics show that a young man who doesn't finish school or go to college in 2005 will likely earn less than half what a college graduate earns. He'll be three times more likely to be unemployed and more likely to be homeless. He'll be more likely to get divorced, more likely to engage in violence against women, and more likely to engage in crime. He'll be more likely to develop substance-abuse problems and to be a greater burden on the economy, statistically, since men who don't attend college pay less in Social Security and other taxes, depend more on government welfare, are more likely to father children out of wedlock, and are more likely not to pay child support.

When I worked as a counselor at a federal prison, I saw these statistics up close. The young men and adult males I worked with were mainly uneducated, had been raised in families that didn't promote education, and had found little of relevance in the schools they had attended. They were passionate people, capable of great love and even possible future success. Many of them told me how much they wanted to get an education. At an intuitive level, they knew how important it was.

Whether in the prison system, in my university classes, or in the schools where I help train teachers, I have noticed a systemic problem with how we teach and mentor boys that I call "industrial schooling" and that I believe is a primary root of our sons' falling behind in school, and quite often in life.

Two hundred years ago, realizing the necessity of schooling millions of kids, we took them off the farms and out of the marketplace and put them in large industrial-size classrooms (one teacher, twenty-five to thirty kids). For many kids, this system worked—and still works. But from the beginning, there were some for whom it wasn't working very well. Initially, it was girls. It took more than 150 years to get parity for them.

Now we're seeing what's wrong with the system for millions of boys. Beginning in very early grades, the sit-still, read-your-book, raise-your-hand-quietly, don't-learn-by-doing-but-by-taking-notes classroom is a

> Studies cited demonstrate seriousness of problem.

> Examines complex causes of current problem.

worse fit for more boys than it is for most girls. This was always the case, but we couldn't see it one hundred years ago. We didn't have the comparative element of girls at par in classrooms. We taught a lot of our boys and girls separately. We educated children with greater emphasis on certain basic educational principles that kept a lot of boys "in line"—competitive learning was one. And our families were deeply involved in a child's education.

Now, however, the boys who don't fit the classrooms are glaringly clear. Many families are barely involved in their children's education. Girls outperform boys in nearly every academic area. Many of the old principles of education are diminished. In a classroom of thirty kids, about five boys will begin to fail in the first few years of preschool and elementary school. By fifth grade, they will be diagnosed as learning disabled, ADD/ADHD, behaviorally disordered, or "unmotivated." They will no longer do their homework (though they may say they are doing it), they will disrupt class or withdraw from it, they will find a few islands of competence (like video games or computers) and overemphasize those.

Boys have a lot of Huck Finn in them—they don't, on average, learn as well as girls by sitting still, concentrating, multitasking, listening to words. For twenty years, I have been taking brain research into homes and classrooms to show teachers, parents, and others how differently boys and girls learn. Once a person sees a PET or SPECT scan[1] of a boy's brain and a girl's brain, showing the different ways these brains learn, they understand. As one teacher put it to me, "Wow, no wonder we're having so many problems with boys."

Yet every decade the industrial classroom becomes more and more protective of the female learning style and harsher on the male, yielding statistics such as these:

> The majority of National Merit scholarships, as well as college academic scholarships, go to girls and young women.
> Boys and young men comprise the majority of high school dropouts, as high as 80 percent in many cities.
> Boys and young men are 1½ years behind girls and young women in reading ability (this gap does not even out in high school, as some have

---

1. **PET or SPECT scan:** Types of brain scans showing sites and levels of brain activity.

[margin note:] Solution may require different approaches tailored to boys and girls.

argued; a male reading/writing gap continues into college and the workplace).

The industrial classroom is one that some boys do fine in, many boys just "hang on" in, many boys fall behind in, many boys fail in, and many boys drop out of. The boys who do fine would probably do fine in any environment, and the boys who are hanging on and getting by will probably reemerge later with some modicum of success, but the millions who fall behind and fail will generally become the statistics we saw earlier.

Explains steps in implementing solution.

Grasping the mismatch between the minds of boys and the industrial classroom is only the first step in understanding the needs of our sons. Lack of fathering and male role models take a heavy toll on boys, as does lack of attachment to many family members (whether grandparents, extended families, moms, or dads). Our sons are becoming very lonely. And even more politically difficult to deal with: The boys-are-privileged-but-the-girls-are-shortchanged emphasis of the last twenty years (an emphasis that I, as a father of two daughters and an advocate of girls, have seen firsthand) has muddied the water for child development in general, pitting funding for girls against funding for boys.

Middle style underscores appeal to general readers, especially parents.

We still barely see the burdens our sons are carrying as we change from an industrial culture to a postindustrial one. We want them to shut up, calm down, and become perfect intimate partners. It doesn't matter too much who boys and men are—what matters is who we think they should be. When I think back to the kind of classroom I created for my college students, I feel regret for the males who dropped out. When I think back to my time working in the prison system, I feel a deep sadness for the present and future generations of boys whom we still have time to save.

Asserts feasibility of solution.

And I do think we can save them. I get hundreds of e-mails and letters every week, from parents, teachers, and others who are beginning to realize that we must do for our sons what we did for our daughters in the industrialized schooling system—realize that boys are struggling and need help. These teachers and parents are part of a social movement—a boys' movement that started, I think, about ten years ago. It's a movement that gets noticed for brief moments by the media (when Columbine happened, when Laura Bush talked about boys) and then goes underground again. It's a movement very much powered by individual women—mainly mothers of sons—who say things to me like the e-mailers who wrote, "I don't know anyone who doesn't have a son struggling in school" or "I thought having a boy would be like having a girl, but when my son was born, I had to rethink things."

We all need to rethink things. We need to stop blaming, suspecting, and overly medicating our boys, as if we can change this guy into the learner we want. When we decide—as we did with our daughters—that there isn't anything inherently wrong with our sons, when we look closely at the system that boys learn in, we will discover these boys again, for all that they are. And maybe we'll see more of them in college again.

ACADEMIC PROPOSAL   Ricky Patel wrote "Mandatory HIV Testing" for a course at the University of Texas at Austin, modifying his first draft to deal with the numerous comments it generated during an in-class editing session. Patel's research-based final version reproduced here would still likely generate much discussion and disagreement. But that's often the point of a proposal.

Patel 1

Ricky Patel

Instructor's Name

Course Title

Date

Mandatory HIV Testing

For many young adults, college is the gateway to freedom.

Some use the opportunity to make new friends, others experiment

with substances like alcohol and marijuana, and still others

experiment with sex. Unfortunately, the decision to have sex could

be the worst mistake of their lives, given the consequences to their

Patel 2

Defines problem on college campuses: continuing danger of HIV and AIDS.

health. Among the many sexually transmitted diseases, HIV remains the most feared and unforeseeable. This virus can lead to AIDS, which takes the lives of millions of individuals each year worldwide, adding new victims each day. In fact, according to the Centers for Disease Control and Prevention (CDC), "1 in 500 college students is infected with HIV" (CDC Pathfinder). Responsible officials at colleges and universities should therefore require each incoming student, solely for the individual's benefit, to take an HIV test.

Proposal targets school officials.

Explains how proposal would re- duce AIDS transmission among young adults.

Many of those who have contracted HIV simply fail to realize it. For some, it may take up to ten years before AIDS symptoms ever show - - plenty of time for an individual to spread the virus to his or her many partners. Additionally, those partners who are infected could just as easily spread the disease to more victims. But if someone knows that he or she has HIV, the likelihood of continued sexual encounters is greatly reduced. According to Dr. Julie Gerberding, director of the CDC, "When people know they're positive [they have the virus], the research has shown they take steps to protect others from infection. People who don't know it continue to transmit the virus" (Smith). By requiring each prospec- tive student to take a test for HIV as an incoming freshman, educational institutions can greatly reduce the spread of this disease in the United States. Obviously, there are those who will engage in promiscuous activity even after they know they have the virus. However, many others will realize they do not want to burden anyone else with the difficult disease.

Cites authorities to support claims and judgments.

Offers second reason for mandatory AIDS testing.

Ignorance about AIDS remains a serious problem. According to a recent survey of a group of students performed by AVERT, a charity for AIDS victims, 38% falsely thought the HIV virus could be

Patel 3

transmitted by kissing, 25% believed the virus could be transmitted
by sharing a glass of wine, and 18% thought the infection could
spread by touching a toilet seat (AVERT). But education should be
the most effective tool to help prevent the spread of HIV. By
mandating an HIV test, schools can be more sure that their students
will be better educated about the risks of AIDS and methods of
prevention available for those who wish to engage in sex.

Additionally, mandatory testing of all students means no
groups are targeted by the program. AIDS specialist Dr. Rochelle
Walensky explains that "when [people] realized you were not asking
them if they wanted an HIV test because of who they were, what
they looked like, or what they came for--but that you were offering it
to them because that was just a service of that clinic--then there
was no stigma" (Smith). Ultimately, university-enforced HIV testing
might encourage potential carriers to take the test without any fear
of discrimination or assumptions. Furthermore, if HIV is detected
early enough, the individual has a greater chance of getting
treatment to live "a long, productive life." Research shows that early
treatment is more effective than treatment after a number of years.

However, there are moral implications when dealing with the
sensitive subject of required testing: Some individuals may feel that
their rights are being violated. Nonetheless, there are many laws in
the United States, like the Patriot Act, by which citizens give up
some of their liberties to ensure the safety of all Americans. With
respect to AIDS, social responsibility clearly overshadows some
privacy rights. All students in the United States have a personal
responsibility to get tested for HIV. The test is simply there to tell
them that they should consider making wise decisions in the future

Anticipating objections, Patel suggests that mandatory testing will remove stigma.

Addresses major objection: potential violation of privacy rights.

Uses emotional style to encourage readers to accept loss of privacy.

Patel 4

and get treatment immediately if they test positive. The average cost of an HIV test is $8 -- a small price, roughly that of a movie ticket, for such life-changing information. How could people live with themselves if they unknowingly infected someone with HIV when such an inexpensive test might have prevented it? Surely the benefits of mandatory testing outweigh the negatives.

Unfortunately, there still isn't a cure for this disease, but through awareness and education, HIV's spread can be greatly limited. A simple, inexpensive test could save dozens of lives at each major university. Since many colleges already require student testing for hepatitis and meningitis, what harm would there be if they also required HIV testing? Every student has a responsibility to themselves and each other to get tested and get treatment.

Argues feasibility by pointing to precedents.

Patel 5

Works Cited

"HIV and AIDS in America." AVERT. AVERT. 20 Nov. 2006 <http://www.avert.org/america.htm>.

"HIV/AIDS and College Students." CDC Pathfinder. Aegis. 20 Nov. 2006 <http://www.aegis.org/PUBS/CDC_FACT_SHEETS/1995/CPATH003.html>.

Smith, Stephen. "US Calls for Making HIV Testing Routine." Boston Globe 22 Sept. 2006. 20 Nov. 2006 <http://www.boston.com/news/nation/articles/2006/09/22/us_calls_for_making_hiv_testing_routine/>.

VISUAL PROPOSAL

In "Carchitecture," artists Tyler Brett and Tony Romano challenge the values of consumerist society, and offer a proposal for making cars more earth-friendly. This piece originally appeared in *Adbusters* magazine (November/December 2004).

CARCHITECTURE

We are all forced to negotiate our way through the everyday car-inundated environment whether on foot, bicycle, or automobile. This project is really about envisioning a way to be more actively and creatively engaged in that environment. We see the potential to imagine a future whose basic structure is tied to the political and economic realities of here and now.

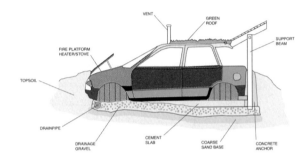

A carchitectural shelter will:

-Provide protection from the elements
-Keep the inside air warm
-Provide ventilation with minimum condensation

Carchitecture is virtually airtight, which is good and bad. Good, because it makes for a superb weatherproof shelter. Bad, because the carbon monoxide gas you produce from cooking and heating will poison you. Ventilation is imperative! Follow these plans to build a carchitectural shelter. To begin, you'll need to replace the car's internal combustion engine with a fire platform consisting of a six-inch bed of flat river stones.

Build a fire from two or three dry logs around two feet in length, allowing plenty of air to get to the fire. Dry kindling, like wood and lichen, can be found under the lower branches of trees, and will usually be dry even during the wettest seasons of the year. The opened hood (positioned 45 degrees to the existing windshield) will reflect the heat into the shelter and also serves as a wind screen. Two carchitectural shelters may be built facing one another with a fire between. When you do this you gain a great advantage. A lot of time is saved, more space is provided, and one fire will heat both shelters.

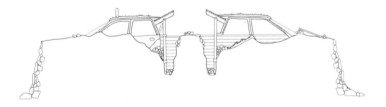

1. **Proposal for Change:** In calling for reducing the drinking age, Barrett Seaman's "How Bingeing Became the New College Sport" (p. 163) offers a solution to alcohol abuse that some might call "politically incorrect." Indeed, many politicians or school officials would likely be reluctant to support a lowered drinking age — even if it might make people more responsible. Choose an issue that you think needs as radical a rethinking as college-age drinking, and write a research-based proposal of your own. Like Seaman, be sure to offer your ideas in language cool and persuasive enough to make responsible adults at least consider them.

2. **Proposal Identifying a Problem:** Michael Gurian was prompted to write "Disappearing Act" (p. 175) after recalling the difficulties he observed young men having in school. Drawing on your own observations and experiences, identify a specific problem on your college campus or in the local community. Research the issue thoroughly, using both human resources and materials such as college manuals and policies, campus newspapers, official records, reports, and so on. Come up with a plausible approach to the problem, and then write a proposal in the form of a detailed letter directed to a person or group with the power to deal with it. Such a letter would likely have to be much shorter, however, than Gurian's article.

3. **Counterproposal:** You likely will find many proposals—such as Ricky Patel's call for mandatory AIDS testing on page 180— totally unacceptable. Identify such a proposal and write a paper in which you counter the idea with good reasons, evidence, and maybe a little humor (if appropriate), explaining why it won't work or why the solution might be worse than the problem.

4. **Visual Proposal:** The artists make a serious point with their humorous cartoon (and commentary) in "Carchitecture" (p. 184). Create a visual text of your own that offers a similarly satirical proposal.

How to start ▶

- Need to **find a text to analyze**?
See page 195.
- Need to come up with **ideas**? See page 198.
- Need to **organize your ideas**? See page 204.

7 Literary Analysis

responds critically to cultural works

Unless you're an English major, the papers you write for Literature 101 may seem as mechanical as chemistry lab reports—something done just to get a degree. But hardly a day goes by when you don't respond strongly to some cultural experience, sharing your thoughts and opinions about the books, music, and entertainment you love. It's worth learning to do this well.

- You write a paper explaining your theory that Lady Macbeth, though a tragic figure by definition, has strong comic elements in her character designed to make her appear more absurd and pathetic than evil.

- Rather than roll your eyes like your companions, you take abstract art seriously. You consider Kayla Mohammadi's painting (on p. 187), and try to explain what you see to someone who "doesn't get it."

- Having spent several seasons watching the TV series *24*, you wonder whether other programs—or maybe stage dramas or novels—have similarly experimented with the passage of time, making it so powerful a factor in telling a story.

UNDERSTANDING LITERARY ANALYSIS. In a traditional literary analysis, you respond to a poem, novel, play, or short story. That response can be analytical, looking at theme, plot, structure, characters, genre, style, and so on. Or it can be critical, theoretical, or evaluative—locating works within their social, political, historic, and even philosophic neighborhoods. Or you might approach a literary work expressively, describing how you connect with it intellectually and emotionally. Or you can combine these approaches or imagine alternative ones—perhaps reflecting new attitudes and assumptions about media.

Other potential genres for analysis include films, TV offerings, popular music, comic books, and games. Distinctions between high and popular culture have not so much dissolved as ceased to be interesting. After all, you can say dumb things about *Hamlet* and smart things about *The Sopranos*. Moreover, every genre of artistic expression—from sonnets to opera to graphic novels—at some point struggled for respectability. What matters is

***Red Tide—Maine* by Kayla Mohammadi** The artist explains that "the intention is not literal portrayal, but rather a visual translation. A translation based on color, value, and space."

the quality of a literary analysis and whether you help readers appreciate the novel *Pride and Prejudice* or, maybe, the video game *Valkyrie Profile 2: Silmeria*. Expect your literary or cultural analyses to do *some* of the following.

Begin with a close reading.   In an analysis, you slow the pace at which people typically operate in a 24/7 world to look deliberately and closely at a text. You might study the way individual words and images connect in a poem, how plot evolves in a novel, or how rapid editing defines the character of a movie. In short, you ponder the *calculated* choices writers and artists make in creating their work. ○

Make a claim or an observation.   Your encounter with a text will ordinarily lead to a thesis. The claim won't always be argumentative or controversial: You may be amazed at the simplicity of Wordsworth's Lucy poems or blown away by Jimi Hendrix's take on "All Along the Watchtower." But more typically, you'll make a statement or an observation that you believe is worth proving either by research or, just as often, by evidence from within the work itself.

Present works in context.   Works of art exist in our real world; that's what we like about them and why they sometimes change our lives. Your analysis can explore these relationships among texts, people, and society.

Draw on previous research.   Your response to a work need not agree with what others have written. But you should be willing to learn from previous scholarship and criticism—readily available in libraries or online. ○

Use texts for evidence.   A compelling analysis unwraps the complexities of a book, movie, poem, drama, or song, explaining it so that readers might better appreciate what they did not notice before. In short, direct them to the neat stuff. For that reason, the well-chosen quotation is the mighty tool of successful literary papers.

read closely
p. 317

plan a project
p. 400

Textual Analysis

In "Distinguishing the *Other* in Two Works by Tolstoy," Melissa Miller assembles evidence from *The Cossacks* and "A Prisoner in the Caucasus" to make one strong claim about author Leo Tolstoy's response to the ethnic peoples he describes. In a paper written for an assignment, she uses a simple comparison structure to organize numerous quotations from the two works to support her point.

Miller 1

Melissa Miller

Instructor's Name

Course Title

Date

Distinguishing the <u>Other</u> in Two Works by Tolstoy

The Cossacks and the Chechens are two very different peoples; they share neither language nor religion. The Cossacks are Russian-speaking Christians, while the Chechens speak a Caucasian language and follow Islam. Certainly, Leo Tolstoy (1828-1910) knew these facts, since he spent a significant length of time in the Caucasus. However, it is difficult to distinguish them as different peoples in Tolstoy's work. The Cossacks in Tolstoy's novel of the same name (1863) and the Chechens in his story "A Prisoner in the Caucasus" (1872) share so many cultural and ethnic features--appearance, reverence for warriors and horses, their behavior--that they appear to be the same people. As a result, their deep cultural differences all but disappear to Tolstoy and his European readers.

From Tolstoy's descriptions of the Cossacks and the Chechens, they appear identical: Both groups are dark in complexion, wear beshmets, and are wild. The Cossack men have black beards and Maryanka has black eyes (<u>Cossacks</u> 30; 55), while Dina has black hair and a face like her father's, "the dark man" ("Prisoner" 316). In

Providing dates of writer's birth/death is a helpful convention.

Title identifies topic and highlights key term.

Thesis is straightforward: Tolstoy doesn't show differences between Cossacks and Chechens.

Miller's close reading of text supports her claim.

Choose a text that you *don't* understand.   Most writers tend to write about works that are immediately accessible and relatively new: Why struggle with a hoary epic poem when you can just watch *The Lord of the Rings* on DVD? One obvious reason may be to figure out how works from different eras can still be powerfully connected to our own; the very strangeness of older and more difficult texts may even prompt you to ask more provocative questions. In short, you'll pay more attention to literary texts that place demands on you.

Stills from *Smoke Signals* (1998) and *Bury My Heart at Wounded Knee* (2007) How much do you know about Native American fiction or film? Use an assignment as an opportunity to learn more.

Understanding your audience

Unless you write book reviews or essays for a campus literary magazine, the readers of your analyses of works of art and culture are likely a professor and other students in your course. But in either situation, assume a degree of expertise among your readers. Moreover, many people will examine your literary analysis simply because they're interested—a tremendous advantage. Be sure to respect the needs of your audience.

Clearly identify the author and works you are analyzing. Seems like common sense, but this consideration is often neglected in academic papers precisely because writers assume that *the teacher must know what I'm doing.* Don't make this mistake. Also briefly recap what happens in the works you are analyzing—especially with texts not everyone has read recently. ○ Follow the model of good reviewers, who typically summarize key elements before commenting on them. Such summaries give readers their bearings at the beginning of a paper. Here's James Wood introducing a novel by Marilynne Robinson that he will be reviewing for the *New York Times.*

> *Gilead* is set in 1956 in the small town of Gilead, Iowa, and is narrated by a seventy-six-year-old pastor named John Ames, who has recently been told he has angina pectoris and believes he is facing imminent death. In this terminal spirit, he decides to write a long letter to his seven-year-old son, the fruit of a recent marriage to a much younger woman. This novel is that letter, set down in the easy, discontinuous form of a diary, mixing long and short entries, reminiscences, moral advice, and so on.

Define key terms. Many specialized and technical expressions are used in a literary analysis. Your instructor will know what an *epithet, peripeteia,* or *rondel* might be, but you may still have to define terms like these for a wider audience—your classmates, for instance. Alternatively, you can look for more accessible synonyms and expressions.

Don't aim to please professional critics. Are you tempted to imitate the style of serious academic theorists you've encountered while researching your paper? No need—your instructor probably won't expect you to write in that way, at least not until graduate school.

sum up ideas
p. 424

Finding and developing materials

▶ **develop ideas**

With an assignment in hand and works to analyze, the next step—and it's a necessary one—is to establish that you have a reliable "text" of whatever you'll be studying. In a course, a professor may assign a particular edition or literary anthology for you to use, making your job easier.

This Bedford/St. Martin's edition of *Frankenstein* provides important textual information and background. Look for texts with such material when studying classic novels, poems, and plays.

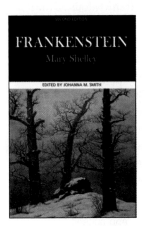

Be aware that many texts are available in multiple editions. (For instance, the novel *Frankenstein* first appeared in 1818, but the revised third edition of 1831 is the one most widely read today.) For classical works, such as the plays of Shakespeare, choose an edition from a major publisher, preferably one that includes thorough notes and perhaps some essays and criticism. When in doubt, ask your professor which texts to use. Don't just browse the library shelves.

Other kinds of media pose interesting problems as well. For instance, you may have to decide which version of a movie to study—the one seen by audiences in theaters or the "director's cut" on a DVD. Similarly, you might find multiple recordings of musical works: Look for widely respected performances. Even popular music may come in both studio (*American Idiot*) and live (*Bullet in a Bible*) versions. Then there is the question of drama: Do you read it on the page, watch a video when one is available, or see it in a theater? Perhaps you do all three. But whatever versions of a text you choose for study, be sure to identify them in your project, either in the text itself or on the Works Cited page. ○

understand citation styles p. 435

Establishing a text is the easy part. How then do you find something specific to write about, an angle on the subject? ○ Following are some strategies and approaches.

Examine the text closely.   Guided by your assignment, begin your project by closely reading, watching, or examining the selected work(s) and taking notes. Obviously, you'll treat some works differently than others. You can read a Seamus Heaney sonnet a dozen times to absorb its nuances, but it's unlikely you'd push through Rudolfo A. Anaya's novel *Bless Me, Ultima* more than once or twice for a paper. But, in either case, you'll need a suitable way to take notes or to annotate what you're analyzing.

Honestly, you should count on a minimum of two readings or viewings of any text, the first to get familiar with the work and find a potential approach, the second and subsequent readings to confirm your thesis and to find supporting evidence for it.

Focus on the text itself.   Your earliest literature papers probably tackled basic questions about plot, character, setting, theme, and language. But these are not simple matters—just the kinds of issues that fascinate most readers. You might, for example, look for moments when the plot of the novel you're examining reinforces its theme or study how characters change in response to specific events. Even the setting of a short story or film might be worth writing about when it becomes a factor in the story: Can you imagine the film *Casablanca* taking place in any other location?

Questions about language loom large in many analyses. How does word choice work with or against the subject of a poem? Does the style of a novel reinforce its story? How does a writer create irony through dialogue? Indeed, any feature of a work might be researched and studied, from the narrators in novels to the rhyme schemes in poetry.

Focus on its meanings, themes, and interpretations.   Although finding themes or meanings in literary works seems like an occupation mostly for English majors, the tendency really is universal and irresistible. If you take any work seriously, you'll discover angles and ideas worth sharing with readers. Maybe *Seinfeld* is a modern version of *Everyman* or *O Brother,*

find a topic
p. 308

Where Art Thou? is a retelling of the *Odyssey* by Homer or maybe not. Observe carefully and open your mind to possible connections: What have you seen like this before? What patterns do you detect? What images recur in the text or what ideas are supported or undercut?

Focus on its authorship and history.   Some artists stand apart from their creations, while others cannot be separated from them. So you might explore in what ways a work reflects the life, education, and attitudes of its author. What psychological forces or religious perspectives might be detected in particular characters or themes? Is the author writing to represent his or her gender, race, ethnicity, or class? Or does the work repudiate its author's identity, class, or religion?

Similarly, consider how a text embodies the assumptions, attitudes, politics, fashions, and even technology of the times during which it was composed. A work as familiar as Jonathan Swift's "A Modest Proposal" still requires readers to know at least a *little* about Irish and English politics in the eighteenth century. How does Swift's satire open up when you learn even more about its world?

Focus on its genre.   Genres are formulas. Take a noble hero, give him a catastrophic flaw, have him make a bad choice, and then kill him off: That's tragedy—or, in the wrong hands, melodrama. With a little brainstorming, you could identify dozens of genres and subcategories: epics, sonnets, historical novels, superhero comics, grand opera, soap opera, and so on. Artists' works often fall between genres, sometimes creating new ones. Readers, too, bring clear-cut expectations to a text: Try to turn a 007 action-spy thriller into a three-hankie chick flick, and you've got trouble in River City.

You can analyze genre in various ways. For instance, track a text backward to discover its literary forebears—the works that influenced its author. Even texts that revolt against previous genres bear traces of what they have rejected. It's also possible to study the way artists combine different genres or play with or against the expectations of audiences. Needless to say, you can also explore the relationships of works within a genre. In fact, it's often a shared genre that makes comparisons interesting or provocative. For example, what do twentieth-century coming-of-age stories such as *A Separate Peace*, *The Catcher in the Rye*, and *Lord of the Flies* have in common?

Focus on its influence.   Some works have an obvious impact on life or society, changing how people think or behave: *Uncle Tom's Cabin*, *To Kill a Mockingbird*, *Roots*, *Schindler's List*. TV shows have broadened people's notions of family; musical genres such as jazz and gospel have created and sustained entire communities.

But impact doesn't always occur on such a grand scale or express itself through social movements. Books influence other books, films other films, and so on—with not a few texts crossing genres. Who could have foreseen all the ties between comic books in the 1930s, TV shows in the 1950s, superhero films in the 1980s, and video games in the new century? And, for better or worse, books, movies, and other cultural productions influence styles, fashions, and even the way people speak. Consider *Fast Times at Ridgemont High* or *Clueless*. You may have to think outside the box, but projects that trace and study influence can shake things up.

Focus on its social connections.   In recent decades, many texts have been studied for what they reveal about relationships between genders, races, ethnicities, and social classes. Works by new writers are now more widely read in schools, and hard questions asked about texts traditionally taught: What do they reveal about the treatment of women or minorities? Whose lives have been ignored in dominant texts, or how are minorities or working classes represented? What responsibility do cultural texts have for maintaining repressive political or social arrangements? These critical approaches have changed how many people view literature and art, and you can follow up on such studies and extend them to texts you think deserve more attention. Such inquiries themselves, however, are as agenda driven as other kinds of analysis and so should also be subjected to the same critical scrutiny.

Find good sources.   Developing a literary paper provides you with many opportunities and choices. Fortunately, you needn't make all your decisions on your own. Ample commentary and research is available on almost any literary subject or method, both in print and online. ○ Your instructor and local librarians can help you focus on the best resources for your project, but the following box lists some possibilities.

refine your search
p. 406

Literary Resources in Print

Abrams, M. H., and Geoffrey Harpham. *A Glossary of Literary Terms*. 8th ed. New York: Heinle, 2004.

Beacham, Walton, ed. *Research Guide to Biography and Criticism*. Washington, DC: Research, 1986.

Crystal, David. *The Cambridge Encyclopedia of Language*. 2nd ed. New York: Cambridge UP, 1997.

Drabble, Margaret, ed. *The Oxford Companion to English Literature*. 6th ed. Oxford: Oxford UP, 2000.

Encyclopedia of World Literature in the 20th Century. 3rd ed. Farmington Hills, MI: St. James, 1999.

Gates, Henry Louis, Jr., et al. *The Norton Anthology of African American Literature*. New York: Norton, 1997.

Gilbert, Sandra M., and Susan Gubar. *The Norton Anthology of Literature by Women: The Traditions in English*. 2nd ed. New York: Norton, 1996.

Harmon, William, and Hugh Holman. *A Handbook to Literature*. 11th ed. New York: Prentice, 2008.

Harner, James L. *Literary Research Guide: A Guide to Reference Sources for the Study of Literature in English and Related Topics*. 4th ed. New York: MLA, 2002.

Hart, James D., ed. *The Oxford Companion to American Literature*. 6th ed. New York: Oxford UP, 1995.

Howatson, M. C. *The Oxford Companion to Classical Literature*. 2nd ed. New York: Oxford UP, 1989.

Leitch, Vincent, et al. *The Norton Anthology of Theory and Criticism*. New York: Norton, 2001.

Preminger, Alex, and T. V. F. Brogan, eds. *The New Princeton Encyclopedia of Poetry and Poetics*. Princeton: Princeton UP, 1993.

Sage, Lorna. *The Cambridge Guide to Women's Writing in English*. Cambridge: Cambridge UP, 1999.

Sampson, George. *The Concise Cambridge History of English Literature*. 3rd ed. Cambridge: Cambridge UP, 1972.

Literary Resources Online

Annotated Bibliography for English Studies (ABES) (http://routledgeabes.com)

Annual Bibliography of English Language and Literature (ABELL) (http://collections.chadwyck.com/home/home_abell.jsp)

Atlantic Unbound (http://www.theatlantic.com) (for book reviews)

The Complete Works of William Shakespeare (http://thetech.mit.edu/Shakespeare)

The English Server (http://eserver.org)

A Handbook of Rhetorical Devices (http://www.virtualsalt.com/rhetoric.htm)

Images: A Journal of Film and Popular Culture (http://www.imagesjournal.com/)

Internet Public Library: Literary Criticism (http://www.ipl.org/div/litcrit/)

Literary Resources on the Net (http://andromeda.rutgers.edu/~jlynch/Lit)

Literature Resource Center (Gale Group – by library subscription)

MIT Literature Resources (http://libraries.mit.edu/guides/subjects/literature/)

MLA on the Web (http://www.mla.org)

New York Review of Books (http://www.nybooks.com/)

New York Times Book Review (http://www.nytimes.com/pages/books)

The Online Books Page (http://digital.library.upenn.edu/books)

Browne Popular Culture Library (http://www.bgsu.edu/colleges/library/pcl)

University of Virginia Library Scholar's Lab (http://www2.lib.virginia.edu/scholarslab)

Voice of the Shuttle (http://vos.ucsb.edu/index.asp)

Yahoo! Arts: Humanities: Literature (http://www.yahoo.com/Arts/Humanities/Literature)

Creating a structure

The shape of your literary analysis evolves as you learn more about your topic and decide how to treat it. Your project takes on the character of a report if you're interested in sharing information or demonstrating a case. Or it becomes an argument if your thesis veers toward a controversial position. ○ Whatever its trajectory, give attention to certain features.

▶ organize
ideas

Focus on a particular observation, claim, or point.   Always have a point firmly in mind as you draft a project, whether you work with individual literary texts or more general cultural questions. Following are some examples of claims or points that literary analyses might explore.

STUDY OF THEME

In Bless Me, Ultima, the youngster Antonio has to find a way to reconcile his traditional values and mystical beliefs with Ultima's prediction that he will become a "man of learning."

CONTRAST OF GENRES

The movie version of Annie Proulx's short story "Brokeback Mountain" actually improves on the original work, making it more powerful, specific, and believable.

CULTURAL ANALYSIS

One likely impact of digital technology will be to eliminate the barriers between art, entertainment, and commerce – with books becoming films, films morphing into games, and games inspiring graphic art.

Imagine a structure.   Here are three simple forms a literary analysis might take, the first developing from a thesis stated early on, the second comparing two works to make a point, and the third building toward a conclusion rather than opening with a thesis. ○

Introduction leading to a **claim**

First supporting reason + textual **evidence**

Second supporting reason + textual **evidence**

Additional supporting reasons + textual **evidence**

Conclusion

understand
argument p. 68

develop a thesis
p. 336

Introduction leading to a **claim** about Texts 1 & 2

> First **supporting reason**

>> Evidence from Text 1

>> Evidence from Text 2

> Next **supporting reason**

>> Evidence from Text 1

>> Evidence from Text 2

> Additional **supporting reasons** . . .

>> Evidence from Text 1

>> Evidence from Text 2

Conclusion or **point**

Introduction presenting an **issue** or a **problem**

> First **point** or **connection**, leading to . . .

> Next **point** or **connection**, leading to . . .

> Next **point** or **connection**, leading to . . .

A **summary observation** or **point**

Work on your opening.   Be certain that your introductory sections provide background for your analysis and identify what works you may be examining, and what you hope to accomplish. ○ Provide enough context so that the project stands on its own and would make sense to someone other than the instructor who assigned it.

shape a beginning
p. 354

Choosing a style and design

As the student examples in this chapter suggest, the literary analyses you write for courses will typically be serious in tone, formal in vocabulary, and, for the most part, impersonal—all markers of a formal or high style. ○ Elements of that style can be identified in this paragraph from an academic paper in which Manasi Deshpande analyzes Emily Brontë's *Wuthering Heights*. Here she explores the character of its Byronic hero, Heathcliff:

Examines Heathcliff from the perspective of a potential reader, not from her own.

In witnessing Heathcliff's blatantly violent behavior, the reader is caught between sympathy for the tormented Heathcliff and shock at the intensity of his cruelty and mistreatment of others. Intent on avenging Hindley's treatment of him, Heathcliff turns his wrath toward Hareton by keeping him in such an uneducated and dependent state that young Cathy becomes "upset at the bare notion of relationship with such a clown" (193). Living

Complex sentences smoothly incorporate quotations and documentation.

first under Hindley's neglect and later under Heathcliff's wrath, Hareton escapes his situation only when Catherine befriends him and Heathcliff dies. In addition, Heathcliff marries Isabella only because Catherine wants to "'torture [him] to death for [her]

Related points are expressed in parallel clauses.

amusement'" and must "'allow [him] to amuse [himself] a little in the same style'"(111). Heathcliff's sole objective in seducing and running away with Isabella is to take revenge on Catherine for abandoning him. Heathcliff's sadism is so strong that he is willing to harm innocent third parties in order to punish those who have caused his misery. He even forces

Vocabulary throughout is accessible, but formal. No contractions.

young Cathy and Linton to marry by locking them in Wuthering Heights and keeping Cathy from her dying father until she has married Linton, further illustrating his willingness to torture others out of spite and vengeance.

Occasionally, you may be asked to write brief essays called *position papers*, in which you record your immediate reactions to poems, short stories, or other readings. ○ In these assignments, an instructor may expect to hear your voice and even encourage exploratory responses. Here is Cheryl Lovelady responding somewhat personally to a literary work in a proposal to revive the Broadway musical *Fiddler on the Roof*:

Question focuses paragraph. Reply suggests strong personal opinion.

How can a play set in a small, tradition-bound Jewish village during the Russian Revolution be modernized? I would argue that <u>Fiddler on the Roof</u> is actually an apt portrayal of our own time. Throughout the show, the conflicted main character, Tevye, is on the brink of pivotal decisions. Perplexed by his daughters' increasingly modern

define your style
p. 366

understand position
papers p. 260

choices, Tevye prays aloud, "Where do they think they are, America?" Tevye identifies America as a symbol of personal freedom––the antithesis of the tradition which keeps his life from being "as shaky as a fiddler on the roof." Forty years after the play's debut, America has become startlingly more like the Anatevka Tevye knows than the America he envisions. Post-9/11 America parallels Anatevka in a multitude of ways: political agendas ideologically separate the United States from most of the world; public safety and conventional wisdom are valued over individual freedoms; Americans have felt the shock of violence brought onto their own soil; minority groups are isolated or isolate themselves in closed communities; and societal taboos dictate whom people may marry.

Basic style remains serious and quite formal: Note series of roughly parallel clauses that follow colon.

A 1964 production of the musical *Fiddler on the Roof.*

Literary papers usually follow MLA documentation style. ○ Here are some guidelines that apply specifically to literary papers.

Describe action in the present tense.   In writing literary analyses, you'll be doing plenty of summarizing and paraphrasing. In most cases, when you narrate the events in a story or poem, set the action in the present tense.

cite in MLA
p. 437

Provide dates for authors and literary works.   The first time you name authors or artists in a paper, give their dates of birth and death in parentheses. Similarly, provide a year of publication or release date for any major work you mention in your analysis.

> Joan Didion (b. 1934) is the author of <u>Play It as It Lays</u> (1970), <u>Slouching Towards Bethlehem</u>
>
> (1968), and <u>The Year of Magical Thinking</u> (2005).

Use appropriate abbreviations.   An English or rhetoric major may want to own a copy of the *MLA Handbook for Writers of Research Papers* if for nothing more than its full chapter on abbreviations common in literary papers. Some of the abbreviations appear chiefly in notes and documentation; others make it easier to refer to very familiar texts; still others identify various parts and sections of literary works.

Follow conventions for quotations.   In a literary paper, you'll be frequently citing passages from novels, short stories, and poems as well as quoting the comments of critics. All of these items need to be appropriately introduced and, if necessary, modified to fit smoothly into your sentences and paragraphs. ○

Cite plays correctly.   Plays are cited by act, scene, and line number. In the past, passages from Shakespeare were routinely identified using a combination of roman and arabic numerals. But more recently, MLA recommends arabic numerals only for such references.

FORMER STYLE

Hamlet's final words are "The rest is silence" (<u>Ham</u>. V.ii.358).

CURRENT STYLE

Hamlet's final words are "The rest is silence" (<u>Ham</u>. 5.2.358).

use quotations
p. 431

Examining models

TEXTUAL ANALYSIS In "Insanity: Two Women," Kanaka Sathasivan examines a poem (Emily Dickinson's "I felt a Funeral, in My Brain") and a short story (Charlotte Perkins Gilman's "The Yellow Wallpaper") to discover a disturbing common theme in the work of these two American women writers. The essay, written in a formal academic style, uses a structure that examines the works individually, drawing comparisons in a final paragraph. Note, in particular, how Sathasivan manages the close reading of the poem by Emily Dickinson, moving through it almost line by line to draw out its themes and meanings. Here's the text of "I felt a Funeral, in my Brain."

> I felt a Funeral, in my Brain,
> And Mourners to and fro
> Kept treading – treading – till it seemed
> That Sense was breaking through –
>
> And when they all were seated,
> A Service, like a Drum –
> Kept beating – beating – till I thought
> My Mind was going numb–
>
> And then I heard them lift a Box
> And creak across my Soul
> With those same Boots of Lead, again,
> Then Space – began to toll,
>
> As all the Heavens were a Bell,
> And Being, but an Ear,
> And I, and Silence, some strange Race
> Wrecked, solitary, here –
>
> And then a Plank in Reason, broke,
> And I dropped down, and down –
> And hit a World, at every plunge,
> And Finished knowing – then –

You can find the full text of "The Yellow Wallpaper" searching online by the title. One such text is available at the University of Virginia Library Electronic Text Center: http://etext.virginia.edu/toc/modeng/public/GilYell.html.

Sathasivan 1

Kanaka Sathasivan

Instructor's Name

Course Title

Date

Insanity: Two Women

The societal expectations of women in the late nineteenth century served to keep women demure, submissive, and dumb. Although women's rights had begun to improve as more people rejected these stereotypes, many women remained trapped in their roles because of the pressures placed on them by men. Their suppression had deep impacts not only on their lives but also on their art as well. At a time when women writers often published under male aliases to gain respect, two of America's well-known authors, Emily Dickinson (1830-1886) and Charlotte Perkins Gilman (1860-1935), both wrote disturbing pieces describing the spiritual and mental imprisonment of women. In verse, Dickinson uses a funeral as a metaphor for the silencing of women and the insanity it subsequently causes. Gilman's prose piece "The Yellow Wallpaper" (1899) gives us a firsthand look into the mental degradation of a suppressed woman. These two works use vivid sensory images and rhythmic narration to describe sequential declines into madness.

In "I felt a Funeral, in My Brain" (first published 1896), Dickinson outlines the stages of a burial ceremony, using them as

Works to be analyzed are set in context: late nineteenth century.

Identifies authors and sets works in thematic relationship.

States thesis for the comparison.

Sathasivan 2

metaphors for a silenced woman's departure from sanity. The first
verse, the arrival of Mourners, symbolizes the imposition of men and
society on her mind. They are "treading" "to and fro," breaking
down her thoughts and principles, until even she is convinced of
their ideas (Dickinson 3, 2). The Service comes next, representing the
closure--the acceptance of fate. Her "Mind was going numb" as they
force her to stop thinking and begin accepting her doomed life. These
first two verses use repetition at parallel points as they describe the
Mourners "treading--treading" and the service like a drum is
"beating--beating" (Dickinson 3, 7). The repetition emphasizes the
incessant insistence of men; they try to control threatening women
with such vigor and persistence that eventually even the women
themselves begin to believe it and allow their minds to be silenced.

    As the funeral progresses, the Mourners carry her casket from
the service. Here Dickinson describes how they scar her very Soul
using the "same Boots of Lead" which destroyed her mind
(Dickinson 11). From the rest of the poem, one can infer that the
service took place inside a church, and the act of parting from a
house of God places another level of finality on the loss of her
spirituality. While the figures in the poem transport her, the church's
chimes begin to ring, and, as if "all the Heavens were a Bell / And
Being, but an Ear," the noise consumes her (Dickinson 13). In this
tremendous sound, her voice finally dissolves forever; her race with
Silence has ended, "wrecked," and Silence has won (Dickinson 16).
Finally, after the loss of her mind, her soul, and her voice, she loses
her sanity as they lower her casket into the grave and bury her. She
"hit a World, at every plunge, / And Finished knowing" (Dickinson
20). The worlds she hits represent further stages of psychosis, and

> Offers close
> reading of
> Dickinson's
> poem.

Sathasivan 3

she plunges deeper until she hits the bottom, completely broken.

Like Dickinson, Gilman in "The Yellow Wallpaper" also
segments her character's descent into madness. The narrator of the
story expresses her thoughts in a diary written while she takes a
vacation for her health. Each journal entry represents another step
toward insanity, and Gilman reveals the woman's psychosis with
subtle hints and clues placed discreetly within the entries. These
often take the form of new information about the yellow room the
woman has been confined to, such as the peeled wallpaper or bite
marks on the bedpost. The inconspicuous presentation of such
details leads the reader to think that these artifacts have long
existed, created by someone else, and only now does the narrator
share them with us. "I wonder how it was done and who did it, and
what they did it for," she says, speaking of a groove that follows the
perimeter of the walls. Here, Gilman reuses specific words at crucial
points in the narration to allude to the state of her character's
mental health. In this particular example, both the narrator and the
maid use the word "smooch" to describe, respectively, the groove in
the wall, and yellow smudges on the narrator's clothes. This
repetition indicates that she created the groove in the room, a fact
affirmed at the end of the story.

Gilman's narrator not only seems to believe other people have
caused the damage she sees but also imagines a woman lives
trapped within the paper, shaking the pattern in her attempts to
escape. "I think that woman gets out in the daytime!" the narrator
exclaims, recounting her memories of a woman "creeping" about
the garden (Gilman 400, 401). Again, Gilman uses repetition to make
associations for the reader as the narrator uses "creeping" to

---

With simple transition, turns to Gilman's short story.

Uses present tense to describe action in "The Yellow Wallpaper."

Sathasivan 4

describe her own exploits. As in the previous example, the end of
the story reveals that the woman in the paper is none other than the
narrator, tricked by her insanity. This connection also symbolizes the
narrator's oppression. The design of the wallpaper trapping the
woman represents the spiritual bars placed on the narrator by her
husband and doctor, who prescribes mental rest, forbidding her from
working or thinking. Even the description of the room lends itself to
the image of a dungeon or cell, with "barred" windows and "rings
and things in the walls" (Gilman 392). Just as the woman escapes
during the daytime, so too does the narrator, giving in to her
sickness and disobeying her husband by writing. Finally, like the
woman in the paper breaking free, the narrator succumbs to her
insanity.

Both Dickinson's and Gilman's works explore society's
influence on a woman's mental health. Like Dickinson's character,
Gilman's narrator has also been compelled into silence by a man.
Although she knows she is sick, her husband insists it isn't so and
that she, a fragile woman, simply needs to avoid intellectual
stimulation. Like a Mourner, "treading--treading," he continually
assures her he knows best and that she shouldn't socialize or work.
This advice, however, only leads to further degradation as her
solitude allows her to indulge her mental delusions. When the
narrator attempts to argue with her husband, she is silenced, losing
the same race as Dickinson's character.

In both these pieces, the characters remain mildly aware of their
declining mental health, but neither tries to fight it. In Dickinson's poem,
the woman passively observes her funeral, commenting objectively on
her suppression and burial. Dickinson uses sound to describe every

Draws attention to common themes and strategies in the two works.

Notes difference in technique between authors.

Sathasivan 5

step, creating the feel of secondary sensory images--images that cannot create a picture alone and require interpretation to do so. Gilman's narrator also talks of her sickness passively, showing her decline only by describing mental fatigue. In these moments she often comments that her husband "loves [her] very dearly" and she usually accepts the advice he offers (Gilman 396). Even on those rare occasions when she disagrees, she remains submissive and allows her suppression to continue. In contrast to Dickinson, Gilman uses visual images to create this portrait, describing most of all how the narrator sees the yellow wallpaper, an approach which allows insight into the narrator's mental state.

Both Dickinson and Gilman used their writing to make profound statements about the painful lives led by many women in the nineteenth century. Through repetition, metaphor, symbolism, and sensory images, both "I felt a Funeral, in My Brain" and "The Yellow Wallpaper" describe a woman's mental breakdown, as caused by societal expectations and oppression. The poetry and prose parallel one another and together give insight into a horrific picture of insanity.

Concludes that writers use similar techniques to explore a common theme in two very different works.

Sathasivan 6

Works Cited

Dickinson, Emily. "I felt a Funeral, in My Brain." Concise Anthology of American Literature. 5th ed. Ed. George McMichael. Upper Saddle River: Prentice, 2001. 1129.

Gilman, Charlotte Perkins. "The Yellow Wallpaper." The American Short Story and Its Writer, An Anthology. Ed. Ann Charters. Boston: Bedford, 2000. 391.

MLA documentation style used for in-text notes and Works Cited.

Liz Miller, a columnist for the popular literary Web site Bookslut, writes about the relationship between books and movies. In "Size Doesn't Matter" (January 2006), edited slightly here for length, Miller explores a general question about film adaptations by examining how one admired short story, Annie Proulx's "Brokeback Mountain," became a celebrated and successful film. Miller nicely walks a line between the personal tone of a blog entry and the serious perspectives of film criticism.

bookslut.com

Posted: January 2006
From: Liz Miller

Size Doesn't Matter: *Brokeback Mountain*

There's a real question when it comes to adaptations as to what length work adapts the best—mainly because there's no pattern to be found. Novels can lose their depth in the course of the condensing process, short stories are stretched to an airy thinness.

> Raises main issue: What length of literary work adapts best to a film script?

An Oprah Winfrey favorite is reduced to long lingering glances, filling in the space left by the passages of inner monologue. Conceptually interesting genre vignettes with weak story lines become the setup for sci-fi action spectaculars, their original resolutions tossed aside and replaced with an extra hour of fisticuffs and wry comebacks.

Recently, I've been reviewing material under consideration for film adaptation, and it's interesting to see how a small and slender book can pop with smart ideas and strong plotting and a much thicker tome will ultimately have less story than the first twenty minutes of *Hitch*. It doesn't surprise me, though, because of Annie Proulx's short story "Brokeback Mountain" and what it became with the guidance of director Ang Lee and writers Larry McMurtry and Diana Ossana. . . .

> Essay has a more personal tone and style than most academic literary analysis.

After reading the story the first time, it became clear that there was no reason why Ang Lee's adaptation shouldn't succeed, at

Provides synopsis of "Brokeback Mountain" to explain why original short story might work as a film.

Argues that movie trailer also provided evidence of successful adaptation.

Examines the two "texts" closely to appreciate adaptation of story to film.

least on a script level. Proulx's brusque prose details the passing of years with brevity and elegance—each intense emotion is given just enough breath to burst with life. The rough-spoken love story of Ennis Del Mar and Jack Twist, two men ultimately kept apart by fear, takes the possibilities promised by a vast expanse of western landscape and reveals how meaningless they are if left unpursued. It's a powerful piece of work. It is also a complete and thorough treatment for a movie.

Seeing the trailer after reading the short story a few more times, I began to suspect that maybe I wasn't the only one who saw that. Every story beat and every line of dialogue of the trailer were straight from the prose, including images that would make no sense to someone who hadn't read the story, like Heath Ledger clenching two button-down shirts to his chest. It was a good omen—a good omen that didn't disappoint.

When I tell people that the entire movie fit totally into Annie Proulx's fifteen pages of prose, they honestly don't believe me. But the passing of years that Proulx so deftly skims over are broadened, enriched by elegant montages, giving the lives of the characters greater detail without feeling out of place (mainly because everything Ang Lee shoots tends to feel a little bit like a montage). And scenes glossed over in the story are given considerable screen time: A casual, after-the-fact reference to a bruise on Jack's jaw, for example, becomes an intensely physical and silent moment between the two characters, something that a few paragraphs of description might have captured, but not nearly so elegantly as the film managed.

The film, for the record, is great across the board. Directing, cinematography, music, and most especially acting. That girl from *Dawson's Creek*! That guy from *10 Things I Hate about You*! That girl from *Princess Diaries*! And all of it simple, understated: in service of the story.

One of the reasons I've read the short story more than once is that I keep finding new details that I overlooked in previous readings—

Actors Heath
Ledger and
Jake Gyllenhaal
in the movie
*Brokeback
Mountain.*

little asides on Proulx's part that continually add to a deeper meaning. *Brokeback Mountain* is a movie made by people who read every word of the story every single day, wringing out its potential for drama like you'd wring out a soaked washcloth. The largest additions are in Jack Twist's passing of years, filling out details unexplored by the story's reliance on the Ennis POV,[1] but of those scenes only one—in which Jack stands up to his rich and domineering father-in-law at Thanksgiving—feels at all out of place.

And the sum of all this is a small love story with an epic feel: a critical favorite, an Oscar front-runner, and the only other film of 2005 that can challenge *Sin City* for the title of Year's Most Faithful Adaptation. A two-hour movie from a fifteen-page short story, with minimal addition.

Sometimes, with adaptations, you sometimes get to see a dull caterpillar transform into a beautiful butterfly, but most of the time you watch a beautiful caterpillar burst from the cocoon as a dull brown moth. *Brokeback* is the rarest of species—it emerged transformed, but still recognizable. Still just as gorgeous as before.

Just a little longer.

1. *POV:* Point of view.

Conclusion still has main point clearly in mind.

PHOTOGRAPHS AS LITERARY TEXTS   Photography attained its status as art in the twentieth century. Even documentary photographs not originally conceived as works of art became prized for their striking depictions of the human condition. Three artists recognized for such work are Dorothea Lange (1895–1965), Walker Evans (1903–1975), and Gordon Parks (1912–2006). During the Great Depression and subsequent years, they produced photographs for the Farm Security Administration (FSA) intended to record all aspects of American life. But their best portraits of people and places often reach beyond the immediate historical context, as the three images below and on pages 219–20 demonstrate. Note how these photographs present and frame their subjects, encouraging viewers to expand and interpret their meanings.

Dorothea Lange, "Jobless on Edge of Pea Field, Imperial Valley, California" (1937)

Walker Evans, "Burroughs Family Cabin, Hale County, Alabama" (1936)

Gordon Parks, "American Gothic" (1942)

Assignments

1. **Textual Analysis:** Study Melissa Miller's "Distinguishing the *Other* in Two Works by Tolstoy" (p. 189). Then examine how a favorite author or filmmaker treats a specific age, gender, ethnic, professional, or political group in a short story, novel, or film. Help readers see a pattern that they (or you) may not have noticed before. If it helps, examine several works by a single artist.

2. **Textual Analysis:** In "Insanity: Two Women" (p. 210) Kanaka Sathasivan does a close analysis of Emily Dickinson's "I felt a Funeral, in My Brain." Do a similar close reading of a favorite short poem. Tease out all the meanings and strategies you can uncover and show readers how the poem works. Alternatively, apply this kind of reading to song lyrics.

3. **Comparing Genres:** Choose a favorite short story and explain why a film adaptation of it would or would not be successful. See Liz Miller's "Size Doesn't Matter: *Brokeback Mountain*" (p. 215) for ideas about what to pay attention to in moving from a literary tale to a visual story.

4. **Analysis of Three Photographs:** Photographers Dorothea Lange, Walker Evans, and Gordon Parks (pp. 218–20) recorded images documenting the long-term effects of the Great Depression. In a short paper, describe the specific scenes you would photograph today if you hoped to leave as important a documentary legacy as Lange, Evans, and Parks. To make the project manageable, focus on your local community. Showcase your own images in a photoessay.

5. **Cultural Analysis:** Compare two literary works in one genre written at least a half-century apart, such as two tragedies, two sonnets, two short stories, two mystery novels. Support your claims with textual evidence.

6. **Cultural Analysis:** Examine several recent works of literature, art, or popular culture that reflect what you find to be an important trend or attitude in society. You may detect, for example, common themes in films, TV series, novels, dance, or even video games. Show how the trend crosses genres or changes how people think or behave.

How to start

- Need to **find a text to analyze**? See page 228.
- Need to come up with **ideas**? See page 230.
- Need to **organize your ideas**? See page 233.

8 Rhetorical Analysis

examines in detail the way texts work

Rhetorical analyses foster the kind of close reading that makes writers better thinkers. Moreover, they're everywhere in daily life, especially in politics and law. In fact, they're hard to avoid.

- An editorial in the college paper calls for yet another fee to support a get-out-the-vote initiative on campus. You respond with an op-ed of your own, pointing out the editor's factual errors and logical inconsistencies.

- As part of a course evaluation, you argue that the assigned history textbook inappropriately endorses a particular interpretation of contemporary European history rather than just stating facts and leaving it for readers to make judgments.

- In your blog, you post a paragraph-by-paragraph refutation of a review published by the *Los Angeles Times* of your favorite band's latest CD. You point to ample textual evidence that the reviewer is neither well-informed nor objective.

- You're pretty sure global warming is the real deal, but you find yourself wishing that news reporters wouldn't blame every spring tornado and summer thunderstorm on the phenomenon.

UNDERSTANDING RHETORICAL ANALYSIS.   You react to what others
say or write all the time. Sometimes an advertisement, speech, or maybe a
political anthem grabs you so hard that you want to take it apart to see how it
works. Put those discoveries into words and you've composed a *rhetorical analysis*.

Rhetoric is the art of using language and media to achieve particular
goals. A rhetorical analysis is an argument that takes a close look at the
strategies of persuasion within a text; it lists and describes specific techniques

"Sun Mad Raisins"
This reworking of the
familiar Sun-Maid
Raisin box by artist
Esther Hernandez
provides plentiful
material for a
rhetorical analysis.
Sun Mad © 1981 Esther
Hernandez.

that a writer, speaker, editor, or advertiser has employed and then assesses their effectiveness. ○ You can take a rhetorical analysis one step further and respond to a particular argument by offering good reasons for agreeing or disagreeing with it. Such a detailed critique of a text is sometimes called a *critical analysis*.

When you write a rhetorical analysis, you'll do the following things.

Take words seriously.   When you compose an analysis, whether admiring or critical, hold writers to a high standard because their ideas may have consequences. Good notions deserve to be identified and applauded. And bad ones should be ferreted out, exposed, and sent packing. Learning to discern one from the other takes practice—which is what rhetorical analyses provide.

Make strong claims about texts.   Of course, you cannot make claims about texts until you know them inside out. The need for close examination may seem self-evident, but we blow through most of what we read (and see) without much thought. Serious critical or rhetorical analysis does just the opposite: It makes texts move like bullets in the movie *The Matrix,* their trajectories slowed and every motion magnified for careful study. ○

Mine texts for evidence.   Not only should you read texts closely in preparing a rhetorical analysis: Use their words (and any other elements) as the evidence for your own claims. That's one of the goals of critical examinations of this sort: to find and cite what other readers of a text may have missed. Expect to use a lot of quotations in a rhetorical analysis. ○

understand argument
p. 68

read closely
p. 317

use quotations
p. 431

This polished and highly entertaining critical analysis is from the "Ad Report Card" series on Slate.com. Seth Stevenson goes after the famous Apple ad campaign comparing Macs and PCs, explaining how it misreads an important audience segment, and gets its facts wrong, too. Notice the personal point of view in this piece: Stevenson has no qualms about using his own experiences as grounds for dissing the ads. He explains exactly why.

Slate.com

Posted: Monday, June 19, 2006, at 6:29 A.M. E.T.
From: Seth Stevenson

Ad Report Card: Mac Attack

Apple's mean-spirited new ad campaign

The Spot: *Two men stand side by side in front of a featureless, white background. "Hello, I'm a Mac," says the guy on the right (who is much younger and dressed in jeans). "And I'm a PC," says the guy on the left (who wears dorky glasses, ill-fitting khakis, and a jacket and tie). The two men discuss the many advantages of using a Mac and seem to agree that Macs are "better" than PCs.*

When I write about ads, I often face an obstacle: I'm not in the target demographic. Am I really in a position to judge whether, say, a Lexus ad is on the mark? The chances that I (driver of a 1996 Saturn with 105,000 miles on it) will buy a luxury sedan are essentially nil. Likewise, who am I to say if those adult-diaper spots are winning mindshare with senior citizens? Incontinence is a health issue that has (knock on wood) not yet hit my radar screen.

In the case of these Mac ads, however, I'm smack in the middle of the target demo. I'm a PC user, and I've often considered switching to an Apple. Thus, I feel equipped to say: These ads don't work on me. They are conceptually brilliant, beautifully

Articles in this series open by describing text to be analyzed.

Written in a middle style, colloquial and personal: Who am I to say.

Explains why he is qualified to assess Mac ads.

executed, and highly entertaining. But they don't make me want to buy a Mac.

Let's talk about the good news first. Directed by Phil Morrison (who also directed *Junebug*—my favorite film last year—and the recent VW ads featuring shocking car crashes), the campaign is a marvel of clarity and simplicity. No slogans. No video effects. No voice-overs. And lots of clean, white space. It's like a bath of cool mineral water when these ads come on after a string of garish, jam-packed spots for other products. (This bare-bones look is right in tune with Apple's consistently stripped-down marketing approach. To understand what makes Apple's aesthetic stand apart, check out this joke video—actually created by Microsoft employees—that envisions what might happen if Microsoft redesigned the iPod's packaging.)

My problem with these ads begins with the casting. As the Mac character, Justin Long (who was in the forgettable movie *Dodgeball* and the forgettabler TV show *Ed*) is just the sort of unshaven, hoodie-wearing, hands-in-pockets hipster we've always imagined when picturing a Mac enthusiast. He's perfect. *Too* perfect. It's like Apple is parodying its own image while also cementing it. If the idea was to reach out to new types of consumers (the kind who aren't already evangelizing for Macs), they ought to have used a different type of actor.

Meanwhile, the PC is played by John Hodgman—contributor to *The Daily Show* and *This American Life,* host of an amusing lecture series, and all-around dry-wit extraordinaire. Even as he plays the chump in these Apple spots, his humor and likability are evident. (Look at that hilariously perfect pratfall he pulls off in the spot titled "Viruses.") The ads pose a seemingly obvious question—Would you rather be the laid-back young dude or the portly old dweeb?—but I found myself consistently giving the "wrong" answer: I'd much sooner associate myself with Hodgman than with Long.

Lists rhetorical strategies that make ads attractive to viewers.

Examines comparison at heart of ad's strategy: cool Mac dude vs. PC dweeb.

Explains why key rhetorical strategy in ad fails.

The writing may have something to do with this, too. Hodgman gets all the laugh lines! And Mr. Mac comes off as a smug little twit, who (in the spot titled "WSJ") just happens to carry around a newspaper that has a great review of himself inside. (Even Norman Mailer usually refrains from such crassness.)

The final straw, for me, is that the spots make unconvincing claims. The one titled "Network" has a funny bit where "that new digital camera from Japan" is represented by a Japanese woman in a minidress. While Hodgman has trouble talking with the woman, Long speaks Japanese and shares giggles with her because "everything just kind of works with a Mac." Now, I happen to have a digital camera from Japan, and it works just fine with my PC. It did from the moment I connected it. Similarly, the spot titled "Out of the Box" (again, a very funny visual metaphor, with Hodgman and Long crouching in cardboard boxes) suggests that new PCs require tons of attention and alteration when you first fire them up. But I bought a new ThinkPad notebook just a few months ago, and it ran on all cylinders pretty much straight out of the gate. Why insult my intelligence by telling me something that I know isn't true?

> Earns credibility by qualifying his own argument.

I suppose the answer is that some people don't know yet. I can see how these ads might be effective with inexperienced computer users. If you're a first-time buyer, the idea that a Mac will make your life immeasurably easier sure does sound appealing. But if you're a PC user, these ads are more likely to irritate you than convert you.

Grade: C+. As usual, Apple hopes to shift the debate away from a battle over specs and value and toward a battle we can all understand: cool kid versus nerd. But these days, aren't nerds like John Hodgman the new cool kids? And isn't smug superiority (no matter how affable and casually dressed) a bit off-putting as a brand strategy?

> Most rhetorical analyses don't include grades, but conclusion is specific and biting.

Exploring purpose and topic

Make a difference. Done right, rhetorical analyses can be as important as the texts they examine. They may change readers' opinions or keep an important argument going. They may also uncover rhetorical strategies and techniques worth imitating or avoiding.

When you write an angry letter to the editor complaining about bias in the news coverage, you don't fret much about defining a purpose or topic—they are given. But when responding to a course assignment and particularly when you can choose a text to analyze rhetorically, you've got to establish the boundaries. Given a choice, select a text to analyze with the following characteristics.

▶ find a text

Choose a text you can work with. Find a gutsy piece that makes a claim you or someone else might actually disagree with. It helps if you have a stake in the issue and already know something about it. The text should also be of a manageable length that you can explore coherently within the limits of the assignment.

Choose a text you can learn more about. Some items won't make much sense out of context. So choose a text that you can research. ○ It will obviously help to know when it was written or published, by whom, and where it first appeared. This information is just as important for visual texts, such as posters and advertisements, as for traditional speeches or articles.

Need help deciding what to write about? See "How to Browse for Ideas" on pp. 312–13.

Choose a text with handles. Investigate arguments that do interesting things. Maybe a speech uses lots of anecdotes or repetition to generate emotional appeals; perhaps a photoessay's commentary is more provocative than the images; or an ad arrests attention by its simplicity but is still full of cultural significance. You've got to write about the piece. Make sure it offers you interesting things to say.

Choose a text you know how to analyze. Stick to printed texts if you aren't sure how to write about ads or films or even speeches. But don't sell yourself short. You don't need highly technical terms to describe poor logic, inept design, or offensive strategies, no matter where they appear. ○ And you can pick up the necessary vocabulary by reading models of rhetorical and critical analysis.

find a topic
p. 308

design your work
p. 517

Understanding your audience

Some published rhetorical analyses are written to ready-made audiences already inclined to agree with the authors. Riled up by an offensive editorial or a controversial ad campaign, people these days, especially on the Web, may even seek and enjoy mean-spirited, over-the-top criticism. But the rhetorical and critical analyses you write for class should be relatively restrained because you won't be able to predict how your readers might feel about the arguments you are examining. So assume that you are writing for a diverse and thoughtful audience, full of readers who prefer reflective analysis to clever put-downs. You don't have to be dull or passionless. Just avoid the easy slide into rudeness. ○

bodybymilk.com

Mind by Masi.
Body by milk.

My hero? Think hard.
It's milk. Some studies suggest
teens who choose it instead
of sugary drinks tend to
be leaner, plus the protein
helps build muscle.
So grab a glass. Then you can
change the future, too.

got milk?

"got milk?" Advertisements in this famous series lend themselves to rhetorical analysis because they are so carefully designed for specific audiences, in this case fans of Masi Oka from the TV series *Heroes*. The character he plays on the show is able to manipulate time.

respect your readers
p. 374

Finding and developing materials

▶ ideas

Before you analyze a text of any kind, do some background research. ○ Discover what you can about its author, creator, publisher, sponsor, and so on. For example, it may be important to know that the TV commercial you want to understand better has aired only on sports networks or lifestyle programs on cable. Become familiar, too, with the contexts in which an argument occurs. If you reply to a *Wall Street Journal* editorial, know what news or events sparked that item and investigate the paper's editorial slant.

Read the piece carefully just for information first, highlighting names or allusions you don't recognize. Then look them up: There's very little you can't uncover quickly these days via a Web search. When you think you understand the basics, you are prepared to approach the text rhetorically. Pay attention to any standout aspects of the text you're analyzing—perhaps how it wins over wary readers through conciliatory language or draws on the life experiences of its author to frame its subject. ○ You might look at any of the following elements.

Consider the topic or subject matter of the text.   What is novel or striking about the topic? How well-defined is it? Could it be clearer? Is it important? Relevant? Controversial? Is the subject covered comprehensively or selectively? What is the level of detail? Does the piece make a point?

Consider the audiences of the text.   To whom is the piece addressed? How is the text adapted to its audience? Who is excluded from the audience and how can you tell? What does the text offer its audience: information, controversy, entertainment? What does it expect from its audience?

Consider its author.   What is the author's relationship to the material? Is the writer or creator personally invested or distant? Is the author an expert, a knowledgeable amateur, or something else? What does the author hope to accomplish?

Consider its medium or language.   What is the medium or genre of the text: essay, article, editorial, advertisement, book excerpt, poster, video, podcast, and so on? How well does the medium suit the subject? How might

appraise your
resources p. 415

read critically
p. 317

the material look different in another medium? What is the level of the language: formal, informal, colloquial? ○ What is the tone of the text—logical, sarcastic, humorous, angry, condescending? How do the various elements of design—such as arrangement, color, fonts, images, white space, audio, video, and so on—work in the text?

Consider its occasion. Why was the text created? To what circumstances or situations does it respond, and what might the reactions to it be? What problems does it solve or create? What pleasure might it give? Who benefits from the text?

Consider its contexts. What purposes do texts of this type serve? Do texts of this sort have a history? Do they serve the interests of specific groups or classes? Have they evolved over time? Does the text represent a new genre?

Consider its use of rhetorical appeals. Persuasive texts are often analyzed according to how they use three types of rhetorical appeal. Typically, a text may establish the character and credibility of its author (*ethos*); generate emotions in order to move audiences (*pathos*); and use evidence and logic to make its case (*logos*).

Ethos—the appeal to character—may be the toughest argumentative strategy to understand. Every text and argument is presented by someone or something, whether an individual, a group, or an institution. Audiences are usually influenced and swayed by writers or speakers who present themselves as knowledgeable, honest, fair-minded, and even likable. Here, for example, Susan Estrich injects herself into a column she wrote about the governor of California to reinforce her own appealing sense of fair play.

> What Schwarzenegger has accomplished in the past eight months, substantively, is remarkable. I'm a lifelong Democrat who was asked to serve on the Schwarzenegger transition team. I did. He also put together a coalition of Democrats and Republicans.
>
> —"Schwarzenegger's California Formula: Bipartisanship + Civility = Progress," *USA Today*, May 27, 2004

define your style
p. 366

Pathos—the emotional appeal—is usually easy to detect. Look for ways that a text generates strong feelings to support its points or win over readers. The strategy is legitimate so long as an emotion fits the situation and doesn't manipulate audiences. For example, columnist Peggy Noonan routinely uses emotions to make her political points.

> We fought a war to free slaves. We sent millions of white men to battle and destroyed a portion of our nation to free millions of black men. What kind of nation does this? We went to Europe, fought, died, and won, and then taxed ourselves to save our enemies with the Marshall Plan. What kind of nation does this? Soviet communism stalked the world and we were the ones who steeled ourselves and taxed ourselves to stop it. Again: What kind of nation does this?
> Only a very great one.
>
> —"Patriots, Then and Now," *Wall Street Journal*, March 30, 2006

Logos—the appeal to reason and evidence—is most favored in academic texts. Look carefully at the claims a text offers and whether they are supported by facts, data, testimony, and good reasons. What assumptions lie beneath the argument? Ask questions about evidence too. Does it come from reliable sources or valid research? Is it up-to-date? Has it been reported accurately and fully? Has due attention been given to alternative points of view and explanations? Has enough evidence been offered to make a valid point?

Creating a structure

In a rhetorical analysis, you'll make a statement about how well the argumentative strategy of a piece works. Don't expect to come up with a thesis immediately or easily: You need to study a speech, editorial, or advertisement closely to figure out how it works and then think about its strengths and weaknesses. Draft a tentative thesis (or hypothesis) and then refine your words throughout the process of writing until they assert a claim you can prove. ○

organize ◀ ideas

Look for a complex and interesting thesis; don't just list some rhetorical features: *This ad has some good logical arguments and uses emotions and rhetorical questions.* Why would someone want to read (or write) a paper with such an empty claim? The following yields a far more interesting rhetorical analysis:

> The latest government antidrug posters offer good reasons for avoiding steroids but do it in a visual style so closely resembling typical health posters that most students will just ignore them.

Develop a structure.   Once you have a thesis or hypothesis, try sketching a design based on a thesis / supporting reason / evidence plan. Focus on those features of the text that illustrate the points you wish to make. You don't have to discuss every facet of the text.

Introduction leading to a **claim**

   First supporting reason + textual **evidence**

   Second supporting reason + textual **evidence**

   Additional supporting reasons + textual **evidence**

Conclusion

Under some circumstances, you might perform what amounts to a line-by-line or paragraph-by-paragraph deconstruction of a text. This structure—though not yet common in classrooms—shows up frequently online. Such analyses practically organize themselves, but your commentary must be smart, factually accurate, and stylish to keep readers on board.

develop a thesis
p. 336

Introduction leading to a **claim**

  First section/paragraph + detailed **analysis**

  Next section/paragraph + detailed **analysis**

  Additional section/paragraph + detailed **analysis**

Conclusion

In this example, political blogger Hugh Hewitt responds paragraph-by-paragraph to a letter from *New York Times* executive editor Bill Keller (June 25, 2006) justifying his newspaper's decision to reveal a top-secret antiterrorist spy program. Keller's remarks are below, followed immediately by Hewitt's critical analysis in italics.

Most Americans seem to support extraordinary measures in defense against this extraordinary threat, but some officials who have been involved in these programs have spoken to the *Times* about their discomfort over the legality of the government's actions and over the adequacy of oversight. We believe the *Times* and others in the press have served the public interest by accurately reporting on these programs so that the public can have an informed view of them.

Without disclosing the officials, we cannot be certain of their rank, their rancor, and their other agendas. We only know they are willing to break the law and their oaths. Mr. Keller's refusal to acknowledge this basic problem is more evidence of the deep dishonesty of his letter. He again asserts a "public interest" that is not his to judge as against the laws passed by Congress, signed by presidents and interpreted by courts. But he doesn't argue why his judgment in this matter trumps that of the government and the people's elected representatives.

Choosing a style and design

The style of your textual analyses will vary depending on audience, but you always face one problem that can sometimes be helped by design: making the text you are analyzing more accessible to readers.

Consider a high style.   Rhetorical and critical analyses you write in school will usually be formal and use a "high" style. ○ Your tone should be respectful, your vocabulary as technical as the material requires, and your perspective impersonal—avoiding *I* and *you*. Such a style gives the impression of objectivity and seriousness. Unless an instructor gives you more leeway, use a formal style for critical analyses.

Consider a middle style.   Oddly, rhetorical and critical analyses appearing in the public arena—rather than in the classroom—will usually be less formal and exploit the connection with readers that a middle style encourages. While still serious, such a style gives writers more options for expressing strong opinions and feelings (sometimes including anger, outrage, and contempt). In much public writing, you can detect a personal voice offering an opinion or advancing an agenda.

Make the text accessible to readers.   A special challenge in any rhetorical analysis is to help readers understand the text you are scrutinizing. At a minimum, furnish basic information about the author, title, place of publication, and date, and briefly explain the context of the work.

When possible, also attach a photocopy of the article directly to your analysis or include a link to it if you are working online. But your analysis should still be written *as if readers do not have that text in hand*. One way to achieve that clarity is to summarize and quote selectively from the text as you examine it. You can see examples of this technique in Matthew James Nance's essay on pages 236–40.

Annotate the text.   When analyzing an image or a text available in digital form, consider attaching your comments directly to the item. Do this by simply inserting a copy of the image or article directly into your project and then using the design tools of your word processor to create annotations.

This poster appears on the Web site of the Navy Environmental Health Center. Does that fact about its context change its message in any way?

define your style
p. 366

Examining models

ANALYSIS OF AN ARGUMENT For a class assignment on rhetorical analysis, Matthew James Nance chose as his subject the award-winning feature article "Can't Die for Trying" by journalist Laura Miller — who later would serve as mayor of Dallas. In the essay, Nance explains in detail how Miller manages to present the story of a convicted killer who wants to be executed to readers who might have contrary views about capital punishment. Nance's analysis is both technical and objective. He does an especially good job helping readers follow the argument of "Can't Die for Trying," a fairly long and complicated article.

Nance 1

Matthew James Nance

Instructor's Name

Course Title

Date

A Mockery of Justice

In 1987, David Martin Long was convicted of double homicide and sentenced to death. He made no attempt to appeal this sentence, and surprisingly, did everything he could to expedite his execution. Nonetheless, due to an automatic appeals process, Long remained on Texas's Death Row for twelve years before he was finally executed. For various reasons, including investigations into whether he was mentally ill, the state of Texas had continued to postpone his execution date. In 1994, when David Long was still in the middle of his appeals process, Dallas Observer columnist Laura Miller took up his case in the award-winning article "Can't Die for Trying." In this article, Miller explores the enigma of a legal system in which a sociopath willing to die continues to be mired in the legal process. The article is no typical plea on behalf of a death-row inmate, and Miller manages to avoid a facile political stance on capital punishment. Instead, Miller uses an effective combination

> Sets scene carefully and provides necessary background information.

> Miller defies expectations and Nance explains why in his thesis.

Nance 2

of logical reasoning and emotional appeal to evoke from readers a
sense of frustration at the system's absurdity.

To show that David Martin Long's execution should be
carried out as soon as possible, Miller offers a reasoned argument
based on two premises: that he wants death and that he deserves
it. Miller cites Long's statement from the day he was arrested: "I
realize what I did was wrong. I don't belong in this society. I never
have. . . . I'd just wish they'd hurry up and get this over with" (5).
She emphasizes that this desire has not changed, by quoting Long's
correspondence from 1988, 1991, and 1992. In this way, Miller
makes Long's argument seem reasoned and well thought out, not
simply a temporary gesture of desperation. "Yes, there are innocent
men here, retarded men, insane men, and men who just plain
deserve another chance," Long wrote [State District Judge Larry]
Baraka in April 1992, "But I am none of these!" (5). Miller also
points out his guilty plea, and the jury's remarkably short deliberation: "The jury took only an hour to find Long guilty of capital
murder--and 45 minutes to give him the death penalty" (5). Miller
does not stop there, however. She gives a grisly description of the
murders themselves, followed by Long's calculated behavior in the
aftermath:

> He hacked away at Laura twenty-one times before going
> back inside where he gave Donna fourteen chops. The
> blind woman, who lay in bed screaming while he savaged
> Donna, got five chops. Long washed the hatchet, stuck it
> in the kitchen sink, and headed out of town in Donna's
> brown station wagon. (5)

Long paragraph furnishes detailed evidence for Miller's two premises.

Provides both summaries and quotations from article so that readers can follow Miller's argument.

Nance 3

Miller's juxtaposition of reasoned deliberation with the bloody
narrative of the murders allows her to show that Long, in refusing to
appeal, is reacting justly to his own sociopathy. Not only is it right
that he die; it is also right that he does not object to his death.

In the midst of this reasoned argument, Miller expresses
frustration at the bureaucratic inefficiency that is at odds with her
logic. She offers a pragmatic, resource-based view of the situation:

> Of course, in the handful of instances where a person is
> wrongly accused . . . this [death-penalty activism] is
> noble, important work. But I would argue that in
> others--David Martin Long in particular--it is a sheer
> waste of taxpayer dollars. And a mockery of justice. (6)

To clarify
Miller's point,
Nance adds
phrase in
brackets to
quotation.

Miller portrays the system as being practically incompatible
with her brand of pragmatism. The figures involved in Long's case are
painted as invisible, equivocal, or both. For instance, in spite of Long's
plea, Judge Baraka was forced to appoint one of Long's attorneys to
start the appeals process. "The judge didn't have a choice. Texas law
requires that a death-penalty verdict be automatically appealed. . . .
[This] is supposed to expedite the process. But the court sat on
Long's case for four long years" (5). Miller also mentions Danny Burn,
a Fort Worth lawyer in association with the Texas Resource Center,
one of the "do-good . . . organizations whose sole feverish purpose is
to get people off Death Row. . . . No matter how airtight the cases"
(6). Burn filed on Long's behalf, though he never met Long in person.
This fact underscores Miller's notion of the death-row bureaucracy as
being inaccessible, and by extension, incomprehensible.

This parade of equivocal incompetence culminates in Miller's

Notice how
smoothly
quotations
merge into
Nance's
sentences.

Nance 4

interview with John Blume, another activist who argued on Long's behalf. Miller paints Blume as so equivocal that he comes across as a straw man. "As a general rule," says Blume, "I tend to think most people who are telling you that are telling you something else, and that's their way of expressing it. There's something else they're depressed or upset about" (6). The article ends with Miller's rejoinder: "Well, I'd wager, Mr. Blume, that something is a lawyer like you" (6). Whereas the article up to this point has maintained a balance between reason and frustration, here, Miller seems to let gradually building frustration get the best of her. She does not adequately address whether Blume might be correct in implying that Long is insane, mentally ill, or otherwise misguided. She attempts to dismiss this idea by repeatedly pointing out Long's consistency in his stance and his own statements that he is not retarded, but her fallacy is obvious: Consistency does not imply sanity. Clearly, Miller would have benefited from citing Long's medical history and comparing his case with those of other death-row inmates, both mentally ill and well. Then her frustrated attack on Blume would seem more justified.

Miller also evokes frustration through her empathetic portrayal of Long. Although the article is essentially a plea for Long to get what he wants, this same fact prevents Miller from portraying Long sympathetically. Miller is stuck in a rhetorical bind; if her readers become sympathetic toward Long, they won't want him to die. However, the audience needs an emotional connection with Long to accept the argument on his behalf. Miller gets around this problem by abandoning sympathy altogether, portraying Long as a cold-blooded killer. The quotation "I've never seen a more cold-blooded, steel-eyed sociopath ever" (5) is set apart from

Nance makes a clear judgment about Miller's objectivity— then offers evidence for his claim.

Nance examines the way Miller deals with the problem she has portraying a cold-blooded killer to readers.

the text in a large font, and Miller notes that "This is a case of a really bad dude, plain and simple. . . . Use any cliché you want. It fits"(5). Miller here opts for a weak appeal; evoking from the audience the same negative emotion that Long feels. She gives voice to Long's frustration over his interminable appeals: "Long stewed. . . . Long steamed. . . . Long fumes. . . ." (6). She also points out Long's fear of himself: "I fear I'll kill again" (6). Clearly, the audience is meant to echo these feelings of frustration and fear. This may seem like a weak emotional connection with Long, but perhaps it is the best Miller could do, given that a primary goal of hers was to show that Long deserves death.

Laura Miller won the H. L. Mencken Award for this article, which raises important questions about the legal process. Part of its appeal is that it approaches capital punishment without taking a simplistic position. It can appeal to people on both sides of the capital punishment debate. The argument is logically valid, and for the most part, the emotional appeal is effective. Its deficiencies, including the weak emotional appeal for Long, are ultimately outweighed by Miller's overarching rationale, which calls for pragmatism in the face of absurdity.

Work Cited

Miller, Laura. "Can't Die for Trying." Dallas Observer 12 Jan. 1994: 5-6.

ANALYSIS OF TWO FILM TRAILERS Ryan Hailey examines the way a movie studio has adjusted a trailer for a blockbuster film to appeal to two different and equally important markets. Those markets, of course, represent the rhetorical concept of "audience."

Hailey 1

Ryan Hailey

Instructor's Name

Course Title

Date

The Die Hard Trailer:

American Version vs. International Version

An unspoken and intangible contract between movie audiences and movie studios is made when viewers watch previews of coming attractions. Audiences know the movie studios have tailored and often manipulated the preview to appeal to the broadest possible demographic, yet the audience still uses the strength of the trailer to decide whether to see the movie. However, most people don't realize how tailored these previews are until they examine the way studios try to persuade different cultures to see the same movie. This summer, 20th Century Fox will release Live Free or Die Hard, or, as it is called in the rest of the world, Die Hard 4.0. Although both the American and international versions of the fourth trailer highlight the film's action, the two trailers are otherwise vastly different. Specifically, the American trailer is characterized by blatant American patriotic themes while the international version makes the film out to be a standard, over-the-top action movie.

"I'm doing America a favor," says a character at the start of the American trailer, presumably a villain. The screen cuts to a shot of the front lawn of the U.S. Capitol in Washington with the

Hailey offers thesis for analysis of movie trailers.

Hailey contrasts the way American and international trailers open.

Hailey 2

American flag waving gracefully in front. While quick shots of various characters loading weapons flash on screen, the bad guy finishes his sentence. "Is the country ready to pay for it?" So in the first twenty seconds of the American trailer, the audience knows the film takes place in the United States. American audiences are immediately given a theme they can relate to and thus are enticed to learn more about the film.

The international trailer for the fourth Die Hard begins with flashy graphics, reminiscent of random surveillance cameras, and this tag superimposed on top of it: "The entire world relies on technology . . . But even technology . . . can be taken hostage." The screen then flashes to a police car flying off a ramp and into a helicopter, spawning a massive and fiery explosion. This collision sets the tone for the rest of the two-minute-and-three-second trailer that's filled with no less than six explosions, seven shoot-outs, four car chases, and two fistfights. The stark contrast between these two beginnings is obvious. The American version sets the trailer up with an ambiguous question about America while the international version opens with a vague scenario that the entire international community can relate to. Hollywood movie studios usually make only a domestic (U.S.) trailer and one trailer to serve the rest of the world. This is why the international trailer has to be so broad in scope that any country could connect with its meaning, and hence the "The entire world relies on technology . . . " tagline. It's useful to note that the theme of terrorism is prevalent in both trailers since, today, everyone in the world can relate to it.

How Bruce Willis and his character John McClane are used in each trailer similarly demonstrates how the studio was trying to persuade American and international audiences differently to see

Using middle style enables Hailey to shift between lighter details and more serious points.

Examines second difference between trailers, focusing on the name *John McClane.*

Hailey 3

the movie. With the premiere of the original <u>Die Hard</u> in 1988, Bruce Willis was catapulted to both domestic and international stardom, becoming one of the most profitable film actors alive today. Both trailers build anticipation about who is going to be the hero in the film--and the payoff is a close-up of Bruce Willis. Since Willis is popular around the world, 20th Century Fox no doubt believes that his image will excite any moviegoer. However, the name of Bruce Willis's famous character in the <u>Die Hard</u> franchise, John McClane, is not mentioned in the international trailer, yet it <u>is</u> used in the American clip. In the international community the presence of Bruce Willis in the movie probably overshadows the fact that he's in a <u>Die Hard</u> film. But in America, John McClane has earned a special place in its pop culture as one of the greatest action characters of all time in one of the greatest action movies of all time. While <u>Die Hard</u> was a megahit worldwide, one could argue that it started a revolution in America and virtually redefined the American action movie. Americans see Bruce Willis in multiple movies every year, but it's not every day that they get to see Bruce Willis don the John McClane character. Although international audiences may see Bruce Willis as "that guy in cool action movies," the name <u>John McClane</u> doesn't immediately pull a delightful trigger in the minds of international audiences as it does for American audiences.

The most interesting distinction between the American and international trailers for the new <u>Die Hard</u> movie is the different names the film is given. In America the film will be called <u>Live Free or Die Hard</u>. Internationally, it will be called <u>Die Hard 4.0</u>. The American title is a play on "Live Free or Die," the state motto of New Hampshire. It is a slogan unique to America and, perhaps, the

Hailey examines why film has two titles.

Hailey 4

Western world. Imagine how foreign the concept of "live free or die" might be to a moviegoer in China or North Korea. While democracy may be spreading throughout the world, it is not widely accepted enough for 20th Century Fox to risk confusing potential ticket purchasers. That may be the reason for the title being changed internationally to Die Hard 4.0, a phrase that also reflects its technology-based plot. In contrast, the title Live Free or Die Hard is uncompromisingly American, aggressively asserting the American dream. It is a title that will surely appeal to many Americans. Taking advantage of the contemporary political climate, the studio is banking on the idea that Americans will come out in droves to watch John McClane kick the butts of terrorists threatening our American way of life of living free.

Since the American and international trailers for movies are shown only in their respective regions, most moviegoers never know that they are being specifically targeted and influenced into buying a ticket for the movies they see. While the movies might be exactly the same domestically as they are globally, the contents emphasized (or omitted) in promotional campaigns often have an extremely specific purpose and reflect how studios view the tastes of particular audiences. The people at 20th Century Fox clearly believe that American audiences are ready for John McClane to be their public defender against global terrorism in the movies this summer. But with the reputation of America dwindling in the international community, Fox doesn't think some moviegoers around the globe will particularly care to pay to see the United States of America be defended from terrorists. That's why the movie looks like just another action-packed, shoot-'em-up, Bruce Willis flick in the trailer that's shown everywhere but America.

ANALYSIS OF A CULTURAL TREND Andy Newman makes an odd visual phenomenon the subject of an essay that appeared in the *New York Times*. Like many rhetorical analyses, he begins with the question *Why?*

They're Soft and Cuddly, So Why Lash Them to the Front of a Truck?

Andy Newman

November 13, 2005

A bear with a prominent grease spot on his little beige nose spends his days wedged behind the bumper guard of an ironworker's pickup in the Gowanus section of Brooklyn. A fuzzy rabbit and a clown, garroted by a bungee cord, slump from the front of a Dodge van in Park Slope. Stewie, the evil baby from *Family Guy,* scowls from the grille of a Pepperidge Farm delivery truck in Brooklyn Heights, mold occasionally sprouting from his forehead.

All are soldiers in the tattered, scattered army of the stuffed: mostly discarded toys plucked from the trash and given new if punishing lives on the prows of large motor vehicles, their fluffy white guts flapping from burst seams and going gray in the soot-stream of a thousand exhaust pipes.

Grille-mounted stuffed animals form a compelling yet little-studied aspect of the urban streetscape, a traveling gallery of baldly transgressive public art. The time has come not just to praise them but to ask the big question. Why?

That is, why do a small percentage of trucks and vans have filthy plush toys lashed to their fronts, like prisoners at the mast? Are they someone's idea of a joke? Parking aids? Talismans against summonses?

Don't expect an easy answer.

Interviews with half a dozen truckers as well as folklorists, art histori-ans, and anthropologists revealed the grille-mounted plush toy to be a

Photo: James Estrin/© The New York Times/Redux.

product of a tangle of physical circumstance, proximate and indirect influence, ethnic tradition, occupational mindset, and Jungian[1] archetype.

Like all adornments, of course, the grille pet advertises something about its owner. The very act of decorating a truck indicates an openness on the driver's part, according to Dan DiVittorio, owner of D & N Services, a carting company in Queens, and of a garbage truck with a squishy red skull on the front.

"It has to do something with their character," said Mr. DiVittorio, twenty-seven. "I don't see anybody that wouldn't be a halfway decent person putting something on their truck."

But a truck can be aesthetically modified in a million ways: *Mom* in spiffy gold letters across the hood; mudflaps depicting top-heavy women; flames painted along the sides. Why use beat-up stuffed animals?

One prevalent theory among truckers is that chicks dig them.

Robert Marbury, an artist who photographed dozens of Manhattan bumper fauna for a project in 2000 (see urbanbeast.com/faq/strapped. html), said he had once asked a trash hauler why he had a family of three mismatched bears strapped to his rig.

"He said: 'Yo, man, I drive a garbage truck. How am I going to get the ladies to look at me?'" Mr. Marbury recalled.

---

1. Jungian: Psychiatrist Carl Jung (1875–1961) theorized that human beings' lives were lived according to innate forms, or archetypes.

Photo: Robert Stolarik/© The New York Times/Redux.

Mr. Marbury, who holds a degree in anthropology, added that the battered bear and his brethren had at least one foot in the vernacular cultures of Latin America, where the festive and the ghoulish enjoy a symbiotic relationship. Most of the drivers whose trucks he photographed were Hispanic, he said.

Monroe Denton, a lecturer in art history at the School of Visual Arts, traced the phenomenon's roots back to the figureheads that have animated bows of ships since the time of the pharaohs.

"There was some sort of heraldic device to deny the fact of this gigantic machine," he said. "You would have these humanizing forms, anthropomorphic forms—a device that both proclaims the identity of the machine and conceals it."

Whatever its origins, the grille-mounted cuddle object is found across the country. It has been spotted in Baltimore, Miami, Chicago, and other cities.

Mierle Laderman Ukeles, the artist in residence at New York City's Department of Sanitation, said that when she noticed the animals on garbagemen's trucks in the late 1970s, she "felt they were like these spirit creatures that were accompanying them on this endless journey in flux."

There are differences, though, between the dragon crowning a Viking ship—or, for that matter, the chrome bulldog guarding the hood of a Mack truck—and the scuzzy bunny bound to the bumper with rubber hose. The main one is that the grille-mounted stuffed animal is almost

How to start

● **Got a test tomorrow?**
Read exam questions carefully. See page 255.

9 Essay Examination

requires answers written within a time limit

Essay examinations test not only your knowledge of a subject but also your ability to write about it coherently and professionally.

- For a class in nursing, you must write a short essay about the role health-care providers play in dealing with patients who have been victims of domestic abuse.

- For an examination in a literature class, you must offer a close reading of a sonnet, explicating its argument and poetic images line by line.

- For a standardized test, you must read a passage by a critic of globalization and respond to the case made and evidence presented.

- For a psychology exam, you must explore the ethical issues raised by two research articles on brain research and the nature of consciousness.

UNDERSTANDING ESSAY EXAMS. You've probably taken enough essay exams to know that there are no magic bullets to slay this dragon, and that the best approach is to know your material well enough to make several credible points in an hour or so. You must also write—*under pressure*—coherent sentences and paragraphs. Here are some specific strategies to increase your odds of doing well.

Anticipate the types of questions you might be asked. What happens in class—the concepts presented, the issues raised, the assignments given—is like a coming-attractions trailer for an exam. If you attend class and do the required readings, you'll figure out at least some of an instructor's habitual moves and learn something to boot. Review any sample essay exams too—they may even be available on a course Web site.

got a test
tomorrow?

Read exam questions carefully. Underscore key words such as *divide, classify, evaluate, compare, compare and contrast,* and *analyze* and then respect the differences between these strategies. Exam questions may be short essays themselves, setting out background information or offering a passage to read before the actual query appears. Respond to that specific question and not to your own take on the preliminary materials.

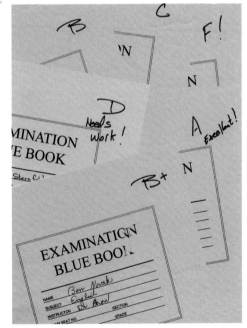

Sketch out a plan for your essay(s). The first part of the plan should deal with *time*. Read all the exam questions carefully and then estimate how many minutes to spend on each—understanding that some will take more effort than others. (Pay attention to point totals too: Focus on essay questions that count more, but don't ignore any. Five points is five points.) Allow time for planning and editing each answer. Sketch outlines and come up with a thesis for each question. ○ Then stick to your time limits.

Organize your answer strategically.   If any form of writing benefits from a pattern of development worn like an exoskeleton, it's a response to an essay question. In your first paragraph, state your main point and pre-view the structure of the whole essay. That way, even if you cannot finish, a reader will know where you were heading and possibly give you partial credit for incomplete work.

Offer strong evidence for your claims.   The overall structure of the essay should convey your grasp of concepts—your ability to see the big picture. Within that structure, arrange details and evidence to show your command of the subject. Use memorable examples culled from class reading to make your points: Cite important names, concepts, and dates; mention critical issues and terms; rattle off the titles of books and articles.

Come to a conclusion.   Even if you run short on time, find a moment to write a paragraph that brings your ideas together. Don't just repeat the topic sentences of your paragraphs. A reader will already have those ideas firmly in mind as he or she assesses your work. So add something new—an implication or extrapolation—to chew on.

Keep the tone serious.   Write essay examinations in a high or middle style. Avoid a personal point of view unless the question invites you to enter your opinion on a controversy. Given the press of time, you can probably get away with contractions and some standard abbreviations. But make sure the essay reads like prose, not a text message.

Don't panic.   Keep your eye on the clock, but *don't panic*. Everyone else is working under the same constraints and will be able to produce only so much prose in an hour or two. If you've prepared for the exam and start with a plan, you may find first-rate ideas materializing in the process of writing. Even if they don't, keep writing. You'll get no credit for blank pages.

develop a thesis
p. 336

Wade Lamb offered the following response to this essay question on a mid-term essay examination in a course entitled Classical to Modern Rhetoric:

> The structure of Plato's *Phaedrus* is dominated by three speeches about the lover and non-lover—one by Lysias (as read by Phaedrus) and two by Socrates. How do these speeches differ in their themes and strategies, and what point do they make about rhetoric and truth?

Lamb 1

Wade Lamb
Instructor's Name
Course Title
Date

Plato's Phaedrus is unique among Platonic dialogues because it takes place in a rural setting between only two characters--Socrates and the youth Phaedrus. It is, however, like Plato's Gorgias in that it is "based on a distinction between knowledge and belief" and focuses on some of the ways we can use rhetoric to seek the truth.

The first speech presented in Phaedrus, written by Lysias and read aloud by Phaedrus, is the simplest of the three. Composed by Lysias to demonstrate the power of rhetoric to persuade an audience, it claims perversely that it is better to have a relationship with a non-lover than with a lover.

Socrates responds with a speech of his own making the same point, which he composes on the spot and which he describes as "a greater lie than Lysias's." Unlike Lysias, however, Socrates begins by carefully defining his terms and organizes his speech more effectively. He does so to teach Phaedrus that in order to persuade an audience, an orator must first understand the subject and divide

Opening focuses directly on issues posed in question.

Short quotation functions as piece of evidence.

Sensibly organized around three speeches to be examined: one paragraph per speech.

Lamb 2

it into its appropriate parts. However, Socrates delivers this speech with a veil over his head because he knows that what he and Lysias have claimed about love is false.

Most important speech gets lengthiest and most detailed treatment.

The third speech--again made by Socrates--is the most important. In it, Socrates demonstrates that persuasion that leads merely to belief (not truth) damages both the orator and the audience. He likens rhetoric such as that used by Lysias to the unconcerned and harmful lust of a non-lover. Good rhetoric, on the other hand--which Socrates says is persuasion that leads to knowledge--is like the true lover who seeks to lead his beloved to transcendent truth. Socrates shows that he believes good rhetoric should ultimately be concerned with finding and teaching truth, not just with making a clever argument someone might believe, as Lysias's speech does.

Conclusion states Lamb's thesis, describing the point he believes Plato wished to make about rhetoric in *Phaedrus*.

By comparing the three speeches in the Phaedrus, Plato shows that he gives some value to rhetoric, but not in the form practiced by orators such as Lysias. Plato emphasizes the importance of the distinction between belief and knowledge and argues for a rhetoric that searches for and propagates the truth.

Getting the details right

Allow a few minutes near the end of the exam period to reread what you have written and insert corrections and emendations. You won't have time to fix large-scale issues: If you've confused the Spanish Armada with Torquemada, you're toast. But a quick edit may catch embarrassing gaffes or omissions. ○ When you write quickly, you probably leave out or transpose some words or simply use the wrong expression. Take a moment to edit these fixable errors. In the process, you may also amplify or repair an idea or two. Here are some other useful strategies to follow.

Use transition words and phrases. Essay examinations are the perfect place to employ such transparent transitional devices as *first, second,* and *third* or *next, even more important, nonetheless, in summary, in conclusion,* and so on. Don't be subtle: The transitions guide you as you write and help keep your instructor on track later. You will seem to be in control of your material.

Do a quick check of grammar, mechanics, and spelling. Some instructors take great offense at mechanical slips, even minor ones. At a minimum, avoid the common errors, covered in Part 9 of this book. Also be sure to spell correctly any names and concepts that you've been reviewing in preparation for the examination. ○ It's *Macbeth*, not *McBeth*.

Write legibly or print. Few people do much handwriting anymore. But most essay examinations still probably use paper or blue books. If you are out of practice or your handwriting is just flat-out illegible, print. Printing takes more time, but instructors appreciate the effort. Write in ink, as pencil can be faint and hard to read. Also consider double-spacing your essay to allow room for corrections and additions. But be careful not to spread your words too far apart. A blue book with just a few sentences per page undermines your ethos: It looks juvenile.

revise and edit
p. 386

common errors
p. 524

How to start

● **Confused?**
Read the assignment carefully. See page 262.

10 Position Paper

requires a brief critical response

A course instructor may ask you to respond to an assigned reading, lecture, film, or other activity with a position paper in which you record your reactions to the material—such as your impressions or observations. Such a paper is usually brief—often not much longer than a page or two—and due the next class session. Typically, you won't have time for more than a draft and quick revision.

- You summarize and assess the findings of a journal article studying the relationship between a full night's sleep and student success on college exams.

- You speculate about how a feminist philosopher of science, whose work you have read for a class, might react to recent developments in genetics.

- You respond to ideas raised by a panel of your classmates discussing a proposition to restore the draft or require national service.

- You offer a gut reaction to your first-ever viewing of *Triumph of the Will*, a notorious propaganda film made for Germany's National Socialist (Nazi) Party in 1935.

UNDERSTANDING POSITION PAPERS.   Instructors usually have several goals in assigning position papers: to focus your attention on a particular reading or class presentation; to measure how well you've understood course materials; to push you to connect one concept or reading with another. Because they may want you to take some risks, instructors often mark position papers less completely than full essays and grade them by different standards.

Because these assignments can be quick, low-stakes items, you might be tempted to blow them off. That would be an error. Position papers give you practice in writing about a subject and so prepare you for other papers and exams; the assignments may even preview the types of essay questions an instructor favors. Position papers also help to establish your ethos in a course, marking you as a careful reader and thinker or, perhaps, someone just along for the ride.

Use a few simple strategies to write a strong position paper.

Protesters taking a position
While some feel that security cameras ensure safety, others believe them to be an invasion of privacy.

△

▶ confused?

Read the assignment carefully.   Understand exactly what your instructor wants: Look for key words such as *summarize, describe, classify, evaluate, compare, compare and contrast,* and *analyze* and then respect the differences between them.

Review assigned material carefully.   Consider photocopying readings so that you can annotate their margins or underscore key claims and evidence. Practice smart reading: Always look for conflicts, points of difference, or issues raised in class or in the public arena—what some writers call *hooks*. Then use the most provocative material to jump-start your own thinking, using whatever brainstorming techniques work best for you. ○

Mine the texts for evidence.   Identify key passages worth quoting or features worth describing in detail. ○ For instance, you may find some startling facts worth repeating, a claim or two you resist heartily, or pithy summaries of complicated issues. Anchor your position paper around such strong passages. Be sure, too, you know how to merge quoted material smoothly with your own writing.

Organize the paper sensibly.   Unless the assignment specifically states otherwise, don't write the position paper off the top of your head. Take the time to offer a thesis or to set up a comparison, an evaluation, or another structure of organization. Give a position paper the same structural integrity you would a longer and more consequential assignment.

Here's a position paper written by Heidi Rogers as an early assignment in a lower-level course on visual rhetoric. Rogers's assignment was to offer an honest response to director Leni Riefenstahl's infamous documentary, *Triumph of the Will,* which showcases the National Socialist Party rallies in Munich in 1934. In the film, we see the German people embracing Hitler and his Nazi regime as they consolidate their power.

get an idea
p. 308

use quotations
p. 431

Rogers 1

Heidi Rogers

Instructor's Name

Course Title

September 22, 2008

Triumph of the Lens

The 1935 film Triumph of the Will, directed by Leni Riefenstahl, masterfully shows how visuals can be a powerful form of rhetoric. In the documentary we see Adolph Hitler, recognized today as one of the greatest mass murderers in history, portrayed as a strong, loving, and inspirational leader who could be the savior of Germany. However, as I was watching this film I was taken aback. I am supposed to hate this man, detest him for his brutal crimes against humanity, and yet I found myself drawn to him, liking him, even smiling as he greeted his fellow Germans on the streets of Munich. How did this filmmaker accomplish this, drawing viewers in and giving them such pride in their leader?

Riefenstahl's technique was to layer selected visuals to create the different emotions she wanted her audience to feel toward Hitler and his regime. Her first step was to introduce locations and natural images that were peaceful and soothing. Next, she would insert images of the German people themselves: children playing and laughing, women cheering and blowing kisses to Hitler, men in uniform proudly united under the Nazi flag. The next step was to weave in images of Hitler himself among these German people, so that even when he wasn't smiling or evoking any emotions at all, it would seem as if he were conveying the happiness, pride, or strength drawn from the images edited around him. The final piece of the puzzle was to put Hitler front and center, usually giving a

Offers a thesis to explain how film makes Hitler attractive.

To explain how film works, describes pattern she sees in Riefenstahl's editing technique.

Rogers 2

rousing speech that would inspire his audience and make him seem larger than life.

A good example of this technique came during the youth rally sequence. First, Riefenstahl presents peaceful images of the area around the Munich stadium, including beautiful trees with the sun streaming between the branches. We then see the vastness of the city stadium, designed by Hitler himself. Then we watch thousands of young boys and girls smiling and cheering in the stands. These masses erupt when Hitler enters the arena and Riefenstahl artfully juxtaposes images of him, usually with a cold, emotionless face, with enthusiastic youth looking up to him as if he were a god. Hitler then delivers an intoxicating speech about the future of Germany and the greatness that the people will achieve under his leadership. The crowd goes wild as he leaves the stage and we see an audience filled with awe and purpose.

What Riefenstahl did in Triumph of the Will is a common technique in film editing. When you have to reach a massive audience, you want to cover all of your bases and appeal to all of them at once. Therefore, the more kinds of ethos, pathos, and logos you can layer onto a piece of film, the better your chances will be of convincing the greatest number of people of your cause. As hard as this is to admit, if I had lived in a devastated 1935 Germany and I saw this film, I might have wanted this guy to lead my country too.

Provides extended example to support claim about how *Triumph of the Will* was edited.

Explores implications of claim—that clever editing enabled Riefenstahl to reach many audiences.

Triumph of the Will features numerous imposing shots of crowds cheering for Hitler.

Getting the details right

Edit the final version.   The assignment may seem informal, but edit and proofread your text carefully before you turn it in. ○ Think of a position paper as a trial run for a longer paper in your course. As such, it should follow the conventions of any given field or major. Even when an instructor seems casual about the assignment, don't ease up.

Identify key terms and concepts and use them correctly and often.   The instructor may be checking to see how carefully you read a book or article. So, in your paper, make a point of referring to the new concepts or terms you've encountered in your reading, as Rogers does with *ethos*, *pathos*, and *logos* in the annotated essay.

Treat your sources appropriately.   Either identify them by author and title within the paper or list them at the end of the paper in the correct documentation form (e.g., MLA or APA). Make sure quotations are set up accurately, properly introduced, and documented. Offer page numbers for any direct quotations you use. ○

Spell names and concepts correctly.   You lose credibility immediately if you misspell technical terms or proper nouns that appear throughout the course readings. In literary papers especially, get characters' names and book titles right.

Respond to your colleagues' work.   Position papers are often posted to electronic discussion boards to jumpstart conversations about ideas or readings. So take the opportunity to reply substantively to what your classmates have written. Don't just say "I agree" or "You've got to be kidding!" Add good reasons and evidence to your remarks. Remember, too, that your instructor may review these comments, looking for evidence of serious engagement with the course material.

revise and edit
p. 386

understand citation
styles p. 435

Want to get the reader's attention?
Choose a sensible subject line. See page 270.

11

E-mail

communicates
electronically

E-mail has quickly become the preferred method for most business (and personal) communication because it is quick, efficient, easy to archive, and easy to search.

- You write to the coordinator of the writing center to apply for a job as a tutor, courtesy copying the message to a professor who has agreed to serve as a reference.

- You send an e-mail to several administrators in which you complain about campus fire safety when you discover there are no smoke alarms in the student lounge.

- You send an e-mail to classmates in a writing class, looking for someone to collaborate on a Web project.

- You e-mail the entire College of Liberal Arts faculty to invite them to attend a student production of Chekhov's *Uncle Vanya*.

UNDERSTANDING E-MAIL.   E-mail is now so common and informal that writers take it for granted, forgetting that e-mail can become important documentation when transacting business. Though usually composed quickly, e-mails have a long shelf life once they're archived. They can also spread well beyond their original audiences. Remember too that e-mails can be printed and filed as hard copy.

You probably know how to handle personal e-mails well enough. But you may not be as savvy about the more specialized messages you send to organizations, businesses, professors, groups of classmates, and so on. The following strategies will help.

Explain your purpose clearly and logically.   Use both the subject line and first paragraph of an e-mail to explain your reason for writing: Be specific about names, titles, dates, places, and so on, especially when your message opens a discussion. Write your message so that it will still make sense a year or more later, specifying references and pronouns (*we, it, them*). ○

Tell readers what you want them to do.   Lay out a clear agenda for accomplishing one task: Ask for a document, a response, or a reply by a specific date. If you have several requests to make of a single person or group, consider writing separate e-mails. It's easier to track short, single-purpose e-mails than to deal with complex documents requiring several different actions.

Write for intended and unintended audiences.   The specific audience in the "To" line is usually the only audience for your message. But e-mail is more public than traditional surface mail, easily duplicated and sent to whole networks of recipients with just a click. So compose your business e-mails as if they *might* be read by everyone in a unit or even published in a local paper. Assume that nothing in business e-mail is private.

Minimize the clutter.   When e-mails run through a series of replies, they grow so thick with headers, copied messages, and

common errors
p. 524

signatures that any new message can be hard to find. Make the latest message stand out, perhaps separating it slightly from the headers and transmission data.

Keep your messages brief.   Lengthy blocks of e-mail prose without paragraph breaks irritate readers. Indeed, meandering or chatty e-mails in business situations can make a writer seem disorganized and out of control. Try to limit your e-mail messages to what fits on a single screen. If you can't, use headings, spacing, and color to create visual pauses. **O**

Distribute your messages sensibly.   Send a copy of an e-mail to anyone directly involved in the message, as well as to those who might need to be informed. For example, if filing a grade complaint with an instructor, you may also copy the chair of his or her academic department or the dean of students. But don't let the copy (Cc) and blind copy (Bcc) lines in the e-mail header tempt you to send messages outside the essential audience.

Here's a fairly informal e-mail announcing a weekend trip, written to members of a department. Despite the relaxed event it describes, the e-mail still provides clear and direct information, gets to the point quickly, and offers an agenda for action.

To: DRW Faculty
From: John Ruszkiewicz
Subject: Annual Big Bend Trip
Cc: Alumni in Rhetoric
Bcc:
Attachments:

Clear, specific subject line makes message easy to find and search: Key search term would be "Big Bend."

Dear Colleagues –

Business letters use colon after greeting, but e-mails are often less formal.

Opening paragraph explains point of e-mail and what colleagues should do.

The Division of Rhetoric and Writing's eighth annual Big Bend trip is scheduled for October 8–11, 2008, at Big Bend National Park in West Texas. If you are considering making the trip this year, please let me know by e-mail and I will put you on the mailing list.

design your work
p. 517

You should know that the trip is neither an official DRW event, nor highly organized — just a group of colleagues enjoying the best natural environment Texas has to offer for a few days. If you've been to Big Bend, you know what to expect. If you haven't, see <http://www.nps.gov/bibe/home.htm>. The weather at Big Bend in October is usually splendid. I say "usually" because we had heavy rains a few years ago and an ice storm in 2000. But such precipitation is rare: It is a desert park.

In the past, most people have camped at the campground, which is first come, first serve. Lodging may be available in the park itself, but rooms are hard to get throughout the fall season. Also available are hotels in nearby Study Butte, Terlingua, and Lajitas.

I'll contact those interested in the trip in a few weeks. We can begin then to plan sharing rides and equipment. And please let other friends of the DRW know about the trip.

Best,
JR

John Ruszkiewicz, Professor
The University of Texas at Austin
Department of Rhetoric and Writing
Austin, TX
Phone: (512) 555-1234
Fax: (512) 555-5678
ruszkiewicz@mail.utexas.edu

Second paragraph provides background information for readers who haven't been on trip before — including helpful Web link.

Tone is professional, but casual, and language is tight and correct. No emoticons.

Final paragraph outlines subsequent actions, letting readers know what to expect.

Signature is complete, opening various routes for communication.

Getting the details right

Because most people receive e-mail messages frequently, make any you send easy to process.

▶ want to get the reader's attention?

Choose a sensible subject line.   The subject line should clearly identify the topic and include helpful keywords that might later be searched. If your e-mail is specifically about a grading policy, your student loan, or mold in your gym locker, make sure a word you'll recall afterward—like *policy, loan,* or *mold*—gets in the subject line. In professional e-mails, subjects such as *A question, Hi!* or *Meeting* are useless.

Arrange your text clearly.   You can do almost as much visually in e-mail as you can in a word-processing program, including choosing fonts, inserting lines, and adding color, images, and videos. But you shouldn't do more than you need. A simple block style with spaces between single-spaced paragraphs works well enough for most messages. If a lengthy e-mail breaks into natural divisions, use boldfaced headings. You might even highlight key information with a readable color (dark blue or red, *not* yellow or lime green).

Check the recipient list before you hit send.   Routinely double-check all the recipient fields—especially when you're replying to a message. The original writer may have copied the message widely: Do you want to send your reply to that entire group or just to the original writer?

Include an appropriate signature.   Professional e-mail of any kind should include a signature that identifies you and provides contact information readers need. Your e-mail address alone may not be clear enough to identify who you are, especially if you are writing to your instructor.

But be careful: You may not want to provide readers with a *home* phone number or address since you don't know precisely who may see your e-mail. When you send e-mail, the recipient can reach you simply by replying.

revise and edit
p. 386

Use standard grammar. Professional e-mails should be almost as polished as business letters: At least give readers the courtesy of a quick review to catch humiliating gaffes or misspellings. ○ Emoticons and smiley faces have also largely disappeared from serious communications.

Have a sensible e-mail address. You might enjoy communicating with friends as HorribleHagar or DaisyGirl, but such an e-mail signature will undermine your credibility with a professor or potential employer. Save the oddball name for a private e-mail account.

Don't be a pain. You just add to the daily clutter if you send unnecessary replies to e-mails—a pointless *thanks* or *Yes!* or *WooHoo!* Just as bad is CCing everyone on a list when you've received a query that needs to go to one person only: For example, when someone trying to arrange a meeting asks members of a group for available times and those members carbon copy their replies to all other members.

How to start

● **Want to get a response?**
Explain your purpose clearly and logically.
See page 273.

12 Business Letter

communicates formally

The formal business letter remains an important instrument for sending information in professional situations. Though business letters can be transmitted electronically these days, legal letters or decisions about admissions to schools or programs often still arrive on paper, complete with a real signature.

● Responding to an internship opportunity at Boeing, you outline your engineering credentials for the position in a cover letter and attach your résumé.

● You send a brief letter to the director of admissions of a law school, graciously declining your acceptance into the program.

● You send a letter of complaint to an auto company, documenting the list of problems you've had with your SUV and indicating your intention to seek redress under your state's "lemon law."

● You write to a management company to accept the terms of a lease, enclosing a check for the security deposit on your future apartment.

UNDERSTANDING BUSINESS LETTERS.

As you would expect, business letters are generally formal in structure and tone, and follow a number of specific conventions, designed to make the document a suitable record or to support additional communication. Yet the principles for composing a business or job letter are not much different from those for a business e-mail. O

Explain your purpose clearly and logically. Don't assume a reader will understand why you are writing. Use the first paragraph to announce your concern and explain your purpose, anticipating familiar *who, what, where, when, how,* and *why* questions. Be specific about names, titles, dates, and places. If you're applying for a job, scholarship, or admission to a program, name the specific position or item. Remember that your letter is a record that may have a long life in a file cabinet. Write your document so that it will make sense later.

want to get a ◀
response?

Tell your readers what you want them to do. Don't leave them guessing about how they should respond to your message. Lay out a clear agenda for accomplishing one task: Apply for a job, request information, or make an inquiry or complaint. Don't hesitate to ask for a reply, even by a specific date when that is necessary.

Write for your audience. Quite often, you won't know the people to whom you are sending a business letter. So you have to construct your letter considering how an executive, an employer, an admissions officer, or a manager of complaints might be most effectively persuaded. Courtesy and goodwill go a long way—though you may have to be firm and impersonal in some situations. Avoid phony emotions or tributes.

An application or cover letter poses special challenges. You need to present your work and credentials in the best possible light without seeming full of yourself. Be succinct and specific, letting achievements speak mostly for themselves—though you

understand e-mail
p. 266

can explain details that a reader might not appreciate. Focus on recent events and credentials and explain what skills and strengths you bring to the job. Speak in your own voice, clipped slightly by a formal style. ○

Keep the letter focused and brief.   Like e-mails, business letters become hard to read when they extend beyond a page or two. A busy administrator or employee prefers a concise message, handsomely laid out on good stationery. Even a job-application letter should be relatively short, highlighting just your strongest credentials: Leave it to the accompanying résumé or dossier to flesh out the details.

Use a conventional form.   All business letters should include your address (called the *return address*), the date of the message, the address of the person to whom you are writing (called the *inside address*), a formal salutation or greeting, a closing, a signature in ink (when possible), and information about copies or enclosures.

Both *block format* and *modified-block format* are acceptable in business communication. In block forms, all elements are aligned against the left-hand margin (with the exception of the letterhead address at the top). In modified-block form, the return address, date, closing, and signature are aligned with the center of the page. In both cases, paragraphs in the body of the letter are set as single-spaced blocks of type, their first lines not indented, and with an extra line space between paragraphs.

In indented form (not shown), the elements of the letter are arranged as in modified-block form, but the first lines of body paragraphs are indented five spaces, with no line spaces between the single-spaced paragraphs.

Distribute copies of your letter sensibly.   Copy anyone involved in a message, as well as anyone who might have a legitimate interest in your action. For example, in filing a product complaint with a company, you may also want to send your letter to the state office of consumer affairs. Copies are noted and listed at the bottom of the letter, introduced by the abbreviation *Cc* (for *courtesy copy*).

Following are two business letters: the first is a concise letter of complaint, while the second is a more detailed letter from a student applying for a scholarship.

define your style
p. 366

Decide on appropriate categories. In most cases, right out of college, you'll use the résumé categories noted above. But you may vary their order and emphasis, depending on the job or career you pursue. In the past, one expensively printed résumé served all occasions; today you can—and should—tailor your electronically crafted résumé to individual job searches.

Arrange the information within categories in reverse chronological order. The most recent attainments come first in each of your categories. If such a list threatens to bury your most significant items, you have several options: Cut the lesser achievements from the list, break out special achievements in some consistent way, or highlight those special achievements in your cover letter.

Design pages that are easy to read. Basic design principles aren't rocket science: Headings and key information should stand out and individual items should be clearly separated. The pages should look substantive but not cluttered. White space makes any document friendly, but too much in a résumé can suggest a lack of achievement. ○

In general, treat the résumé as a conservative document. This is not the time to experiment with fonts and flash or curlicues. Don't include a photograph either, even a good one.

want to ◀
get a job?

Proofread every line in the résumé several times. Careful editing isn't a "detail" when it comes to résumés: It can be the whole ball game. When employers have more job candidates than they can handle, they may look for reasons to dismiss weak cases. Misspelled words, poor design of headings and text, and incomplete or confusing chronology are the kinds of mistakes that can terminate your job quest. ○

Applying for a job
need not be as dreary
as it once was—
or as sexist.

The following résumé, by Andrea Palladino, is arranged in reverse chronological order. Palladino uses a simple design that aligns the major headings and dates in a column down the left-hand margin and indents the detailed accomplishments to separate them, making them highly readable.

design your work
p. 517

common errors
p. 524

Contact information centered at top of page for quick reference. If necessary, give both school and permanent addresses.

Optional "career objective" functions like thesis.

Alignments further emphasize headings and dates.

Ample, but not excessive, white space enhances readability.

Andrea Palladino
600 Oak St.
Austin, TX 78705
(281) 555-1234

CAREER OBJECTIVE   Soon-to-be college graduate seeking full-time position that allows for regular interpersonal communication and continued professional growth.

EDUCATION
8/02–5/06   University of Texas at Austin – Psychology, B.A.

EXPERIENCE
3/04–Present   Writing Consultant
University of Texas at Austin Undergraduate Writing Center – Austin, TX
Tutor students at various stages of the writing process. Work with a variety of assignments. Attend professional development workshops.

5/04–Present   Child Care Provider
CoCare Children's Services – Austin, TX
Care for infants through children age ten, including children with physical and mental disabilities. Change diapers, give food and comfort, engage children in stimulating play, and clean/disinfect toys after childcare. Work on standby and substitute for coworkers when needed.

5/03–12/04   Salesperson/Stockperson
Eloise's Collectibles – Katy, TX
Unpacked new shipments, prepared outgoing shipments, and kept inventory. Interacted with customers and performed the duties of a cashier.

ACCOMPLISHMENTS
2003–Present   College Scholar for 3 yrs. – acknowledgment of in-residence GPA of at least 3.50

10/05–Present   Big Brothers Big Sisters of Central Texas

Fall 2003   University of Texas at Austin Children's Research Lab – Research Assistant

Getting the details right

With its fussy dates, headings, columns, and margins, a résumé is all about the details. Fortunately, it is brief enough to make a thorough going-over easy. Here are some important considerations.

Don't leave unexplained gaps in your education or work career.
Readers will wonder about blanks in your history (Are you a spy? slacker? felon?) and so may dismiss your application in favor of candidates whose career chronology raises no red flags. Simply account for any long periods (a year or so) you may have spent wandering the capitals of Europe or flipping burgers. Do so either in the résumé or in the job-application letter—especially if the experiences contributed to your skills. ○

Be consistent.   Keep the headings and alignments the same through-out the document. Express all dates in the same form: For example, if you abbreviate months and seasons, do so everywhere. Use hyphens between dates.

Protect your personal data.   You don't have to volunteer information about your race, gender, age, or sexual orientation on a job application or résumé. Neither should you provide financial data, Social Security or credit card numbers, or other information you don't want in the public domain and that is not pertinent to your job search. However, you do need to be accurate and honest about the relevant job information: Any disparity about what you state on a résumé and your actual accomplishments may be a firing offense down the road.

Consider having your résumés designed and printed professionally.
You may save time by letting someone else design and print your document, especially if you aren't particularly computer savvy. If you do produce your own résumé, be sure to print it on high-quality paper. Ordinary typing paper won't cut it.

understand business
letters p. 272

14 Personal Statement

**explains a
person's
experiences
and goals**

Preparing a short personal statement has become almost a ritual among people applying for admission to college, professional school, or graduate school, or for jobs, promotions, scholarships, internships, and even elective office.

● An application for an internship asks for an essay in which you explain how your career goals will contribute to a more tolerant and diverse society.

● All candidates for the student government offices you're interested in must file a personal statement explaining their positions. Your statement, limited to 300 words, will be printed in the campus newspaper and posted online.

● You dust off the personal statement you wrote to apply to college to see what portions you can use in an essay required for admission to upper-division courses in the College of Communication.

UNDERSTANDING PERSONAL STATEMENTS.   Institutions that ask for personal statements are rarely interested in who you are. Rather, they want to see whether you can *represent* yourself as a person with whom they might want to be affiliated. That may seem harsh, but consider the personal statements you have already written. At best, they are a slice of your life—the verbal equivalent of you in full-dress mode.

If you want a sense of what a school, business, or other institution expects in the essays they request from applicants, read whatever passes for that group's statement of mission or core values. If the words sound a little stiff, inflated, and unrealistic, you've got it—except that you shouldn't actually sound as pretentious as an institution. A little blood has to flow through the veins of your personal statement, just not so much that someone in an office gets nervous about your emotional pitch.

Hitting the right balance between displaying overwhelming competence and admitting human foibles in a personal statement is tough. Here's some advice for composing a successful essay.

Present yourself in your personal statement the same way you would in an interview: confident, professional, and pleasant.

Read the essay prompt carefully.   Essay topics are often deliberately open-ended to give you some freedom in pursuing a topic, but only answer the question actually posed, not one you'd prefer to deal with. Ideally, the question will focus on a specific aspect of your work or education; try to write about this even if the question is more general.

Be realistic about your audience.   Your personal statements are read by strangers. That's scary, but you can usually count on them to be reasonable people, and well-disposed to give you a fair hearing. They measure you against other applicants—not unreachable standards of perfection.

▶ feeling lost?

Gather your material.   In most cases, a personal statement is part of an application package that may already include an application letter or résumé. If that's the case, don't waste your essay repeating what's already on record elsewhere. Instead, look for incidents and anecdotes in your life that bring your résumé lines to life. Talk about the experiences that prepared you for the work you want to do or, perhaps, determined the direction of your life. If the prompt encourages personal reminiscences (e.g., *the person who influenced you the most*), think hard about how to convey those experiences concretely to a perfect stranger.

Decide on a focus or theme.   Personal statements are short, so decide how to make best use of a reader's time. Don't ramble about your opinions or educational career. Instead, choose a theme that builds on the strongest aspects of your application. If you're driven by a passion for research, arrange the elements of your life to illustrate this. If your best work is extracurricular, explain in a scholarship application how your commitment to people and activities makes you a more estimable student. You may find it odd to turn your life into a thesis statement, but you need to make a clear point about yourself in any personal essay.

Organize the piece conventionally.   Many personal statements take a narrative form, though they may also borrow some elements of reports and even proposals. Whatever structures you adopt for the essay, pay attention to the introduction, conclusion, and transitions: You cannot risk readers getting confused or lost. ○

Try a high or middle style.   You don't want to be breezy or casual in an essay for law school or medical school, but a *personal* statement does invite a human voice. So a style that marries the correctness and formal vocabulary of a high style with the occasional untailored feel of the middle style might be perfect for many personal statements.

The Academic Service Partnership Foundation asked candidates for an internship to prepare an essay addressing a series of questions. The prompt and one response to it follows.

connect ideas
p. 350

ASPF NATIONAL INTERNSHIP PROGRAM

Please submit a 250–500 word typed essay answering the following three questions:

1. Why do you want an internship with the ASPF?
2. What do you hope to accomplish in your academic and professional career goals?
3. What are your strengths and skills, and how would you use these in your internship?

Specific questions limit reply, but also help to organize it.

Michael Villaverde

April 14, 2008

The opportunity to work within a health-related government agency alongside top-notch professionals initially attracted me to the Academic Service Partnership Foundation (ASPF) National Internship Program. I was excited after reading about the program's success and its extensive network of alumni. Participating in the ASPF's internship program would enable me to augment the health-services research skills I've gained through work at the VERDICT Research Center in San Antonio and the M. D. Anderson Cancer Center in Houston. This ASPF internship could also give me the chance to gain experience in health policy and administration.

I support the ASPF's mission to foster closer relations between formal education and public service and believe that I could contribute to this mission. If selected as an ASPF intern, I will become an active alumnus of the program. I would love to do my part by advising younger students and recruiting future ASPF interns. Most importantly, I make it a point to improve the operations of programs from which I benefit. Any opportunities provided to me by the ASPF will be repaid in kind.

Opening sentence states writer's thesis or intent; First two paragraphs address first question.

Essay uses first person (*I, me*) but is fairly formal in tone and vocabulary, between high and middle style.

Personal note slips through in enthusiasm author shows for internship opportunity.

This statement transitions smoothly into second issue raised in prompt.

Formidable and *specific* goals speak for themselves in straightforward language.

Another transition introduces third issue raised by prompt.

Qualifications offered are numerous and detailed.

Special interest/concern is noted, likely to impress reviewers of statement.

Final sentence affirms enthusiasm for technical internship.

Other strengths I bring to the ASPF's National Internship Program are my broad educational background and dedication. My undergraduate studies will culminate in two honors degrees (finance and liberal arts) with additional pre-med coursework. Afterward, I wish to enroll in a combined M.D./Ph.D. program in health-services research. Following my formal education, I will devote my career to seeing patients in a primary-care setting, researching health-care issues as a university faculty member, teaching bioethics, and developing public policy at a health-related government agency.

The coursework at my undergraduate institution has provided me with basic laboratory and computer experience, but my strengths lie in oral and written communication. Comparing digital and film-screen mammography equipment for a project at M.D. Anderson honed my technical-writing skills and comprehension of statistical analysis. Qualitative analysis methods I learned at VERDICT while evaluating strategies used by the Veterans Health Administration in implementing clinical practice guidelines will be a significant resource to any prospective employer. By the end of this semester, I will also possess basic knowledge of Statistical Package for the Social Sciences (SPSS) software.

During my internship I would like to research one of the following topics: health-care finance, health policy, or ethnic disparities in access to quality health-care. I have read much about the Medicare Prescription Drug, Improvement, and Modernization Act of 2003 and would especially enjoy studying the implications of this legislation. I would learn a great deal from working with officials responsible for the operation and strategic planning of a program like Medicare (or a nonprofit hospital system). The greater the prospects for multiple responsibilities, the more excited I will be to show up to work each day.

Getting the details right

As with résumés, there's no room for errors or slips in personal statements. ○ They are a test of your writing skills, plain and simple, and so you need to get the spelling, mechanics, and usage right. In addition, consider the following advice.

Don't get too artsy.   A striking image or two may work well in the statement, as may the occasional metaphor or simile. But don't build your essay around a running theme, an extended analogy, or a pop-culture allusion that a reader might dismiss as hokey or simply not get. If a phrase or feature stands out too noticeably, change it, even though *you* may like it.

Use commonsense.   You probably already have the good grace not to offend gender, racial, religious, and ethnic groups in your personal statements. You should also take the time to read your essay from the point of view of people from less protected groups who may take umbrage at your dismissal of *old folks*, *fundamentalists*, or even Republicans. You don't know who may be reading your essay.

Write the essay yourself.   It's the ethical thing to do. If you don't, and you're caught, you're toast. You might ask someone to review your statement or take a draft to a writing center for a consultation. ○ This review or consult by a parent or English-major roommate should not purge your *self* from the essay. Remember, too, that wherever you arrive, you'll need to write at the level you display in the statement that got you there.

common errors
p. 524

peer review
p. 392

15

Lab Report

**records a
scientific
experiment**

In most courses in the natural or social sciences, you are expected to learn how to describe experiments systematically and report information accurately. It goes with the territory. The vehicle for such work is the familiar lab report.

- For a physics course, you describe an experiment that uses a series of collisions to demonstrate the conservation of energy.

- In an organic chemistry lab, you try to produce chemical luminescence and report your results.

- For a psychology class, you describe the results of an experiment you created to determine whether students taking examinations benefit from a good night's sleep the night before the test.

UNDERSTANDING LAB REPORTS. Formal scientific papers published in academic journals have conventional features designed to convey information to readers professionally interested in the results of studies and experiments. The key elements of such a scientific paper are the following:

- Descriptive title clearly describing the content of the paper

- Introduction explaining the purpose of the study or experiment and reviewing previous work on the subject (called a literature review)

- Description of materials and methods, explaining the factual and procedural details of the experiment

- Results section, tabulating and reporting the data

- Discussion of the results, interpreting the data

- References list or bibliography, documenting articles and books cited in the paper

- Abstract (not always required) condensing a summary of the main points in your report

For details about composing full scientific papers, consult the handbooks used in your particular field (and recommended by your instructor), such as *The CSE Manual for Authors, Editors, and Publishers* (7th edition, 2006), or the *Publication Manual of the American Psychological Association* (5th edition, 2001).

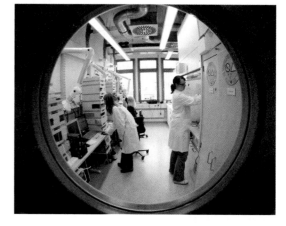

Lab reports borrow many of the features of the scientific papers published in academic journals, but are generally much shorter and tailored to specific situations. Typically, you prepare lab reports to describe the results of experiments you're assigned to perform in science courses. But you may also write lab reports to document original research done with colleagues or professors.

△

Follow instructions to the letter.   In a course with a lab, you typically receive precise instructions on how to compile a lab notebook or prepare and submit reports. Read these guidelines carefully and ask the instructor or teaching assistant questions about any specifications you do not understand. Each section of a lab report provides a specific kind of information that helps a reader understand and, possibly, repeat a procedure or an experiment.

▶ first time
writing a lab
report?

Look at model reports.   Lab report requirements may vary not only from subject to subject but also from course to course. So ask the instructor whether sample reports might be available for a particular lab section. If so, study them closely. The best way to understand what your work should look like is to see a successful model.

Be efficient.   If an abstract is required, keep it brief. Use charts, tables, and graphs (as required) to report information and then don't repeat that data elsewhere. Keep your reporting of results separate from the discussion and commentary.

Edit the final version.   In a lab report, editing means not only proofreading your language but also reviewing the structure of equations or formulas, assessing the clarity of methods or procedures sections, and checking any numbers, calculations, equations, or formulas. ○ Be sure to label all sections and items accurately, numbering any figures, tables, and charts. Use these numbers to refer to these items in the body of your report.

Following is a lab report produced for a course in organic chemistry. It follows a structure defined in a full page of instructions. Some sections — such as "Main Reactions and Mechanisms" — are clearly tied to the specific subject matter of the chemistry class. Other sections — such as "Data and Results" — would be found in lab reports in many disciplines.

Like any lab report, this one is mostly business. But there are informal moments ("Did it glow? Yes!"), probably reflecting the fact that the writer had already gained a sense of what was acceptable in this course: This was the seventh of more than a dozen required reports.

○

revise and edit
p. 386

Sandra Ramos

3/22/2008

Synthesis of Luminol

CH 210C Syllabus, Supplement I.

INTRODUCTION

The purpose of this lab is to synthesize a chemiluminescent product

and observe chemiluminescence.

MAIN REACTIONS AND MECHANISMS

a.

b.

Almost all lab reports use
headings for their structure.
"Introduction" functions as
thesis.

"Materials and Methods"
section starts here. (As-
signment instructions
specified different lan-
guage for these headings.)

Ramos 2

c.

3- aminophthalate
Singlet state

3- aminophthalate
Triplet state

Proposed peroxide

3- aminophthalate
Ground state

TABLE OF REACTANTS AND PRODUCTS

Included 3-nitrophthalic acid, hydrazine solution, triethylene glycol,

NaOH, sodium hydrosulfite dihydrate, acetic acid, luminol,

potassium ferricyanide, hydrogen peroxide

SYNOPSIS OF PROCEDURE

APPARATUS:

5 ml conical vial, hot plate, heating block, spin vane, Hirsch funnel,

250 ml Erlenmeyer flask, and thermometer

Abbreviations are not followed by periods.

SYNTHESIS OF LUMINOL:

1. Heated 5 ml vial containing 200 mg 3-nitrophthalic acid and 0.4

ml aq 8% hydrazine sol'n until solid dissolved.

Ramos 3

2. Once dissolved, add 0.6 ml triethylene glycol and clamped vial in vertical position. Added spin vane and inserted thermometer into vial.

3. Brought sol'n to vigorous boil to boil away excess water. During this time, temperature should be around 110°C.

4. Once water boiled off, temperature rose to 215°C in a 3–4 minute period. Maintained the 215–220°C temperature for 2 minutes.

5. Removed the vial and cooled it to 100°C. While cooling, placed 10 ml water in Erlenmeyer flask and heated to boiling.

6. Once sample cooled to 100°C, added 3 ml boiling water.

7. Collected yellow crystals by vacuum filtration using a Hirsch funnel.

8. Transferred solid back to vial and added 1 ml of 3.0 M NaOH and stirred with a stirring rod until the solid was dissolved. Then added 0.6 g of fresh sodium hydrosulfite dihydrate to the deep brown-red solution.

9. Heated solution slightly under boiling for 5 minutes, taking care not to cause bumping. Then added 0.4 ml acetic acid.

10. Cooled tube in beaker of cool water, and collected solid luminol by vacuum filtration using Hirsch funnel.

LIGHT-PRODUCING REACTION:

1. Combined two samples of luminol. Dissolved them in 2 ml of 3 M NaOH and 18 ml water (sol'n A).

2. Next, prepared a sol'n of 4 ml 3% aqueous potassium ferricyanide, 4 ml 3% H_2O_2 and 32 ml H_2O (sol'n B).

3. Now, diluted 5 ml sol'n A with 35 ml water. In a dark place, poured diluted sol'n and sol'n B simultaneously into an Erlenmeyer flask. Swirled flask; looking for blue-green light.

Standard notation is used to describe chemical reactions.

Ramos 4

Data sections are rarely this simple. Most would require tables, charts, etc.

DATA AND RESULTS

Did it glow?   Yes!

DISCUSSION AND CONCLUSION

When a chemical reaction generates light, chemiluminescence has occurred. The product of such a reaction is in an excited electronic state and emits a photon. One example of chemiluminescence is the luciferase-catalyzed reaction of luciferin with molecular oxygen in the male firefly. Chemiluminescence occurring through biochemical processes is also called bioluminescence.

Luminol is synthesized through two steps. 4-nitrophthalic acid and hydrazine react to produce 5-nitrophthalhydrazide, which is reduced by sodium dithionite to form luminol. In alkaline solution, luminol emits blue-green light when mixed with H_2O_2 and potassium ferricyanide.

Although the mechanism of this reaction isn't fully understood, chemists believe that a peroxide decays to form 3-diaminophthalate in an excited triplet state (two unpaired electrons with the same spin). Slowly, the 3-diaminophthalate converts to a singlet state (two unpaired electrons now have different spins), which then decays to the ground state, emitting light through fluorescence. In contrast, phosphorescence occurs in reactions where a triplet state emits photons while converting to a singlet state.

Blue-green light glowed for a fraction of a second when I mixed solutions A and B. This indicates that I successfully synthesized enough luminol to run the chemiluminescent reaction. Only a small amount of dissolved luminol was required, so a high yield was not necessary.

Getting the details right

Even the conventions of scientists vary, so it helps to know what sorts of issues may come up in preparing a lab report for a given course. Again, ask questions when you aren't sure what conventions to follow.

Keep the lab report impersonal.   Keep yourself and any lab partners out of the work. In fact, most instructors will *require* that you use the third person and passive voice throughout: *The beaker was heated* rather than *We heated the beaker*. Though some instructors do allow the use of first-person pronouns in undergraduate work—preferring the clarity of active sentences—always check before using *I* or *we*. O

Keep the style clear.   Written for knowledgeable readers, lab reports needn't apologize for using technical terms, jargon, and scientific notation. However, sentences still need to be coherent and grammatical in structure and free of clutter. Avoid contractions, however, as well as any trendy or slang terms.

Follow the conventions.   Learn the rules as they apply in particular fields. In general, however, you should italicize scientific names expressed in Latin, write out formulas and equations on separate lines, use only metric quantities and measures, use standard abbreviations, and narrate the materials and methods section in the past tense.

Label charts, tables, and graphs carefully.   Any data you present graphically should make sense at a glance if your design is sensible and the labels are thorough and accurate. Don't leave readers wondering what the numbers in a column represent or what the scale of a drawing might be. O

Document the report correctly.   Most lab reports won't require documentation or a list of references. But a scientific paper will. Determine the documentation style manual used in the subject area and follow its guidelines closely. O

define your style
p. 366

display data
p. 514

understand citation
styles p. 435

How to start ● **Adapting material?**
Organize your presentation. See page 299.

16 Oral Report

presents information to a live audience

For an oral report, you must not only research a subject and organize information but also find ways to convey your points powerfully and sometimes graphically to an audience listening and watching rather than reading.

- For a government class, you use your technical expertise and a series of slides to explain why you believe electronic voting equipment is far from secure.

- For a psychology exam, you use presentation software to review the results of an experiment you and several colleagues designed to test which types of music were most conducive to studying for examinations.

- For a group of middle-school children, you and three colleagues from a college drama club use lots of props to demonstrate how you stage a full Shakespeare production every spring.

- Prepping a crowd for a protest march, you use a bullhorn and a little humor to review the very serious ground rules for staging a peaceful demonstration on the grounds of the state capitol.

UNDERSTANDING ORAL REPORTS.   Oral reports can be deceptive. To watch someone give an effective three-minute talk, you may assume they spent less time preparing it than they would a ten-page paper. But be warned: Oral presentations require all the research, analysis, and drafting of any other type of assignment, and then some. After all the background work is done, the material needs to be distilled into its most important points and sold to an audience. Here is some advice for preparing effective oral reports.

Know your stuff.   Having a strong grasp of your subject will make your presentation more effective. Knowledge brings you confidence that will ease your anxieties about speaking in public. You'll appear believable and persuasive to an audience. And you'll feel more comfortable improvising and taking questions.

What's more, even the best-prepared reports can run into problems. Equipment may fail or perhaps you won't be able to find your note cards. But if you are in command of your subject, you'll survive.

Organize your presentation.   If your report is based on material you've already written, reduce it to an outline, memorize the key points (or put them on a card), and then practice speaking to each point. ○ If it helps, connect each point to one or two strong examples listeners will later remember. Make the report seem spontaneous, but plan every detail.

adapting ◀
material?

The process is similar for an oral report built from scratch. First, study your subject. Then list the points you want to cover and arrange them in a way that will make sense to listeners—choosing a pattern of organization that fits your topic. Either note cards or the outlining tools that you'll find in programs like Word or PowerPoint are ideal for exploring options for arranging your talk.

The best equipment
can't save a poorly
prepared report.

Once into your subject, tell your audience briefly what you intend to cover and in what order. Then, throughout the report at critical transition points, tell the audience where you are by simply explaining what comes next: *The second issue I want to discuss. . . . ; Now that we've examined the phenomenon,*

order ideas
p. 342

let's look at its consequences. ○ Don't be shy about stating your main points this directly or worry about repetition. In an oral report, strategic repetition is your friend.

Finally, signal your conclusion when you get there and end the report shortly thereafter, as promised. If you're taking questions after your presentations, follow up with *Any questions?*

Adapt your material to the time available.   Don't worry about running out of things to say if you know your subject: Few speakers have that problem once they get rolling. But be realistic about how much material you can cover within the assigned limit, especially if you have to answer questions at the end. Tie your key ideas to fixed points on a clock. Know where you need to be at a quarter, half, and three-quarters of the way through the available time.

Practice your presentation.   Complete several dry runs for an oral report. Each session will increase your confidence and alert you to problems you can then steer around. You'll know immediately where the report works and where to make adjustments. Whenever possible, have one or more friends or colleagues watch you practice and give you feedback on how to improve.

Practice sessions are needed, too, to time the presentation. Speak any material aloud *exactly* as you intend to deliver it and go through all the motions, especially if you have accompanying media such as slides or video clips. If you practice only in your head, you will greatly underestimate the duration of the report.

If your presentation is collaborative, choreograph the report with the full group, agreeing on the introductions, handoffs, and interactions with the audience. Who runs the slide projector? Who distributes the handouts and when? Who handles the question-and-answer session? Details like these seem minor until they are mishandled on game day.

connect ideas
p. 350

At least one run-through should, if possible, occur at the actual location for the report. You'll feel far more comfortable during the presentation if you've stood on the stage, handled the microphone and podium, found places to plug in the media equipment, and heard your voice from the front of the room, even if it is a classroom you've been sitting in all term.

The PowerPoint presentation on this page was created by Terri Sagastume, a resident of a small Florida town who opposes a proposed real-estate development, Edenlawn Estates on property near his home. J&M Investments, the real-estate developer that recently purchased the property, hopes to create a new multistory condominium complex, known as Edenlawn Estates, in place of the property's existing single-family homes. Sagastume's goal is to inform the public of the damage such a development would do to the surrounding area, and he is trying to convince his audience to sign a petition, which he will present to the local government in an effort to shut the project down.

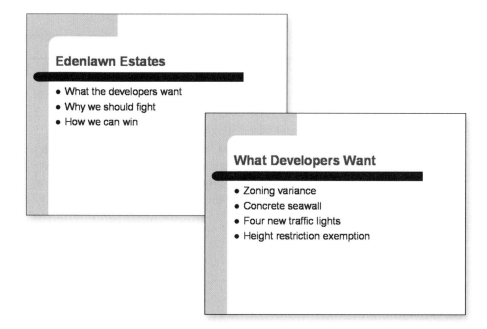

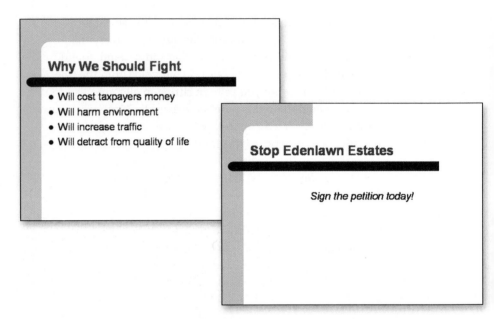

The slides themselves are extremely simple and brief: They are merely the bullet points that Sagastume uses to ground his presentation. **O**

With the first slide as his backdrop, Sagastume provides a preview of his speech in three broad sections. First, he explains to his audience that the real-estate developer—a Miami-based conglomerate with no personal ties to the area—wants to change the existing building codes and zoning laws in order to maximize profits. Second, he reminds his audience of the reason those codes and laws are there, and that much could be lost if exceptions are made. And finally, he convinces his audience that, together, they can fight the big developer and win.

create slides
p. 510

Getting the details right

An oral report, whether onstage, in school, or at work, is a performance. You aren't just reading information aloud; you're working an audience in a more physical way.

Fortunately, as a speaker you have some advantages. You stand front and center in the room, possibly with a microphone to amplify your voice and a PowerPoint slide presentation to illustrate your points. And, for about thirty seconds, you'll probably have the automatic goodwill of an audience. After that, you've got to earn every minute of their continued attention. Here's how to do it.

Stay connected to your listeners. Once the oral presentation begins, consult your notes as you need them, but spend most of your report looking at the crowd. Make eye contact with individuals and sweep the room. Watch their reactions. When it's clear you've made a point, move on. If you see puzzled looks, explain more. No speaker charms everyone, so don't let a random yawn or frown throw you. But if the whole crowd starts to snooze, you *are* the problem. Connect or lose 'em.

Be sure to speak *to* your listeners, not to a text or notes. If you look downward too often, you lose eye contact and your voice may be muffled, even with a microphone. Print your notes in a font and type size large enough to read easily from a distance so that you can look up without worrying about losing your place.

Use your voice. Speak clearly and deliberately, and be sure people in back can hear you. Nervous speakers unconsciously accelerate until they're racing to their conclusions, and their voices will sometimes be higher-pitched than usual. If you get skittish, take a deep breath and smile. You'll calm down a bit and be better able to continue.

If in rehearsal you find yourself punctuating every few words in your sentences with *uh*, *um*, *ok*, *like*, or *you know*, you've got a problem that you'll want to fix. Try recording your presentations to discover any annoying repetitions. Then make a conscious effort to eliminate them, continuing to record your speech to gauge your progress. You won't eliminate *you know* overnight, but it can be done.

Use your body. If the room is large and a fixed microphone doesn't confine you, try moving around on the stage to reach more of the audience. Use gestures too. They are a natural part of public speaking, especially for arguments and personal narratives.

If you are stuck behind a podium, you can still use your voice, posture, and gestures to keep listeners engaged. If the occasion and your paper are very academic, at least look steady onstage. Don't rock as you read.

Dress for the occasion too. A little spit and polish earns you the goodwill of most audiences. Your classmates may razz you about the tie or skirt, but it just proves they're paying attention. And that's a good thing.

Use humor. In longer reports to less familiar groups, consider easing into your material with an anecdote that connects you, your subject, and your listeners. Self-deprecating humor sometimes helps. And don't forget to introduce yourself if there is no one to perform that task. (Short, in-class presentations won't need much, if any, warm-up material.)

Use appropriate props. There's nothing wrong with a report that relies on the spoken word alone. Still, audiences appreciate supporting material, including flip charts that summarize key points; handouts that duplicate passages, texts, or data germane to the presentation; visual or audio samplings; and so on. All such materials, clearly labeled and handsomely reproduced, should also be genuinely relevant to the report. Resist the temptation to show something just because it's cool.

reference

Ideas

3

part three

Need help organizing or drafting? See page 334.

17 Brainstorming

find a topic/
get an idea

A great deal of thinking occurs at the beginning of a project or assignment. How exactly will you fill ten or twenty pages with your thoughts on Incan architecture, the life cycle of dung beetles, or what you did last summer? What hasn't already been written about religion in America, cattle in Africa, or the cultural hegemony of iTunes? What do you do when you find yourself clueless or stuck or just overwhelmed by the possibilities—or lack thereof? Simple answer: Brainstorm.

Put a notion on the table and see where it goes—and what you might do with it or learn about it. Toy with an idea like a kitten with a catnip mouse. Push yourself to think through, around, over, and under a proposition. Dare to be politically incorrect or, alternatively, so conventional that your good behavior might scare even your elders.

But don't think of brainstorming as disordered and muddled. Consider the metaphor itself: Storms are awesomely organized events. They generate power by physical processes so complex that we're just beginning to understand them. Similarly, a first-rate brainstorming session spins ideas from the most complex chemistry in our bodies, the tumult of the human brain.

Naturally, you'll match brainstorming techniques to the type of writing you hope to produce. Beginning a personal tale about a trip to Wrigley Field, you might make a list of sensory details to jog your memory—the smell of hot dogs, the catcalls of fans, the green

Chalkboards, flip charts, and even sticky notes can help you rapidly record your ideas.

grass of the outfield. But for an assigned report on DNA fingerprinting, your brainstorming might itemize things you still must learn about the subject: what DNA fingerprinting is, how it is done, when it can be used, how reliable it is, and so on.

Find routines that support thinking.   Use whatever brainstorming techniques get you invested in a project. Jogging, swimming, knitting, or sipping brew at the coffeehouse may be your stimulus of choice. Such routine activities keep the body occupied, allowing insights to mature. Your thoughts do need to be captured and recorded, either in notes or, perhaps, voice memos.

One warning: Brainstorming activities of this kind can become simple procrastination. That comfortable chair in Starbucks might evolve into a spot too social for much thinking or writing. Recognize when your productivity has been compromised and change tactics.

> Ideas won't keep; something must be done about them.

—Alfred North Whitehead

Build lists.   Brainstorm to list potential topics or, if you already have a subject, to explore the major points you might cover. Add all items that come to mind: If you're too picky or detailed at the start, you defeat the power of brainstorming—in which one idea, written on paper or on a screen, suggests another, then another. Even grocery lists work this way.

Lists work especially well when you already know something about a subject. For instance, preparing a letter to the editor in defense of collegiate sports, you can first inventory the arguments you've heard from friends or have made yourself. Then list the counterarguments you come up with as well. Write down everything that bubbles up, both reasonable and off-the-wall. Finally, winnow out the better items based on their quality or plausibility, and arrange them tentatively, perhaps pairing arguments and counterarguments. Even when you don't know much about a potential topic, assemble a list of basic questions that might lead to greater knowledge, to stimulate your ideas and thinking.

Map your ideas.   If you find a list too static as a prompt for writing, another way may be to explore the relationships between your ideas *visually*. Some writers use logic trees to represent their thinking, starting with a single general concept and breaking it into smaller and smaller parts. You can find examples of "tree diagrams" from many fields by using a search engine to investigate a keyword and then clicking the Image option.

Try freewriting.   Freewriting is a brainstorming technique of nonstop composing designed to loosen the bonds we sometimes use to clamp down on our own thinking. Typically, freewriting sessions begin slowly, with disconnected phrases and words. Suddenly, there's a spark and words stream onto the paper—but slow or fast you must still keep writing. The moment you settle back in your chair, you break the circuit that makes freewriting work. By forcing yourself to write, you push yourself to think and, perhaps, to discover what really matters in a subject.

Like other brainstorming techniques, freewriting works best when you already have some knowledge of your subject. You might freewrite successfully about standardized testing or working at fast-food restaurants if you've experienced both; you'll stumble trying to freewrite on subjects you know next to nothing about, maybe thermodynamics, ergonomics, or the career of Maria Callas. Freewriting tends to work best for personal narratives, personal statements, arguments, and proposals, and less well for reports and technical projects.

Although freewriting comes in many forms, the basic formula is simple.

STAGE ONE

- Start with a blank screen or sheet of paper.
- Put your subject or title at the top of the page.
- Write on that subject nonstop for ten minutes.
- Don't stop typing or lift your pen from the paper during that time.
- Write nonsense if you must, but keep writing.

STAGE TWO

- Stop at ten minutes and review what you have written.
- Underscore or highlight the most intriguing idea, phrase, or sentence.
- Put the highlighted idea at the top of a new screen or sheet.
- Freewrite for another ten minutes on the new, more focused topic.

Use memory prompts.   When writing personal narratives, institutional histories, or even résumés, you might trigger ideas with photographs, yearbooks, diaries, or personal memorabilia. An image from a vacation may bring events worth writing about flooding back to you. Even checkbooks or credit card statements may help you reconstruct past events or see patterns in your life worth exploring in writing.

Search online for your ideas.   You can get lots of ideas simply by exploring most topics online through keywords. Indeed, determining those initial keywords and then following up with new terms you discover while browsing is a potent form of brainstorming in itself.

A photo album is a great place to look for writing ideas, because we tend to document meaningful moments.

How to... *Browse for ideas*

Uncle Bob, who's a cop, complains about the "*CSI* effect." What is that?

Wikipedia isn't an academic source, but it gives me a new term: "*CSI* syndrome."

Web   Images   Video   News   Maps   Gmail   mor

Google csi effect

Web

1 **CSI Effect** - Wikipedia, the free encyclopedi
The "**CSI Effect**" (sometimes referred to as the "**CSI**
phenomenon of popular television shows such as the
en.wikipedia.org/wiki/**CSI**_Effect - 45k - Cached - Sin

2 USATODAY.com - '**CSI effect**' has juries w
Like viewers across the nation, folks in Galveston, T
crime-scene investigators. Jury consultant Robert Hi
www.usatoday.com/news/nation/2004-08-05-**csi**-effe

3 "**CSI**' Effect" Is Mixed Blessing for Real Cr
Popular television shows like **CSI**: Crime Scene Inve
in forensics. So what is the job of a crime-scene inve
news.nationalgeographic.com/news/2004/09/0923_04
Cached - Similar pages

The **CSI effect**: On TV, it's all slam-dunk ev

Your continued donations keep Wikipedia running!

| article | discussion | edit this page | history |

CSI Effect

From Wikipedia, the free encyclopedia

The "**CSI Effect**" (sometimes referred to as the "**CSI syndrome**") i
phenomenon of popular television shows such as the *CSI* franchise
jury members' real-world expectations of forensic science, especia
and DNA testing.[1] Much of these concerns stem from the "drama
writers of forensic science television--glamorizing the field, overstat
techniques, and exaggerating the abilities of forensic science.[2] Th
the way many trials are presented today, in that prosecutors are p
forensic evidence in court.[3][4]

WIKIPEDIA
The Free Encyclopedia

navigation
- Main Page
- Contents
- Featured content
- Current events
- Random article

interaction
- About Wikipedia
- Community portal
- Recent changes
- Contact Wikipedia
- Donate to Wikipedia
- Help

search

[Go] [Search]

toolbox
- What links here
- Related changes

Contents [hide]
1 Manifestations of the CSI Effect
1.1 Influence on jurors
1.2 Influence on the criminal mind
1.3 Influence on forensic science training programs
2 See also
3 References

Manifestations of the CSI Effect

Influence on jurors

Although speculation as to the validity of the *CSI* effect abounds,[5]

Consider the source.

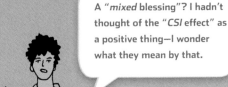

It looks like lawyers and juries are affected—and juries think trials should be like *CSI* episodes.

A "*mixed* blessing"? I hadn't thought of the "*CSI* effect" as a positive thing—I wonder what they mean by that.

USA TODAY, August 5, 2004. Reprinted with permission.

USA TODAY Classifieds: | careerbuilder.com | Marketplace

Home
News
Travel
Money
Sports
Life
Tech
Weather
Search

powered by YAHOO! GO

Wash/Politics
Washington home
Washington briefs
Government guide
Health&Behavior
H&B home
Medical resources
Health information
Opinion
Opinion home
Columnists
Cartoons
More News
Top news briefs
Nation briefs
World briefs

Nation

E-MAIL THIS · PRINT THIS · SAVE THIS · MOST POPULAR · S
Posted 8/5/2004 1:05 AM Updated 8/5/2004 1:06 AM

'CSI effect' has juries wanting more evidence

By Richard Willing, USA TODAY

Like viewers across the nation, folks in Galveston, Texas, watch a lot of TV shows about crime-scene investigators. Jury consultant Robert Hirschhorn couldn't be happier about that.

CSI: Miami characters sort through evidence. It seems the crime show franchise has given jurors an incomplete picture of forensics. CBS

NATIONAL GEOGRAPH
REPORTING YOUR WORLD DA

MAIN ANIMAL NEWS ANCIENT WORLD ENVIRONMENT NEWS CULTURES NEWS

'"CSI" Effect" Is Mixed Blessing for Real Crime Labs

Stefan Lovgren
for National Geographic News
September 23, 2004

A few months ago, a crime scene investigator from the Los Angeles County Sheriff's Department was dusting for fingerprints at the scene of a residential burglary. The victim of the crime was not impressed, however. "That's not the way they do it on television," she told the investigator.

Capt. Chris Beattie, who heads the L.A. County's Scientific Services Bureau—or "the crime lab"—calls it the "*CSI* effect." The popularity of television shows like *CSI: Crime Scene Investigation* and *Forensic Files,* he says, has turned millions of viewers into real-life science sleuths.

Printer Friendly
Email to

The phenomenon has reached into both classrooms and courtrooms. Universities have

2

Determine who has something at stake.

3

Question claims.

18 Brainstorming with Others

You've probably seen films or TV series that mock groupthink in corporations—wherein cowering yes-men and -women gather around a table to rubber-stamp the dumb ideas of a domineering CEO. Real group brainstorming is just the opposite. It encourages a freewheeling discovery and sharing of ideas among people with a stake in the outcome.

Group brainstorming comes in several varieties. The notorious college dorm-room bull session is a famous example, though with obvious defects. Such boozy late-night talk is likely to be frank,

collaborate

open-ended, wide-ranging, and passionate. But it typically doesn't lead anywhere or produce an agenda for action.

In academic or professional situations, formal brainstorming within a group requires specific strategies to produce solid results.

Choose a leader.   Leaders should be strong enough to keep discussions moving, cordial enough to encourage everyone to participate, and modest enough to draw out a range of opinions without pursuing agendas of their own. The leader probably shouldn't be the person with the most power in the group—not the CEO, chair of the department, or president of the student government. In fact, in serious brainstorming sessions, an outsider or trained facilitator might be the best choice.

Begin with a goal and set an agenda.   Most groups don't brainstorm for the pleasure of it. Some need or concern brings participants to the table— for instance, an assignment that requires a committee's response or, maybe, decision-making for a project that's more work than one person can handle. The leader should get the group to agree on a goal and a simple agenda. Even if that goal is open-ended, it will help keep discussions on track. And both the goal and agenda can be written on a board or flip chart to keep the group on-message. Without an agenda, brainstorming activity can dissolve into a bull session.

As the session evolves, a leader should help the group understand what it is accomplishing by stating and restating positions as they develop from discussion, posing important questions, and recording ideas as they emerge.

Set time limits.   Groups are most productive when working against reasonable time restraints. Given open-ended sessions (such as those dorm-room all-nighters), nothing productive may ever occur. But with only an hour or two for brainstorming, a group serious about its work will focus mightily. Time restraints also give a leader leverage to stifle the chatterers.

Encourage everyone to participate.   A leader or facilitator can call on the quiet types, but other participants can help too just by asking a colleague, "What do you think?" In a group setting, a reluctant participant's first contribution is usually the toughest, but it's worth any prodding: The silent observer in a group may come up with the sharpest insight.

Avoid premature criticism.   Leaders and participants alike need to encourage outside-the-box thinking and avoid a tendency to cut off contributions at the knees. No sneering, guffawing, or eye-rolling—even when ideas *are* stupid. Early on, get every scheme, suggestion, and proposal on the blackboard or flip chart. Criticism and commentary can come later.

It might even help to open the session with everyone freewriting on a key idea for five or ten minutes as a warmup, then reading their best ideas aloud. ○

Test all ideas.   Sometimes, a group agrees too readily when a sudden good idea gains momentum. Such a notion should be challenged hard—even if it means someone has to play devil's advocate, that is, raise arguments or objections just to test the leading idea or claim. Even good ideas need to have their mettle proved.

Keep good records.   Many brainstorming sessions fail not because the ideas didn't emerge, but because no one bothered to catch them. Someone competent should take notes detailed enough to make sense a month later, when memories start to fade. Here again a flip chart may be useful, since points written on it don't get erased. The facilitator should follow up on the session by seeing that the notes get organized, written up, and promptly distributed to the group.

Agree on an end product.   Effective brainstorming sessions should lead to action of some kind or, at least, a clear agenda for further discussion. Keeping an eye on the clock, the leader of the group should wind up general discussion early enough to push the group toward conclusions and plans for action. Not every brainstorming session reaches its goals, but participants will want closure on their work.

get an idea
p. 308

Smart Reading

We get antsy when our written work gets criticized (or even edited) because ideas we put on a page or screen emerge from our own thinking—writing is *us*. Granted, our words rarely express *exactly* who we are, or what we've been imagining, but such distinctions get lost quickly when someone points to our work and says, "That's stupid" or "What nonsense!" The criticism cuts deep; it feels personal.

Challenges to a writer's assumptions, strategies, or evidence are part of the give-and-take of academic and professional life. You'll survive criticism and controversy if your work has integrity. But you'll have no defense at all if your writing is found thoughtless or careless when, in fact, *it is*.

Fortunately the surest way to avoid embarrassing criticism is also the best way to come up with fine ideas and impressive writing: *reading*. Reading can deepen your impressions of a subject, enrich your understanding, sharpen your critical acumen, and introduce you to alternative views. Reading also places you within a community of writers who have thought about a subject.

Of course, not all reading serves the same purposes.

- You pack a romance novel for pleasure reading on the beach.

- You consult stock market quotes or baseball box scores because you need info *now*.

read critically/read closely

317

- You check out a dozen scholarly books to do research for a paper.

- You read an old diary or memoir to imagine what life was like in the past.

- You thumb a graphic novel to move into a different reality.

Yet any of these reading experiences, as well as thousands of others, might lead to ideas for projects.

You've probably been thoroughly schooled in basic techniques of critical reading: Survey the table of contents; preread to get a sense of the whole; look up terms or concepts you don't know; and so on. It's good advice, especially for difficult scholarly or professional texts. Following is advice for using reading to boost your college-level writing.

Read to deepen what you already know.   Whatever your interests or experiences in life, you're not alone. Others have explored similar paths and probably written about them. Reading such work may give you confidence to bring your own thoughts to public attention. Whether your passion is tintype photography, skateboarding, or film fashions of the 1930s, you'll find excellent books on the subjects by browsing library catalogs or even just checking Amazon.com. ○

For example, if you have worked at a fast-food franchise and know what goes on there, you might find a book like Eric Schlosser's *Fast Food Nation: The Dark Side of the All-American Meal* engrossing. You'll be drawn in because your experience makes you an informed critic. You can agree and disagree intelligently with Schlosser and, perhaps, see how his arguments might be extended or amended. At a minimum, you'll walk away from the book knowing even more about the fast-food industry and knowing the titles of dozens of additional sources, should you want to learn more.

Read above your level of knowledge.   It's comfortable to connect with people online who share your interests, but you'll often be chatting with people who don't know much more than you do. To find new ideas, push your reading to a higher and more demanding level. Spend some time with

refine your search
p. 406

books and articles you can't blow right through. You'll know you are there when you find yourself looking up names, adding terms to your vocabulary, and feeling humbled at what you still need to learn about a subject. That's when thinking occurs and ideas germinate.

> If you don't have the time to read, you don't have the time or tools to write.
>
> —Stephen King

Don't get in a rut.   It's easy to shut down intellectually by always foraging in the same topics—like baby boomers who haven't moved on from Dylan and the Beatles. But most of us now have access to technologies that connect us to endless paths of information. So why, especially when you're young, restrict your life to superficial topics of immediate current interest: sports, celebrities, fashion, music, or politics?

But even these topics can take on texture if you examine them critically. The car guy who tricks out Civics or Lancers might start wondering about the economics of motor sports or the auto industry. A fan of contemporary music might suddenly wonder how genres like punk or hip-hop developed and what inspired the artists who created them. The information is out there and worth pursuing.

Be curious.   You'll never be at a loss for ideas if you learn to read the world critically. *Critically* does not mean finding fault with everything but rather letting nothing you experience breeze by without scrutiny. You can *read* the architecture of your dorm room, the latest trends in women's politics, the changing menu options in local restaurants, and ponder their meanings. Why are there so few men in liberal-arts courses? What topics does your campus newspaper studiously avoid and why? How have your friends changed now that most come equipped with earbuds and cell phones? The world you inhabit is a text to be read and reread.

Read for claims, reasons, and evidence.   Browsing online has made many of us superficial readers. For serious texts, forget speed-reading and slow down. Read more systematically and analytically. ○ Begin by identifying the claims writers make and the reasons they make them. Then examine the assumptions they work from and the evidence they present.

○

understand argument
p. 68

Claims are the passages in a text where a writer makes an assertion, offers an argument, or presents a hypothesis, for which the writer will provide evidence.

> Using a cell phone while driving is dangerous.
>
> Playing video games can improve intelligence.

Some assertions early in a work may seem to state a thesis or goal for a project, but that's only one type of claim. Sentences that assert or advance a writer's ideas about a topic may occur just about anywhere in an article, report, or book. So look for claims in the topic sentences of paragraphs, in transitional sentences, or in summary materials at the end of sections or the entire work. (The exception may be formal scientific writing, in which the hypothesis, results, and discussion will occur in specific sections of an article.) ○

Most major claims in a text are accompanied by supporting *reasons* either in the same sentence or in adjoining material. These reasons may be announced by expressions such as *because, if, to,* and *so.* Or look for more elaborate connective phrases that similarly imply a causal or logical link. The statement of a reason provides a rationale or a condition for accepting a claim.

> Using a cell phone while driving is dangerous *because* distractions are a proven cause of auto accidents.
>
> Playing video games can improve intelligence *if* they teach young gamers to make logical decisions quickly.

Supporting all important claims and reasons are *assumptions* or *premises.* In oral arguments when people say *I understand where you're coming from,* they signal that they get your assumptions. You want similar clarity when reading serious reports and arguments yourself, especially when claims are controversial or argumentative. Premises and assumptions are the values upon which writers and researchers base their work. They can be specific or general, conventional or highly controversial, such as the following.

> We should discourage behaviors that contribute to accidents.
>
> Improving intelligence is a desirable goal.

○

understand lab reports
p. 290

The physical world is organized by coherent and predictable principles.

Freedom is better than tyranny.

Developing the environment is better than preserving it.

Writers typically assume that they share basic premises with at least some of their readers. Or they take time to explain and defend their assumptions. As you read a serious work, try to locate or put into your own words its key assumptions—either stated outright in source material or, much more often, merely implied.

Finally, as you read, be sure that all major claims and assumptions are supported by *evidence* to confirm them. A claim without evidence attached is just that—a barefaced assertion no better than a child's "Oh yeah?" You should review evidence skeptically, always judging whether it is sufficient, complete, reliable, and unbiased. Does the source offer enough evidence to make a convincing case? Has the author done original research and drawn on respectable sources or, instead, relied on evidence that seems flimsy or anecdotal? These are questions to ask routinely and single-mindedly.

Read to expose logical fallacies.   Reasonable texts by honest writers have nothing to hide. They name names, identify sources, and generate appropriate emotions. They acknowledge weakness in their arguments and concede readily when the opposition has a point. Look for these qualities in the texts you read and use as sources.

However, be alert for the opposite strategy, often expressed through various logical fallacies. *Fallacies* are rhetorical moves that corrupt solid reasoning—the verbal equivalent of sleight of hand. When you read a text, look for the following devices and remain aware that they can undermine the credibility of a text.

- **Appeals to false authority.** Be suspicious of writers who may not actually have the knowledge, authority, or credentials to deal with their subjects: *I'm not a doctor, but I play one on television.*

- **Dogmatism.** Writers fall back on dogmatism whenever they want to give the impression, usually false, that they control the party line on an issue and know what all the correct answers are. The tip-off for dogma-tism can be the phrase *No serious person would disagree.* . . .

- **Ad hominem attacks.** Writers sometimes attempt to bolster their own credentials or authority by attacking the character of their opponents when character isn't an issue in the argument. They may even resort to name-calling or character assassination.

- **Either/or choices.** When complex issues are reduced to simple choices, look closer. Be deeply suspicious whenever you encounter some version of this collocation: *Either we . . . or we will surely.* . . . Also, writers reducing complicated issues to black-and-white will typically present one side as completely wrong.

"Either you left the TV on downstairs or we have whales again."

● **Scare tactics.** An argument that makes its appeal chiefly by raising fears—usually of the unknown—is automatically suspect. Examine such a claim carefully to see whether its warnings are backed by facts and good reasons. If not, point out the deficiency or don't cite the source.

● **Sentimental appeals.** Maybe it's fair for the Humane Society to decorate its pleas for cash with pictures of puppies, but you can see how the tactic might be abused. Be wary, too, of language that pushes buttons the same way, *oohing* and *aahing* readers out of their best judgment.

● **Hasty generalizations.** It is remarkably tempting to draw conclusions from one or two examples or instances, particularly when they are dramatic and fit the writer's preconceived notions. Ask questions whenever a writer seems too eager to make his or her point based on scant evidence.

● **Faulty causality.** Just because two events or phenomena occur close together in time doesn't mean that one caused the other. (The Tigers didn't start hitting *because* you put on the lucky boxers.) People are fond of leaping to such easy conclusions, but causal situations involving issues of science, health, politics, and culture are almost always too complicated to explain simply. Review closely any texts that push readers to make quick judgments. ○

understand causal
analysis p. 128

● **Equivocations and evasions.** *Equivocations* are lies that look like truths; *evasions* simply avoid the truth entirely. You'll find the statements of politicians and bureaucracies filled with such interesting uses of language: "It depends on what the meaning of the word *is* is." When you find these kinds of examples, take them apart to figure out what's really being said—or not said.

● **Straw men.** *Straw men* are easy or habitual targets that a writer aims at to win an argument. Often the issue in such an attack has long been defused or discredited: for example, welfare recipients driving Cadillacs; immigrants taking jobs from hard-working citizens; the rich not paying a fair share of taxes. Writers who resort to straw-man arguments may not have much else in their arsenals.

● **Slippery-slope arguments.** Take one wrong step off the righteous path and you'll slide all the way down the hill: That's the warning that a slippery-slope argument makes. They aren't always inaccurate, but be wary, particularly when the imagined chain of events begins to sound plausible. Will buying an SUV really doom the planet? Maybe not.

● **Bandwagon appeals.** People who want to be in on the latest trend or fad are easy targets, and advertisers know it. But be alert for feeding frenzies in the media or public arena too. When a writer suggests that it's time to stop debate and jump aboard the bandwagon, push back.

● **Faulty analogies.** Similes and analogies are worth applauding when they illuminate ideas or make them comprehensible or memorable. But analogies deserve more scrutiny when they have serious implications. Calling a military action either "another Vietnam" or a "crusade" might raise serious issues, as does comparing one's opponents to "Commies" or Nazis. Be skeptical of writers who use such tactics.

Experts

Forget about *expert* as an intimidating word. When you need help with your writing, you should consult knowledgeable people who either know more about your subject than you do or more about how to handle the project. Admittedly, those answers may come from different people, but that's not a problem: The more people you talk to, the better.

Knowledgeable people can get you on track quickly, confirming the merit of your topic ideas, cutting through issues irrelevant to your work, and directing you to the best sources.

ask for help

Talk with your instructor.   Don't be timid. Instructors hold office hours to answer your questions, especially about assignments. Save yourself time and, perhaps, much grief by getting feedback early on your ideas and topic. It's better to learn immediately that your thesis is hopeless, before you compose a first draft.

Just as important, your instructor might help you see aspects of a topic you hadn't noticed or direct you to indispensable sources. Don't try to write a paper only to please instructors, but you'd be foolish to ignore their counsel.

Take your ideas to the writing center.   Many student writers think the only time to use a campus writing center is when their teacher returns a draft on life support. Most writing center tutors prefer not to be seen as emergency room personnel. So they are eager to help at the start of a project, when you're still developing ideas and thinking about strategies. Tutors may not be experts on your subject, but they have seen enough bad papers to offer sensible advice for focusing a topic, shaping a thesis, or adapting a subject to an audience. ○ They also recognize when you're so clueless that you need to talk with your instructor pronto.

Find local experts.   Don't consult an expert for information you could find easily yourself in the library or online: Save human contacts for when you need serious help on a major writing project—a senior thesis, an important story for a campus periodical, a public presentation on a controversial subject. But then do take advantage of the human resources you have. Campuses are thick with knowledgeable people and that doesn't just include faculty in their various disciplines. Staff and administrative personnel at your school can advise you on everything from trends in college admissions to local crime statistics.

Look to the local community for expertise and advice as well. Is there a paper to be written about declining audiences for feature films? You couldn't call Steven Spielberg and get through, but you could chat with a few local theater owners or managers to learn what they think about the business. Their perceptions might change the direction of your project.

Check with librarians.   Campus librarians have lots of experience helping writers find information, steering you toward fertile topics and away from ideas that may not have much intellectual standing. They can't be as specific or directive as, for example, your instructor, but they have just as firm a grasp on the resources available for a project and what sorts of topic ideas the library's resources will and will not support.

Chat with peers.   Peers aren't really experts, but an honest classroom conversation among fellow students can be an eye-opening experience. You'll likely see a wide spectrum of opinions (if the discussion is frank) and even be surprised by objections to your ideas that you hadn't anticipated.

develop a thesis
p. 336

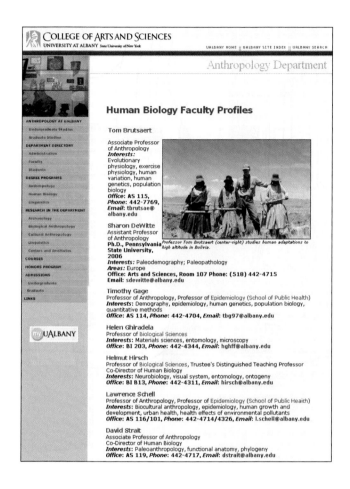

Peers often have a surprising range of knowledge and, if the group is diverse, your friends will bring a breadth of life experiences to the conversation. You might be eager to champion advances in medical technology, but someone from a community where hospitals can't afford high-tech gear might add a wrinkle to your thinking.

Shaping & Drafting

Need help developing your ideas? See page 346.   /   Need style help? See page 366.

22 Thesis

develop a thesis

A *thesis* is a statement in which a writer affirms or defends the specific idea that will focus or organize a paper. Typically, the thesis appears in an opening paragraph or section, but it may also emerge as the paper unfolds. In some cases, it may not be stated in classic form until the very conclusion. A thesis can be complex enough to require several sentences to explain, or a single sentence might suffice. But a thesis will be in the writing somewhere.

Offering a thesis is a move as necessary and, eventually, as instinctive to a writer as stepping on a clutch before shifting is to drivers. No thesis, no forward motion.

How do you write and frame a thesis? Consider the following advice.

Write a complete sentence.   Phrases can identify topic areas, even intriguing ones, but they don't make the assertions or claims that provoke thinking and require support. Sentences do. ⭕ None of the following phrases comes close to providing direction for a paper.

Polygamy in the United States

Reasons for global warming

Economist Steven D. Levitt's controversial theory about declining crime rates

common errors
p. 524

Make a significant claim or assertion.   *Significant* here means that the notion provokes discussion or inquiry. Give readers substance or controversy—in other words, a reason to spend time with your writing.

> Until communities recognize that polygamy still exists in parts of the United States, girls and young women will be exploited by the practice.
>
> Global warming won't stop until industrial nations either lower their standards of living or acknowledge the inevitability of nuclear power.

Write a declarative sentence, not a question.   Questions may focus attention, but they are not assertions. So, while you might use a question to introduce a topic, don't rely on it to state your claim. A humdrum question acting as a thesis can provoke simplistic responses. There's always the danger, too, that in offering your thesis as a question, you invite strong reactions from readers—and not the ones you want. But introduce an idea as a statement and you gain more control. One exception to this guideline: Provocative questions can often help structure personal and exploratory writing.

Expect your thesis to mature.   Your initial thesis will likely grow more complicated as you learn more about your subject. That's natural. But even at the outset, resist the notion that a thesis is simply a statement that breaks a subject into three parts. Conventional theses too often read like shopping lists, with few connections between the ideas presented. Just putting the claims in such a statement into a relationship often makes for a more compelling thesis. The items in olive type do that job in the second example below.

ORIGINAL THESIS

Crime in the United States has declined because more people are in prison, the population is growing older, and DNA testing has made it harder to get away with murder.

REVISED THESIS

It is much more likely that crime in the United States has declined because more people are in prison than because the population is growing older or DNA testing has made it harder to get away with murder.

Introduce a thesis early in a project.   This sound guideline is especially relevant for academic term papers. Instructors will usually want to know up front what the point of a paper will be, especially in reports and some arguments. Whether phrased as a single sentence or several, a thesis typically follows an introductory paragraph or two. Here's the thesis (highlighted in yellow) of Andrew Kleinfeld and Judith Kleinfeld's essay "Go Ahead, Call Us Cowboys," bringing up the rear of an opening paragraph that explains the context for their claim.

> Everywhere, Americans are called *cowboys*. On foreign tongues, the reference to America's Western rural laborers is an insult. Cowboys, we are told, plundered the earth, arrogantly rode roughshod over neighbors, and were addicted to mindless violence. So some of us hang our heads in shame. We shouldn't. The cowboy is in fact our Homeric hero, an arche-type that sticks because there's truth in it.

Or state a thesis late in a project.   In high school, you may have heard that the thesis statement is *always* the last sentence in the first paragraph. That may be so in conventional five-paragraph essays, but you'll rarely be asked to follow so predictable a pattern in college or elsewhere.

In fact, it is not unusual, especially in some arguments, for a paper to build toward a thesis—and that statement may not appear until the final paragraph or sentence. ○ Such a strategy makes sense when a claim might not be convincing or rhetorically effective if stated baldly at the opening of the piece. Bret Stephens uses this strategy in an essay entitled "Just Like Stalingrad" to debunk frequent comparisons between President George W. Bush and either Hitler or Stalin. Stephens's real concern turns out to be not these exaggerated comparisons themselves but rather what happens to language when it is abused by sloppy writers. The final two paragraphs of his essay summarize this case and, arguably, lead up to a thesis in the very last sentence of the essay—more rhetorically convincing there because it comes as something of a surprise.

> Care for language is more than a concern for purity. When one describes President Bush as a fascist, what words remain for real fascists? When one describes Fallujah as Stalingrad-like, how can we express, in the words that remain to the language, what Stalingrad was like?

understand arguments
p. 68

George Orwell wrote that the English language "becomes ugly and inaccurate because our thoughts are foolish, but the slovenliness of our language makes it easier for us to have foolish thoughts." In taking care with language, we take care of ourselves.

—*Wall Street Journal*, June 23, 2004

Write a thesis to fit your audience and purpose.   Almost everything you write will have a purpose and a point (see following table), but not every piece will have a formal thesis. In professional and scientific writing, readers want to know your claim immediately. For persuasive and exploratory writing, you might prefer to keep readers intrigued or have them track the path of your thinking, and delay the thesis until later.

Type of Assignment	Thesis or Point
Narrative	Usually implied, not stated. (See thesis example on p. 8.)
Report	Thesis usually previews material or explains its purpose. (See thesis example on p. 60.)
Argument	Thesis makes an explicit and arguable claim. (See thesis example on p. 73.)
Evaluation	Thesis makes an explicit claim of value based on criteria of evaluation. (See thesis example on p. 105.)
Causal analysis	Thesis asserts or denies a causal relationship, based on an analysis of evidence. (See thesis example on p. 131.)
Proposal	Thesis offers a proposal for action. (See thesis example on p. 165.)
Literary analysis	Thesis explains the point of the analysis. (See thesis example on p. 189.)
Rhetorical analysis	Thesis explains the point of the analysis. (See thesis example on p. 236.)
Essay examination	Thesis previews the entire answer, like a mini-outline. (See thesis example on p. 258.)
Position paper	Thesis makes specific assertion about reading or issue raised in class. (See thesis example on p. 263.)
E-mail	Subject line may function as thesis or title. (See thesis example on p. 268.)
Business letter	Thesis states the intention for writing. (See thesis example on p. 276.)
Résumé	"Career objective" may function as a thesis. (See thesis example on p. 282.)
Personal statement	May state an explicit purpose or thesis or lead readers to inferences about qualifications. (See thesis example on p. 287.)
Lab report	Thesis describes purpose of experiment. (See thesis example on p. 293.)
Oral report	Introduction or preview slide describes purpose. (See thesis example on p. 301–02.)

24 Outlines

Outlines are supposed to make writing easier, not harder, as they help you put ideas in manageable form. And you'll feel more confident when you begin with a plan. The trick is to start simple and let outlines evolve to fit your needs.

Begin with scratch outlines.   Many writers prefer working first with scratch, or informal, outlines—the verbal equivalent of the clever mechanical idea hurriedly sketched on a cocktail napkin. In fact, the analogy is especially apt because good ideas often do evolve from simple, sometimes crude, notions that begin to make sense only when seen on paper. Both the Internet and the structure of the DNA molecule began with the visual equivalents of scratch outlines.

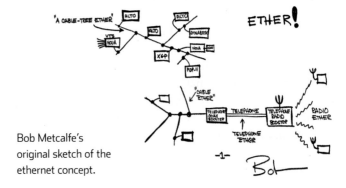

Bob Metcalfe's original sketch of the ethernet concept.

List key ideas.   Write down your preliminary thoughts so you can see what they are exactly, eliminating any that obviously overlap. Keep these notes brief but specific, using words and phrases rather than complete sentences. Your initial scratch outline will likely resemble a mildly edited brainstorming list, like the one that follows.

> <u>Fuel-efficient vehicles</u>
>
> Hybrids
> Electric cars haven't worked well
> Europeans prefer diesels
> Strengths and weaknesses
> Costs might be high
> Mechanically reliable?

Once you have ideas, begin applying the three principles that make outlining such a powerful tool of organization: *relationship, subordination,* and *sequence.*

Look for relationships.   Examine the initial items on your list and try grouping *like* with *like*—or look for opposites and contrasts. Experiment with various arrangements or clusters. In the brief sketch outline above, for example, you might decide that the items fall into two distinct categories. The three types of fuel-efficient cars are obviously related, while the remaining items represent aspects of these vehicles.

Hybrids	Strengths
Electric cars	Weaknesses
Diesels	Costs
	Reliability

Subordinate ideas.   Some ideas belong not only grouped with others but also under them—that is to say, they belong to a smaller subset within a larger set. Outlines are built on this principle of subordination or hierarchy: You are systematically dividing a subject into topics and subtopics.

For instance, looking again at those simple groupings of fuel-efficient vehicles, you could argue that *cost* and *reliability* are items that fit better under either *strengths* or *weaknesses*. They are aspects of these larger categories. So you remove them from the outline for the moment.

You might notice, too, that your notes so far suggest a comparison/ contrast structure for your project. (See "Compare and contrast" on p. 114 of Chapter 4, "Evaluation.") Deciding to replace *strengths* and *weaknesses* with the slightly more aggressive terms *advantages* and *disadvantages*, you sketch out a rather more complex outline.

<u>Fuel-efficient vehicles</u>
Advantages
    Hybrids
    Electric cars
    Diesels
Disadvantages
    Hybrids
    Electric cars
    Diesels

Decide on a sequence.   Now that you've moved from an initial list of ideas to a basic design, consider in which order to present the material. You might arrange the items chronologically or by magnitude. Or your order may be determined rhetorically—by how you want readers to respond.

Let's say you drive a Prius and have done enough research to believe that hybrids represent the best option for saving on fuel costs. So you arrange the paper to end on that note, understanding that readers are most likely to remember what they read last. Reading the end of your paper, the audience will focus on the advantages of gas-electric hybrid vehicles.

A. Disadvantages of fuel-efficient vehicles
    1. Electrics
    2. Diesels
    3. Gas-electric hybrids
B. Advantages of fuel-efficient vehicles
    1. Electrics
    2. Diesels
    3. Gas-electric hybrids

Move up to a formal outline.   You may be required to submit a formal outline with your final paper. By adhering to the following outline conventions, you can ferret out weaknesses in your thinking. ○

- Align the headings at every level (see example).

- Present at least two items at every heading level (I, A, and 1). If you can't find a second item to match the first in a new level of heads, perhaps the new level isn't needed.

- Present all items (except the thesis) as complete and parallel statements (not questions), properly punctuated.

- Place a topic sentence above the outline, underlined or italicized. That topic sentence sitting atop the project may keep you from wandering off-subject.

Thesis: <u>Though all fuel-efficient vehicles have technological strengths and weaknesses, hybrids currently represent the best option for drivers today.</u>

I.   Currently available fuel-efficient vehicles have different technological problems.
    A. Electric vehicles lack versatility.
        1. Their batteries limit them to city use, preferably in flat regions.
        2. Their electric batteries are heavy, expensive, and slow to charge.
    B. Diesel vehicles can be truck-like.
        1. Their emissions are laden with harmful particulates.
        2. They smoke when cold.
        3. Their fuel is smelly and toxic.
    C. Gas-electric hybrids are technologically risky.
        1. They are expensive.
        2. Their dual propulsion systems (gas and electric) are complex.
II. Fuel-efficient vehicles have significant strengths.
    A. Electric vehicles are simple and civilized machines.
        1. They emit no measurable pollution where they are used.
        2. Their motors are almost silent and free of vibration.
    B. Diesels are robust vehicles suitable for all road conditions.
        1. Their engines are based on well-proven and robust technology.
        2. They use fuel efficiently.
    C. Gas-electric hybrids combine advantages of other fuel-efficient vehicles.
        1. They work like electric vehicles in the city.
        2. They are as strong as diesels on the highway.
        3. They combine well-proven electric and internal-combustion technologies.

develop a thesis
p. 336

25 Paragraphs

develop
ideas

Paragraphs are a practical invention, created to make long continuous blocks of writing easier to read by dividing them up. Because they give writers a physical way to shape ideas and transmit them to readers, paragraphs are a powerful tool. You've heard many rules and definitions over the years, but the fact is that paragraphs exist to help you develop and structure your ideas, not the other way around. Here are some helpful ways to think about them.

Make sure paragraphs lead somewhere. Sometimes you'll use an explicit topic sentence to state your point and introduce a claim that the rest of your paragraph will develop. ○ But, just as often, you may wait until the concluding sentences to make your point, or you may weave a key idea into the fabric of the entire paragraph (as in the first paragraph of the example below). Whatever your strategy, all paragraphs should do significant work: introduce a subject, move a narrative forward, offer a new argument or claim, provide support for a claim already made, contradict another point, amplify an idea, furnish more examples, even bring discussion to an end. It has to do *something* that readers see as purposeful and connected to what comes before and after.

For instance, reviewing the third album of the rock band Coldplay, music critic Jon Pareles leads his readers through an opening paragraph demanding enough to try any rocker's patience. Where's he going with this? But then he delivers his

346

develop a thesis
p. 336

deathblow in a second, much shorter, paragraph. Suddenly, you have no doubt where Pareles stands—and probably want to read the entire review, even if you like the band.

> There's nothing wrong with self-pity. As a spur to songwriting, it's right up there with lust, anger, and greed, and probably better than the remaining deadly sins. There's nothing wrong, either, with striving for musical grandeur, using every bit of skill and studio illusion to create a sound large enough to get lost in. Male sensitivity, a quality that's under siege in a pop culture full of unrepentant bullying and machismo, shouldn't be dismissed out of hand, no matter how risible it can be in practice. And building a sound on the lessons of past bands is virtually unavoidable.
>
> But put them all together and they add up to Coldplay, the most insufferable band of the decade.
>
> —"The Case Against Coldplay," *New York Times,* June 5, 2005

Develop ideas adequately. Instructors who insist that paragraphs run a minimum number of sentences (say 6–10) are usually just tired of students who don't back up claims with details and evidence. ○ In fact, most writers don't count sentences when they build paragraphs. Instead, they develop a sense for paragraph length, matching the swell of their ideas to the habits of their intended readers.

Consider the following paragraph, which describes the last moments of the final Apollo moon mission in December 1972. The paragraph might be reduced to a single sentence: *All that remained of the 363-foot Saturn V* Apollo 17 *launch vehicle was a 9-foot capsule recovered in the ocean.* But what would be lost? The pleasure of the full paragraph resides in the details the writer assembles to support the final sentence, which contains his point.

> A powerful Sikorsky Sea King helicopter, already hovering nearby as they [the *Apollo 17* crew] hit the water, retrieved the astronauts and brought them to the carrier, where the spacecraft was recovered shortly later. The recovery crew saw not a gleaming instrument of exotic perfection, but a blasted, torn, and ragged survivor, its titanic strength utterly exhausted, a husk now a shell. The capsule they hauled out of the ocean was all that remained of the *Apollo 17* Saturn V. The journey had spent, incinerated, smashed, or blistered into atoms every other part of the colossal, 363-foot white rocket, leaving only this burnt and brutalized 9-foot capsule. A great

understand argument
p. 68

△

shining army had set out over the horizon, and a lone squadron had
returned, savaged beyond recognition, collapsing into the arms of its
rescuers, dead. Such was the price of reaching for another world.

—David West Reynolds, *Apollo: The Epic Journey to the Moon*

Organize paragraphs logically.   It would be surprising if paragraphs
didn't borrow structural strategies used by full essays: thesis and support,
sequence, and division. But ideas drive the shape of paragraphs, not patterns
of organization. Most writers don't pause to wonder whether their next
paragraph should follow a narrative or cause-effect plan. They just write it,
making sure it makes a point and offers sufficient evidence to keep readers
engaged.

In fact, individual paragraphs in any longer piece can be organized
many different ways. And because paragraphs are relatively short, you
usually see their patterns unfold right before your eyes. Following are some
paragraphs from an essay by Jon Katz entitled "Do Dogs Think?" Each uses
the structure Katz needs at that given moment.

Narrative paragraph
describes changes in Blue's
behavior.

Blue, Heather's normally affectionate and obedient Rottweiler, began
tearing up the house shortly after Heather went back to work as an
accountant after several years at home. The contents of the trash cans
were strewn all over the house. A favorite comforter was destroyed. Then
Blue began peeing all over Heather's expensive new living-room carpet
and systematically ripped through cables and electrical wires.

Katz uses *causal* pattern to
explore Blue's behavioral
problem.

Lots of dogs get nervous when they don't know what's expected of
them, and when they get anxious, they can also grow restless. Blue hadn't
had to occupy time alone before. Dogs can get unnerved by this. They
bark, chew, scratch, destroy. Getting yelled at and punished later doesn't
help: The dog probably knows it's doing something wrong, but it has no
idea what. Since there's nobody around to correct behaviors when the dog
is alone, how could the dog know which behavior is the problem? Which
action was wrong?

Paragraph uses simple
statement-proof structure.

I don't believe that dogs act out of spite or that they can plot
retribution, though countless dog owners swear otherwise. To punish or
deceive requires the perpetrator to understand that his victim or object has
a particular point of view and to consciously work to manipulate or thwart
it. That requires mental processes dogs don't have.

Why will Clementine come instantly if she's looking at me, but not if she's sniffing deer droppings? Is it because she's being stubborn or, as many people tell me, going through "adolescence"? Or because, when following her keen predatory instincts, she simply doesn't hear me? Should my response be to tug at her leash or yell? Maybe I should be sure we've established eye contact before I give her a command, or better yet, offer a liver treat as an alternative to whatever's distracting her. But how do I establish eye contact when her nose is buried? Can I cluck or bark? Use a whistle or hoot like an owl?

I've found that coughing, of all things, fascinates her, catches her attention, and makes her head swivel, after which she responds. If you walk with us, you will hear me clearing my throat repeatedly. What can I say? It works. She looks at me, comes to me, gets rewarded.

—Slate.com, October 6, 2005

> These two paragraphs follow *problem-solution* structure common in *proposal* arguments.

Design paragraphs for readability.   Paragraph breaks work best when they coincide with shifts or breaks within the writing itself. Readers understand that your thoughts have moved in some different direction. But paragraphs are often at the mercy of a text's physical environment as well. When you read a news items on the Web, the short paragraphs used in these single-column stories look fine. But hit the "print this article" link and the text suddenly sprawls across the screen, becoming difficult to read.

The point? You can manipulate the length and shape of paragraphs to suit the environment in which your words will appear.

Use paragraphs to manage transitions.   Paragraphs often provide direction in a paper. An opening paragraph can be used to set the scene in a narrative or to preview the content in a report. ○ You might occasionally use very brief paragraphs—sometimes just a sentence or two long—to punctuate a piece by drawing attention to a turn in your thinking or offering a strong judgment. You've likely seen paragraphs that consist of nothing more than an indignant "Nonsense!" or a sarcastic "Nuts" or "Go figure." There's a risk in penning a paragraph with so much attitude, but it's an option when the occasion calls for it. In longer papers, you might need full transitional paragraphs to summarize what has already been covered or to point the project in new directions.

shape a beginning
p. 354

26

Transitions

What exactly makes words, sentences, and ideas flow from paragraph to paragraph as fluidly as Tour de France champion Lance Armstrong cycling through the French Alps? *Transitional words and phrases,* many writers would reply—thinking of words such as *and, but, however, neither . . . nor, first . . . second . . . third,* and so on. Placed where readers need them, these connecting words make a paper read smoothly. But they are only part of the story.

connect ideas

Almost any successful piece of writing is held together by more devices than most writers can consciously juggle. Fortunately, a few of the devices—such as connections between pronouns and their referents—almost take care of themselves. Here are some guidelines for making smooth transitions between ideas in paragraphs and sections of your writing.

Common Transitions

Connection or Consequence	Contrast	Correlation	Sequence or Time	Indication
and	but	if . . . then	first . . . second	this
or	yet	either . . . or	and then	that
so	however	from . . . to	initially	there
therefore	nevertheless		subsequently	for instance
moreover	on the contrary		before	for example
consequently	despite		after	in this case
hence	still		until	
	although		next	
			in conclusion	

Use appropriate transitional words and phrases.   There's nothing complicated or arcane about them: You'll recognize every word in any list of transitions. But be aware that they have different functions and uses, with subtle differences even between words as close in meaning as *but* and *yet*.

Transitional words are often found at the beginnings of sentences and paragraphs, simply because that's the place where readers expect a little guidance. There are no rules, per se, for positioning transitions—though they can be set off from the rest of the sentence with commas.

Use the right word or phrase to show time or sequence.   Readers often need specific words or phrases to help keep events in order. Such expressions can simply mark off stages: *first, second, third.* Or they might help readers keep track of more complicated passages of time.

Use sentence structure to connect ideas.   When you build sentences with similar structures, readers will infer that the ideas in them are related. Devices you can use to make this kind of linkage include *parallelism* and *repetition*.

In the following example, the final paragraph in Catherine Crier's *The Case Against Lawyers*, you can see both strategies at work. Though its structure is more elaborate than you would ordinarily use, the paragraph brings a lengthy book to a rousing conclusion. Parallel items are highlighted.

> Despite the horror, September 11 was an amazing example of the best we can be. It was not rules or regulations that made us great that day. It certainly wasn't lawyers or lawsuits. It was just an emotion and feeling of unity that gave us strength in the face of such tragedy. It is time to do more than fly the flag. We must understand and proclaim American principles that have given life to hopes and dreams around the world. We must actively rescue our liberties from those who would tyrannize us. Finally, we must restore the rule of law to its proper place as our safeguard in a government created of and by and for the American people.

Pay attention to nouns and pronouns.   Understated transitions in a piece can occur between pronouns and their antecedents, but make sure the relationships between the nouns and pronouns are clear. ○ And, fortunately, readers usually don't mind encountering a pronoun over and over—except maybe *I*. Note how effortlessly Adam Nicolson moves between *George Abbot, he,* and *man* in the following paragraph from *God's Secretaries* (2003), in which the writer describes one of the men responsible for the King James translation of the Bible:

> George Abbot was perhaps the ugliest of them all, a morose, intemperate man, whose portraits exude a sullen rage. Even in death, he was portrayed on his tomb in Holy Trinity, Guilford, as a man of immense weight, with heavy, wrinkled brow and coldly open, staring eyes. He looks like a bruiser, a man of such conviction and seriousness that anyone would think twice about crossing him. What was it that made George Abbot so angry?

Use synonyms.   Simply by repeating a noun from sentence to sentence, you make an obvious and logical connection within a paper—whether you are naming an object, an idea, or a person. To avoid monotony, vary terms you have to use frequently. But don't strain with archaic or inappropriate synonyms which will distract the reader.

○

common errors
p. 524

Note the sensible variants on the word *trailer* in the following paragraph.

> Hype and hysteria have always been a part of movie advertising, but the frenzy of film trailers today follows a visual style first introduced by music videos in the 1980s. The quick cut is everything, accompanied by a deafening soundtrack. Next time you go to a film, study the three or four previews that precede the main feature. How are these teasers constructed? What are their common features? What emotions or reactions do they raise in you? What might trailers say about the expectations of audiences today?

Use physical devices for transitions.   You know all the ways movies manage transitions between scenes, from quick cuts to various kinds of dissolves. Writing has fewer visual techniques to mark transitions, but they are important. Titles and headings in lab reports, for instance, let your reader know precisely when you are moving from "Method" to "Results" to "Discussion." ○ In books, you'll encounter chapter breaks as well as divisions within chapters, sometimes marked by asterisks or perhaps a blank space. Seeing these markers, readers expect that the narration is changing in some way. Even the numbers in a list or shaded boxes in a magazine can be effective transitional devices, moving readers from one place to another.

Read a draft aloud to locate weak transitions.   The best way to test your transitions in a paper or project may be to listen to yourself. As you read, mark every point in the paper where you pause, stumble, or find yourself adding a transitional word or phrase not in the original text. Record even the smallest bobble because tiny slips have a way of cascading into bigger problems.

understand lab reports
p. 290

27

Introductions

An introduction has to grab and hold a reader's attention, but that's not all. It also must introduce a topic, a writer, and a purpose. Like the music over a film's opening credits, an introduction tells readers what to expect. Any doubts about where the following opening lines are heading?

shape a
beginning

> Use this package to figure and pay your estimated tax. If you are not required to make estimated tax payments for 2005, you can discard this package.
>
> —Form 1040-ES/V (OCR) Estimated Tax for Individuals, Department of the Treasury, Internal Revenue Service

> The shell game that political professionals play with the campaign laws has taken an encouraging hit in the House. Enough Democrats joined Republicans to pass a bill to plug the egregious soft-money loophole used in 2004 to flood the presidential campaign with hundreds of millions of dollars in attack ads and voter drives.
>
> —"Political Animal Bites Fat Cat," Editorial, *New York Times*, April 8, 2006

Of course, you will want to write introductions that fit your projects. In some cases a single line may be enough—as in an e-mail request for information. ○ A paragraph can provide all the push you need to get a short paper rolling. In a senior thesis or

understand e-mail
p. 266

book, a preface or an entire chapter can set the
stage for your project. Realize, too, that in longer
projects, you'll write what amounts to an introduction for every new section or major division.

What should your introductory paragraphs
accomplish? Following are some options.

Announce your project.   In academic papers,
introductions typically declare a subject directly
and indicate how it will be developed. Quite often,
an introductory paragraph or section leads directly
to a thesis statement or a hypothesis. ○ This is a
pattern you can use in many situations.

> In her novel *Wuthering Heights* (1847), Emily Brontë presents the story
> of the families of Wuthering Heights and Thrushcross Grange through the
> seemingly impartial perspective of Nelly Dean, a servant who grows up with
> the families. Upon closer inspection, however, it becomes apparent that
> Nelly acts as much more than a bystander in the tragic events taking place
> around her. In her status as an outsider with influence over the families,
> Nelly strikingly resembles the Byronic hero Heathcliff and competes with
> him for power. Although the author depicts Heathcliff as the more overt
> gothic hero, Brontë allows the reader to infer from Nelly's story her true
> character and role in the family. The author draws a parallel between Nelly
> Dean and Heathcliff in their relationships to the Earnshaw family, in their
> similar roles as tortured heroes, and in their competition for power within
> their adoptive families.
>
> —Manasi Deshpande, "Servant and Stranger: Nelly and Heathcliff in
> *Wuthering Heights*"

Paper opens by identifying
its general topic or theme.

Detailed thesis states what
paper will prove.

Preview your project.   Sometimes you'll have to use an introductory
section to set up the material to follow, helping readers to understand why
an issue deserves their attention. You might, for example, present an anecdote, describe a trend, or point to some change or development readers may
not have noticed. Then you can explore its significance or implications. In
the following example, Gabriela Montell, a writer for *The Chronicle of Higher*

○
develop a thesis
p. 336

Education, first describes a research study to then explain why she is interested in whether looks matter for college professors.

News article opens by getting readers interested in research study.

Researchers identified and study described in sufficient, but limited, detail.

Professors aren't known for fussing about their looks, but the results of a new study suggest they may have to if they want better teaching evaluations.

Daniel Hamermesh, a professor of economics at the University of Texas at Austin, and Amy Parker, one of his students, found that attractive professors consistently outscore their less comely colleagues by a significant margin on student evaluations of teaching. The findings, they say, raise serious questions about the use of student evaluations as a valid measure of teaching quality.

In their study, Mr. Hamermesh and Ms. Parker asked students to look at photographs of ninety-four professors and rate their beauty. Then they compared those ratings to the average student evaluation scores for the courses taught by those professors. The two found that the professors who had been rated among the most beautiful scored a point higher than those rated least beautiful (that's a substantial difference, since student evaluations don't generally vary by much).

Full story will examine implications of study for educators.

While it's not news that beauty trumps brains in many quarters, you would think that the ivory tower would be relatively exempt from such shallowness.

—"Do Good Looks Equal Good Evaluations?" October 15, 2003

Provide background information.   Decide what your readers need to know about a subject and then fill in the blanks. Provide too little background information on a subject and readers may find the remainder of the project confusing. Supply too much context and you lose readers quickly: They may assume that the paper has nothing new to offer them or may simply grow impatient.

And yet, even when readers know a subject well, you still need, especially in academic papers, to answer basic questions about the project or topic—*who, what, where, when, how,* and *why.* Name names in your introduction, offer accurate titles, furnish dates, and explain what your subject is. Imagine readers from just slightly outside your target audience who might not instantly recall, for instance, that Shakespeare wrote a play titled *Henry V* or that Hurricane Katrina struck New Orleans on August 29, 2005.

Catch the attention of readers.   Offer your readers a reason to enter a text. You can invite them any number of ways—with a compelling incident or amusing story, with a recitation of surprising or intriguing facts, with a dramatic question, with a provocative description or quotation.

For visual texts like a brochure or poster, a cover, masthead, or headline can lead readers inside the project. Naturally, any opening has to be in synch with the material that follows—not outrageously emotional if the argument is sober; not lighthearted and comic if the paper has a serious theme. It is hard to imagine a reader even modestly interested in history not being caught by the opening paragraph of Barbara Tuchman's *The First Salute* (1998):

> White puffs of gun smoke over a turquoise sea followed by the boom of cannon rose from an unassuming fort on the diminutive Dutch island of St. Eustatius in the West Indies on November 16, 1776. The guns of Fort Orange on St. Eustatius were returning the ritual salute on entering a foreign port of an American vessel, the *Andrew Doria*, as she came up the roadstead, flying at her mast the red-and-white-striped flag of the Continental Congress. In its responding salute the small voice of St. Eustatius was the first officially to greet the largest event of the century—the entry into the society of nations of a new Atlantic state destined to change the direction of history.

Set a tone.   Introductory material sends readers all sorts of signals, some of them almost subliminal. Make noticeable errors in grammar and usage in an opening section and you immediately lose credibility with your readers.

More typically, though, readers use your opening material to determine whether they belong to the audience you are addressing. A paper opening with highly technical language indicates that the territory is open to specialists only, while a more personal or colloquial style signals a broader audience. O

Follow any required formulas.   Many genres of writing specify how you may enter a subject. This is especially the case for technical material (lab reports, research articles, scholarly essays) and highly conventional genres

refine your tone
p. 374

such as business letters, job-application letters, and even e-mail. Quite often, these conventions are simple: A business letter opens with a formal salutation; a job letter announces that you are applying for a specific announced position. You cannot ignore these details without raising eyebrows and doubts. To get such introductions right, review models of the genre and follow them.

Write an introduction when you're ready.   The opening of a project—especially of longer efforts such as research papers and theses—can be notoriously difficult to compose. If you are blocked at the outset of a project, plunge directly into the body of the paper and see where things go. You can even write the opening section last. No one will know.

Similarly, if you write your introduction first, review it when you come to the end of the paper—and revise as necessary. ○ Sometimes, the promises you made at the beginning aren't the same ones you delivered on. When that's the case, recast the opening to reflect the paper's new content or revise the body of the paper to conform to important commitments made in the introduction.

revise and edit
p. 386

Conclusions 28

Composing introductions carries all the trepidations of asking for a first date. So conclusions should be much easier, right? By the time you write it, you've established a relationship with readers, provided necessary background, laid down arguments, and discussed important issues. All that remains is the verbal equivalent of a good-night kiss. . . . Okay, maybe conclusions aren't that simple.

Like introductions, conclusions serve different purposes and audiences. A brief e-mail or memo may need no more sign-off than a simple closing: *regards*, *best*, *later*. A senior thesis, however, could require a whole chapter to wrap things up. Here are some of the options when writing conclusions.

shape an
ending

Summarize your points, then connect them.   In reports and arguments, use the concluding section to recap what you've covered and tie your major points together. Following is the systematic conclusion of a college report on a childhood developmental disorder, Cri Du Chat Syndrome (CDCS). Note that this summary paragraph also leads where many other scientific and scholarly articles do: to a call for additional research.

> Though research on CDCS remains far from abundant, existing studies prescribe early and ongoing intervention by a team of specialists, including speech-language pathologists, physical and occupational therapists, various medical and

Major point

educational professionals, and parents. Such intervention has been shown to allow individuals with CDCS to live happy, long, and full lives. The

Major point

research, however, indicates that the syndrome affects all aspects of a child's development and should therefore be taken quite seriously. Most children require numerous medical interventions, including surgery (especially to correct heart defects), feeding tubes, body braces, and repeated treatment of infections. Currently, the best attempts are being made to help young children with CDCS reach developmental milestones earlier, communicate effectively, and function as independently as possible.

Conclusion ties together main points made in paper, using transitional words and phrases.

However, as the authors of the aforementioned studies suggest, much more research is needed to clarify the causes of varying degrees of disability, to identify effective and innovative treatments/interventions (especially in the area of education), and to individualize intervention plans.

— Marissa Dahlstrom, "Developmental Disorders: Cri Du Chat Syndrome"

Reveal your point. In some writing, including many arguments, you may not want to reveal your key point until the very end, following a full presentation of claims and evidence. ○ The paper unfurls a bit like a mystery, keeping readers eager to discover your point. You don't open with a thesis, nor do you tip your hand completely until the conclusion.

Here, for example, are the concluding paragraphs of an article in which Andrew Sullivan has been guiding readers through a city he argues has grown more self-absorbed and alienated because of technologies like the Internet and iPod. In his conclusion, Sullivan raises important questions that lead toward his chief belief that we need to turn outward again to enrich our lives.

We become masters of our own interests [thanks to technology], more connected to people like us over the Internet, more instantly in touch with anything we want, need, or think we want and think we need. Ever tried a Stairmaster in silence? But what are we missing? That hilarious shard of an overheard conversation that stays with you all day; the child whose chatter on the pavement takes you back to your early memories; birdsong;

Details give argument power: Plugged in, we're missing a lot.

weather; accents; the laughter of others. And those thoughts that come not by filling your head with selected diversion, but by allowing your mind to wander aimlessly through the regular background noise of human and mechanical life.

understand argument
p. 68

External stimulation can crowd out the interior mind. Even the boredom that we flee has its uses. We are forced to find our own means to overcome it.

And so we enrich our life from within, rather than from white wires. It's hard to give up, though, isn't it?

Not so long ago I was on a trip and realized I had left my iPod behind. Panic. But then something else. I noticed the rhythms of others again, the sound of the airplane, the opinions of the taxi driver, the small social cues that had been obscured before. I noticed how others related to each other. And I felt just a little bit connected again and a little more aware.

Try it. There's a world out there. And it has a soundtrack all its own.

— "Society Is Dead: We Have Retreated into the iWorld"

> Sullivan anticipates readers' objections and acknowledges his own weakness.

> Final anecdote drives home key point.

> Three short concluding sentences punctuate the essay.

Finish dramatically.   Arguments, personal narratives, and many other kinds of writing often call for conclusions that will influence readers and maybe change their opinions. Since final paragraphs are what many readers remember, it makes sense that they be powerfully written. Here's the conclusion of a lengthy personal essay by Shane McNamee that leads up to a poignant political appeal. (To read the entire essay, see Chapter 3, p. 91.)

Forget for the moment the rainbow flags and pink triangles. Gay pride is not about being homosexual; it's about the integrity and courage it takes to be honest with yourself and your loved ones. It's about spending life with whomever you want and not worrying what the government or the neighbors think. Let's protect that truth, not some rigid view of sexual orientation or marriage. Keep gay marriage out of your church if you like, but if you value monogamy as I do, give me an alternative that doesn't involve dishonesty or a life of loneliness. Many upstanding gay citizens yearn for recognition of their loving, committed relationships. Unless you enjoy being lied to and are ready to send your gay friends and family on a Trail of Queers to Massachusetts or Canada — where gay marriage is legal — then consider letting them live as they wish.

— "Protecting What Really Matters"

> Deliberate repetition focuses readers on serious point.

> Conclusion makes direct appeal to readers, addressed as *you.*

> Final sentence appeals emotionally through both images and language.

29 Titles

Titles may not strike you as an important aspect of organization, but they can be. Of course, a proper title tells readers what a paper is about, but it can play a role during the writing process and make a document easier to locate later. Titles *can* be provocative, but more often their goal is to let readers know what they're about to read or see.

name your work

Use titles to focus documents. A too-broad title early on in a project can determine whether you have identified a workable subject. If all you have is "Sea Battles in World War II" or "Children in America," do more reading and research. If no title comes to mind, you don't have a subject. ○ You're still exploring ideas.

Titles for academic papers need only be descriptive. Consider these items culled at random from one issue of the *Stanford Undergraduate Research Journal* (Spring 2005). As you might expect, scientific papers aimed at a knowledgeable audience of specialists have highly technical titles. Titles in the social sciences and liberal arts are slightly less intimidating, but just as focused on providing information about their subjects. And a few papers do have titles designed, perhaps, to simply attract attention.

> "Hydrogenation Energies and Vibration Frequencies of Hydrogenated Carbon Nanotubes: Exploring Possibilities for Hydrogen Storage"
>
> — Ashok Kumar

develop a thesis
p. 336

"Married Women and AIDS Vulnerability"

— Jenny Tolan

"Druze and Jews"

— Adi Greif

Create searchable titles. For academic or professional papers, a title should make sense standing on its own and out of context. That way if the paper winds up in someone's bibliography or in an online database, readers know what your subject is. Your title should also include keywords by which it might be searched in a database or online.

"Rethinking the Threat of Domestic Terrorism"

If you must be clever or allusive, follow the cute title with a colon and an explanatory subtitle.

"Out, Damn'd Spot!': Images of Conscience and Remorse in Shakespeare's *Macbeth*"

"Out, Damn'd Spot: Housebreaking Your Puppy"

Avoid whimsical or suggestive titles. A bad title will haunt you like a silly screen name. At this point you may not worry about publication, but documents take on a life of their own when uploaded to the Web or listed on a résumé. Any document posted where the public can search for it online needs a levelheaded title, especially when you approach the job market.

Capitalize and punctuate titles carefully. The guidelines for capitalizing titles vary between disciplines. See Chapters 44 and 45 for the MLA and APA guidelines, or consult the style manual for your discipline.

Your titles should avoid all caps, boldface, underscoring, and italics (except for titles within titles; see *Macbeth* above). For Web sites, newsletters, PowerPoint presentations, and so on, you can be bolder graphically. ○

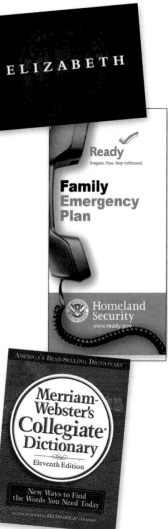

Titles tell readers what to expect.

design your work
p. 517

Style

Need help with revising and editing? See page 384. / Need help with common errors? See page 524.

30

High, Middle, and Low Style

define your
style / refine
your tone

We all have an ear for the way words work in sentences and paragraphs, for the distinctive melding of voice, tone, rhythm, and texture some call *style*. You might not be able to explain exactly why one paragraph sparkles and another is flat as day-old soda, but you know when writing feels energetic, precise, and clear or stodgy, lifeless, and plodding. Choices you make about sentence type, sentence length, vocabulary, pronouns, and punctuation *do* create distinctive verbal styles—which may or may not fit particular types of writing. ○

In fact, there are as many styles of writing as of dress. In most cases, language that is clear, active, and economical will do the job. But even such an essential style has variations. Since the time of the ancient Greeks, writers have imagined a "high" or formal style at one end of a scale and a "low" or colloquial style at the other, bracketing a just-right porridge in the middle. Style is more complex than that, but keeping the full range in mind reveals some of your options.

High, middle, and low styles
of weddings: formal and
traditional, less formal, and
totally informal.

improve your sentences
p. 378

Use high style for formal, scientific, and scholarly writing.   You
will find high style in professional journals, scholarly books, legal briefs, formal
addresses, many editorials, some types of technical writing, and some wedding
invitations. Use it yourself when a lot is at stake—in a scholarship application,
for example, or a job letter, term paper, or thesis. High style is signaled by some
combination of the following features—all of which can vary.

- Serious or professional subjects
- Knowledgeable or professional audiences
- Dominant third-person (*he, she, it, they*) or impersonal point of view
- Relatively complex and self-consciously patterned sentences (that display *parallelism, balance, repetition*), often in the passive voice
- Professional vocabulary, often abstract and technical
- No contractions, colloquial expressions, or nonstandard forms
- Conventional grammar and punctuation; standard document design
- Formal documentation, when required, often with notes and a bibliography

Following is an example from a scholarly journal. The article uses a
formal scientific style, appropriate when an expert in a field is writing for an
audience of his or her peers.

> Temperament is a construct closely related to personality. In human
> research, temperament has been defined by some researchers as the
> inherited, early appearing tendencies that continue throughout life and
> serve as the foundation for personality (A. H. Buss, 1995; Goldsmith et al.,
> 1987). Although this definition is not adopted uniformly by human re-
> searchers (McCrae et al., 2000), animal researchers agree even less about
> how to define temperament (Budaev, 2000). In some cases, the word
> *temperament* appears to be used purely to avoid using the word *personality*,
> which some animal researchers associate with anthropomorphism. Thus,
> to ensure that my review captured all potentially relevant reports,
> I searched for studies that examined either personality or temperament.
>
> – Sam D. Gosling, "From Mice to Men: What Can We Learn About Personality from
> Animal Research?" *Psychological Bulletin*

Technical term introduced and defined.

Sources documented.

Perspective generally impersonal—though *I* is used.

The *New York Times* editorial below also uses a formal style. This is common when dealing with serious political or social issues.

Tone of first paragraph is sober and direct.

Haiti, founded two centuries ago by ex-slaves who fought to regain their freedom, has again become a hub of human trafficking.

Today, tens of thousands of Haitian children live lives of modern-day bondage. Under the system known as *restavek,* a Creole word meaning "stay with," these children work for wealthier families in exchange for education and shelter. They frequently end up cruelly overworked, physically or sexually abused, and without access to education.

Key term is defined.

Vocabulary is fairly abstract.

The most effective way to root out this deeply oppressive but deeply ingrained system would be to attack the conditions that sustain it — chiefly, impoverished, environmentally unsustainable agriculture and a severe shortage of rural schools.

This is an area in which America can and should help. Washington has been quick to respond to political turmoil in Haiti, with its accompanying fears of uncontrollable refugee flows. But the frenzied flurries of international crisis management that follow typically leave no lasting results.

Borrows technical language of diplomacy and government.

A wiser, more promising alternative would be to help create long-term economic options by improving access to schools and creating sustainable agriculture. Meanwhile, the United States should work with nongovernmental organizations to battle the resigned acceptance by many Haitians of the restavek system. They could, for example, help local radio stations broadcast programs of open dialogue about how damaging the system is, and include restavek survivors or human-rights experts.

Voice throughout is that of a serious institution, not an individual.

The primary responsibility for eliminating the restavek system lies with the Haitian people and their government. After years of political crisis, there is a new democratically elected government. Eradicating the restavek system should be one of its top priorities, combining law enforcement efforts with attacks on the root social and economic causes.

Tone of final paragraph is more emotional than rest of editorial.

The former slaves who won Haiti's freedom two hundred years ago dreamed of something better for their children than restavek bondage. The time is overdue for helping those dreams become reality.

— "The Lost Children of Haiti," *New York Times*

Use middle style for personal, argumentative, and some academic writing.   This style, perhaps the most common, falls between the extremes. It is the language of journalism, popular books and magazines, professional memos and nonscientific reports, instructional guides and manuals, and most commercial Web sites. Use this style in position papers, letters to the editor, personal statements, and business e-mails and memos—even in some business and professional work, once you are comfortable with the people to whom you are writing. Middle style doesn't so much claim features of its own as walk a path between formal and everyday language. It may combine some of the following characteristics:

- Full range of topics, from serious to humorous
- General audiences
- Range of perspectives, including first (*I*) and second (*you*) person points of view
- More often a human rather than an institutional voice
- Sentences in active voice varied in complexity and length
- General vocabulary, more specific than abstract, with concrete nouns and action verbs and with unfamiliar terms or concepts defined
- Informal expressions, some dialogue, slang, and contractions
- Conventional grammar and reasonably correct formats
- Informal documentation, usually without notes

In the following article for the online magazine *Slate* Joel Waldfogel, a professor of business and public policy, explains recent research in his field to a general audience—people who are not experts in either business or public policy.

It is well-documented that short people earn less money than tall people do. To be clear, pay does not vary lockstep by height. If your friend is taller than you are, then it's nearly a coin toss whether she earns more. But if you compare two large groups of people who are similar in every respect but

Readers addressed familiarly as "you" and example offered to clarify principle of causality.

height, the average pay for the taller group will be higher. Each additional inch of height adds roughly 2 percent to average annual earnings, for both men and women. So, if the average heights of our hypothetical groups were 6 feet and 5 feet 7 inches, the average pay difference between them would be 10 percent.

> Transition between paragraphs reads like spoken English: easy and natural.

But why? One possibility is height discrimination in favor of the tall. A second involves adolescence. A few years ago, Nicola Persico and Andrew Postlewaite of the University of Pennsylvania and Dan Silverman of the University of Michigan discovered that adult earnings are more sharply related to height at age sixteen than to adult height – suggesting, scarily, that the high-school social order determined the adult economic order.

> Sources cited, but not documented.

For boys at least, height at sixteen affects things like social and athletic success – scoring chicks and baskets or, as the authors put it, "participation in clubs and athletics." And maybe those things affect later earning power.

> Highlights difference between his informality and high style of scholars.

That wasn't likely to make short people feel good, but the latest explanation is worse. In a new study, Anne Case and Christina Paxson, both of Princeton University, find that tall people earn more, on average, because they're smarter, on average. Yikes.

> Surprisingly colloquial term punctuates paragraph.

–Joel Waldfogel, "Short End," Slate.com

Next, in this excerpt from an article that appeared in the popular magazine *Psychology Today*, Ellen McGrath uses a conversational middle style to present scientific information to a general audience.

> Vocabulary is sophisticated but not technical.

Families often inherit a negative thinking style that carries the germ of depression. Typically it is a legacy passed from one generation to the next, a pattern of pessimism invoked to protect loved ones from disappointment or stress. But in fact, negative thinking patterns do just the opposite, eroding the mental health of all exposed.

> Familiar example (fictional son is even named) illustrates technical term: *cognitive distortion*.

When Dad consistently expresses his disappointment in Josh for bringing home a B minus in chemistry although all the other grades are As, he is exhibiting a kind of cognitive distortion that children learn to deploy on themselves – a mental filtering that screens out positive experience from consideration.

    Or perhaps the father envisions catastrophe, seeing such grades as foreclosing the possibility of a top college, thus dooming his son's future. It is their repetition over time that gives these events power to shape a person's belief system.

– Ellen McGrath, "Is Depression Contagious?" *Psychology Today*

> Phrase following dash offers further clarification helpful to educated, but nonexpert, readers.

Use a low style for personal, informal, and even playful writing.
Don't think of "low" here in a negative sense: A colloquial or informal style is fine on occasions when you want or need to sound more at ease and open. Low style can be right for your personal e-mails and instant messaging, of course, as well as in many blogs, advertisements, magazines trying to be hip, personal narratives, and in humor writing. Low style has many of the following features.

- Everyday or off-the-wall subjects, often humorous or parodic
- In-group or specialized readers
- Highly personal and idiosyncratic points of view; lots of *I, me, you, us,* and dialogue
- Shorter sentences and irregular constructions, especially fragments
- Vocabulary from pop culture and the street—idiomatic, allusive, and obscure to outsiders
- Colloquial expressions resembling speech
- Unconventional grammar and mechanics and alternative formats
- No systematic acknowledgment of sources

Note the relaxed style this former college instructor uses in her blog.

TUESDAY, JANUARY 03, 2006

Dumpster diving

Stuff and *kids* immediately signal casual tone—as does sentence fragment.

Stuff I've found in or near the dumpsters after the college kids move out of our apartment complex between semesters:

- Brand new HP printer, all cords still attached
- Tall oak computer-printer stand on wheels
- Blank computer discs and CD-ROMs
- China tea set
- Funky 1950s plates and saucers, left in a box beside the garbage bin
- Unopened bottle of semi-expensive champagne (still in my fridge)
- Nearly full bottles of expensive shampoos and conditioners
- Leather camera bag
- Replacement car antenna, still in unopened package
- Framed movie posters

Highly personal parenthetical remark—and slangy *fridge*.

"Really made out bigtime" is deliberately low, echoing student chatter.

Pause marked by ellipsis.

Article omitted at beginning of sentence makes advice seem casual.

One of my students told me about one of the rare perks of being a resident assistant in the dorm. She really made out bigtime with stuff left behind. One girl moved out and left all the dresser drawers loaded with clothes (and not by accident . . . she just didn't want to pack the stuff). Lots of students abandon bicycles, stereos, VCRs, TVs, sofas, and futons. Best days for scavenging are during final exams and right after.

The very serious story told in the *9/11 Commission Report* was retold in *The 9/11 Report: A Graphic Adaptation*. Creators Sid Jacobson and Ernie Colón use the colloquial visual style of a comic book to make the formidable data and conclusions of a government report accessible to a wider audience.

THE PORT AUTHORITY, AT ITS OWN EXPENSE, INSTALLED A REPEATER SYSTEM IN 1994 TO ENHANCE THE FDNY'S RADIO COMMUNICATIONS IN THE TOWER.

IN 1996, MAYOR GIULIANI CREATED THE OFFICE OF EMERGENCY MANAGEMENT (OEM) TO MONITOR THE CITY'S KEY COMMUNICATIONS CHANNELS, TO IMPROVE THE CITY'S RESPONSE TO MAJOR INCIDENTS, AND TO PLAY A CRUCIAL ROLE IN MANAGING THE CITY'S OVERALL RESPONSE TO AN INCIDENT.

HOWEVER, AS OF 9/11, THE CITY WAS NOT PREPARED TO COMPREHENSIVELY COORDINATE EFFORTS IN RESPONDING TO A MAJOR INCIDENT. THE OEM HAD NOT OVERCOME THIS PROBLEM.

AT 8:46:40, HIJACKED AMERICAN AIRLINES FLIGHT 11 FLEW INTO THE UPPER PORTION OF THE NORTH TOWER, CUTTING THROUGH FLOORS 93 TO 99.

A JET FUEL FIREBALL ERUPTED UPON IMPACT AND SHOT DOWN AT LEAST ONE BANK OF ELEVATORS.

THE FIREBALL EXPLODED ONTO NUMEROUS FLOORS, INCLUDING THE 77TH, THE 22ND, THE LOBBY LEVEL, AND FOUR STORIES BELOW.

SHOOM!

EVIDENCE SUGGESTS THAT ALL THREE OF THE BUILDING'S STAIRWELLS BECAME IMPASSABLE FROM THE 92ND FLOOR UP.

HUNDREDS WERE KILLED INSTANTLY BY THE IMPACT.

HUNDREDS MORE REMAINED ALIVE BUT TRAPPED.

THE BURNING JET FUEL IMMEDIATELY CREATED THICK BLACK SMOKE THAT ENVELOPED THE UPPER FLOORS OF THE NORTH TOWER. THE ROOF OF THE SOUTH TOWER WAS ALSO ENGULFED IN SMOKE BECAUSE OF THE PREVAILING WINDS.

HUNDREDS OF CIVILIANS TRAPPED ON OR ABOVE THE 92ND FLOOR GATHERED IN LARGE AND SMALL GROUPS BETWEEN THE 103RD AND 106TH FLOORS.

CIVILIANS WERE TRAPPED IN ELEVATORS, WHILE OTHERS BELOW THE IMPACT ZONE WERE TRAPPED OR WAITING FOR ASSISTANCE.

Panels combine verbal and visual elements to tell story.

Political figures become characters in drama.

Sounds (*Shoom!*) are represented visually—as in superhero tales.

Real images (the photograph on the left) are sometimes juxtaposed with cartoon panels as part of collage.

Inclusive and Culturally Sensitive Style

Writers in school or business today need to remember how small and tightly connected the world has become and how readily people may be offended. When you compose any document electronically (including a Word file), it may sail quickly around the Web. You can't make every reader in this potential audience happy, but you can at least write respectfully, accurately, and, yes, honestly. Language that is both inclusive and culturally sensitive can and should have these qualities.

respect your readers

Avoid expressions that stereotype genders. Largely purged from contemporary English usage are job titles that suggest that they are occupied exclusively by men or women. Gone are *poetess* and *stewardess*, *policeman* and *congressman*, *postman* and *woman scientist*. When referring to professions, even those still dominated by one gender or another, avoid using a gendered pronoun.

Don't strain sense to be politically correct. *Nun* and *NFL quarterback* are still gendered, as are *witch* and *warlock*—and *surrogate mother*. Here are some easy solutions.

STEREOTYPED	The postman came up the walk.
INCLUSIVE	The letter carrier came up the walk.
STEREOTYPED	Amongst all her other tasks, a nurse must also stay up-to-date on her medical education.
INCLUSIVE	Amongst all their other tasks, nurses must also stay up-to-date on their medical education.

Outdated Terms	Alternatives
postman	letter carrier, postal worker
mankind	humankind, people, humans
congressman	congressional representative
chairman	chair
policeman	police officer
stewardess	flight attendant
actress, poetess	actor, poet
fireman	firefighter

Avoid expressions that stereotype races, ethnic groups, or religious groups. Deliberate racial slurs these days tend to be rare in professional writing. But it is still not unusual to find well-meaning writers noting how "hard-working," "articulate," "athletic," "well-groomed," or "ambitious" members of minority and religious groups are. The praise rings hollow because it draws on old and brutal stereotypes. You have an obligation to learn the history and nature of such ethnic caricatures and grow beyond them. It's part of your education, no matter what group or groups you belong to.

Refer to people and groups by the expressions used in serious publications, understanding that almost all racial and ethnic terms are contested: *African American, black* (or *Black*), *Negro, people of color, Asian American, Hispanic, Mexican American, Cuban American, Native American, Indian, Inuit, Anglo, white* (or *White*). Even the ancient group of American Indians once called Anasazi now go by the more culturally and historically accurate Native Puebloans. While shifts of this sort may seem fussy or politically correct to some, it costs little to address people as they prefer, acknowledging both their humanity and our differences.

Be aware, too, that being part of an ethnic or racial group usually gives you license to say things about the group not open to outsiders. Chris Rock and Margaret Cho can joke about topics Jay Leno can't touch, using epithets that would cost the *Tonight Show* host his job. In academic and professional settings, show similar discretion in your language—though not in your treatment of serious subjects. Sensitivities of language should not become an excuse for avoiding open debate, nor a weapon to chill it. In the table below are suggestions for inclusive, culturally sensitive terms.

Outdated Terms	Alternatives
Eskimo	Inuit
Oriental	Asian American (better to specify country of origin)
Hispanic	Specify: Mexican, Cuban, Nicaraguan, and so on
Negro (acceptable to some)	African American, black
colored	people of color
a gay, the gays	gay, lesbian, gays and lesbians
cancer victim	person who has had cancer
boys, girls (to refer to adults)	men, women
woman doctor	doctor
male nurse	nurse

Treat all people with respect.   This policy makes sense in all writing. Some slights may not be intended—against the elderly, for example. But writing that someone drives *like an old woman* manages to offend two groups. In other cases, you might mistakenly think that most readers share your prejudices or narrow vision when describing members of campus groups, religious groups, the military, gays and lesbians, athletes, and so on. You know the derogatory terms and references well enough and you should avoid them if for no other reason than the golden rule. Everyone is a member of some group that has at one time or another been mocked or stereotyped. So writing that is respectful will itself be treated with respect.

Avoid sensational language. It happens every semester. One or more students asks the instructor whether it's okay to use four-letter words in their papers. Some instructors tolerate expletives in personal narratives, but it is difficult to make a case for them in academic reports, research papers, or position papers unless they are part of quoted material—as they may be in writing about contemporary literature or song lyrics.

Certain kinds of writing do effectively push the limits of their audience or, rather, appreciate that their readers might occasionally enjoy seeing a subject justly skewered by a few well-chosen words. You'll see this gleeful meanness in book, movie, or music reviews, for example. ○ Following is the opening paragraph of a film review written by a critic taking her scalpel to the movie version of teen-author Christopher Paolini's novel *Eragon*. Note that, for the most part, the writer avoids offensive language, but she doesn't mince words either.

> *Eragon* is what happens when misguided studio executives option a novel written by a teenager (Christopher Paolini) with a head full of Anne McCaffrey and Ursula K. Le Guin. Not full enough, however; this boy-and-his-dragon fantasy set in a land bristling with Tolkienesque nomenclature and earnest British actors is as lacking in fresh ideas as Tim Allen's manager. Even the scaly star, a Delft-blue beastie whose tint suggests either royal lineage or hypothermia, seems unsure of her motivation.
>
> —Jeanette Catsoulis, "A Boy and His Dragon," *New York Times*

understand evaluation
p. 102

32

Vigorous, Clear, Economical Style

improve your sentences

Ordinarily, tips and tricks don't do much to enhance your skills as a writer. But a few guidelines, applied sensibly, can improve your sentences and paragraphs noticeably—and upgrade your credibility as a writer. You sound more professional and confident when every word and phrase pulls its weight.

Always consider the big picture in applying the following tips: Work with whole pages and paragraphs, not just individual sentences. Remember, too, that these are guidelines, not rules. Ignore them when your good sense suggests a better alternative.

Use strong, concrete subjects and objects. Scholar Richard Lanham famously advised writers troubled by tangled sentences to ask, "Who is kicking who?" That's a memorable way of suggesting that readers shouldn't have to puzzle over what they read.

Lower the level of generality to add interest. Nouns should be as specific as possible so that sentences create images for readers.

ABSTRACT	SPECIFIC
bird	roadrunner
cactus	prickly pear
animal	coyote

Most readers can more readily imagine *students* than *constituencies*; they can picture a *school*, not an *academic institution*. A wordy sentence can seem almost hopeless until you start translating phrases like "current fiscal pressures" into everyday English.

WORDY   All of the separate constituencies at this academic institution must be invited to participate in the decision making process under the current fiscal pressures we face.

BETTER   Faculty, students, and staff at this school must all have a say during this current budget crunch.

Avoid clumsy noun phrases.   It's too easy to build massive noun phrases that sound impressive but give readers fits, especially as they accumulate over an entire page. You can spot such phrases by various markers:

- Strings of prepositional phrases
- Verbs turned into nouns via endings such as *-ation* (*implement* becomes *implementation*)
- Lots of articles (*the, a*)
- Lots of heavily modified verbals

Such expressions are not always inaccurate or wrong, just tedious. They make your reader work hard for no reason. They are remarkably easy to pare down once you notice them.

WORDY   members of the student body at Arizona State

BETTER   students at Arizona State

WORDY   the manufacturing of products made up of steel

BETTER   making steel products

WORDY   the prioritization of decisions for policies of the student government

BETTER   the student government's priorities

Avoid sentences with long windups.   Get to the point quickly. The more stuff you pile up ahead of the main verb, the more readers have to remember. Most people today prefer sentences that defer their lengthy modifying phrases and clauses until after the main verb. This sentence

Don't use words too big for the subject. Don't say "infinitely" when you mean "very," otherwise you'll have no word left when you want to talk about something really infinite.

—C. S. Lewis

from the Internal Revenue Service Web site piles up too many prepositional phrases before the verb. It's easy to fix.

ORIGINAL   A new scam e-mail that appears to be a solicitation from the IRS and the U.S. government for charitable contributions to victims of the recent Southern California wildfires has been making the rounds.

REVISED   A new scam e-mail making the rounds asks for charitable contributions to victims of the recent Southern California wildfires. It appears to be from the IRS and the U.S. government, but it is not legitimate.

Use action verbs when possible.   Verbs get as tangled up as nouns if you lose track of the action. Cut through the clutter.

WORDY VERB PHRASE   We must make a decision soon.

BETTER   We must decide soon.

WORDY VERB PHRASE   Students are reliant on credit cards.

BETTER   Students rely on credit cards.

WORDY VERB PHRASE   Engineers proceeded to reinforce the levee.

BETTER   Engineers reinforced the levee.

Avoid strings of prepositional phrases.   Prepositional phrases consist of a preposition and its object, which may take modifiers: *under* the spreading chestnut tree; *between* you and me; *in* the line *of* duty. You can't write without prepositional phrases. But use more than two or, rarely, three, in a row and they drain the energy from your sentences. Try moving the prepositions or turning them into more compact modifiers. Sometimes you can alter the verb to eliminate a preposition, or it might be necessary to revise the sentence even more substantially.

TOO MANY PHRASES   We stood in line at the observatory on the top of a hill in the mountains to look in a huge telescope at the moons of Saturn.

BETTER   We lined up at the mountaintop observatory to view Saturn's moons through a huge telescope.

Don't repeat key words close together. You can often improve the style of a passage just by making sure you haven't used a particular word or phrase too often or in too close proximity—unless you repeat it deliberately for effect (*government of the people, by the people, for the people*). When you edit to fix unintentional repetition, the resulting variety will make your sentences sound fresher.

This is a guideline to apply sensibly: Sometimes to be clear, especially in technical writing, you must repeat key nouns and verbs sentence after sentence.

> The New Horizons payload is incredibly power efficient, with the instruments collectively drawing only about 28 watts. The payload consists of three optical instruments, two plasma instruments, a dust sensor, and a radio science receiver/radiometer.
>
> —NASA, "New Horizons Spacecraft Ready for Flight"

Avoid doublings. In speech, we tend to repeat ourselves or say things two or three different ways to be sure listeners get the point. Such repetitions are natural, even appreciated. But in writing, the habit of doubling can be irritating. And it is very much a habit, backed by a long literary tradition comfortable with pairings such as *home and hearth, friend and colleague, tried and true, clean and sober, neat and tidy*, and so on.

Often, writers will add an extra noun or two to be sure they have covered the bases: *colleges and universities; books and articles; ideas and opinions.* There may be good reasons for a second (or third) item. But not infrequently, the doubling is just extra baggage that slows down the train. Leave it at the station.

Turn clauses into more direct modifiers. If you are fond of *that, which*, and *who* clauses, be sure you need them. You can sometimes save a word or two by pulling the modifiers out of the clause and moving them ahead of the words they embellish. Or you may be able to tighten a sentence just by cutting *that, which*, or *who.*

WORDY   Our coach, who is nationally renowned, expected a raise.

BETTER   Our nationally renowned coach expected a raise.

WORDY   Our coach, who is nationally renowned and already rich, still expected a raise.
BETTER Our coach, nationally renowned and already rich, still expected a raise.

Cut introductory expressions such as *it is* and *there is/are* when you can.   Such expressions, called *expletives,* are just part of the way we say some things: *It is going to rain today; There is a tide in the affairs of men.* Cut them to save a few words, though, and you sound like Yoda: *Rain it will today.* But don't let an expletive substitute for a clearer expression.

WORDY   It is necessary that we reform the housing policies.
BETTER We need to reform the housing policies.

WORDY   There were many incentives offered by the company to its sales force.
BETTER The company offered its sales force many incentives.

Vary your sentence lengths and structures.   Sentences, like music, have rhythm. If all your sentences run about the same length or rarely vary from a predictable subject–verb–object pattern, readers grow bored without even knowing why. Every so often, surprise readers with a really short statement. Or begin with a longer-than-usual introductory phrase. Or try compound subjects or verbs, or attach a series of parallel modifiers to the verb or object. Or let a sentence roll toward a grand conclusion, as in the example below.

> [Carl] Newman is a singing encyclopedia of pop power. He has identified, cultured, and cloned the most buoyant elements of his favorite Squeeze, Raspberries, Supertramp, and Sparks records, and he's pretty pathological about making sure there's something unpredictable and catchy happening in a New Pornographers song every couple of seconds—a stereo flurry of *ooohs,* an extra beat or two bubbling up unexpectedly.
>
> —Douglas Wolk, "Something to Talk About," *Spin*

Listen to what you have written.   Read everything that matters aloud at least once. Then fix the words or phrases that cause you to pause or stumble. This is a great way to find problem spots. If you can't follow your own writing, a reader won't be able to either. Better yet, persuade a friend or roommate to read your draft to you and take notes.

Cut a first draft by 25 percent—or more.   If you tend to be wordy, try to cut your first drafts by at least one-quarter. Put all your thoughts down on the page when drafting a paper. But when editing, cut every unnecessary expression. Think of it as a competition. However, don't eliminate any important ideas and facts. If possible, ask an honest friend to read your work and point out where you might tighten your language.

I believe more in the scissors than I do in the pencil.

—Truman Capote

If you ~~are aware that you~~ tend to ~~say more than you need to in your writing,~~ *be wordy,*

~~then get in the habit of~~ trying to cut ~~the~~ first drafts ~~that you have written~~ by *your*

at least one-quarter. ~~There may be good reasons for you to~~ put all your

thoughts ~~and ideas~~ down on the page when ~~you are in the process of~~

drafting a paper ~~or project~~. But when ~~you are in the process of~~ editing, ~~you~~

~~should be sure to~~ cut every unnecessary ~~word that is not needed or~~ *expression.*

~~necessary. You may find it advantageous to~~ think of it as a competition ~~or a~~ *T* .

~~game. In making your cuts, it is important that you~~ don't eliminate any *However,*

important ideas ~~that may be essential or~~ facts ~~that may be important.~~ If you *and* .

~~find it~~ possible, ~~you might consider~~ asking an honest friend ~~whom you trust~~

to read your ~~writing~~ and ~~ask them to~~ point out ~~those places in your writing~~ *work*

where you might ~~make~~ your language ~~tighter.~~ *tighten* .

Revising & Editing

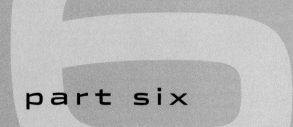

part six

how

It is amazing much of our day-to-day lives now depend on increasingly

sp (seemless) kinds of communication, our cell phones talking to our PDAs,

drawing e-mails from the air, sharing texts with each other, down loading

images, and taking pictures. Our communications now seem infinitely

layered a real life <u>Alice in Wonderland</u> experience Messages don't begin or

end somewhere; they are part of a magical stream of information that

extends the reach of human intelligence, to make us all connected to

anything we want.

Keep comments tactful.   Treat another writer's work the way you'd
like to have your own efforts treated. Slips in writing can be embarrassing
enough without an editor making sport of them.

How to... Insert a comment in a Word document

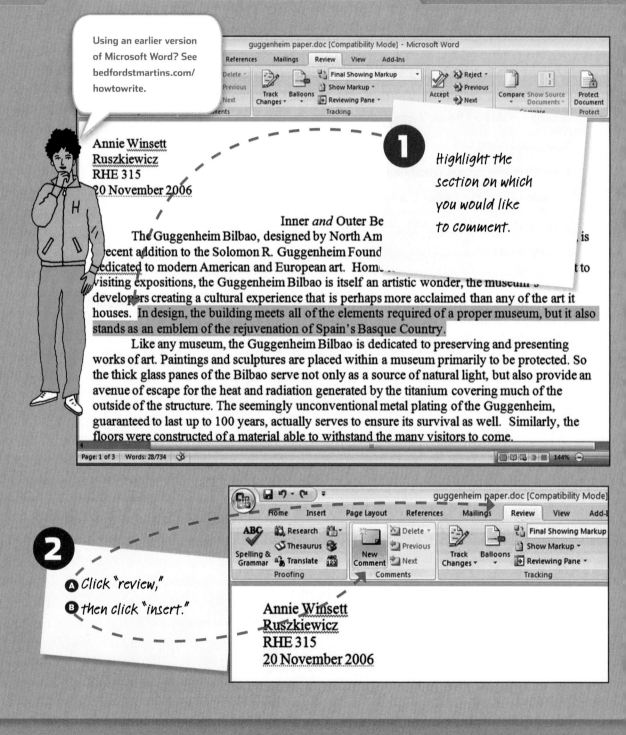

Using an earlier version of Microsoft Word? See bedfordstmartins.com/howtowrite.

1 Highlight the section on which you would like to comment.

guggenheim paper.doc [Compatibility Mode] - Microsoft Word

References Mailings Review View Add-Ins

Final Showing Markup
Show Markup
Reviewing Pane

Track Changes Balloons Tracking

Accept Reject Previous Next

Compare Show Source Documents Protect Document

Annie Winsett
Ruszkiewicz
RHE 315
20 November 2006

Inner *and* Outer Be

The Guggenheim Bilbao, designed by North Am... is recent addition to the Solomon R. Guggenheim Found... dedicated to modern American and European art. Hom... to visiting expositions, the Guggenheim Bilbao is itself an artistic wonder, the museum developers creating a cultural experience that is perhaps more acclaimed than any of the art it houses. In design, the building meets all of the elements required of a proper museum, but it also stands as an emblem of the rejuvenation of Spain's Basque Country.

Like any museum, the Guggenheim Bilbao is dedicated to preserving and presenting works of art. Paintings and sculptures are placed within a museum primarily to be protected. So the thick glass panes of the Bilbao serve not only as a source of natural light, but also provide an avenue of escape for the heat and radiation generated by the titanium covering much of the outside of the structure. The seemingly unconventional metal plating of the Guggenheim, guaranteed to last up to 100 years, actually serves to ensure its survival as well. Similarly, the floors were constructed of a material able to withstand the many visitors to come.

Page: 1 of 3   Words: 28/734   144%

2

Ⓐ Click "review,"

Ⓑ then click "insert."

guggenheim paper.doc [Compatibility Mode]

Home Insert Page Layout References Mailings Review View Add-I

ABC Research Thesaurus Translate

Spelling & Grammar

Proofing

New Comment Delete Previous Next

Comments

Track Changes Balloons

Final Showing Markup
Show Markup
Reviewing Pane

Tracking

Annie Winsett
Ruszkiewicz
RHE 315
20 November 2006

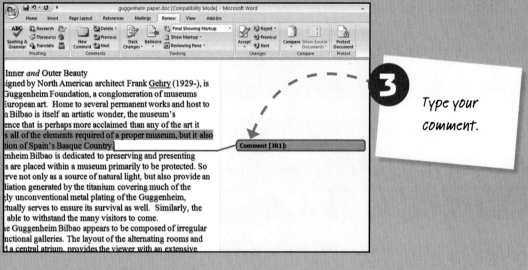

3 Type your comment.

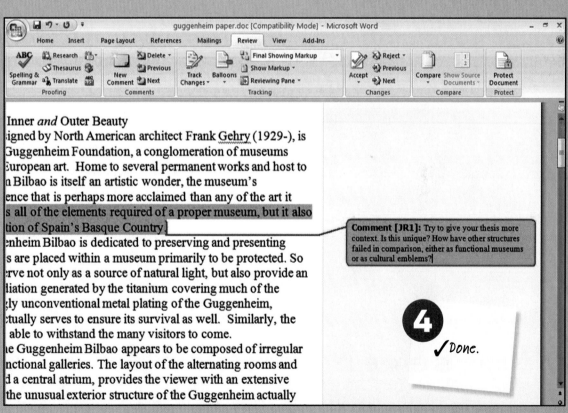

4 ✓ Done.

Research & Sources

7

35 Beginning Your Research

plan a project

Research can be part of any major writing project. Creative writers spend hours in a library gathering data about historical periods or contemporary events. Authors of reports conduct surveys and studies to confirm what they believe about a topic. And people engaged in arguments (ideally, at least) consult dozens of professional sources to be sure their claims are accurate and fully supported. ○

When doing research, you uncover what is already known about a topic. For humanities courses, this involves examining a wide range of books, articles, and Web sources. In the social and natural sciences, you may also perform experiments or do field research to create and share new knowledge about a topic.

So where do you begin your research project and how do you keep from being swamped by the sheer weight of information available? You need smart research strategies.

Know your assignment. Begin by reviewing the assignment sheet for a term paper or research project, when one is provided, and be sure you understand the kinds of research the paper requires. For a one-page position paper related to a class discussion, you might use only the reference section of the library and your textbook. An argument about current events will likely send you to newspapers, magazines, and various Web sites, while a full-length term paper is researched by seeking out academic books

understand argument
p. 68

and journals. (For details and advice on a wide variety of assignments, refer to Parts One and Two.)

Come up with a plan.   Research takes time. You have to find sources, read them, record your findings, and then write about them. Most research projects also require formal documentation and some type of formal presentation, either as a research paper or, perhaps, an oral report. This stuff cannot be scammed the night before. You can avoid chaos by preparing a calendar that links specific tasks to specific dates. Simply creating the schedule (and you should keep it *simple*) might even jump-start your actual research. At a minimum, record important due dates in your day planner. Here's a basic schedule for a research paper with three deadlines.

Research is formalized curiosity. It is poking and prying with a purpose.

—Zora Neale Hurston

Schedule: Research Paper

February 19: Topic Proposal Due
___ *Explore and select a topic*
___ *Do preliminary library research*
___ *Define a thesis or hypothesis*
___ *Prepare an annotated bibliography*
March 26: First draft due
___ *Read, summarize, and paraphrase sources*
___ *Organize the paper*
April 16: Final draft due
___ *Get peer feedback on draft*
___ *Revise the project*
___ *Check documentation*
___ *Edit the project*

Find a manageable topic.   Keep in mind that any topic and thesis for a research project should present you with a reasonable problem to solve.

(For ample advice on finding and developing topics, see Part Three.) Look for an idea or a question you can explore sensibly within the scope of the assignment and the allotted time, and with the resources available to you.

When asked to submit a ten- or twenty-page term paper, some writers panic, thinking they need a topic broad or general enough to fill up all these blank pages. But the opposite is true. You will have more success finding useful sources if you break off small but intriguing parts of much larger subjects.

> *not* Military Aircraft, *but* The Development of Jet Fighters in World War II
>
> *not* The History of Punk Rock, *but* The Influence of 1970s Punk Rock on Nirvana
>
> *not* Developmental Disorders in Children, *but* Cri Du Chat Syndrome

Read broadly at first in order to find a general subject to then narrow down to a topic. Then brainstorm this topic to come up with focused questions you might ask in your preliminary research. By the end of this early stage of the research process, your goal is to have turned a topic idea or phrase into a claim at least one full sentence long. ○

In the natural and social sciences, topics sometimes evolve from research problems already on the table in various fields. Presented with this research agenda in a course, you then ordinarily begin with a "review of the literature" to determine what others have published on this issue in the major journals. Then create an experiment in which your research question—offered as a claim called a *hypothesis*—either confirms the direction of ongoing work in the field or perhaps advances or changes it. In basic science courses, get plenty of advice from your instructor about framing sensible research questions and hypotheses.

Seek professional help.   During your preliminary research phase, you'll quickly discover that not all sources are equal. ○ They differ in purpose, method, media, audience, and credibility. Until you get your legs as a researcher, never hesitate to ask questions about research tools and strategies: Get recommendations about the best available journals, books, and authors from teachers and reference librarians. Ask them which publishers, institu-

develop a thesis
p. 336

find reliable sources
p. 415

tions, and experts carry the most intellectual authority in their fields. If your topic is highly specialized, plan to spend additional time tracking down sources outside of your own library.

Distinguish between *primary* and *secondary* sources.   This basic distinction is worth keeping in mind as you approach a new subject and project: A *primary source* is a document that provides an eyewitness account of an event or phenomenon; a *secondary source* is a step or two removed, an article or book that interprets or reports on events and phenomena described in primary sources. The famous Zapruder film of the John F. Kennedy assassination in Dallas (November 22, 1963) is a memorable primary historical document; the many books or articles that draw on the film to comment on the assassination are secondary sources. Both types of sources are useful to you as a researcher.

Use primary sources when doing research that breaks new ground. Primary sources represent raw data—letters, journals, newspaper accounts, official documents, laws, court opinions, statistics, research reports, audio and video recordings, and so on. Working with primary materials, you generate your own ideas about a subject, free of anyone else's opinions or explanations. Or you can review the actual evidence others have used to make prior claims and arguments, perhaps reinterpreting their findings or bringing a new perspective to the subject.

Web sites featuring government resources, such as Thomas or FedStats, and corporate annual reports provide primary material for analysis.

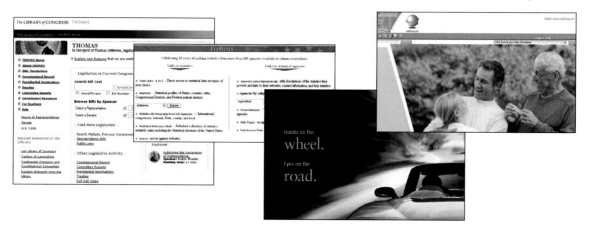

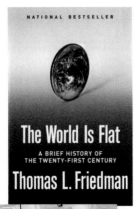

Reprinted by permission from Macmillan Publishers Ltd.: NATURE, © January 2008.

Books and magazines often provide secondary, not primary, information.

Use secondary sources to learn what others have discovered or said about a subject. In many fields, you spend most of your time reviewing secondary materials, especially when researching areas of knowledge new to you. Secondary sources include scholarly books and articles, encyclopedias, magazine pieces, and many Web sites. In academic assignments, you may find yourself moving easily between different kinds of materials, first reading a primary text like *Hamlet* and then reading various commentaries on it.

Record every source you examine.   Most writers and researchers download or photocopy sources rather than examine original copies in a library and take notes. However you plan on working, *you must* accurately record every source you encounter right from the start, gathering the following information:

- Authors, editors, translators, sponsors (of Web sites) or other major contributors

- Titles, subtitles, edition numbers, volumes

- Publication information, including places of publication and publishers (for books); titles of magazines and journals, volume and page numbers; dates of publication and access (the latter for online materials)

- Page numbers, URLs, electronic pathways, or other locators

You'll need these details later to document your sources.

It might seem obsessive to collect basic bibliographic data on books and articles you know you are unlikely to use. But when you expect to spend weeks or months on an assignment, log all material you examine so that later you won't have to backtrack, wondering "Did I miss this source?" A log also comes in handy if you need to revisit a source later in your research.

Prepare a topic proposal.   Your instructor may request a topic proposal. Typically, this includes a topic idea, a draft thesis or hypothesis, potential sources, your intended approach, and a list of potential problems.

Remember that such proposals are written to get feedback about your project's feasibility, and that even a good idea raises questions. Following is a sample proposal for a short project directed chiefly to peers invited to respond via electronic discussion board.

Eades 1

Micah Eades

Instructor's Name

Course Title

Date

Causal Analysis Proposal: Awkward Atmospheres

People don't like going to the doctor's office. You wait in an office room decorated from the 1980s reading Highlights or last year's Field & Stream and listen to patients in the next room talking about the details of their proctology exam. Since I am planning a future as a primary care physician, I don't want people to dread coming to see me.

My paper will propose that patient dissatisfaction with visits to their physicians may not be due entirely to fear of upcoming medical examinations but rather to the unwelcoming atmosphere of most waiting and treatment rooms. More specifically, I will examine the negative effect that noise, poor interior design, and unsympathetic staff attitudes may have on patient comfort. I will propose that these factors have a much larger impact on patient well-being than previously expected. Additionally, I will propose possible remedies and ways to change these negative perceptions.

My biggest problem may be finding concrete evidence for my claims. For evidence, I do intend to cite the relatively few clinical studies that have been conducted on patient satisfaction and atmosphere. My audience will be a tough crowd: doctors who have neither an awareness of the problems I describe nor much desire to improve the ambience of their offices.

Opening paragraph offers rationale for subject choice.

Title indicates that proposal responds to specific assignment.

Describes planned content and structure of paper.

Has done enough research to know that literature on subject is not extensive.

Paper will be directed to specific audience.

36

Finding Print and Online Sources

refine your
search

When beginning an academic research project, whether a brief report or a full term paper or thesis, you'll likely turn to three resources: local and school libraries, informational databases and indexes, and the Internet.

At the library are books, journals, and newspapers and other printed materials in a collection overseen by librarians to preserve information and support research. Often, the help of these librarians is necessary to locate and evaluate sources.

Also at a library or among its online resources are databases and indexes with electronic access to abstracts or full-text versions of up-to-date research materials in professional journals, magazines, and newspaper archives. Your library or school purchases licenses to allow you to use these password-protected resources—services such as EBSCOhost, InfoTrac, and LexisNexis.

And, of course, you can find endless streams of information with your computer simply by exploring the Web, using search engines such as Google and Yahoo! to locate data. Information on the Web varies hugely in quality, but covers just about every subject imaginable.

Whether working in a physical library, within a library catalog or an electronic database, or at home on your computer, you need to know how to use the full capacity of research tools designed to search large bodies of information.

Learn to navigate the library catalog.   All but the smallest or most specialized libraries now organize their collections electronically. Be sure you know how the electronic catalog works: It tells you if the library has an item you need, where it is on the shelves, and whether it has been checked out. You can search for most items by author, title, subject, keywords, and even call number.

Pay special attention to the terms or keywords by which an item you've located in an electronic catalog has been indexed: You can then use those terms to search for similar materials, an important way of generating leads on a topic.

In addition to author, title, and publication information, the full entry for an item in a library catalog will include subject headings. These terms may suggest additional avenues of research.

Locate research guides.   Another excellent option for starting an academic project is to use research sites prepared by libraries or universities to help researchers working in specific fields. Check to see whether your institution has developed such materials. Or simply search the phrase "library research guides" on Google. Such sites identify resources both within and outside of academic institutions, and may also give you suggestions for topic ideas or research areas. Use these guides carefully, since they may contain links to sites that libraries and schools cannot vouch for entirely. The charts on pages 408 and 411 will help you find databases for your subject.

You will probably begin your search with one or more multidisciplinary databases such as *LexisNexis Academic, Academic OneFile,* or *Academic Search Premier*. These resources cover a wide range of materials, including newspapers, respected magazines, and some professional journals. Most libraries subscribe to one or more such information services, and these can be searched using keywords.

But for more in-depth work, focus on the databases within your specific discipline. There are, in fact, hundreds of such databases and tools, far too many to list here. Look for databases that present current materials at a level you can understand: Some online resources may be too specific or technical for your project. When working with a database for the first time, review

Research Guides and Databases	
Institution	**Subject Guides at**
Columbia University Library	www.columbia.edu/cu/lweb/ eresources
New York Public Library	www.nypl.org/research/electronic/ subject.cfm
The Ohio State University	library.osu.edu/sites/thegateway
Stanford University	http://library.stanford.edu/ research_help/res_quick_start
University of Chicago	www.lib.uchicago.edu/e/su
The University of Texas at Austin	www.lib.utexas.edu/subject
University of Virginia	www.lib.virginia.edu/resguide.html
Yale University Library	www.library.yale.edu/guides
Electronic Books	www.lib.utexas.edu/books/etext.html
Infomine	http://infomine.ucr.edu
The Internet Public Library	www.ipl.org
Librarians' Internet Index	http://lii.org
Library of Congress Research Centers	http://lcweb.loc.gov/rr/ research-centers.html

the Help section or page to find the most efficient way to conduct your searches. Librarians, too, can offer professional advice on refining your search techniques.

Identify the best reference tools for your needs.   For encyclopedias, almanacs, historical records, maps, and so on, head to the reference section of your library and ask the librarian to direct you to the appropriate items.

Quite often, for instance, you'll need to trace the biographical facts of important people—dates of birth, countries of origin, schools attended, career paths, and so on. For current newsmakers, you might find enough fairly reliable data from a Google or Yahoo! search or a Wikipedia entry. But to get the most accurate information on historical figures, consult

Integrating Sources into Your Work

42

When you integrate sources effectively into your work, you give readers information they need to identify paraphrased or quoted items and to understand how they may have been edited for clarity or accuracy.

Signal the introduction of all borrowed material, whether summarized, paraphrased, or quoted directly.   Readers always need to be able to distinguish between your ideas and those you've borrowed from other authors. So you must provide a signal whenever source material is introduced. Think of it as framing this material to set it off from your own words. Framing also enables you to offer an explanation or context for borrowed material, giving it the weight and power you believe it should have.

Often, all that's required for a frame is a brief signal phrase that identifies the author, title, or source you are drawing on.

> President Clinton explained at a press conference that ". . .
>
> According to a report in *Scientific American*, . . .
>
> . . ." said the former CEO of General Electric, arguing that ". . .
>
> In *Blink*, Malcolm Gladwell makes some odd claims. For example, he . . .

At other times you'll need a few words or a complete sentence or more to incorporate borrowed material into a paper. Readers

avoid plagiarism / use quotations

MLA and APA Style
The examples in this section follow MLA (Modern Language Association) style, covered in Chapter 44. For information on APA (American Psychological Association) style, see Chapter 45.

431

should never be in doubt about your use of a source. Your frame can introduce, interrupt, follow, or even surround the words or ideas taken from sources, but be sure that your signal phrases are grammatical and lead naturally into the material.

Select an appropriate "verb of attribution" to frame borrowed material. Note that source material is often introduced or framed by a "verb of attribution" or "signal verb." These verbs influence what readers think of borrowed ideas or quoted material.

Use more neutral signal verbs in reports and descriptive or even biased terms in arguments. Note that, by MLA convention, verbs of attribution are usually in the present tense when talking about current work or ideas. (In APA, these verbs are generally in the past or present perfect tense.)

Verbs of Attribution		
Neutral	**Descriptive**	**Biased**
adds	acknowledges	admits
explains	argues	charges
finds	asserts	concedes
notes	believes	confuses
offers	claims	derides
observes	confirms	disputes
says	disagrees	evades
shows	responds	insists
states	reveals	pretends
writes	suggests	smears

Use ellipsis marks [. . .] to shorten a lengthy quotation. When quoting a source in your paper, it's not necessary to use every word or sentence, so long as the cuts you make don't distort the meaning of the original material. An ellipsis mark, formed from three spaced periods, shows where words, phrases, full sentences, or more have been removed from a quotation. The mark doesn't replace punctuation within a sentence. Thus you might see a period or a comma immediately followed by the ellipsis mark.

ORIGINAL PASSAGE

Although gift giving has been a pillar of Hopi society, trade has also flourished in Hopi towns since prehistory, with a network that extended from the Great Plains to the Pacific Coast, and from the Great Basin, centered on present-day Nevada and Utah, to the Valley of Mexico. Manufactured goods, raw materials, and gems drove the trade, supplemented by exotic items such as parrots. The Hopis were producers as well, manufacturing large quantities of cotton cloth and ceramics for the trade. To this day, interhousehold trade and barter, especially for items of traditional manufacture for ceremonial use (such as basketry, bows, cloth, moccasins, pottery, and rattles), remain vigorous.

–Peter M. Whiteley, "Ties That Bind: Hopi Gift Culture and Its First Encounter with the United States," *Natural History,* Nov. 2004, p. 26

Highlighting shows words to be deleted when passage is quoted.

PASSAGE WITH ELLIPSES

Whiteley has characterized the practice this way:

Although gift giving has been a pillar of Hopi society, trade has also flourished in Hopi towns since prehistory. . . . Manufactured goods, raw materials, and gems drove the trade, supplemented by exotic items such as parrots. The Hopis were producers as well, manufacturing large quantities of cotton cloth and ceramics for the trade. To this day, interhousehold trade and barter, especially for items of traditional manufacture for ceremonial use, . . . remain vigorous. (26)

Ellipses show where words have been deleted.

Use brackets [ ] to insert explanatory material into a quotation.   By convention, readers understand that the bracketed words are not part of the original material.

Writing in the *London Review of Books* (January 26, 2006), John Lancaster describes the fears of publishers: "At the moment Google says they have no intention of providing access to this content [scanned books still under copyright]; but why should anybody believe them?"

Use ellipsis marks, brackets, and other devices to make quoted materials suit the grammar of your sentences. Sometimes, the structure of sentences you want to quote won't quite match the grammar, tense, or perspectives of your own surrounding prose. If necessary, cut up a quoted passage to slip appropriate sections into your own sentences, adding bracketed changes or explanations to smooth the transition.

ORIGINAL PASSAGE

Words to be quoted are highlighted.

Among Chandler's most charming sights are the business-casual dads joining their wives and kids for lunch in the mall food court. The food isn't the point, let alone whether it's from Subway or Dairy Queen. The restaurants merely provide the props and setting for the family time. When those kids grow up, they'll remember the food court as happily as an older generation recalls the diners and motels of Route 66—not because of the businesses' innate appeal but because of the memories they evoke.

—Virginia Postrel, "In Defense of Chain Stores," *Atlantic Monthly*, December 2006

MATERIAL AS QUOTED

Words quoted from source are highlighted.

People who dislike chain stores should ponder the small-town America that cultural critic Virginia Postrel describes, one where "business-casual dads [join] their wives and kids for lunch in the mall food court," a place which future generations of kids will remember "as happily as an older generation recalls the motels and diners of Route 66."

Use [sic] to signal an obvious error in quoted material. You don't want readers to blame a mistake on you, and yet you are obligated to reproduce a quotation exactly—including blunders in the original. You can highlight an error by putting *sic* (the Latin word for "thus") in brackets immediately following the mistake. The device says, in effect, that this is the way you found it.

Senator Kennedy took Supreme Court nominee Samuel Alito to task for his record: "In an era when America is still too divided by race and riches, Judge Alioto [sic] has not written one single opinion on the merits in favor of a person of color alleging race discrimination on the job."

Documenting Sources

43

Required to document your research paper? It seems simple: Just list your sources and note where and how you use them. But the practice can be intimidating. For one thing, you have to follow rules for everything from capitalizing titles to captioning images. For another, documentation systems differ between fields. What worked for a Shakespeare paper won't transfer to your psychology class research project. Bummer. What do you need to do?

Understand the point of documentation. Documentation systems differ to serve the writers and researchers who use them. Modern Language Association (MLA) documentation, which you probably know from composition and literature classes, highlights author names and books and article titles, and assumes that writers will be quoting a lot—as literature scholars do. American Psychological Association (APA) documentation, gospel in psychology and social sciences, focuses on publication dates because scholars in these fields value the latest research. Council of Science Editors (CSE) documentation, used in the hard sciences, provides predictably detailed advice for handling formulas and numbers.

So systems of documentation aren't arbitrary. Their rules simply anticipate problems researchers face when dealing with sources.

Understand what you accomplish through documentation. First, you clearly identify your sources. In a world awash with information, readers really do need to have reliable author, title, and publication information.

By identifying your sources, you provide evidence for your claims. You also certify the quality of your research, and receive due credit for your labor. A shrewd reader or instructor can tell a lot from your bibliography alone.

Finally, when you document a paper, you encourage readers to follow up on your work. When you've done a good job on a paper, serious readers will want to know more. Both your citations and your bibliography enable them to take the next step in the research.

Style Guides Used in Various Disciplines

Field or Discipline	Documentation and Style Guides
Anthropology	*Chicago Manual of Style* (15th ed., 2003)
Biology	*Scientific Style and Format: The CSE Manual for Authors, Editors, and Publishers* (7th ed., 2006)
Business and management	*The Business Style Handbook: An A-to-Z Guide for Writing on the Job* (2002)
Chemistry	*The ACS Style Guide: Effective Communication of Scientific Information* (3rd ed., 2006)
Earth sciences	*Geowriting: A Guide to Writing, Editing, and Printing in Earth Science* (5th ed., 1995)
Engineering	Varies by area; *IEEE Standards Style Manual* (2007) (online)
Federal government	*United States Government Printing Office Manual* (29th ed., 2000)
History	*Chicago Manual of Style* (15th ed., 2003)
Humanities	*MLA Handbook for Writers of Research Papers* (6th ed., 2003)
Journalism	*The AP Stylebook and Briefing on Media Law* (2008); *UPI Stylebook and Guide to Newswriting* (4th ed., 2004)
Law	*The Bluebook: A Uniform System of Citation* (18th ed., 2005)
Mathematics	*A Manual for Authors of Mathematical Papers* (8th ed., 1990)
Music	*Writing about Music: An Introductory Guide* (3rd ed., 2001)
Nursing	*Writing for Publication in Nursing* (2001)
Political science	*The Style Manual for Political Science* (2006)
Psychology	*Publication Manual of the American Psychological Association* (5th ed., 2001)
Sociology	*ASA Style Guide* (2nd ed., 1998)

MLA Documentation and Format

44

The style of the Modern Language Association (MLA) is used in many humanities disciplines. For complete details about MLA style, consult the *MLA Handbook for Writers of Research Papers* (2003) by Joseph Gibaldi. The basic details for documenting sources and formatting research papers in MLA style are presented below.

Document sources according to convention.   When you use sources in a research paper, you are required to cite the source, letting readers know that the information has been borrowed from somewhere else, and showing them how to find the original material if they would like to study it further. An MLA-style citation includes two parts: a brief in-text citation and a more detailed works cited entry to be included in a list at of the end of your paper.

cite in MLA

In-text citations must include the author's name as well as the number of the page where the borrowed material can be found. The author's name (shaded in orange) is generally included in the signal phrase that introduces the passage, and the page number (shaded in yellow) is included in parentheses after the borrowed text.

> Frazier points out that the Wetherill-sponsored expedition to explore Chaco Canyon was roundly criticized (43).

Alternatively, the author's name can be included in parentheses along with the page number.

The Wetherill-sponsored expedition to explore Chaco Canyon was roundly criticized (Frazier 43).

At the end of the paper, in the works cited list, a more detailed citation includes the author's name as well as the title and publication information about the source.

Frazier, Kendrick. People of Chaco: A Canyon and Its Culture. Rev. ed. New York: Norton, 1999.

Both in-text citations and works cited entries can vary greatly depending on the type of source cited (book, periodical, Web site, etc.). The following pages give specific examples of how to cite a wide range of sources in MLA style.

Directory of MLA In-Text Citations

1. Author named in signal phrase 434
2. Author named in parentheses 439
3. With block quotations 439
4. Two or three authors 440
5. Four or more authors 440
6. Group, corporate, or government author 440
7. Two or more works by the same author 440
8. Authors with same last name 441
9. Unidentified author 441
10. Multivolume work 441
11. Work in an anthology 441
12. Entry in a reference book 442
13. Literary work 442
14. Sacred work 443
15. Entire work 443
16. Secondary source 443
17. No page numbers 443
18. Multiple sources in the same citation 444

MLA in-text citation

1. Author Named in Signal Phrase

Include the author's name in the signal phrase that introduces the borrowed material. Follow the borrowed material with the page number of the source in parentheses. Note that the period comes after the parentheses. For a source without an author, see item 9; for a source without a page number, see item 17.

> According to Seabrook, "astronomy was a vital and practical form of knowledge" for the ancient Greeks (98).

2. Author Named in Parentheses

Follow the borrowed material with the author and page number of the source in parentheses, and end with a period. For a source without an author, see item 9; for a source without a page number, see item 17.

> For the ancient Greeks, "astronomy was a vital and practical form of knowledge" (Seabrook 98).

Note: Most of the examples below follow the style of item 1, but naming the author in parentheses (as shown in item 2) is also acceptable.

3. With Block Quotations

For quotations of four or more lines, MLA requires that you set off the borrowed material as indented text. Include the author's name in the introductory text (or in the parentheses at the end). End the block quotation with the page number(s) in parentheses, *after* the end punctuation of the quoted material.

> Jake Page, writing in American History, underscores the significance of the well-organized Pueblo revolt:
>
>> Although their victory proved temporary, in the history of Indian-white relations in North America the Pueblo Indians were the only Native Americans to successfully oust European invaders from their territory. . . . Apart from the Pueblos, only the Seminoles were able to retain some of their homeland for any length of time, by waging war from the swamps of the Florida Everglades. (36)

4. Two or Three Authors

If your source has two or three authors, include all of their names in either the signal phrase or parentheses.

> Muhlheim and Heusser assert that the story "analyzes how crucially our actions are shaped by the society . . . in which we live" (29).

> According to some experts, "Children fear adult attempts to fix their social lives" (Thompson, Grace, and Cohen 8).

5. Four or More Authors

If your source has four or more authors, list the first author's name followed by "et al." (meaning "and others") in the signal phrase or parentheses.

> Hansen et al. estimate that the amount of fish caught and sold illegally worldwide is between 10% and 30% (974).

6. Group, Corporate, or Government Author

Treat the name of the group, corporation, or government agency just as you would any other author, including the name in either the signal phrase or the parentheses.

> The United States Environmental Protection Agency states that if a public water supply contains dangerous amounts of lead, the municipality is required to educate the public about the problems associated with lead in drinking water (3).

7. Two or More Works by the Same Author

If your paper includes two or more works by the same author, add a brief version of the works' titles (shaded in green) in parentheses to help readers locate the right source.

> Mills suggests that new assessments of older archaeological work, not new discoveries in the field, are revising the history of Chaco Canyon ("Recent Research" 66). She argues, for example, that new analysis of public spaces can teach us about the ritual of feasting in the Puebloan Southwest (Mills, "Performing the Feast" 211).

MLA works cited entries

AUTHOR INFORMATION

1. Single Author

Author's Last Name, First Name. Book Title. Publication City: Publisher, Year
of Publication.

Will, George. Men at Work: The Craft of Baseball. New York: Macmillan,
1990.

2. Two or Three Authors

List the authors in the order shown on the title page.

First Author's Last Name, First Name, and Second Author's First and Last
Name. Book Title. Publication City: Publisher, Year of Publication.

Mortenson, Greg, and David Oliver Relin. Three Cups of Tea: One Man's
Mission to Promote Peace . . . One School at a Time. New York: Penguin,
2007.

Clark, Ricky, George W. Knepper, and Ellice Ronsheim. Quilts in
Community: Ohio's Traditions. Nashville: Rutledge, 1991.

3. Four or More Authors

When a source has four or more authors, list only the name of the first
author (last name first), followed by a comma and the Latin term *et al.*
(meaning "and others").

First Author's Last Name, First Name, et al. Book Title. Publication City:
Publisher, Year of Publication.

Roark, James L., et al. The American Promise: A History of the United States.
4th ed. Boston: Bedford, 2009.

4. Corporate Author

If a group or corporation rather than a person appears to be the author,
include that name as the work's author in your list of works cited.

Name of Corporation. Book Title. Publication City: Publisher, Year of
Publication.

Congressional Quarterly. <u>Presidential Elections: 1789-2004</u>. Washington: CQ, 2005.

5. Unidentified Author

If the author of a work is unknown, begin the works cited entry with the title of the work.

Note that in the example given, "The New York Times" is not underscored because it is a title within a title (see item 19).

Book Title. Publication City: Publisher, Year of Publication.

The New York Times <u>Guide to Essential Knowledge: A Desk Reference for the Curious Mind</u>. New York: St. Martin's, 2004.

6. Multiple Works by the Same Author

To cite two or more works by the same author in your list of works cited, organize the works alphabetically by title (ignoring introductory articles such as *The* and *A*). Include the author's name only for the first entry; for subsequent entries, type three hyphens followed by a period in place of the author's name.

Author's Last Name, First Name. Title of Work. Publication City: Publisher, Year of Publication.

---. Title of Work. Publication City: Publisher, Year of Publication.

Friedman, Thomas L. <u>The Lexus and the Olive Tree: Understanding Globalization</u>. New York: Farrar, 1999.

---. <u>The World Is Flat: A Brief History of the Twenty-First Century</u>. New York: Farrar, 2005.

BOOKS

7. Book: Basic Format

The example here is the basic format for a book with one author. For author variations, see items 1–6. For more information on the treatment of authors, dates, titles, and publication information, see the box on page 446. After listing the author's name, include the title (and subtitle, if any) of the book, underscored. End with the publication city, publisher's name, and year.

Author. Book Title: Book Subtitle. Publication City: Publisher, Publication Year.

Mah, Adeline Yen. Falling Leaves: The True Story of an Unwanted Chinese Daughter. New York: Wiley, 1997.

8. Author and Editor

Include the author's name first if you are referring to the text itself. If, however, you are citing material written by the editor, include the editor's name first, followed by a comma and *ed.*

Author's Last Name, First Name. Book Title. Year of Original Publication. Ed. First and Last Name of Editor. Publication City: Publisher, Year of Publication.

Editor's Last Name, First Name, ed. Book Title. Year of Original Publication. By Author's First Name Last Name. Publication City: Publisher, Year of Publication.

Dickens, Charles. Great Expectations. 1861. Ed. Janice Carlisle. Boston: Bedford, 1996.

Carlisle, Janice., ed. Great Expectations. 1861. By Charles Dickens. Boston: Bedford, 1996.

9. Edited Collection

Last Name, First Name of Editor, ed. Book Title. Publication City: Publisher, Year of Publication.

Abbott, Megan, ed. A Hell of a Woman: An Anthology of Female Noir. Houston: Busted Flush, 2007.

10. Work in an Anthology or a Collection

Author Last Name, First Name. "Title of Work." Book Title. Ed. First and Last Name of Editor. Publication City: Publisher, Year of Publication. Page Numbers of Work.

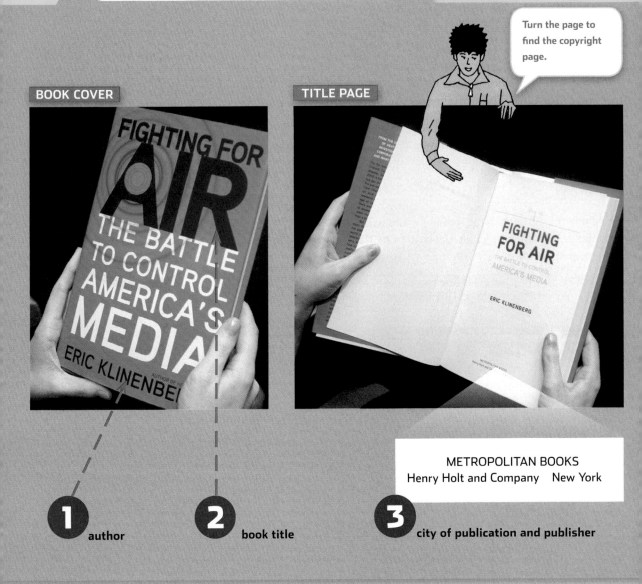

BOOK COVER

TITLE PAGE

Turn the page to find the copyright page.

FIGHTING FOR AIR
THE BATTLE TO CONTROL AMERICA'S MEDIA
ERIC KLINENBERG

FIGHTING FOR AIR
THE BATTLE TO CONTROL AMERICA'S MEDIA
ERIC KLINENBERG

METROPOLITAN BOOKS
Henry Holt and Company   New York

1 author

2 book title

3 city of publication and publisher

COPYRIGHT PAGE

Copyright © 2007 by Eric Klinenberg

4 year of publication

QUOTED PAGE

33

5 page number

MLA in-text citation

Some politicians might fear that "the industry's influence determines the fate of policy proposals, political campaigns, and, in turn, their own careers" (Klinenberg 33).

1 **1** **5** **2**

MLA works cited entry

Klinenberg, Eric. Fighting for Air: The Battle to Control America's Media.

New York: Metropolitan, 2007.

3 **4**

> Okpewho, Isidore. "The Cousins of Uncle Remus." The Black Columbiad:
>   Defining Moments in African American Literature and Culture. Ed.
>   Werner Sollors and Maria Diedrich. Cambridge: Harvard UP, 1994. 15-27.

11. Multivolume Work

To cite one volume of a multivolume work, include the volume number after the title. Note that by including the volume number in your list of works cited, you do not need to list it in your in-text citation. To cite two or more volumes, include the number of volumes after the title. In this case, you would need to include the specific volume number in each of your in-text citations for this source.

> Author or Editor. Title of Work. Vol. Number. Publication City: Publisher, Year
>   of Publication.

> Odekon, Mehmet, ed. Encyclopedia of World Poverty. Vol. 2. Thousand Oaks,
>   CA: Sage, 2006.

> Author or Editor. Title of Work. Number of Vols. Publication City: Publisher,
>   Year of Publication.

> Odekon, Mehmet, ed. Encyclopedia of World Poverty. 3 vols. Thousand Oaks,
>   CA: Sage, 2006.

12. Part of a Series

Include the series title from the title page and number (if any) after the title of the book.

> Author or Editor. Title of Work. Title and Number of Series. Publication City:
>   Publisher, Year of Publication.

> Dixon, Kelly J. Boomtown Saloons: Archaeology and History in Virginia City.
>   Wilbur S. Shepperson Ser. in Nevada Hist. Reno: U of Nevada
>   P, 2005.

13. Republished Book

If the book you are citing was previously published, include the original publication date after the title. If the new publication includes additional text, such as an introduction, include that, along with the name of its author, before the current publication information.

Author Last Name, First Name. Title of Work. Original Year of Publication.
New Material Author First Name Last Name. Publication City: Publisher,
Year of Publication.

Twain, Mark. Life on the Mississippi. 1883. Introd. Justin Kaplan. New York:
Penguin, 2001.

14. Later Edition

Include the edition number as a numeral with letters (*2nd*, *3rd*, *4th*, etc.) followed by *ed.* after the book's title. If the edition is listed on the title page as *Revised*, without a number, include *Rev. ed.* after the title of the book.

Author(s). Title of Work. Number ed. Publication City: Publisher, Year of
Publication.

Hartt, Frederick, and David G. Wilkins. History of Italian Renaissance Art:
Painting, Sculpture, Architecture. 4th ed. New York: Abrams, 2006.

15. Sacred Work

Include the title of the work as it is shown on the title page. If there is an editor or a translator listed, include the name after the title with either *Ed.* or *Trans.*

Title of Work. Editor or Translator. Publication City: Publisher, Year of
Publication.

The New American Bible. New York: Catholic Book Publishing, 1987.

The Qu'ran: A New Translation. Trans. M. A. S. Abdel Haleem. New York:
Oxford UP, 2004.

16. Translation

Original Author Last Name, First Name. Title of Work. Trans. First Name Last
Name. Publication City: Publisher, Year of Publication.

Fasce, Ferdinando. An American Family: The Great War and Corporate
Culture in America. Trans. Ian Harvey. Columbus: Ohio State UP, 2002.

17. Article in a Reference Book

If there is no article author, begin with the title of the article.

> Last Name, First Name of Article Author. "Title of Article." Book Title.
>   Publication City: Publisher, Year of Publication.

> Lutzger, Michael A. "Peace Movements." The Encyclopedia of New York
>   City. New Haven: Yale UP, 1995.

> "The History of the National Anthem." The World Almanac and Book of
>   Facts 2004. New York: World Almanac, 2004.

18. Introduction, Preface, Foreword, or Afterword

> Last Name, First Name of Book Part Author. Name of Book Part. Book Title.
>   Book Author or Editor. Publication City: Publisher, Year of Publication.
>   page numbers.

> Groening, Matt. Introduction. Best American Nonrequired Reading 2006. Ed.
>   Dave Eggers. Boston: Houghton, 2006. xi-xvii.

19. Title within a Title

If a book's title includes the title of another long work (play, book, or
periodical) within it, do not underline the internal title.

> Last Name, First Name of Author. Book Title Title within Title. Publication City:
>   Publisher, Year of Publication.

> Norris, Margot. A Companion to James Joyce's Ulysses. Boston: Bedford,
>   1998.

PERIODICALS

20. Article in a Journal Paginated by Volume

List the author(s) first, then include the article title, the journal title, the
volume number, the publication year, and the page numbers.

Author(s). "Title of Article." Title of Journal Volume Number (Year of
    Publication): page numbers.

Burt, Stephen, et al. "Does Poetry Have a Social Function?" Poetry 189
    (2007): 297-309.

21. Article in a Journal Paginated by Issue

Include the issue number after the volume number, separated by a period.

Author(s). "Title of Article." Title of Journal Volume Number.Issue Number (Year
    of Publication): page numbers.

Lynn, Susan. "The Case for Daily Physical Education: Concerns about
    Budget, Time, and Staffing Can All Be Satisfied." Journal of Physical
    Education, Recreation & Dance 18.4 (2007): 18-21.

22. Magazine Article

Include the date of publication rather than volume and issue numbers. (See
abbreviation rules in the box on p. 446.)

Author(s). "Title of Article." Title of Magazine Date of Publication: page numbers.

Fredenburg, Peter. "Mekong Harvests: Balancing Shrimp and Rice Farming
    in Vietnam." World and I Mar. 2002: 204+.

23. Newspaper Article

If a specific edition is listed on the newspaper's masthead, such as *Late
Edition* or *National Edition*, include an abbreviation of this after the date. If
page numbers are not consecutive, add "+" after the initial page.

Author(s). "Title of Article." Title of Newspaper Date of Publication: page
    numbers.

Smith, Stephen. "Taunting May Affect Health of Obese Youths." Boston
    Globe 11 July 2007: A1+.

Author(s). "Title of Article." Title of Newspaper Date of Publication, spec. ed.:
    page numbers.

Rohde, David. "Taliban Push Poppy Production to a Record Again." New
    York Times 26 Aug. 2007, natl. ed.: 3.

How to...
Cite from a magazine (MLA)

MAGAZINE COVER

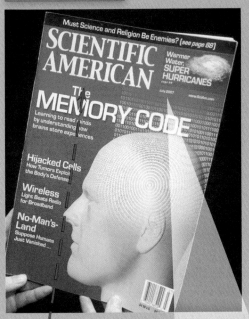

ARTICLE

July 2007

By Joe Z. Tsien

1 magazine title

2 publication date

3 author

4 article title

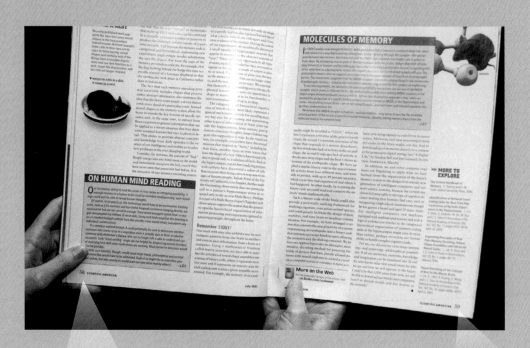

58

5 page number of quoted passage

52 **59**

6 first and last pages of article

MLA in-text citation

Analysis of one research team's recent findings "reinforces the idea that the brain is not simply a device that records every detail of a particular event" (Tsien 58).

3 **6**

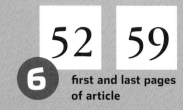

MLA works cited entry

3 **4** **1** **2** **6**

Tsien, Joe Z. "The Memory Code." Scientific American July 2007: 52-59.

If a paper numbers each section individually, without attaching letters to the page numbers (as on p. 455), include the section number in your citation.

Author(s). "Title of Article." Title of Newspaper Date of Publication, sec.
   Section Number: page numbers.

Bowley, Graham. "Keeping Up with the Windsors." New York Times 15 July
   2007, sec. 3: 1+.

24. Editorial

For a newspaper editorial, do not include an author, but do include the word *Editorial*, followed by a period, after the title of the article.

"Title of Article." Editorial. Title of Newspaper Date of Publication: page
   number(s).

"Living on Iraq Time." Editorial. New York Times 28 May 2007: A15.

25. Letter to the Editor

Last Name, First Name of Letter Writer. Letter. Title of Newspaper Date of
   Publication: page number.

Zita, Ken. Letter. Financial Times 16 Aug. 2006: 8.

26. Unsigned Article

"Title of Article." Title of Newspaper Date of Publication: page number.

"Justice Probes Lenders." Washington Post 26 July 2007: D02.

27. Review

Add *Rev. of* before the title of the work being reviewed.

Review Author. "Title of Review." Rev. of Title of Work Being Reviewed, by
   Author of Work Being Reviewed. Title of Publication in Which Review
   Appears. Volume.Issue (Year of Publication): page numbers.

Levin, Yuval. "Diagnosis and Cure." Rev. of Sick: The Untold Story of
   America's Health-Care Crisis and the People Who Pay the Price, by
   Jonathan Cohn. Commentary 124.1 (2007): 80-82.

ELECTRONIC SOURCES

28. Short Work from a Web Site

Last Name, First Name of Short Work Author. "Title of Short Work." Title of
  Web Site. Date of Publication or Most Recent Update. Name of
  Sponsoring Organization (if needed). Date of Access <URL>.

McFee, Gord. "Why 'Revisionism' Isn't." The Holocaust History Project.
  15 May 1999. 10 Sept. 2007 <http://www.holocaust-history.org/
  revisionism-isnt/>.

29. Entire Web Site

Last Name, First Name of Web Site Author. Title of Web Site. Date of
  Publication or Most Recent Update. Name of Sponsoring Organization.
  Date of Access <URL>.

Myers, Robert, et al. Exploring the Environment. 28 Apr. 2005. Wheeling
  Jesuit U. 12 Sept. 2007 <http://www.cotf.edu/ete/>.

30. Entire Weblog

Include any of the following elements that are available.

Author's Last Name, First Name. Title of Weblog. Weblog. Date of most recent
  post. Name of Sponsoring Organization (if any). Date of Access <URL>.

Sellers, Heather. Word after Word. Weblog. 21 Jun. 2008. 24 Jun. 2008
  <http://heathersellers.com/blog/index.php>.

31. Entry in a Weblog

Include any of the following elements that are available.

Author's Last Name, First Name. "Title of Entry. " Weblog post.
  Title of Weblog. Date. Name of sponsoring organization. Date of Access
  <URL>.

Sellers, Heather. "East Coast." Weblog post. Word after Word. 7 Nov. 2007
  30 Jan. 2008 <http://www.heathersellers.com/blog/2007/11/07/
  east-coast/>.

32. Online Book

Last Name, First Name of Book Author. Title of Book. Book Publication City: Book Publisher, Book Publication Year. Title of Web Site. Date of Online Publication or Most Recent Update. Name of Sponsoring Organization (if any). Date of Access <URL>.

Riis, Jacob. How the Other Half Lives. New York: Scribner's, 1890. Bartleby.com: Great Books Online. 2000. 6 Nov. 2007 <http:// www.bartleby.com/208/>.

33. Work from a Library Subscription Service (such as InfoTrac or FirstSearch)

The example below is for a scholarly journal paginated by issue. For more details on citing various types of periodical articles, see items 20–27, above.

Author(s) of Article. "Title of Article." Title of Periodical. Volume Number.Issue Number (Year of Publication): page numbers. Name of Database. Name of Subscription Service. Name, City, and State of Subscribing Library. Date of Access <URL>.

Cotugna, Nancy, and Connie Vickery. "Educating Early Childhood Teachers about Nutrition: A Collaborative Venture." Childhood Education 83.4 (2007): 194-98. Academic OneFile. InfoTrac. Martin County Lib., Stuart, FL. 10 July 2007 <http://find.galegroup.com>.

34. Work from an Online Periodical

The example below is for a popular magazine. For more details on citing various types of periodical articles, see items 20–27, above.

Author(s) of Article. "Title of Article." Title of Periodical. Publication Date page numbers (if any). Date of Access <URL>.

Gogoi, Pallavi. "The Trouble with Business Ethics." BusinessWeek Online 25 June 2007. 3 Oct. 2007 <http://www.businessweek.com/bwdaily/ dnflash/content/jun2007/db20070622_221291.htm>.

35. Online Posting

Author of Post. "Title (or Subject) of Post." Online posting. Date of Post. Title of Bulletin Board. Date of Access <URL>.

Winkleman, Tallulah. "Reducing Your Food Miles." Online posting.
13 July 2007. Farm Folk City Folk Bulletin. 10 Sept. 2007 <http://
tech.groups.yahoo.com/group/FFCFBulletin/message/220>.

36. E-mail

E-mail Author Last Name, First Name. "Subject of E-mail." E-mail to the author
(or Name of Recipient). Date Sent.

Gingrich, Newt. "Drill here. Drill now." E-mail to the author. 20 May 2008.

37. CD-ROM

Last Name, First Name of CD-ROM author (if any). Title of CD-ROM.
CD-ROM. Publication City: Publisher, Publication Year.

History through Art: The Twentieth Century. CD-ROM. San Jose: Fogware,
2001.

38. Podcast

Include any of the following elements that are available.

Author's or Speaker's Name, Last Name First. "Title of Podcast." Podcast.
Names of Performers or Host. Title of Site on which podcast is posted.
Date podcast is posted. Sponsoring Organization. Date of access < URL>.

Graham, Lester (Prod.). "Capping Pollution at the Source." Podcast.
Host Graham. The Environment Report. 31 July 2006. The Nature
Conservancy. 25 June 2008 <http://www.environmentreport.org/
story.php3?story_id=3102>.

39. Entry in a Wiki

Wiki content is continually edited by its users, so there is no author to cite.

"Title of Entry." Name of the Wiki. Date of last update (if available). Sponsoring
Organization, if any. Date of access. <URL>.

"Emo." Wikipedia. Wikimedia Foundation. 24 June 2008 <http://
en.wikipedia.org/wiki/Emo>.

How to...
Cite from a Web site (MLA)

1 Web site title

2 article title

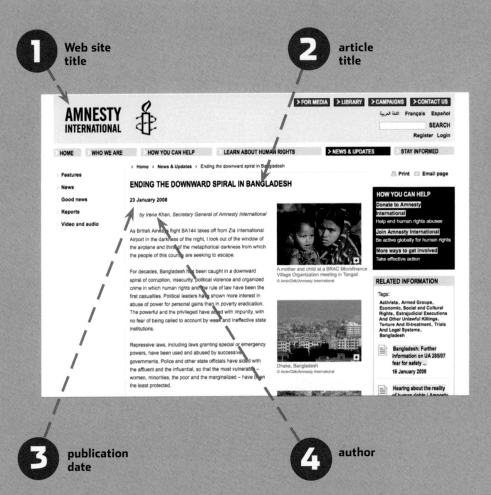

3 publication date

4 author

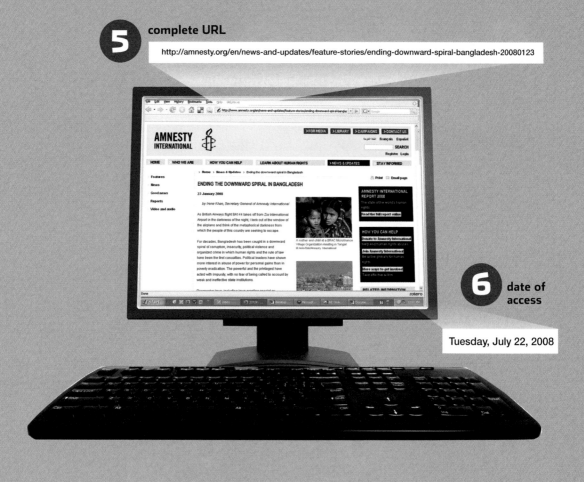

5 complete URL

http://amnesty.org/en/news-and-updates/feature-stories/ending-downward-spiral-bangladesh-20080123

6 date of access

Tuesday, July 22, 2008

MLA in-text citation

The Secretary General of Amnesty International argues that "the right question is not whether the human rights situation today is better or worse than last year. It is whether one should be more hopeful or less that this country will turn a corner on human rights" (Khan).

4 **2** **4** **1**

Khan, Irene. "Ending the Downward Spiral in Bangladesh." Amnesty

3 **6** **5**

MLA works cited entry

International. 23 Jan. 2008. 22 July 2008 <http://

www.amnesty.org/en/news-and-updates/feature-stories/

ending-downward-spiral-bangladesh-20080123>.

How to...
Cite from a database (MLA)

1 author   **2** article title   **3** volume and issue number

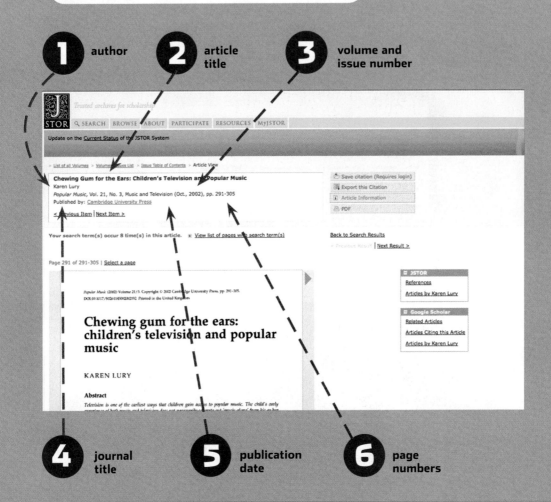

4 journal title   **5** publication date   **6** page numbers

7 database name

8 database URL

http://jstor.org/

9 library through which you accessed the article

Emerson College

10 date of access

Tuesday, July 22, 2008

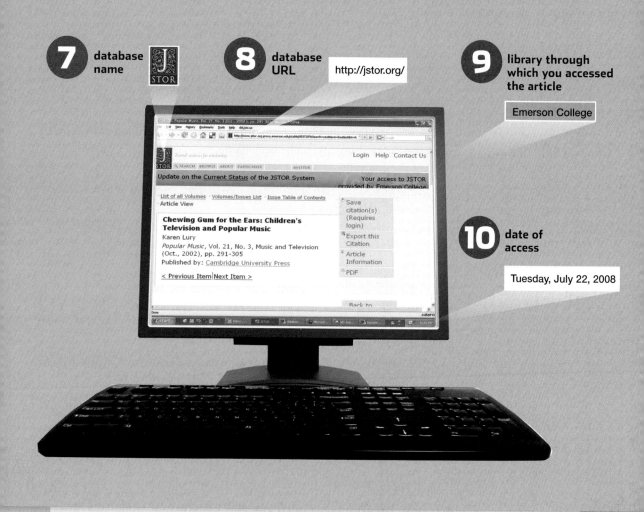

MLA in-text citation

Children accept even nonsensical lyrics as legitimate musical expression, and one researcher calls their tolerance "a mode of engagement carried productively into the adult's experience of popular songs" (Lury 300).

1   **2**   **1** **6**

Lury, Karen. "Chewing Gum for the Ears: Children's Television and

MLA works cited entry

4   **3** **5**   **6**   **7**

Popular Music." Popular Music 21.3 (2002): 291-305. JSTOR.

9   **10**   **8**

Emerson Coll. Lib., Boston. 22 July 2008 <http://www.jstor.org>.

OTHER

40. Dissertation

If the dissertation is published, the title should be underlined or italicized, and the publication city, publisher's name, and year should be listed at the end of the citation.

> Author Last Name, First Name. "Dissertation Title." Diss. Name of University, Year.

> Mooney, John Alfonso. "Shadows of Dominion: White Men and Power in Slavery, War, and the New South." Diss. U of Virginia, 2007.

41. Published Conference Proceedings

List the editor(s) name(s), followed by *ed.* or *eds.* and the underlined title of the proceedings. Before the conference information, add *Proc. of* and follow with the conference title, dates, and location.

> Editor Names, eds. Title of Proceedings. Proc. of Conference Title, Conference Date, Conference Location. Publication City: Publisher, Year.

> Westfahl, G., and George Slusser, eds. Nursery Realms: Children in the World of Science Fiction, Fantasy, and Horror. Proc. of J. Lloyd Eaton Conf. on Science Fiction and Fantasy Lit., Jan. 1999, U of California, Riverside. Athens: U of Georgia P, 1999.

42. Government Document

Begin by listing the government (usually a country or state) that issued the document, and then list the specific department or agency. Most U.S. government documents are published by the Washington-based Government Printing Office (GPO).

> Government. Department or Agency. Title of Document. Publication City: Publisher, Date of Publication.

> United States. Dept. of Labor. Summary Data from the Consumer Price Index News Release. Washington, DC: GPO, Oct. 2006.

Cri Du Chat Syndrome 6

References

Campbell, D., Carlin M., Justen, J., III, & Baird, S. (2004). Cri-du-chat
  syndrome: A topical overview. Retrieved from http://
  www.fivepminus.org/online.htm

Denny, M., Marchand-Martella, N., Martella, R., Reilly, J. R., & Reilly,
  J. F. (2000, November). Using parent-delivered graduated
  guidance to teach functional living skills to a child with cri du
  chat syndrome. *Education & Treatment of Children, 23*(4), 441.

Five P-Minus Society. (n.d.). *About 5P-syndrome.* Retrieved from
  http://www.fivepminus.org/about.htm

Kugler, M. (2006). Cri-du-chat syndrome: Distinctive kitten-like cry in
  infancy. Retrieved from http://rarediseases.about.com/cs/
  criduchatsynd/a/010704.htm

McClean, P. (1997). Genomic analysis: *In situ* hybridization. Retrieved
  from http://www.ndsu.nodak.edu/instruct/mcclean/plsc431/
  genomic/genomic2.htm

Sarimski, K. (2003, February). Early play behavior in children with
  5p-syndrome. *Journal of Intellectual Disability Research, 47*(2),
  113-120.

Sondheimer, N. (2005). Cri du chat syndrome. In *MedlinePlus medical
  encyclopedia.* Retrieved from http://www.nlm.nih.gov/
  medlineplus/ency/article/001593.htm

Media & Design

part eight

46 Understanding Images

think visually

Most of us realize how powerful images can be, particularly when they perfectly capture a moment or make an argument that words alone struggle to express. The famous "Blue Marble" shot of the Earth taken by *Apollo 17* in 1972 is one such image—conveying both the wonder and fragility of our planet hanging in space.

More recently, the numerous still and video shots of human suffering following Hurricane Katrina galvanized a nation and altered the political landscape (for an example, see p. 90).

But media need not be spectacular or inimitable to effectively communicate ideas. We routinely use images of all kinds, from simple photographs to CT scans of human organs, to organize and present information. Consider how the average campus map easily directs users to the buildings and services they need, relying on nothing more than drawings, colors, symbols, and various legends or keys—all important communication devices.

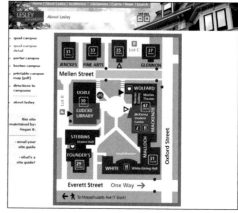

Lesley College campus map

When enhanced by sound and action, images become complex multimedia experiences. A sports fan can watch virtual baseball and football games on ESPN.com, thanks to an interface that mimics the actions and sounds on the remote playing field.

Images relate different kinds of experiences and achieve a variety of results: The riveting and emotional photograph clinches an argument, as does the cool-headed and clear chart's display of data. Following are a few strategies to keep in mind when designing and using images, to reach readers effectively and powerfully.

Design an image showing a sequence.   Like a narrative, an image can show information in stages or steps. ○ The sequence might be alphabetical, chronological, or by degree or magnitude (for example, greater to lesser, cheap to expensive)—whatever works for the material. ○ However, the arrangement of data should be self-evident to readers, whether in a chart, Web page, or map. They should never have to guess how the material works or what the sequence illustrates. The American Red Cross, for example, depicts its history on its Web museum through a visual timeline. The reader simply clicks on any of the scrolling panels for more information about a specific period.

Visual timeline from the Web site of the American Red Cross

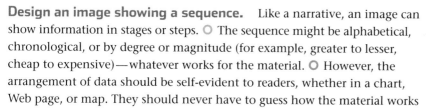

understand narrative
p. 4

shape your work
p. 340

**Seating plan for the
Santa Fe Opera House.**

Design an image displaying differences.   Many types of images use boundaries of various kinds—lines, boxes, columns, contrasting colors, and so on—to highlight divisions. A simple seating guide to an auditorium mimics its floor plan to guide you to your box. An online weather map shows the entire country marked off into states, counties, climatic regions, and so on.

Color-coding is often added to such images to convey even further information. The colors in that seating guide tell you that there is a price difference between the loge and the mezzanine sections; on a weather map, colors indicate temperatures or storm fronts.

Design an image demonstrating a process.   Sometimes processes are easier to understand if they are broken down into components and displayed visually. In a flowchart, a reader follows a series of distinct steps, often making one or more choices along the way, in order to reach a conclusion.

Even complex cause-and-effect relationships can be displayed visually, either as static images or more elaborate animations. ○ For example, *USA Today*—one of the leaders in innovative information design—uses an animated sequence online to show how cat-dander allergies can occur and be overcome. The graphic allows readers to pick several options and then "play" the item to see the results. Note that the image explains to readers where to start and what to do.

This *USA Today* interactive graphic enables readers to see how scientists are learning to shut down allergic reactions.

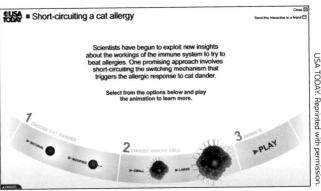

understand causal
analysis p. 128

Design an image showing how information is related.   Quite often, information needs to be presented in diagrams that show hierarchies and other relationships. A family tree illustrates the genealogical connections among a person's ancestors. A site map displays the main pages and sub-pages of a Web site. An organizational chart (or "org chart," as it is commonly called) lets readers know who reports to whom within an organization.

PENNSYLVANIA DEPARTMENT OF STATE ORGANIZATIONAL CHART

Secretary of the Commonwealth
Pedro A. Cortés

Executive Deputy Secretary
Thomas J. Weaver

Office of Chief Counsel
Albert H. Masland

Office of Communications and Press
Leslie Amorós

Office of Legislative Affairs
Meredith M. Biggica

Office of Policy
Kathleen Kotula

Deputy Secretary for Administration
Harry A. VanSickle

Deputy Secretary for Regulatory Programs
Sara Manzano-Diaz

Deputy Secretary for Planning and Service Delivery
David P. Burgess

Bureau of Commissions/Elections/Legislation
Chet Harhut

Bureau of Charitable Organizations
Tracy L. McCurdy

Bureau of Management Information Systems
Timothy S. Ruppert

Bureau of Finance and Operations
Cynthia K. Gnech

Bureau of Enforcement and Investigation
Claude A. Shields

Human Resource Office
Patrick M. Striggle

Bureau of Professional/Occupational Affairs
Basil L. Merenda

State Athletic Commission
Greg P. Sirb

Corporation Bureau
Richard K. House

Design an image displaying three dimensions.   Many images, particularly in the fields of science and engineering, attempt to convey three-dimensional information in two dimensions, enabling viewers to understand how objects work, how parts mesh, or how the natural world functions. Consider how cutaway drawings enable viewers to see relationships that would be very difficult to explain in words alone.

47 Using Images

Use images in various academic papers and projects to help illustrate a topic or argue a point. ○ The images may be embedded in a paper or other print document, appear on a Web page, or become part of a multimedia project. In order to use images sensibly and effectively in your work, consider the following guidelines.

work with visuals

Have a good reason for using every image. A photograph or clip should do what words cannot. For instance, a verbal description of the unique style of a Frank Gehry or Santiago Calatrava building probably wouldn't do justice to the subject. Readers should benefit from seeing a photograph in your text—which is exactly why Annie Winsett includes the photograph of the Guggenheim Bilbao in her report on page 60. On the other hand,

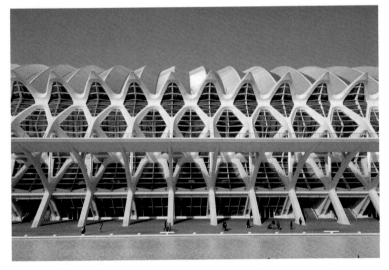

think visually
p. 500

what would be gained from downloading images of the president or secretary of state into a report for a government class: Who doesn't already know what they look like? Using unnecessary images contributes to *clutter*, the visual equivalent of wordiness. ○

Download and save images.   Most images on the Web can be saved on your computer simply by control clicking (or right clicking) on them. You can also purchase whole libraries of clip art and stock photography, which you can then use without worrying about copyright infringement. If you are working with a digital camera, download your own images onto your computer, where you can edit them and import them into various documents.

To import an image into a Word or PowerPoint document, select Picture (or another option) from the Insert menu, find the appropriate image file, and click on it. Alternatively, you can copy an online image directly from its source (by right clicking or control clicking) and paste it into your document. If you choose this method, be *extremely careful* to document the source site; obtain permission if necessary. ○

Keep careful tabs on the images you collect for your project. Create a dedicated folder on your desktop or other memorable place on your hard drive, and save each image with a new name that will remind you exactly where it came from. Keeping a printed record of images, with more detailed background about copyright and source information, will be a great time-saver later, when you are putting your project or paper together.

Use digital images of an appropriate size.   Even if you have limited knowledge of image file formats (such as JPG, GIF, or TIFF), you probably understand that digital files come in varying sizes. The size of a digital-image file is directly related to the quality, or resolution, of the image. Attach a few high resolution photos to an e-mail, and you'll quickly clog the recipient's mailbox.

For most Web pages and online documents, compressed or lower resolution images will be acceptable. On the other hand, if you intend to print an image — in a paper or brochure, for example — use the highest

At this size, the image downloaded from the Web is clear enough. But it would become distorted if you tried to enlarge it, because its resolution is too low.

improve your sentences
p. 378

understand citation
styles p. 435

PART 8   MEDIA & DESIGN

resolution image (the greatest number of pixels) available to assure maximum sharpness and quality.

Use tools to crop and improve an image.   Even the simplest image-editing software enables you to adjust the tint, contrast, saturation, and sharpness of your digital photographs. For instance, heightening the contrast of a PowerPoint image so that it projects better. Or adjusting the tint in a portrait to get the green out of skin tones. More sophisticated programs such as iPhoto, Photoshop, or Photo Editor allow you to do even more. Don't, however, tinker with the settings on professional photographs, even if you have permission to use them. Unless you have purchased the images from a stock photography library, they belong to someone else.

Use the cropping tool to select just the portion of an image you need for your project. Be aware, though, that when you enlarge a section of a larger digital image, it loses sharpness. And never crop an image in a way that distorts its meaning.

Improving a Photo Using Photo Editor   Image-editing software offers numerous options for enhancing picture files. Look for them on palettes, toolbars, or dropdown menus.

Caption an image correctly.   When using images in an academic paper, number, label, and caption them. Captions provide context for readers, so they know why they're looking at the image. MLA and APA styles have different guidelines for captioning images and referring to them in the text, so consult the relevant guidebook before writing your captions. In general, however, captions should include the source of the image and any copyright and publication information. The photo below has not been previously published, but note we still had to ask the photographer for permission to reprint.

Respect copyrights.   The images you find, whether online or in print, are someone else's property. You cannot use them for commercial purposes—Web sites, brochures, posters, magazine articles, and so on—without permission.

Fig. 1. The Floating Market in Phuket, Thailand. (Courtesy Sid Darion.)

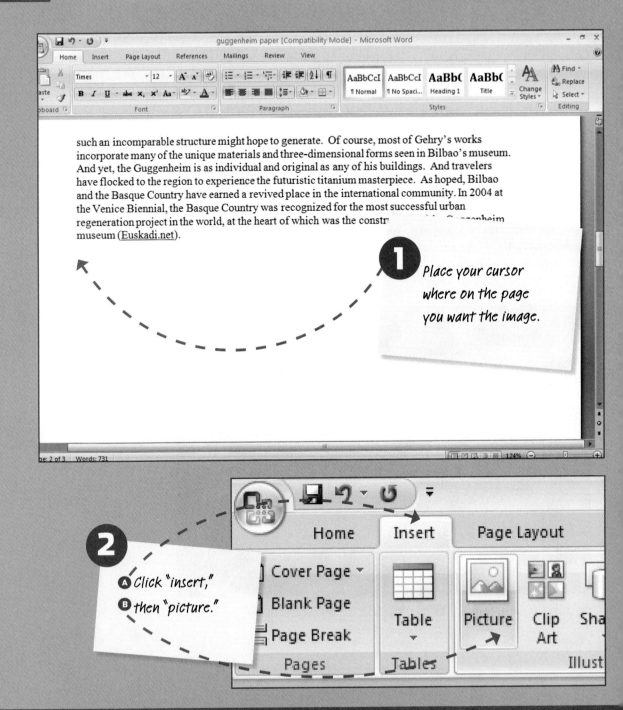

such an incomparable structure might hope to generate. Of course, most of Gehry's works incorporate many of the unique materials and three-dimensional forms seen in Bilbao's museum. And yet, the Guggenheim is as individual and original as any of his buildings. And travelers have flocked to the region to experience the futuristic titanium masterpiece. As hoped, Bilbao and the Basque Country have earned a revived place in the international community. In 2004 at the Venice Biennial, the Basque Country was recognized for the most successful urban regeneration project in the world, at the heart of which was the constr... ...zenheim museum (Euskadi.net).

1 Place your cursor where on the page you want the image.

2
A Click "insert,"
B then "picture."

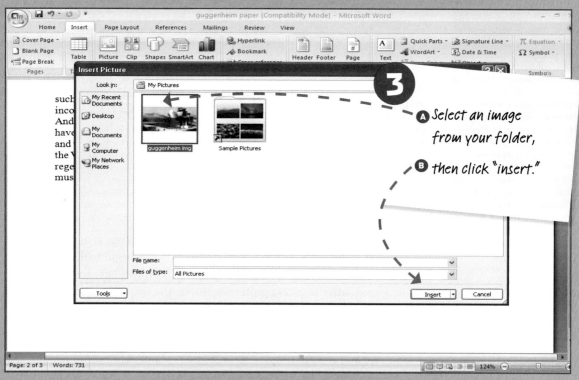

3

Ⓐ Select an image from your folder,

Ⓑ then click "insert."

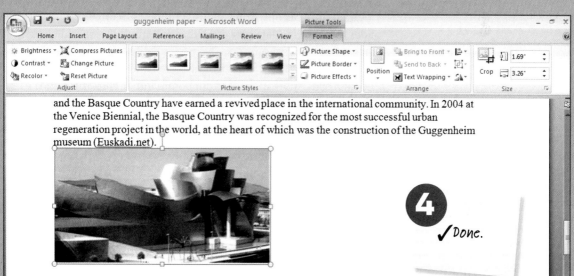

and the Basque Country have earned a revived place in the international community. In 2004 at the Venice Biennial, the Basque Country was recognized for the most successful urban regeneration project in the world, at the heart of which was the construction of the Guggenheim museum (Euskadi.net).

4 ✓ Done.

48 Presentation Software

PowerPoint is the dominant software used in public presentations, perhaps as often as tens of millions of times a day. When asked to do an oral report, most people automatically begin with Power-Point or a comparable product such as Keynote. Easy to use, these programs can give a professional look to any presentation. For an example of a PowerPoint presentation, see page 301 in Chapter 16 on oral reports.

With presentation software, you create a sequence of slides to accompany an oral report, building the slides yourself or picking them from a gallery of ready-made designs and color schemes that fit different occasions. You can also choose individual layouts for slides to accommodate text only, text and photos, text and charts, images only, and so on.

Once created, the slides can be edited and rearranged. Set up the final slide show to run at your command or click through the slides yourself, with the transitions accompanied by various sound effects and animations.

Those are just the basics. Presentation software offers so many bells and whistles that novices tend to overdo it, allowing the software to dominate the report. Here's how to make PowerPoint or Keynote work for you.

create slides

PART 8 MEDIA & DESIGN

For presentations, PowerPoint offers both design templates (left) and individual slide layouts (right).

Be certain you need presentation software.   A short talk that makes only one or two points probably works better if viewers focus on you, not on a screen. Use presentation software to keep audiences on track through more complicated material, to highlight major issues or points, or to display images viewers really need to see. A little humor or eye candy is fine once in a while, but don't expect audiences to be impressed by glitz. What matters is the content of the report. ⊙

Use slides to introduce points, not cover them.   If you find yourself reading your slides, you've put too much material on them. And you'll bore your audience to distraction. Put material on-screen that audiences need to see: main points, charts, and images directly relevant to the report. It's fine, too, for a slide to outline your presentation at the beginning and to summarize your points at the end. In fact, it's helpful to have a slide that obviously signals a conclusion.

Use a simple and consistent design.   Select one of the design templates provided or create a design of your own that fits your subject. A consistent design scheme will unify your report and minimize distractions. ⊙
     For academic presentations, choose simple designs and fonts. Make the text size large enough for viewers at the back of the room to read easily. For reasons of legibility, avoid elegant, playful, or eccentric fonts, including

understand oral
reports p. 298

design your work
p. 517

Make your slides readable

- Avoid fonts so fancy that they are hard to read.

- Avoid eccentric or cursive fonts.

- Don't crowd your slide with more words than you need.

- Don't put everything you expect to say on a slide because readers will be bored.

- **Boldface for emphasis, but rarely!**

- Be sure to show enough contrast between words and background.

Make your slides readable

- Use readable fonts.

- Avoid eccentric or cursive fonts.

- Don't crowd your slides.

- Maintain contrast between font and background.

those that resemble handwriting or Old English styles. And don't use more than one or two fonts within the presentation. Use boldface very selectively for emphasis. If you have to boldface a font to make it visible at a distance, simply find a thicker font. Italics are fine for occasional use, but in some fonts they are hard to read at a distance.

Check, too, that you have plenty of contrast between words and background on a screen so that your points don't fade away. For academic reports, keep colors sober and compatible. Avoid dark backgrounds and bright fonts. Look for an opportunity to preview your slides in the room where they'll be presented, and under the actual lighting conditions. Be familiar with the slideshow equipment.

Keep transitions between slides simple.   PowerPoint offers numerous options for transitions between slides, many of them animated and accompanied by sound effects. Simple transitions such as *dissolve* and *appear* are restrained enough for academic reports. But many of the other choices are better suited to cartoons and rock videos. Browse these special effects to get them out of your system. Then avoid them unless you have a compelling reason to use one. For example, *camera* nicely mimics the sound of a shutter closing. When you are presenting just one or two special photographs, the transition can work nicely and won't seem gimmicky.

Edit your slides ruthlessly.   Errors in spelling and punctuation never look good. But when projected in living color on a screen in front of an audience, they are just plain embarrassing and destroy your credibility. Make sure to review and proofread your work for careless mistakes. O

proofread
p. 386

49 Charts, Tables, and Graphs

Just as images and photographs are often the media of choice for conveying visual information, charts, graphs, and tables are usually your best bet for displaying numerical and statistical data.

In programs like Word and PowerPoint, you can create charts with the various tools on the drawing toolbar. A spreadsheet application such as Excel automatically creates charts and graphs for you once you input your information. Excel charts can then be inserted into Word or PowerPoint as needed.

Use tables to present statistical data. Tables consist of horizontal rows and vertical columns into which you drop data.

display data

> Often the most effective way to describe, explore, and summarize a set of numbers—even a very large set—is to look at pictures of those numbers.
> —Edward R. Tufte

Table A. Expectation of life by age, race, and sex: United States, 2002
[Race categories are consistent with the 1977 Office of Management and Budget guidelines]

Age	All races			White			Black		
	Total	Male	Female	Total	Male	Female	Total	Male	Female
0	77.3	74.5	79.9	77.7	75.1	80.3	72.3	68.8	75.6
1	76.8	74.1	79.4	77.2	74.6	79.7	72.4	68.8	75.6
5	72.9	70.2	75.4	73.3	70.7	75.8	68.5	65.0	71.7
10	67.9	65.3	70.5	68.3	65.7	70.8	63.6	60.1	66.8
15	63.0	60.3	65.5	63.4	60.8	65.9	58.7	55.2	61.8
20	58.2	55.6	60.7	58.6	56.1	61.0	53.9	50.5	57.0
25	53.5	51.0	55.8	53.8	51.4	56.1	49.3	46.0	52.1
30	48.7	46.3	51.0	49.0	46.7	51.2	44.7	41.6	47.4
35	44.0	41.6	46.1	44.3	42.0	46.4	40.1	37.1	42.7
40	39.3	37.0	41.4	39.6	37.4	41.6	35.6	32.8	38.1
45	34.8	32.6	36.7	35.0	32.9	36.9	31.3	28.5	33.7
50	30.3	28.3	32.2	30.5	28.5	32.4	27.3	24.6	29.5
55	26.1	24.1	27.7	26.2	24.3	27.9	23.4	21.0	25.4
60	22.0	20.2	23.5	22.1	20.3	23.6	19.9	17.6	21.6
65	18.2	16.6	19.5	18.2	16.6	19.5	16.6	14.6	18.0
70	14.7	13.2	15.8	14.7	13.3	15.8	13.5	11.8	14.7
75	11.5	10.3	12.4	11.5	10.3	12.3	10.9	9.5	11.7
80	8.8	7.8	9.4	8.7	7.7	9.3	8.6	7.5	9.2
85	6.5	5.7	6.9	6.4	5.7	6.8	6.6	5.8	7.0
90	4.8	4.2	5.0	4.7	4.1	4.9	5.1	4.5	5.3
95	3.6	3.2	3.7	3.4	3.0	3.5	3.9	3.6	4.0
100	2.7	2.5	2.8	2.4	2.3	2.5	3.0	2.9	3.0

Table

514

They are ideal for organizing lots of information without actually interpreting it. A table may show trends and suggest comparisons, but readers must find them on their own—one of the pleasures of reading tables.

You can make tables using a word processing program, either drawing them yourself or via an automatic function in which you specify the number of columns and rows you will need and select a design template. Some of the ready-made designs use color and even 3-D effects to highlight information. But good tables can be very plain. In fact, many of the tables on federal government Web sites, though packed with information, are dirt simple and yet very clear.

Use graphs to plot relationships within sets of data.   Graphs highlight relationships you choose to draw out of data by plotting one significant variable against another. Column and bar graphs emphasize comparisons; if well designed, they enable readers to grasp relationships that would otherwise take many words to explain.

Line graphs are more dynamic, plotting changes in variables, often over a period of time, so that readers can see both relationships and trends. Line graphs often are used to show the heart of many political and social arguments: for example, changes in employment, average world temperatures, or stock prices.

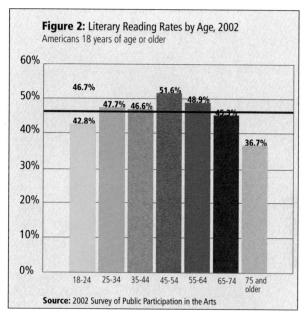

Figure 2: Literary Reading Rates by Age, 2002
Americans 18 years of age or older

Source: 2002 Survey of Public Participation in the Arts

Bar Chart

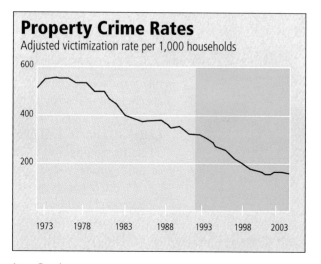

Line Graph

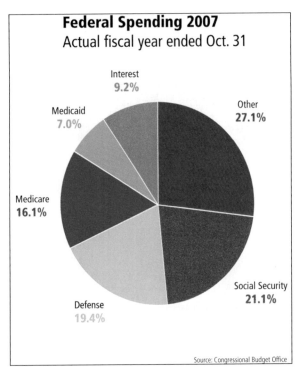

Federal Spending 2007
Actual fiscal year ended Oct. 31

Interest
9.2%

Medicaid
7.0%

Other
27.1%

Medicare
16.1%

Social Security
21.1%

Defense
19.4%

Source: Congressional Budget Office

Pie Chart

Use pie charts to display proportions.

Pie charts show how groups within a larger whole stand in relationship to one another. For instance, you might use a pie chart to show the relative size of major ethnic groups (white, Hispanic, black, Asian) within the total U.S. population. Keep in mind that the segments in a pie chart should always total 100 percent. To finish this ethnic pie, you would need to include a segment called "Other" to account for groups not represented in the major categories.

Pie-chart sections can be cut only so thin before they begin to lose clarity. If you wanted to use a pie chart to depict all the specific religious groups in the United States, you'd find yourself with hundreds of slivers readers couldn't possibly distinguish. Better to transfer the data to a table, which would handle each creed in a separate row.

Use maps to depict varying types of information.

A plain old atlas or road map delivers an immense amount of information, from the location of cities and mountains to the distances between them. But many other kinds of data can be laid atop geographic boundaries. Consider how hikers use a topographical map that shows elevations and trails. Maps are also helpful in displaying social and political data.

Label all charts and graphs.

In an academic paper, label and number all charts, graphs, and tables. Include publication information for any chart or graph you reproduce from another source.

APA style has its own detailed guidelines for constructing and labeling tables and charts. Be sure to use the *Publication Manual of the American Psychological Association*, Fifth Edition, when preparing graphics for a major paper in APA style.

Designing Print and Online Documents

Much advice about good visual design is common sense: You could guess that the design of most academic and professional documents should be balanced, consistent, and uncluttered. But it is not always simple to translate abstract principles into practice. Nor are any visual qualities absolute. A balanced and consistent design is exactly what you want for government documents and research reports, but to create newsletters or brochures, you need more visual snap. As always, purpose and audience determine what works.

Keep page designs simple and uncluttered. Simple doesn't mean a design should be simplistic, only that you shouldn't try to do more on a page than it (or your design skills) can handle. You want readers to find information they need, navigate your document without missteps, and perceive the structure of your project. Key information should stand out. If you keep the basic design uncomplicated, you can present lots of information without a page feeling cluttered.

Consider, for example, how cleverly Anthro Technology Furniture uses design cues as simple as *Step 1, Step 2,* and *Step 3* to guide consumers on a Web page through the complex process of configuring a workstation. A reader simply moves left to right across a page making specific choices. They don't feel overwhelmed by the options, even though the material is detailed.

Keep the design balanced.   Think of balance as a dynamic term—what you hope to achieve *overall* in a design. You probably don't want many pages that, if split down the middle, would show mirror images. Strive for active page designs, in which, for example, a large photograph on one side of a page is countered on the other by blocks of print and maybe several smaller images. The overall effect required is balance, even though the individual page elements may all differ in size and shape.

You can see basic design principles at work on the front pages of most newspapers, where editors try to come up with a look that gives impact to the news. They have many elements to work with, including their paper's masthead, headlines of varying size, photographs and images, columns of copy, screened boxes, and much more. The pages of a newspaper can teach you a lot about design.

Use templates sensibly.   If you have the time and talent to design all of your own documents, that's terrific. But for many projects, you could do worse than to begin with the templates offered by many software products. The Project Gallery in Microsoft software, for example, helps you create business letters, brochures, PowerPoint presentations, and more. It sets up a generic document, placing its margins, aligning key elements and graphics, and offering an array of customizations. No two projects based on the same template need look alike.

If you resist borrowing such materials from software, not wanting yet another part of your life packaged by corporate types, know that it is tough to design documents from scratch. Even if you intend to design an item yourself, consider examining a template to figure out how to assemble a complex document. Take what you learn from the model and then strike out on your own.

Front page of the *San Francisco Chronicle,* May 11, 2008

On slow news days without big headlines, masthead dominates front page.

Colorful column of boxes and photos previews paper content.

Below masthead, candidate photo (in shaded box) separates two visually balanced stories on politics.

Large photo on fold (with secondary photo and pull quote below) provides lead-in for a feature.

Print-heavy right-hand column helps balance many images on page.

For variety, column width changes for feature story.

Coordinate your colors.   Your mother was right: Pay attention to colors and patterns when you dress and when you design color documents. To learn elementary principles of color coordination, try searching "*color* wheel" on the Web, but recognize that the subject is both complicated and more art than science. As an amateur, keep your design work simple.

For academic papers, the text is black and the background is white. You may use one additional color for headings, but make it a highly readable choice. Avoid flashy or gaudy tints, such as reverse lime green and bright purple. For Web sites and other projects, keep background colors pale, if you use them at all, and maintain adequate contrast between text and background.

Use headings if needed.   Readers really appreciate headings. In academic work, they should be descriptive more than clever. If you have prepared a good scratch or topic outline, the major points may provide you with headings almost ready-made. ○ Like items in an outline, headings at the same level should be roughly parallel in style. ○

A short paper (3–5 pages) doesn't require much more than a title. For longer papers (10–20 pages), it's possible to use top-level items from your outline as headings. For some projects, especially in the sciences, you must use the headings you're given. This is especially true for lab reports and scientific articles, and you shouldn't vary from the template. For an example of a report with headings, see pages 56–60 in Chapter 2.

Choose appropriate fonts.   There are likely dozens or even hundreds of fonts to work with on your computer, but, as with most other design elements, simple is generally best. Here is some basic information to help you choose the best font for your needs.

Serif fonts, such as Century, show thin flares and embellishments (called serifs; circled in the illustration on p. 522) at the tops and bottoms of their letters and characters. These fonts have a traditional look: Note the newspaper masthead on page 521. In contrast, *sans serif* fonts, such as Helvetica, lack the decorations of serif fonts. They are smoother and more contemporary-looking. For an example, see the article headlines on page 521.

order ideas
p. 342

common errors
p. 524

Century

Helvetica

Century, a serif font

Helvetica, a sans serif font

Serif fonts are more readable than sans serif, for extended passages of writing, such as papers. A sans serif font heading often contrasts well for a document using serif-font text. Some designers prefer sans serif fonts for Web sites and PowerPoint presentations, especially for headings and smaller items.

Display and decorative fonts are designed to attract attention. Avoid them for academic and professional writing, but you may want to explore their use when creating posters, brochures, or special PowerPoint presentations. Beyond the few words of a heading, display fonts are hard to read: Never use them for extended passages of writing.

For typical academic projects, all text, headings, and other elements—including the title—are set in one font size, either 10 or 12 point. In professional or business projects, such as résumés, newsletters, or PowerPoint slides, you'll need to vary type sizes to distinguish headings, captions, and headlines from other elements. Examine your pages carefully in the draft stage to see that there is a balance between the larger and smaller fonts. The impact of a résumé in particular can be diluted by headings that overwhelm the career data. Be careful, too, with smaller sizes. Some fonts look crowded (and strain eyesight) as they dip below 10 points.

Boldfaced items stand out clearly on a page but only if they are rare. Too many boldfaced headings too close together (or too much highlighting) and your page looks heavy and cluttered. Don't use boldface as the regular text throughout your project. If you want an emphatic font, find one that looks that way in its regular form.

Common Errors

part nine

Capitalization

You know to capitalize most proper nouns (and the proper adjectives formed from them), book and movie titles, the first words of sentences, and so on. In principle, the guidelines can seem straightforward, but the fact is you make many judgment calls when capitalizing, some of which will require a dictionary (ask your instructor if he or she can advise you on a good one). Here are just a few of the special cases that can complicate your editing.

Spring or
spring?

Capitalize the names of ethnic, religious, and political groups. The names of these groups are considered proper nouns. Nonspecific groups are lowercase.

South Korean	Mexican American	American Indians
Buddhists	Presbyterians	Muslims
Green Party	Republicans	
the Quincy City Council		the city council

Capitalize modifiers formed from proper nouns. In some cases, such as "french fry," the expressions have become so common that the adjective does not need to be capitalized. When in doubt, consult a dictionary.

PROPER NOUN	PROPER NOUN USED AS MODIFIER
French	French thought
Navajo	Navajo rug
Jew	Jewish lore
American	American history

Capitalize all words in titles except prepositions, articles, or conjunctions. This is the basic rule for the titles of books, movies, long poems, and so on.

> *Dickens and the Dream of Cinema*
>
> *All Quiet on the Western Front*

The variations and exceptions to this general rule, however, are numerous. MLA style specifies that the first and last words in titles always be capitalized, including any articles or prepositions.

> *The Guide to National Parks of the Southwest*
>
> *To the Lighthouse*
>
> *Such Stuff as Dreams Are Made Of*

APA style doesn't make that qualification, but does specify that all words longer than four letters be capitalized in titles—even prepositions.

> *A Walk Among the Tombstones*
>
> *Sleeping Through the Night and Other Lies*

In all major styles, any word following a colon (or, much rarer, a dash) in a title is capitalized, even an article or preposition:

> *Bob Dylan: In His Own Words*
>
> *2001: A Space Odyssey*

Finally, note that in APA style *documentation*—that is, within the notes and on the References page, titles are capitalized differently. Only the first word in most titles, any proper nouns or adjectives, and any words following a colon are capitalized. All other words are in lowercase:

> *Bat predation and the evolution of frog vocalizations in the neotropics*
> *Human aging: Usual and successful*

Take care with compass points, directions, and specific geographical areas.   Points of the compass and simple directions are not capitalized when referring to general locations.

north	southwest
northern Ohio	eastern Canada
southern exposure	western horizons

But these same terms *are* capitalized when they refer to specific regions that are geographically, culturally, or politically significant (keep that dictionary handy!). Such terms are often preceded by the definite article, *the.*

the West	the Old South
the Third Coast	Southern California
Middle Eastern politics	the Western allies

Understand academic conventions.   Academic degrees are not capitalized, except when abbreviated.

bachelor of arts	doctor of medicine
M.A.	Ph.D.

Specific course titles are capitalized, but they are lowercase when used as general subjects. Exception: Languages are always capitalized when referring to academic subjects.

Art History 101	Civil Engineering
an art history course	an English literature paper

Capitalize months, days, holidays, and historical periods.   But not the seasons.

January	winter
Monday	fall
Halloween	autumn
the Renaissance	

Apostrophes

52

Like gnats, apostrophes are small and irritating. They have two major functions: to signal that a noun is possessive and to indicate where letters have been left out in contractions.

Use apostrophes to form the possessive. The basic rules for forming the possessive aren't complicated: For singular nouns, add *'s* to the end of the word:

> the wolf's lair
>
> the woman's portfolio
>
> IBM's profits
>
> Bush's foreign policy

it's or *its?*

Some possessives, while correct, look or sound awkward. In these cases, try an alternative:

ORIGINAL	REVISED
the class's photo	the class photo; the photo of the class
Bright Eyes's latest single	the latest single by Bright Eyes
in Kansas's budget	in the Kansas budget; in the budget of Kansas

For plural nouns that do not end in *s*, also add *'s* to the end of the word:

> men's shoes   the mice's cages   the geese's nemesis

529

For plural nouns that do end in *s*, add an apostrophe after that terminal *s*:

the wolves' pups

the Bushes' foreign policies

three senators' votes

Use apostrophes in contractions.   An apostrophe in a contraction takes the place of missing letters. Edit carefully, keeping in mind that a spell checker doesn't help you with such blunders. It only catches words that make no sense without apostrophes, such as *dont* or *Ive*.

ORIGINAL	Its a shame that its come to this.
REVISED	It's (It is) a shame that it's (it has) come to this.
ORIGINAL	Whose got the list of whose going on the trip?
REVISED	Who's (Who has) got the list of who's (who is) going on the trip?

Don't use apostrophes with possessive pronouns.   The following possessives do not take apostrophes: *its, whose, his, hers, ours, yours,* and *theirs.*

ORIGINAL	We shot the tower at it's best angle.
REVISED	We shot the tower at its best angle.
ORIGINAL	The book is her's, not his.
REVISED	The book is hers, not his.
ORIGINAL	Their's may be an Oscar-winning film, but our's is still better.
REVISED	Theirs may be an Oscar-winning film, but ours is still better.

There is, inevitably, an exception. Indefinite pronouns such as *everybody, anybody, nobody,* and so on show possession via *'s.*

The film was everybody's favorite.

Why it was so successful is anybody's guess.

Commas

53

The comma has more uses than any other punctuation mark—
uses which can often seem complex. Below are some of the most
common comma situations in academic writing.

**Use a comma and a coordinating conjunction to separate
two independent clauses.**   Independent clauses can stand on
their own as a sentence. To join two of them, you need two things:
a coordinating conjunction and a comma.

need to
connect ideas?

> Fiona's car broke down. She had to walk two miles to the train
> station.

> Fiona's car broke down, so she had to walk two miles to the
> train station.

There are several key points to remember here. Be sure you truly
have two independent clauses, and not just a compound subject or
verb. Also, make certain to include both a comma and a coordinating conjunction (*and, but, for, nor, or, so, yet*). Leaving out the
coordinating conjunction creates an error known as a comma splice
(see p. 534).

Use a comma after an introductory word group.   Introductory word groups are descriptive phrases or clauses that open a
sentence. Separate these introductions from the main part of the
sentence with a comma.

> Within two years of getting a degree in journalism, Nobuko was writing for the *New York Times*.

For very brief introductory phrases, the comma may be omitted, but it is not wrong to leave it in.

> After college I plan to join the Peace Corps.
>
> After college, I plan to join the Peace Corps.

Use commas with transitional words and phrases.   Transitional expressions such as *however* and *for example* should be set off from a sentence with a pair of commas.

> These fans can be among the first, however, to clamor for a new stadium to boost their favorite franchise.

If a transitional word or phrase opens a sentence, it should be followed by a comma.

> Moreover, studies have shown that trans fats can lower the amount of good cholesterol found in the body.

Put commas around nonrestrictive (that is, nonessential) elements.   You'll know when a word or phrase is functioning as a non-restrictive modifier if you can remove it from the sentence without destroying the overall meaning of the sentence.

> Cicero, ancient Rome's greatest orator and lawyer, was a self-made man.
>
> Cicero was a self-made man.

The second sentence is less informative, but still functions. See also the guideline below, "Do not use commas to set off restrictive elements."

Use commas to separate items in a series.   Commas are necessary when you have three or more items in a series.

> American highways were once ruled by powerful muscle cars such as Mustangs, GTOs, and Camaros.

Do not use commas to separate compound verbs. Don't confuse
a true compound sentence (with two independent clauses) with a sentence
that has two verbs.

> ORIGINAL They rumbled through city streets, and smoked down drag strips.

> REVISED They rumbled through city streets and smoked down drag strips.

They rumbled through city streets is an independent clause, but *and smoked
down drag strips* is not, because it doesn't have a subject. To join the two
verbs, use *and* with no comma. The only exception to this rule is if you have
three or more verbs, which should be treated as items in a series and separated with commas.

> Muscle cars guzzled gasoline, polluted incessantly, and drove parents crazy.

Do not use a comma between subject and verb. Perhaps it's obvious
why such commas don't work when you try one in a short sentence.

> Keeping focused, can be difficult.

When a subject gets long and complicated, you might be more tempted to
insert the comma, but it would still be both unnecessary and wrong.

> Keeping focused on driving while simultaneously trying to operate a cell phone,
> can be difficult.

Do not use commas to set off restrictive elements. Phrases you
cannot remove from a sentence without significantly altering meaning are
called restrictive or essential. They are modifiers that provide information
needed to understand the subject.

> The canyon that John Wesley Powell explored in 1869 has been inhabited by
> Native Americans for thousands of years.

> The Native Puebloans who built Tusayan Pueblo around 1185 abandoned it
> within a century.

Delete the highlighted phrases in the above examples, and you are left with
sentences that are vague or confusing.

54 Comma Splices, Run-ons, and Fragments

need a complete sentence?

The sentence errors marked most often in college writing are comma splices, run-ons, and fragments.

Identify comma splices and run-ons. A *comma splice* occurs when only a comma is used to join two independent clauses (an independent clause contains a complete subject and verb).

Identify a comma splice simply by reading the clauses on either side of a doubtful comma. If *both* clauses stand on their own as sentences (with their own subjects and verbs), it's a comma splice.

COMMA SPLICE   Officials at many elementary schools are trying to reduce childhood obesity on their campuses, research suggests that few of their strategies will work.

A *run-on* sentence is similar to a comma splice, but it doesn't even include the comma to let readers take a break between independent clauses. The clauses knock together, confusing readers.

RUN-ON SENTENCE   Officials at many elementary schools are trying to reduce childhood obesity on their campuses research suggests that few of their strategies will work.

Fix comma splices and run-ons. To fix comma splices and run-ons, you can include a comma and a coordinating conjunction after the first independent clause to join it with the second clause.

> Officials at many elementary schools are trying to reduce childhood obesity on their campuses, **but** research shows that few of their strategies will work.

Or you can use a semicolon to join the two clauses.

> Officials at many elementary schools are trying to reduce childhood obesity on their campuses; research shows that few of their strategies will work.

Common Coordinating Conjunctions

and	or
but	so
for	yet
nor	

Less frequently, colons or dashes may be used if the second clause summarizes or illustrates the main point of the first clause.

> Some schools have taken extreme measures: They have banned cookies, snacks, and other high-calorie foods from their vending machines.

Along with the semicolon (or colon or dash), you may wish to add a transitional word or phrase (such as *however* or *in fact*). If you do so, set off the transitional word or phrase with commas. ○

> Officials at many elementary schools are trying to reduce childhood obesity on their campuses; research, **however,** shows that few of their strategies will work.

> Other schools emphasize a need for more exercise—**in fact,** some have even gone so far as to reinstate recess.

You can also rewrite the sentence to make one of the clauses subordinate. Using a subordinating conjunction, revise so that one of the clauses in the sentence can no longer stand as a sentence on its own.

> **Although** officials at many elementary schools are trying to reduce childhood obesity on their campuses, research shows that few of their strategies will work.

Common Subordinating Conjunctions

after	once
although	since
as	that
because	though
before	unless
except	until
if	when

Or use end punctuation to create two independent sentences.

> Officials at many elementary schools are trying to reduce childhood obesity on their campuses. Research shows that few of their strategies will work.

Identify sentence fragments.   A sentence fragment is a word group that lacks a subject, verb, or possibly both. As such, it is not a complete sentence and is not appropriate for most academic and professional writing.

FRAGMENT   Climatologists see much physical evidence of global warming. **Especially in the receding of glaciers around the world.**

connect ideas
p. 350

Fix sentence fragments in your work.   You have two options for fixing sentence fragments. Attach the fragment to a nearby sentence:

COMPLETE SENTENCE   Climatologists see much physical evidence of global warming, especially in the receding of glaciers around the world.

Turn the fragment into its own sentence:

COMPLETE SENTENCE   Climatologists see much physical evidence of global warming. They are especially concerned by the receding of glaciers around the world.

Watch for fragments in the following situations.   Often a fragment will follow a complete sentence and start with a subordinating conjunction.

FRAGMENT   Global warming seems to be the product of human activity. Though some scientists believe sun cycles may explain the changing climate.

COMPLETE SENTENCE   Global warming seems to be the product of human activity, though some scientists believe sun cycles may explain the changing climate.

Participles (such as *breaking, seeking, finding*) and infinitives (such as *to break, to seek, to find*) can also lead you into fragments.

FRAGMENT   Of course, many people welcome the warmer weather. Confounding scientists who fear governments will not act until climate change becomes irreversible.

COMPLETE SENTENCE   Of course, many people welcome the warmer weather. Their attitude confounds scientists who fear governments will not act until climate change becomes irreversible.

Use deliberate fragments only in appropriate situations.   Use deliberate fragments, such as the following colloquial expressions or clichés, in informal or popular writing only after considering your audience and purpose.

In your dreams.   Excellent.   Not on your life.

Subject / Verb Agreement

55

Verbs take many forms to express changing tenses, moods, and voices. To avoid common errors in choosing the correct verb form, follow these guidelines.

Be sure the verb agrees with its real subject. It's tempting to link a verb to the nouns closest to it (in olive below) instead of the subject, but that's a mistake.

none are or
none is?

ORIGINAL	Liftport, one of several private **companies** working on space ladder technologies, anticipate a working prototype by 2018.
REVISED	Liftport, one of several private companies working on space ladder technologies, anticipates a working prototype by 2018.
ORIGINAL	Bottles of water sold at the grocery store usually costs as much as gasoline.
REVISED	Bottles of water sold at the grocery store usually cost as much as gasoline.

Some indefinite pronouns are exceptions to this rule. See the chart on page 538.

In most cases, treat multiple subjects joined by *and* as plural. But when a subject with *and* clearly expresses a single notion, that subject is singular.

Hip-hop, rock, and country are dominant forms of popular music today.

Blues and folk have their fans too.

Peanut butter and jelly is the sandwich of choice in our house.

Rock and roll often strikes a political chord.

When singular subjects are followed by expressions such as *along with, together with,* or *as well as,* the subjects may feel plural, but technically they remain singular.

ORIGINAL   Mariah Carey, along with Gwen Stefani, Kanye West, and Green Day, were competing for "Record of the Year."

REVISED   Mariah Carey, along with Gwen Stefani, Kanye West, and Green Day, was competing for "Record of the Year."

If the corrected version sounds awkward, try revising the sentence.

REVISED   Mariah Carey, Gwen Stefani, Kanye West, and Green Day were all competing for "Record of the Year."

Indefinite Pronouns		
Singular	**Plural**	**Variable**
anybody	both	all
anyone	few	any
anything	many	more
each	others	most
everybody	several	none
everyone		some
everything		
nobody		
no one		
nothing		
one		
somebody		
someone		
something		

When compound subjects are linked by *either . . . or* **or** *neither . . . nor,* **make the verb agree with the nearer part of the subject.**
Knowing this rule will make you one person among a thousand.

> Neither my sisters nor my mother is a fan of Kanye West.

When possible, put the plural part of the subject closer to the verb to make it sound less awkward.

> Neither my mother nor my sisters are fans of Kanye West.

Confirm whether an indefinite pronoun is singular, plural, or variable.   Most indefinite pronouns are singular, but consult the chart on page 538 to double-check.

> Everybody complains about politics, but nobody does much about it.
>
> Each of the women expects a promotion.
>
> Something needs to be done about the budget crisis.

A few indefinite pronouns are obviously plural: *both, few, many, others, several.*

> Many complain about politics, but few do much about it.

And some indefinite pronouns shift in number, depending on the prepositional phrases that modify them.

> All of the votes are in the ballot box.
>
> All of the fruit is spoiled.
>
> Most of the rules are less complicated.
>
> Most of the globe is covered by oceans.
>
> None of the rules makes sense.
>
> On the Security Council, none but the Russians favor the resolution.

Be consistent with collective nouns.   Many of these words describing a group can be treated as either singular or plural: *band, class, jury, choir, group, committee.*

> The jury seems to resent the lawyer's playing to its emotions.
>
> The jury seem to resent the lawyer's playing to their emotions.
>
> The band was unhappy with its CD.
>
> The band were unhappy with their CD.

A basic principle is to be consistent throughout a passage. If *the band* is singular the first time you mention it, keep it that way for the remainder of the project. Be sensible too. If a sentence sounds odd to your ear, modify it:

AWKWARD   The band were unhappy with their CD.

BETTER   The members of the band were unhappy with their CD.

Irregular Verbs

Verbs are considered regular if they form the past and past participle—which you use to form various tenses—simply by adding –*d* or –*ed* to the base of the verb. Below are several regular verbs.

Base form	Past tense	Past participle
smile	smiled	smiled
accept	accepted	accepted
manage	managed	managed

lie or *lay?*

Unfortunately, the most common verbs in English are irregular. The chart on page 542 lists some of them. When in doubt about the proper form of a verb, check a dictionary.

Base form	Past tense	Past participle
be	was, were	been
become	became	become
break	broke	broken
buy	bought	bought
choose	chose	chosen
come	came	come
dive	dived, dove	dived
do	did	done
drink	drank	drunk
drive	drove	driven
eat	ate	eaten
get	got	gotten
give	gave	given
go	went	gone
have	had	had
lay (to put or place)	laid	laid
lie (to recline)	lay	lain
ride	rode	ridden
ring	rang, rung	rung
rise	rose	risen
see	saw	seen
set	set	set
shine	shone, shined	shone, shined
sing	sang, sung	sung
sink	sank, sunk	sunk
speak	spoke	spoken
swear	swore	sworn
throw	threw	thrown
wake	woke, waked	woken, waked
write	wrote	written

Pronoun / Antecedent Agreement

57

You already know that pronouns take the place of nouns. Antecedents are the words pronouns refer to. Since pronouns in their many forms stand in for nouns, they also share some of the same markers, such as gender and number.

SINGULAR / FEMININE	The **nun** merely smiled because **she** had taken a vow of silence.
SINGULAR / MASCULINE	The **NASCAR champion** complained that **he** got little media attention.
SINGULAR / NEUTER	The **jury** seemed to take **itself** too seriously.
PLURAL	The **members of the jury** seemed to take **themselves** too seriously.
PLURAL	**They** seemed awfully subdued for **pro athletes**.
PLURAL	The **bridge and groom** wrote **their** own ditzy vows.
PLURAL	**Many** in the terminal resented searches of **their** luggage.

their or his or hers?

The basic rule for managing pronouns and antecedents couldn't be simpler: Make sure pronouns you select have the same number and gender as the words they stand for.

ORIGINAL	When a **student** spends too much time on sorority activities, **they** may suffer academically.

REVISED   When a **student** spends too much time on sorority activities, **she** may suffer academically.

As always, though, there are confusing cases and numerous exceptions. Following are the common problems.

Check the number of indefinite pronouns.   Some of the most common singular indefinite pronouns—especially *anybody, everybody, everyone*—may seem plural, but they should be treated as singular. (For the complete list of indefinite pronouns, see the chart on p. 538 in Chapter 55.)

ORIGINAL   Has **everybody** completed **their** assignment by now?

REVISED   Has **everybody** completed **his or her** assignment by now?

If using *his or her* sounds awkward, revise the sentence.

Have **all students** completed **their** assignments by now?

Correct sexist pronoun usage.   Using *his* alone (instead of *his or her*) to refer to an indefinite pronoun is considered sexist unless it clearly refers only to males. ○

Treat collective nouns consistently.   Collective nouns—such as *team, herd, congregation, mob,* and so on—can be treated as either singular or plural.

The **legion** marched until **it** reached **its** camp in Gaul.

The **legion** marched until **they** reached **their** camp in Gaul.

Just be consistent and sensible in your usage. Treat a collective noun the same way, as either singular or plural, throughout a paper or project. And don't hesitate to modify a sentence when even a correct usage sounds awkward.

AWKWARD   The **team** smiled as **it** received **its** championship jerseys.

BETTER   **Members of the team** smiled as **they** received **their** championship jerseys.

respect your readers
p. 374

Pronoun Reference

58

A pronoun should refer back clearly to a noun or pronoun (its *antecedent*), usually the one nearest to it that matches it in number and, when necessary, gender.

> Consumers will buy a Rolex because they covet its snob appeal.
>
> Nancy Pelosi spoke instead of Harry Reid because she had more interest in the legislation than he did.

If connections between pronouns and antecedents wobble within a single sentence or longer passage, readers will struggle. Following are three common problems you should avoid.

Clarify confusing pronoun antecedents. Revise sentences in which readers will find themselves wondering *who is doing what to whom*. Multiple revisions are usually possible, depending on how the confusing sentence could be interpreted.

CONFUSING The batter collided with the first baseman, but he wasn't injured.

BETTER The batter collided with the first baseman, who wasn't injured.

BETTER The batter wasn't injured by his collision with the first baseman.

sure what *it* means?

Make sure a pronoun has a plausible antecedent. Sometimes the problem is that the antecedent doesn't actually exist—it is only implied. In these cases, either insert an antecedent or replace the pronoun with a noun.

CONFUSING   Grandmother had hip-replacement surgery two months ago, and it is already fully healed.

In the above sentence, the implied antecedent for *it* is *hip,* but the noun *hip* isn't in the sentence (*hip-replacement* is an adjective describing *surgery*).

BETTER   Grandmother had her hip replaced two months ago, and it is already fully healed.

BETTER   Grandmother had hip-replacement surgery two months ago, and her hip is already fully healed.

Don't leave the antecedent of *this, that,* or *which* deliberately vague. In the following example, a humble *this* is asked to shoulder the burden of a writer who hasn't quite figured out how to pull together all the ideas raised in the preceding sentence. What exactly might the antecedent for *this* be? It doesn't exist. To fix the problem, the writer needs to replace *this* with a more thoughtful analysis.

The university staff is underpaid, the labs are short on equipment, and campus maintenance is neglected. Moreover, we need two or three new parking garages to make up for the lots lost because of recent construction projects. Yet students cannot be expected to shoulder additional costs because tuition and fees are high already. This is a problem that must be solved.

REVISED FINAL SENTENCE

How to fund both academic departments and infrastructure needs without increasing students' financial outlay is a problem that must be solved.

Pronoun Case

In spoken English, you hear it when you run into a problem with pronoun case.

> "Let's just keep this matter between you and . . . *ummmm* . . . me."

> "To who . . . I mean, uh . . . whom does this letter go?"

> "Hector is more of a people person than her . . . than she is."

Like nouns, pronouns can be subjects, objects, or possessives, and their forms vary to show which case they express in a sentence. Unfortunately, determining case is the problem. Here are some strategies for dealing with these common situations.

I or *me? who* or *whom?*

Subjective pronouns	Objective pronouns	Possessive pronouns
I	me	my, mine
you	you	your, yours
he, she, it	him, her, it	his, her, hers, its
we	us	our, ours
they	them	their, theirs
who	whom	whose

Use the subjective case for pronouns that are subjects.
When pronouns are the only subject in a clause, they rarely cause a problem. But double the subject, and there's trouble.

> Sara and . . . me . . . , or is it Sara and I wrote the report?

To make the right choice, try answering the question for one subject at a time. You quickly recognize that *Sara* wrote the report, and *I* did the same thing. So one possible revision is:

> Sara and I wrote the report.

Or, you can recast the sentence to avoid the difficulty in the first place.

> We wrote the report.

Use the objective case for pronouns that are objects.   Again, choosing one objective pronoun is generally obvious, but with two objects, the choice is less clear. How do you decide what to do in the following sentence?

> The corporate attorney will represent both Geoff and I . . . Geoff and me?

Again, deal with one object at a time. Since the attorney will represent *me*, and will also represent *Geoff*, a possible revision is:

> The corporate attorney will represent Geoff and me.

Or, to be more concise:

> The corporate attorney will represent us.

Use *whom* when appropriate.   One simple pronoun choice brings many writers to their knees: *who* or *whom*. The rule, however, is the same as for other pronouns: Use the subjective case (*who*) for subjects and the objective case (*whom*) for objects. In some cases, the choice is obvious.

ORIGINAL   Whom wrote the report?

REVISED   Who wrote the report?

ORIGINAL   By who was the report written?

REVISED   By whom was the report written?

But this choice becomes tricky when you're dealing with subordinate clauses.

ORIGINAL   The shelter needs help from whomever can volunteer three hours per week.

The previous above example may sound right because *whomever* immediately follows the preposition *from*. But, because the pronoun is the subject of a subordinate clause, it needs to be in the subjective case.

REVISED   The shelter needs help from whoever can volunteer three hours per week.

Finish comparisons to determine the right case.   Many times when writers make comparisons, they leave out some understood information.

I've always thought John was more talented than Paul.

(I've always thought John was more talented than Paul *was*.)

But leaving this information out can lead to confusion when it comes to choosing the correct pronoun case. Try the sentence, adding *him*.

ORIGINAL   I've always thought John was more talented than him.

I've always thought John was more talented than him *was*.

REVISED   I've always thought John was more talented than he.

If it sounds strange to use the correct pronoun, complete the sentence.

REVISED   I've always thought John was more talented than he was.

Don't be misled by an appositive.   An *appositive* is a word or phrase that amplifies or renames a noun or pronoun. In the example below, *Americans* is the appositive. First, try reading the sentence without it.

ORIGINAL   Us Americans must defend our civil rights.

We must defend our civil rights.

REVISED   We Americans must defend our civil rights.

When the pronoun is contained within the appositive, it follows the case of the word or words it renames.

SUBJECTIVE   The bloggers who were still in the running, Lucy, Cali, and I, wrote all night trying to outdo each other.

OBJECTIVE   The site was dominated by the bloggers who were still in the running, Lucy, Cali, and me.

Misplaced and Dangling Modifiers

In general, modifiers need to be close and obviously connected to the words they modify. When they aren't, readers may become confused—or amused.

Position modifiers close to the words they modify.

> MISPLACED   Tiered like a wedding cake, Mrs. DeLeon unveiled her model for the parade float.

Mrs. DeLeon is not tiered like a wedding cake; the model for the parade float is.

> REVISED   Mrs. DeLeon unveiled her model for the parade float, which was tiered like a wedding cake.

Place adverbs such as *only*, *almost*, *especially*, and *even* carefully.   If these modifiers are placed improperly, their purpose can be vague or ambiguous.

> VAGUE   The speaker almost angered everyone in the room.
>
> CLEARER   The speaker angered almost everyone in the room.
>
> AMBIGUOUS   Joan only drove a stick shift.
>
> CLEARER   Only Joan drove a stick shift.
>
> CLEARER   Joan drove only a stick shift.

Don't allow a modifier to dangle.   A modifying word or phrase at the beginning of a sentence should be followed immediately by the subject it modifies. When it doesn't, the modifier is said to dangle.

DANGLING   **After picking me up at the airport,** San Francisco was introduced to me by my future business partner.

San Francisco didn't pick me up at the airport; my future business partner did. So *my future business partner* needs to be the subject of the sentence.

REVISED   **After picking me up at the airport,** my future business partner introduced me to San Francisco.

61 Parallelism

making a list?

When items in sentences follow similar patterns of language, they are described as parallel. Parallel structure makes your writing easier to read and understand.

When possible, make compound items parallel. Don't confuse your readers by requiring them to untangle subjects, verbs, modifiers, or other items that could easily be parallel:

NOT PARALLEL	Becoming a lawyer and to write a novel are Leslie's goals.
PARALLEL	Becoming a lawyer and writing a novel are Leslie's goals.
NOT PARALLEL	The university will demolish its old stadium and bricks from it are being sold.
PARALLEL	The university will demolish its old stadium and sell the bricks.
NOT PARALLEL	The TV anchor reported the story thoroughly and with compassion.
PARALLEL	The TV anchor reported the story thoroughly and compassionately.

Keep items in a series parallel. A series should consist of all nouns, all adjectives, all verbs, and so on.

NOT PARALLEL	She was a fine new teacher—eager, very patient, and gets her work done.
PARALLEL	She was a fine new teacher—eager, very patient, and conscientious.
NOT PARALLEL	We expected to rehabilitate the historic property, break even on the investment, and to earn the goodwill of the community.
PARALLEL	We expected to rehabilitate the historic property, to break even on the investment, and to earn the good will of the community.
PARALLEL	We expected to rehabilitate the historic property, break even on the investment, and earn the goodwill of the community.

Keep headings and lists parallel.   If you use headings to break up the text of a document, use a similar language pattern and design for all of them. It may help to type the headings out separately from the text to make sure you are keeping them parallel. Items in a printed list should be parallel as well.

Art credits (in order of appearance):

Page 125: TM and Copyright © 20th Century Fox Film Corp. All rights reserved. Courtesy: The Everett Collection.

Page 126: Columbia/Courtesy of the Everett Collection.

Page 129: Courtesy of the EPA.

Page 132: © Loretta Rae/Corbis.

Page 137: Stephen Schauer/Stone/Getty Images.

Page 143: Mary Evans Picture Library/Everett Collection.

Page 145: USA TODAY. June 30, 2006. Reprinted with permission.

Page 154: © Bettmann/CORBIS.

Page 155: © John Springer Collection/CORBIS.

Page 156: © Bettmann/CORBIS.

Page 157: © Bettmann/CORBIS.

Page 161: Reprinted with permission of AdBusters.

Page 165: Lauren Greenfield/VII/AP.

Page 168: David Young-Wolff/PhotoEdit.

Page 169: © CORBIS.

Page 174: Massachusetts Turnpike Authority. Used with permission.

Page 184: Tyler Brett and Tony Romano (T&T). Reprinted with permission.

Page 187: Courtesy of Kayla Mohammadi. Reprinted with permission.

Page 196: Top: MIRAMAX/The Kobal Collection/Jill Sabella. Bottom: HBO/Courtesy of Everett Collection.

Page 207: PhotoFest. Copyright notice: © United Artists.

Page 217: Focus Features/The Kobal Collection.

Pages 218–20: Library of Congress Prints and Photographs Division, Washington, D.C.

Page 226: Courtesy of Dell, Inc.

Page 227: George Nikitin/Associated Press.

Page 229: Masi Oka © 2007 America's Milk Processors.

Page 235: Courtesy of the Navy Environmental Health Center.

Page 255: ©Bill Aron/PhotoEdit, Inc.

Page 256: Jim Zook/© Images.com/Corbis.

Page 261: © George Steinmetz/Corbis.

Page 264: NSDAP/The Kobal Collection.

Page 267: Ziga Soleil/Iconica/Getty Images.

Page 273: Mario Villafuerte/Bloomberg/Landov.

Page 279: © Bob Daemmrich/The Image Works.

Page 281: © Hulton-Deutsch Collection/Corbis.

Page 285: Jerome Tisne/Iconica/Getty Images

Page 291: © Christian Charisius/Reuters/Landov.

Page 299: © Hulton-Deutsch Collection/Corbis.

Page 309: Photo by Jacob Botter. Reprinted with permission.

Page 310: Library of Congress.

Page 312: Wikipedia image used with permission under the terms of the GNU Free Documentation License.

Page 313: CBS/Robert Voets/Landov.

Page 313: Stefan Lovgren/National Geographic Image Collection.

Page 314: NBC/PhotoFest. © Copyright NBC.

Page 327: Used by permission David Strait, Anthropology Dept., University at Albany.

Index